TOPICS IN COGNITIVE PSYCHOLOGY

TOPICS IN COGNITIVE PSYCHOLOGY

SERGE P. SHOHOV (EDITOR)

Nova Science Publishers, Inc.
New York

Senior Editors: Susan Boriotti and Donna Dennis
Coordinating Editor: Tatiana Shohov
Office Manager: Annette Hellinger
Graphics: Wanda Serrano and Matt Dallow
Editorial Production: Maya Columbus, Alexis Klestov, Vladimir Klestov,
                 Matthew Kozlowski and Lorna Loperfido
Circulation: Ave Maria Gonzalez, Vera Popovic, Sean Corkery, Raymond Davis,
            Melissa Diaz, Magdalena Nuñez, Marlene Nuñez and Jeannie Pappas
Communications and Acquisitions: Serge P. Shohov
Marketing: Cathy DeGregory

Library of Congress Cataloging-in-Publication Data

Topics in cognitive psychology / Serge P. Shohov, editor.
   p. cm.
Includes bibliographical references and index.
     ISBN: 1-59033-836-7.
1. Cognitive psychology. I. Shohov, Serge P.

BF201.T67 2003
153—dc22   2003017280

CONTENTS

PREFACE

Cognitive psychology is concerned with several mental processes, including those involved in perception, attention, learning, memory, problem solving, decision making and the use of language. It is often said that cognitive psychology tries to understand how people represent their experience and then use these representations to operate effectively. Cognitive psychology holds that people are not passive organisms whose mental representations are simple or direct reflections of the outside world. Rather, they are active processors of environmental events, and as such they bring their past knowledge and their biases to bear on how they perceive and understand all current events. Thus perceiving, imagining, thinking, remembering, forming concepts, and solving problems, indeed all aspects of people's mental lives, define the domain of cognitive exploration.

In this book, we present important research which was carefully selected and screened for both current relevance and long-term advancement of the field.

In chapter 1 advances in designing questionnaires to measure self-concept are described. Recent evidence involving the proper linear measurement of academic self-concept for university students (using the new questionnaires and a recently developed computer program based on a Rasch measurement model) support a different model of the formation and creation of academic self-concept. It is suggested that self-concept formation is dependent on at least four views of a subject or performance: an idealistic view, a capability view, a realistic view, and a self-view of their corresponding achievement in the subject or performance.

For many decades higher education pedagogic has been speaking about the need to consider students primarily the subject of teaching. But the realities of life outside and inside institutions of higher education have made these talks declarative for a long time. Have there been any changes in the motivation, contents and level of classroom and cognitive activity of modern students since then? In chapter 2 the authors tried to answer this question, having at our disposal the results of our studies of the *dynamics of classroom and cognitive activity* of the students of Samara State University (SSU), carried out for almost two decades.

In chapter 3 the factor structure of the WAIS-III in the 13 normative age samples was examined using principal components analysis for 1-factor (general), 2-factor (Verbal and Performance), and 4-factor (Verbal Comprehension, Perceptual Organization, Working Memory, and Processing Speed) solutions. For the 2-factor and 4-factor solutions an orthogonal procrustes rotation was used to rotate the loadings to the least squares best fit of the hypothesis matrix. Congruence coefficients and root mean square differences were used to assess consistency of the subtest loadings across age groups and goodness of fit with the hypothesized structure.

Chapter 4 targets the topic of remembering the delayed execution of an intention, i.e. prospective memory. After specifying the significance of this research area, a model of prospective remembering is described identifying four phases in the process of forming and executing a delayed intention. The main part of the chapter summarizes recent work of the author concerning the question whether and how the importance of an intention influences the delayed execution. Three studies with five experiments are integrated presenting evidence for the author's resource-allocation-conflict-hypothesis.

In chapter 5 on the hypothesis of biologically conditioned intellectual giftedness in the monozygotic male-twins is suggested on basis of data on the strong connection between high intelligence in pre/adolescents and high testosterone level in the prenatal fetus development and also on the increased concentration of testosterone in the amniotic liquid in the case of pregnancy with monozygotic male-twins. The prenatal developmental peculiarities and unfavorable psychosocial factors during postnatal twins' development are discussed as the reasons for the phenomenological absence of talented male-twins in human history.

Family socialization practices, especially parent-child conversational interactions, play a paramount role in mediating children's acquisition of culture-appropriate modes of thinking, remembering, feeling, and behaving. In chapter 6, the authors draw upon empirical evidence on parent-child reminiscing in European American and East Asian families to analyze cultural variation in the cognitive, social, and emotional aspects of sharing memory narratives. It is demonstrated that parents in these cultures show different patterns and tendencies when conversing with their children about the shared past.

Many studies show that intended thought suppression often paradoxically leads to higher frequencies of unwanted thoughts. This effect has been linked to the development and/or maintenance of anxiety disorders. One important issue is whether the ability to suppress unwanted thoughts is generally impaired or specifically for thoughts related to the disorder. Chapter 7 discusses a clinical study of patients with agoraphobia and patients with social phobia who were compared with a control group without mental disorders. All participants were instructed to suppress two target thoughts related to the respective central fear of the two disorders and one non-specific item. During the suppression period, all occurrences of unwanted thoughts had to be signaled. Agoraphobics showed a rather specific deficit in thought suppression, while social phobics seem to be characterized by a general impairment of mental control, affecting specific as well as non-specific stimuli. Strategies used during the suppression task did not differ between target thoughts nor groups.

Most research on the important role of knowledge of results has been done on continuous spatiotemporal movements like in tracking tasks. However, few studies concentrate on the effects of training and feedback in discrete timing tasks. Chapter 8 gives an overview of studies examing the timing of movements in different tasks like the coincidence-anticipation task and the synchronization task as well as the effects of training in these tasks. A study is presented that analyzes the influence of knowledge of results on the timing of repetitive movements in a sensorimotor synchronization task. Informative feedback about the asynchrony between keypress and pacing signal is presented to test the hypothesis that the availability of augmented feedback is a precondition for learning in such timing tasks. The results obtained in the experiments clearly show that informative feedback is highly effective in reducing the (usually observed) anticipatory tendency, whereas no practice effects were obtained when subjects tapped without getting any feedback at all or with non-informative visual feedback.

Chapter 9 examined the effects of vocal and instrumental music upon the performance of introverts and extraverts on two different cognitive tasks. In the presence of either vocal or instrumental music or in silence, participants completed a reading comprehension and a phonological task. A significant interaction was found only for the phonological task possibly because of ceiling effects on the reading comprehension task. As hypothesised, music impaired performance of introverts more than extraverts, but extraverts' performance was not enhanced by the music as predicted. The study also examined study habit preferences and found, as predicted, introverts reported preferring to study in environments free of distraction.

In chapter 10 six experiments examine effects of overtraining on reversal learning in concurrent discriminations in rats. The findings of the six experiments in the study make it clear that stimulus-stimulus associations (i.e., stimulus classes) between the discriminative stimuli are formed in concurrent discriminations after overtraining, but not after criterion training.

Chapter 11 presents an approach to item pool design that has the potential to improve on the quality of current item pools in educational and psychological testing and hence to increase both measurement precision and validity. The approach consists of the application of mathematical programming techniques to calculate optimal blueprints for item pools. Three different types of design problems are discussed, namely for item pools for linear tests, item pools computerized adaptive testing (CAT), and systems of rotating item pools for CAT.

Cognitive psychology is concerned with several mental processes, including those involved in perception, attention, learning, memory, problem solving, decision making and the use of language. Therefore, it is very extensive and of great relevance to other areas of psychology. This book presents research on the leading edge of cognitive psychology.

In: *Topics in Cognitive Psychology*   ISBN 1-59033-836-7.
Serge P. Shohov (Editor) pp. 1-11   © 2003 Nova Science Publishers, Inc.

Chapter 1

THE STRUCTURE AND MEASUREMENT OF SELF-CONCEPT FOR UNIVERSITY STUDENTS

*Russell F. Waugh**
Edith Cowan University
Western Australia

ABSTRACT

The current model of the structure of academic self-concept involving separate maths and verbal domains plus separate subject self-concepts linked with a hierarchical general academic self-concept that is related strongly to each of the separate subject self-concepts, as proposed by Marsh and Shavelson (1985), is called into question.

Advances in designing questionnaires to measure self-concept are described. Recent evidence involving the proper linear measurement of academic self-concept for university students (using the new questionnaires and a recently developed computer program based on a Rasch measurement model) support a different model of the formation and creation of academic self-concept. It is suggested that self-concept formation is dependent on at least four views of a subject or performance: an idealistic view, a capability view, a realistic view, and a self-view of their corresponding achievement in the subject or performance.

* * *

The literature on academic self-concept is voluminous and academic self-concept is generally considered to be an important educational variable. Its importance mainly lies in its reported connection with academic achievement and academic behavior (see for example, Chapman & Tunmer, 1997, 1995; Chapman, Turner & Prochnow, 2000; Eccles & Wigfield, 1995; Marsh & Yeung, 1997a, 1997b; Muijs, 1997; Waugh, 2002b). Generally, students with positive self-concepts are more likely to have high academic achievement and to have positive academic behaviors towards studying and learning, and time-on-task: and the

* Address: Edith Cowan University, Pearson Street, Churchlands 6018 Western Australia. E-mail: r.waugh@ecu.edu.au.

converse is generally true. This leads, in turn, to the importance of the structure of self-concept and how self-concept is formed.

The structures that have been given most attention in recent times are the ones proposed by Shavelson, Hubner and Stanton (1976), and the revised version that separately considers maths and verbal domains proposed by Marsh and Shavelson (1985). These structures propose a multi-dimensional set of separate subject self-concepts, with a hierarchical general academic self-concept that is related strongly to each of the separate subject self-concepts. There is a great deal of literature published in relation to the multi-dimensional (subject) nature of academic self-concept. Using True Score Theory to measure self-reported realistic academic self-concept, it has been shown time-and-again that students have different subject self-concepts (see for example Byrne, 1996; Byrne & Gavin, 1996; Harter, 1996; Hattie, 1992; Marsh, 1993, 1987; Marsh, Byrne & Shavelson, 1988; Vispoel, 1995). So there doesn't seem to be much question that academic self-concept is multi-dimensional, in the sense that students have different self-concepts for different subjects.

The question of whether academic self-concept is hierarchical in structure is more questionable than its multi-dimensional structure. There is much less evidence about its hierarchical structure, probably because a hierarchy is more difficult to test with True Score Theory measurement. There are three recent studies on the hierarchical structure, each providing some support for a hierarchy. In the first study, Yeung, Chui, Lau, McInerney and Russell-Bowie (2000) collected evidence to support; (one) a higher order global Creative Arts self-concept factor to represent Music, Visual Art, Dance and Drama for teacher education students; (two) a higher order global English self-concept factor to represent Speaking, Reading and Writing English for students learning English as a Second Language in a Hong Kong university; (and three) a higher order global Commerce self-concept factor to represent Accounting, Maths, Economics, English and Chinese for Commerce students in a Hong Kong university. In the second study, Marsh, Hey, Johnson, and Perry (1997) collected evidence to support a higher order Physical self-concept factor to represent six specific physical aspects for elite athletes from Australian representative teams and from a sports high school. In the third study, Vispoel (1995) collected evidence to support a hierarchical representation of a global artistic self-concept within a number of art subject domains, but not for a single higher-order factor that would 'explain' all the individual subject domains.

STRUCTURE CALLED INTO QUESTION

There are at least three aspects of these studies that can be called into question. One relates to the lack of a proper linear measure of self-concept. The use of True Score Theory only enables a rank measure to be obtained, not a proper interval-scale measure. Researchers need to obtain data for self-concept items that fit a linear measurement model of self-concept, not build a model from items that seem like they ought to make a good model. Two relates to how self-concept is formed and the lack of inclusion of ideal self-concept and self-efficacy (self-reported capability) in its theoretical structure and formation. How can it possibly be correct that students don't use an ideal self-concept or aim for some standard, using the standards they see on television and elsewhere, and their own self-capability, as depicted in the current models? The current structural models of academic self-concept are just not believable. Three relates to the proposed hierarchical structure that is not supported when proper interval-scale measures are used. A hierarchical structure implies a top-down or bottom-up formation, none of which is supported when proper interval-scale measures are used.

Nearly all the studies of academic self-concept have used True Score Test Theory in the measures of self-concept and Confirmatory Factor Analysis to test for the hierarchy. Because a proper linear scale has not been constructed and used in these studies, the results are called into question. Wright (1999) argues the case for the use of proper linear measures in education and psychology. He suggests that no 'laws' of educational psychology have been discovered so far, as there are in physics and chemistry, for example, and 'laws' are unlikely to be discovered until researchers use proper linear measures of educational variables, such as Rasch measures (see Andrich, 1988a; Rasch, 1960/1980). This means that unless researchers use proper linear measures for academic self-concept, they are unlikely to find any 'laws' that link it to achievement or behavior, or which find out its structure and formation. There are available some Rasch computer programs that are easy to use and interpret, and they are reasonably cheap. One of the best is Rasch Unidimensional Measurement Models (RUMM) (Andrich, Sheridan, Lyne & Luo, 2002) and it has been used with a number of educational psychological variables such as motivation, approaches to study and self-concept (see for example, Waugh, 2002a, 2001, 2000, 1999). Not only can a Rasch computer program help test for a unidimensional interval-level scale, it can also test for a hierarchical structure.

The models of self-concept proposed by Shavelson, Hubner and Stanton (1976), and the revised version that separately considers maths and verbal domains proposed by Marsh and Shavelson (1985), do not involve ideal or capability self-views. Most of the measures of self-concept use only realistic items. Items relating to an ideal self-view and a capability self-view are rarely used. This comes about, at least partly, because there are strong positive correlations between real and ideal views. Marsh and Hattie (1996, p.77) have written, for example, that "ideal ratings typically do not contribute beyond what can be explained by actual ratings alone, and mean discrepancy scores have no more and, perhaps, less explanatory power than the mean of actual ratings". These comments are based on results from measures of self-concept that use True Score Theory and, as such, are called into question. There is a strong argument that people create their self-concept from an ideal self-view (see Waugh, 2001, 2000, 2002a, 2002b, 2002c), a capability self-view (see Bandura 1997; Waugh, 2002a, 2002b), and a real self-view. If one accepts this, and self-concept is related to achievement and behavior, then the self-concept measures, and the structural models behind these measures, should include all three aspects (ideal, capability and real).

While to some people, it may be reasonable to propose a general academic self-concept that is related to individual subject self-concepts in a hierarchical structure, the only test of this is by measurement. Do studies that use proper interval-level measures of academic self-concept provide evidence that support this proposed hierarchical structure? Up to 2002, there is only one study that uses Rasch measures of self-concept to test the hierarchical nature of the self-concept structure (see Waugh, 2002a). While this study does not support the hierarchical structure, there is a clear need for other studies to investigate this question.

VALUE OF RASCH MEASUREMENT

Rasch measurement produces data from which valid and reliable inferences can be made. Rasch measures produce interval-level data; it produces scale-free measures and sample-free item difficulties; it calculates person measures and item difficulties on the same scale; it checks that persons answer the response categories logically and consistently; and it checks that a uni-dimensional trait influences all the responses to all the items. True Score Test Theory does not make all these checks and hence is inadequate in helping researchers construct a proper scale. Researchers want a scale in which self-concept items are ordered from easy to hard, and calibrated on the same scale with the person self-concept measures from low to high. They want all the persons to agree that the same self-concept items are easy, that the same other items are moderately hard, and that the same other items are very hard. That is, researchers want persons with different measures of self-concept to agree on the difficulties of the self-concept items. They want persons with a high self-concept to have a higher probability of answering a self-concept item positively than persons with a low self-concept, for any item along the scale. Only when there are such measures can researchers make valid and reliable inferences, and deduce some 'laws' of academic self-concept in educational psychology (a claim supported by Wright, 1999 and Waugh, 2002c).

Scale-Free Measures and Sample-Free Item Difficulties

When data fit a Rasch measurement model, scale-free measures and sample-free item difficulties are produced (Andrich, 1988b; Wright & Masters, 1982). This means that the differences between pairs of measures and pairs of item difficulties are sample independent and the mathematics behind the Rasch model support this. This means that the probability of answering a self-concept item is dependent on the difference between the person measure and the item difficulty on the same scale. In contrast, in True Score Test Theory, the sums of scores on the items and the item difficulties are not calibrated on the same scale, and the total score (which is a measure of the variable) is strictly sample dependent. Strictly, True Score Test Theory cannot produce anything better than a ranking scale that will vary from sample to sample. If researchers want to make a linear measurement of academic self-concept, this cannot be performed through True Score Test Theory (a claim made, for example, by Wright, 1999, amongst others).

Uni-dimensional Data

When all the items fit a Rasch measurement model, there is a uni-dimensional trait 'covering' and influencing all the items. Mathematically, this means that the probability of answering a self-concept item positively is only dependent on the difference between the person measure of self-concept and the item difficulty, for all persons and all items. This means that the measure estimated in Rasch modeling should be different from that calculated in True Score Test Theory. This could come about because the Rasch model will produce a different set of items contributing to the uni-dimensional trait than will True Score Test Theory based on inter-item correlation data. An ideal Guttman pattern of responses would fit a Rasch measurement model. The argument is that a Rasch measurement model is needed to produce a proper linear scale in which both person measures and item difficulties are calibrated together on the same scale where a single dominant trait of self-concept influences all the items. True Score Test Theory does not make this test and hence cannot produce a proper linear measure. The main difference here is that, in Rasch modelling, only items that produce data that fit the measurement model are retained, whereas in True Score Test Theory, only items that produce good inter-item correlation data are retained. A recent movement in academic self-concept research is towards Rasch analysis that uses a uni-dimensional trait.

Check on Response Format

The RUMM computer program (Andrich et alia, 2002) uses a mathematically ordered threshold structure that corresponds with the conceptual ordering of the response categories for the items. The thresholds are boundaries located between the response categories. At a threshold, there are odds of 1:1 of answering in adjacent response categories. If respondents answer the categories consistently and logically, the thresholds should be ordered in correspondence with the order of the response categories. If thresholds are not ordered, then the item is discarded as not being able to produce valid and reliable data. In measuring variables like self-concept, there is a move to use response categories that are ordered from low to high, such as *never, sometimes, mostly,* or *a low standard, a moderate standard* or *a high standard*. No check is normally made on the logical and consistent answering of response formats in True Score Test Theory. So checking on consistency of data from response formats provides another test for good measurement and indicates why different items will be used in Rasch measurement, compared to those used in True Score Test Theory.

It needs to be noted here that Likert (1932) response categories (such as SDA, DA, U, A, SA) are not ordered from low to high, and they contain a discontinuity between DA and A. Although they have been widely used in the past, they should not generally be used in modern measurement. It is better to use an ordered response format.

Zero Point on the Scale

The zero point on a Rasch scale does not represent zero academic self-concept, necessarily. In a Rasch analysis, the zero point is usually artificial and represents the mean of the item difficulties, calibrated to be zero. It is possible to calibrate a true zero point, if it can be shown that an item represents zero self-concept. In True Score Test Theory there is no true zero point either. The difficulties of the items are not calibrated against the total scores (measures), and the items are not conceptualised or calibrated to form a scale from 'easy' to 'hard'. A zero score is usually the lowest score and is artificially made since there is no item measuring zero self-concept. In Rasch designed scales, items are now initially conceptualised and written in a number of sub-groups, from easy to hard (like several sets of Guttman patterns). The Rasch data analysis tests this conceptualisation and a zero point is not designed to be part of the scale, although it could be, if the researcher is clever enough.

Person-Item Interaction Tests

The RUMM program substitutes the parameter estimates back into the model and allows the researcher to examine the difference between the expected values predicted from the model and the observed values, using two tests of fit: one is the item-trait interaction and the second is the item-student interaction.

If the standardised residual between the observed and expected person parameters are not significantly different according to the item-trait test-of-fit (a chi-square), then there is no significant interaction between the responses to the items and the measures of the persons along the trait (see Andrich and van Schoubroeck, 1989, pp. 479-480 for the equations). This shows whether there is a collective agreement between persons of differing measures along the scale, over items of differing difficulty. That is, it provides a check that people with low, medium and high measures agree that certain items are easy, and that certain items are hard. It checks that there is a uni-dimensional trait that influences this ordering of the items. This is the main check that is performed to indicate a single global trait, if the items pass all the other fit statistics for forming a proper linear scale. No such check is normally done on this aspect in True Score Test Theory.

The item-person test-of-fit examines both the response patterns for persons across items and for items across persons. It examines the residual between the expected estimate and the actual values for each person-item summed over all items for each person and summed over all persons for each item (see Styles and Andrich, 1993, p. 914 or Andrich and van Schoubroeck, 1989, p. 482 for the equations). The fit statistics approximate a distribution with a mean expected near zero and a standard deviation near one when the data fit the measurement model. Negative values indicate a response pattern that fits the model too closely (probably because response dependencies are present, see Andrich, 1985) and positive values indicate a poor fit to the model (probably because other measures ('noise') are present). Again, no checks are normally done on this aspect in True Score Theory measurement.

The Rasch RUMM computer program automatically produces all these statistics and they can be checked to see that a good linear scale is produced, from which valid and reliable inferences can be made.

ADVANCES IN QUESTIONNAIRE DESIGN

Advances in questionnaire design involve ordering the items by difficulty in their initial conceptual design, and having each item answered in a number of ordered perspectives (such as an idealistic view, a capability view and a realistic view). This has advantages in data collection, checking construct validity, and measurement and interpretation. A particular problem, though, is collecting true data in line with the structure of the questionnaire. The structure has to be explained to the students and the students have to be counselled to answer the questionnaire correctly and truthfully, and be given, or allocated, sufficient time to do so. Students need to think about what they are answering. The common computer comment, *garbage in, garbage out*, is also true for measurement.

Ordering the Items by Difficulty

Measurement of academic self-concept implies that the items are ordered by difficulty from easy to hard, so that we can measure student self-concept from low to high (on the same scale). This means that the self-concept items are conceptualised and designed from easy to hard. Some examples of this are given in Appendix A (measuring English self-concept) and in Appendix B (measuring Physical Education self-concept). In Appendix A, for example, item 1 is *Have an interest and ability in Reading.* Item 2 is *Have an interest and ability, and work hard to achieve in Reading.* Item 2 is conceptual harder than item 1, because it involves item 1 and more, the more being *working hard to achieve in Reading.* Item 3 is *Have a natural flair and ability in, and feel good doing, Reading.* Item 3 is conceptually harder than item 2, because it involves item 2 and more, the more involves *having a natural flair and feeling good doing Reading.* So items 1 to 3 under the sub-heading Reading are conceptually ordered from easy to hard and this order can be tested from the student data analysed with a Rasch computer program, where the item difficulties and student measures are calibrated on the same scale. Items under the other sub-headings (Writing, Listening and Speaking) are similarly ordered from easy to hard.

Ordering the Item Perspectives by Difficulty

In Appendix A (measuring English self-concept), each item is answered in four perspectives: an idealistic self-concept, a capability self-concept, a realistic self-concept, and a self-reported achievement. It is expected that most students will order these perspectives from high (idealistic) to low (self-reported achievement). This is because an idealistic self-view involves what students would like, which is usually higher than their capability self-view, which in turn is usually higher than their actual self-view, which in turn is usually higher than their self-reported achievement. This order can be tested with student data, analysed with a Rasch computer program, where all the item difficulties and the person measures of self-concept are calibrated on the same scale.

SOME NEW RESULTS FOR SELF-CONCEPT FORMATION

Recently, Waugh (2002a, 2002b) has tested whether academic self-concept can be represented by a uni-dimensional trait when ideal self-concept, capability self-concept and real self-concept, together with self-reported corresponding subject achievement, are measured together on the same scale using a Rasch measurement model. Examples of the questionnaire that represent a new structure of self-concept are given in Appendices A and B. Samples were analysed in nine separate studies involving 15 subjects and 847 university students.

Drama students (N=135) were measured for separate Art, Music, Dance and Acting self-concepts, and a global self-concept covering these four subjects. Art students (N=103) were measured for separate Art, Music, Dance and Acting self-concepts, and a global self-concept. Music students (N=103) were measured for separate Art, Music, Dance and Acting self-concepts, and a global self-concept. These three groups were combined (N=343) and measured for separate Art, Music, Dance and Acting self-concepts, and a global self-concept. The results clearly supported three main conclusions. One is that ideal, capability and real self-concepts are linked and influenced by a single trait for each of the four subjects (Art, Music, Dance and Acting) for each of the three groups of students (Drama, Art and Music). Two is that single subject self-concepts could not be represented by a global self-concept for the combined students of Drama, Art and Music, except for Acting; that is, the data did not support the hierarchical structure postulated in the literature. Where the global structure was supported for Acting, an alternative hypothesis to the hierarchical structure is that this occurs for students who are trained to think and act in similar ways, only in subject combinations that are closely aligned by content and methods. Three is that ideal, capability and real self-concept are linked to corresponding self-reported achievement by a uni-dimensional trait for each of the four subjects (Art, Music, Dance and Acting) for each of the three groups of students (Drama, Art and Music).

Science students (N=174) were measured for separate English, Science, Maths and Social Science self-concepts, and a global self-concept covering all four subjects. Maths students (N=118) were measured for separate English, Science, Maths and Social Science self-concepts, and a global self-concept. These two groups were combined (N=294) and measured for separate English, Science, Maths and Social Science self-concepts, and a global self-concept. The results supported three main conclusions. One is that ideal, capability and real self-concepts are linked and influenced by a uni-dimensional trait for each of the four subjects (English, Science, Maths and Social Science) for the groups of Maths and Science students. Two is that single subject self-concepts could be represented by a global self-concept for the combined students of Science and Maths for English, Maths and Social Science, but not for Science, and not for these four subjects and two classes combined; that is, the data provides some partial support for the hierarchical structure postulated in the literature. Where the global structure is partially supported, an alternative hypothesis to the hierarchical structure is that the global self-concept link occurs for students who are trained to think and act in similar ways, only in subject combinations that are closely aligned by content and methods. Three is that ideal, capability and real self-concept are linked to corresponding self-reported achievement by a uni-dimensional trait for each of the four subjects (Music, Dance and Acting) for each of the three groups of students (Drama, Art and Music).

Physical Education students (N=109) were measured for separate Physical Education, Sport and Health Science self-concepts, and a global self-concept covering all three subjects. The results supported three main conclusions. One is that ideal, capability and real self-concepts are linked and influenced by a uni-dimensional trait for each of the three subjects (Physical Education, Sport and Health Science) for the group of Physical Education students. Two is that single subject self-concepts could not be represented by a global self-concept for the combined subjects of Physical Education, Sport and Health Science. Three is that ideal, capability and real self-concept are linked to corresponding self-reported achievement by a uni-dimensional trait for each of the three subjects (Physical Education, Sport and Health Science) for Physical Education students.

English Language students (N=103) were measured for separate Reading, Writing, Speaking and Listening self-concepts, and a global self-concept covering all four subjects. The results supported three main conclusions. One is that ideal, capability and real self-concepts are linked and influenced by a uni-dimensional trait for each of the three subjects (Reading, Writing and Speaking) for the group of English Language students, and that a dominant trait was present for Listening. Two is that single subject self-concepts could be represented by a global self-concept for the combined subjects of Reading, Writing, Listening and Speaking. Three is that ideal, capability and real self-concept are linked to corresponding self-reported achievement by a uni-dimensional trait for each of the four subjects (Reading, Writing, Listening and Speaking) for English Language students.

SOME PRINCIPLES OF SELF-CONCEPT FORMATION AND LINKS WITH ACHIEVEMENT

The current model of the structure of academic self-concept involving separate maths and verbal domains plus separate subject self-concepts linked with a hierarchical general academic self-concept that is related strongly to each of the separate subject self-concepts, as proposed by Marsh and Shavelson (1985), is called into question. Recent studies with university students, using proper linear measures (Rasch measurement, see Waugh, 2002a, 2002b, 2002c, 2001, 2000, 1999) support a different method of the creation and formation of academic self-concept than is involved in the structure proposed by Marsh and Shavelson (1985). These studies support the following principles of self-concept, its creation as a latent trait by students, and its links with self-reported achievement.

1. Students create separate self-concepts about academic subjects (like Science) and their performances (like Acting) that they study at university, or watch on television, DVD or video. A particular student may create different subject and performance self-concepts that are not dependent on each other. In some cases the different self-concepts may be correlated because they are good (or bad, or mediocre) in a number of subjects, because they are trained to think in similar ways for the different (and perhaps related) subjects, or performances.

2. Self-concept formation is dependent on at least four views of a subject or performance: an idealistic view, a capability view, a realistic view, and a self-view of their corresponding achievement in the subject or performance. Students think about what they can do (an idealistic self-concept), what they think that they might be able to do, given their abilities and interests (a capability self-concept), and what they think they can actually do (a realistic self-concept). Most students find it easiest to have a higher ideal self-concept than a capability self-concept, which in turn is higher than their perceived realistic self-concept.

3. Students' academic self-concepts are not just based on a view of their abilities or achievements. While realistically perceived achievement may be causally predominate on self-concept for some students, both idealistic and capability self-concept both influence the creation and formation of academic self-concept.

4. Students do not create a general academic self-concept that then influences the creation and formation of specific subject self-concepts, such as those for English, Science, Maths and Social Science. There is no common 'top-down' creation from general to specific academic self-concept used by students, although this could occur to some extent, in some situations of light indoctrination, such as religion classes.

5. Students do not create specific subject academic self-concepts that then influence the creation and formation of a general academic self-concept. There is no 'bottom-up' creation of academic self-concept as a common method used by students, although this could occur to some extent, in some situations of light indoctrination or training where subjects or performances are content and method related.

6. Students create their individual subject self-concepts, and their global self-concepts, from their idealistic, capability and realistic self-views, and their self-views of their achievements. These, in turn, depend on their particular and different personalities, their different experiences and ways of viewing events, and their different up-brings, including social and cultural differences.

REFERENCES

Andrich, D. (1988a). A General Form of Rasch's Extended Logistic Model for Partial Credit Scoring. *Applied Measurement in Education,* 1(4), 363-378.

Andrich, D. (1988b). *Rasch models for measurement.* Sage university paper on quantitative applications in the social sciences, series number 07/068. Newbury Park, California: Sage Publications.

Andrich, D. (1985). A latent trait model for items with response dependencies: Implications for test construction and analysis. In S.E. Embretson (Ed.), *Test design: developments in psychology and psychometrics* (pp. 245-275). Orlando: Academic Press.

Andrich, D., Sheridan, B., Lyne, A., & Luo, G. (2002). *RUMM: A windows-based item analysisprogram employing Rasch unidimensional measurement models.* Perth: Murdoch University.

Andrich, D. & van Schoubroeck, L. (1989). The General Health Questionnaire: a psychometricanalysis using latent trait theory. *Psychological Medicine,* 19, 469-485.

Bandura, A. (1997). *Self-Efficacy: The exercise of control.* New York, NY: W.H. Freeman and Company.

Byrne, B.M. (1996). Academic self-concept: Its structure, measurement and relation to academic achievement. In B.A. Bracken (Ed.), *Handbook of self-concept* (pp. 287-316). New York: Wiley.

Bryne, B.M. & Gavin, D.A.W. (1996). The Shavelson model revisited: Testing for the structure of academic self-concept across pre-, early and late adolescents. *Journal of Educational Psychology,* 88, 215-228.

Chapman, J.W. & Tunmer, W.E. (1997). A longitudinal study of beginning reading achievement and reading self-concept. *British Journal of Educational Psychology,* 67 (3), 279-291.

Chapman, J.W. & Tunmer, W.E. (1995). Development of young children's reading self-concept: An examination of emerging subcomponents and their relationship with reading achievement. *Journal of Educational Psychology*, 87 (1), 154-167.

Chapman, J.W., Tunmer, W.E. & Prochnow, J.E. (2000). Early reading-related skills and performance, reading self-concept, and the development of academic self-concept: A longitudinal study. *Journal of Educational Psychology*, 92 (4), 703-718.

Eccles, J.S. & Wigfield, A. (1995). In the mind of the actor: The structure of adolescents' achievement task values and expectancy-related beliefs. *Personality and Social Psychology Bulletin*, 21, 215-225.

Forsterling, F. & Morgenstern, M. (2002). Accuracy of self-assessment and task performance: Does it pay to know the truth. *Journal of Educational Psychology*, 94 (3), 576-585.

Guay, F., Bowin, M. & Hodges, E.V.E. (1999). Predicting change in academic achievement: A model of peer experiences and self-system processes. *Journal of Educational Psychology*, 91 (1), 105-115.

Harter, S. (1996). Historical rootsof contemporary issues involving self-concept. In B.A. Bracken (Ed.), *Handbook of self-concept* (pp. 1-37). New York: Wiley.

Hattie, J. (1992). *Self-concept*. Hillsdale, NJ: Lawrence Erlbaum Associates.

Likert, R. (1932). *Archives of Psychology*, 140.

Marsh, H.W. (1987). The hierarchical structure of self-concept and the application of hierarchical confirmatory factor analysis. *Journal of Educational Measurement*, 24, 17-39.

Marsh, H.W. (1986). Verbal and math self-concepts: An inertnal/external frame of reference model. *Educational Research Journal*, 23, 129-149.

Marsh, H.W. (1993). Academic self-concept: Theory, measurement and research. In J. Suls (Ed.), *Psychological perspectives on the self* (Vol.4, pp.59-88). Hillsdale, NJ: Lawrence Erlbaum Associates.

Marsh, H.W., Byrne, B.M. & Shavelson, R.J. (1988). A multifaceted academic self-concept: Its hierarchical structure and its relation to academic achievement. *Journal of Educational Psychology*, 80, 366-380.

Marsh, H.W., Hey, J., Johnson, S., & Perry, C. (1997). Elite athlete Self-Description Questionnaire: Hierarchical confirmatory factor analysis of responses by two distinct groups of elite. *International Journal of Sport Psychology*, 28, 237-258.

Marsh, H.W. & Shavelson, R.J. (1985). Self-concept: Its multi-faceted, hierarchical structure. *Educatioanl Psychologist*, 20, 107-125.

Marsh, H.W. & Yeung, A.S. (1998). Longitudinal structural equation models of academic self-concept and achievement: gender differences in the development of math and English constructs. *American Educational Research Journal*, 35 (4), 705-738.

Marsh, H.W. & Yeung, A.S. (1997). Causal effects of academic self-concept on academic achievement: Structural equation models of longitudinal data. *Journal of Educational Psychology*, 89 (1), 41-54.

Muijs, R.D. (1997). Predictors of academic achievement and academic self-concept: A longitudinal perspective. *British Journal of Educational Psychology*, 67 (3), 263-277.

In: *Topics in Cognitive Psychology*
Serge P. Shohov (Editor) pp. 13-18

ISBN 1-59033-836-7.
© 2003 Nova Science Publishers, Inc.

Chapter 2

THE DYNAMICS OF CLASSROOM AND COGNITIVE ACTIVITY OF STUDENTS

*V. P. Garkin and I. Y. Stolyarova**
Samara State University

For many decades higher education pedagogic has been speaking about the need to consider students primarily the subject of teaching. But the realities of life outside and inside institutions of higher education have made these talks declarative for a long time. Have there been any changes in the motivation, contents and level of classroom and cognitive activity of modern students since then? We have tried to answer this question, having at our disposal the results of our studies of the *dynamics of classroom and cognitive activity* of the students of Samara State University (SSU), carried out for almost two decades. In 1981 the laboratory of sociological research of our university studied the situation with classroom and cognitive activity of students. There were questioned 400 students of 5 undergraduate courses (Mathematics, Physics, History, the Russian Language and Literature and English and German departments). In 1997 and 1998 the survey of classroom and cognitive activity of students of SSU and their professional orientation was repeated according to almost the same program; the number of students questioned had grown up to 852, the number of courses made 13 then. We suppose the results of this research to be of any interest primarily because they reveal the *dynamics* of the phenomenon studied during the 80ies and the 90ies that reflects the formation of some new tendencies in contemporary higher education.

It is necessary to say a few words about the approach to studying classroom and cognitive activity. In our research it is objectively characterised by two groups of indices: according to the classroom work results (marks during exam sessions) and the classroom work process (how students plan their classroom activity, how they work at lectures, how well and often they prepare their home work, their participation in research and scientific work, how they develop their classroom skills). As for the subjective aspect we believe it is basically the

* Vitaly P. Garkin –Doctor of Chemistry, Vice-rector of Samara State University. Iren Y. Stolyarova – Doctor of Philosophy, senior research assistant of the Sociology and Political Science Chair of the same University.

students' evaluation of how interesting and informative their classes are as well as their motivation to acquire higher education.

In the 60ies and 80ies numerous studies of the problems mentioned above performed by sociological centres of our country located in institutions of higher education persistently proved that classroom and cognitive activity of students have unlimited unrealised possibilities as the most important means of increasing the quality of training. Thus, the research held in 1990 within the program "Public Opinion"[1] supported by the State Committee of Education of the Soviet Union found out that no more than 10-20% of students have well developed skills of independent work. Only one of ten students knew how to work on the computer. Only 16% of the students could (as they thought) bring data obtained from different sources together to prepare a report or a speech.

Have there been any changes since then? Let us turn to the comparative analysis data of the results of the research held in SSU in 1981 and in 1997-1998. The *level of progress in studies* in late 90ies proved to be as high as it had been before: 44.4% of the students of Natural Sciences and 64.5% of the students of the Humanities have satisfactory or good marks. *The character of students' planning their classroom activity* has not changed significantly either, though more students began to study independently according to a wider specified program: in 1981 their number was only 32%, but in 1997-1998 it grew up to about 45%. One-fifth of all the students of the 90ies paid extra time and attention to the preparation in the field of their particular course and studied the problems of related sciences. Nearly the same number of students (17.8%) spent much time on foreign languages and computer. Even in early 90ies in SSU there appeared, though not numerous, a group of students who studied at two institutes or universities or attended two faculties or took paid courses in Economics and Management simultaneously. Today the share of such students is about 2% of all students of Natural Sciences and 1% of the students of the Humanities and Management. The amount is small, but it proves the existence of new ways of realisation of their creative potential. It is worth while mentioning that such determined and diligent students quickly and easily find their way in science choosing interdisciplinary themes for their research work.

As for the lectures, they still remain an important form of meeting cognitive needs of young people. *Lecture attendance* of the students is rather high: lectures on the Humanities, Social and Economic subjects were attended by 71.8% of the students of Natural Sciences and by 92.4% of the students of the Humanities and Management; as for lectures on Mathematics and General Natural Sciences the numbers were 90.7% and 90.5% respectively; for General Professional Subjects the numbers were 86.2% of the students of Natural Sciences and 82.3% of those studying Humanities and Management. The activity level of the students of Natural Sciences has not changed since 1981, while with the students of the Humanities (further on for the purposes of this survey the students of Management will be included into this group) this level has slightly decreased. The evaluation of the quality of presentation of lectures by the students of the Humanities on the whole is much higher than that of the students of Natural Sciences. At the same time students of both groups appreciated above all such aspects as "the connection of the studied subject with the future professional activity" and the fact that "lectures give an idea of perspective science developments".

---

[1] The sociological laboratory of our university became the organizer of this research. 834 students from 36 different types of institutions of higher education were questioned in many regions of the Russian Federation. 26% of them were students of *classical* universities. The results of the research performed in other Russian universities were the same as those received in SSU in 1981.

Answering the question "What forms of class work meet your cognitive needs most of all?" students gave the first place to seminars, practical training and laboratory works (taken all together) but not to lectures. The efficiency of students' work at lectures did not prove to be very high. Only 13.9% of the students of Natural Sciences and 19.1% of the students of the Humanities analyse the information received at a lecture and ask questions. There are many reasons decreasing the students' activity: their tiredness, sometimes inconvenient timetable, etc. Students as well as lecturers treat these circumstances with patience. It is more important to emphasise that the habit of passive learning typical for the secondary school, in institutions of higher education is developing stronger.

One of the most important indicators of the students' classroom and cognitive activity is their *participation in research work*. According to the results of the survey, it is this very index that has gone through serious changes in its substantial aspect. In 1981 about 60% of the students questioned took part in different forms of research work. The most popular form was the Chair Circles (mentioned by 26.2% of respondents). The second most popular group was speaking at students' conferences -18.4%, as well as participation in theoretical seminars held by the Chair - 11.9%. The data of the survey carried out in 1997-1998 are as follows: 54.8% of the students of Natural Sciences and 75% of the students of the Humanities took part in research work. The most popular form was independent work at course papers and diploma theses (28.1% of the students of Natural Sciences and 22.5% of the students of the Humanities). The second most popular form was speaking at students' scientific conferences and participation in contests (18.5% of the students of Natural Sciences and 34.1% of the students of the Humanities). Scientific circles held by chairs were scarcely mentioned by the students as they stopped their existence. In general, the students' attitude to research work has improved, as well as changed. Now the students of SSU (at least 30% of them) consider it an honour to make their course paper creative, to present it at a students' conference, make a brilliant display at a diploma viva voce.

The comparison of all indices of classroom and cognitive activity makes it possible to get a wider picture of classroom processes, have a look into the "students' soul", to know their motivation to study, the importance of getting higher education. Today the studies are *of any interest* for 72% of the students of Natural Sciences and 86.5% of the students of the Humanities (in 1981 the figures were 62.1% and 78% respectively).

Knowledge, skills and abilities, that a student acquires while studying in institutions of higher education do not exist separately from his/her personality. On the one hand, the degree of development *of classroom skills and abilities* reflects the level of the institution's requirements towards the students, on the other hand, it reflects the students' conscientious attitude towards the process of preparation for their future professional activity. In 1981 only 24% of the students questioned could (in their opinion) work efficiently with books, in 1997-1998 50.4% of the students of Natural Sciences and 69.5% of the students of the Humanities highly evaluated their ability to work with books (95.9% of the students of Natural Sciences and 96.9% of the students of the Humanities are able to do it on the whole). Let us continue the comparison. In 1981 only 18.8% of the students were quite able to use data obtained from different sources, in late 90ies those were 92.5% of the students of Natural Sciences and 97% of students of the Humanities. In so doing 42.1% of the first group and 58.6% of the second evaluated their skills as "good". In 1981 most of the students only heard about the existence of computers. Nowadays 76.3% of the students of Natural Sciences and 68% of the students of the Humanities know how to work on them (21.4% of the former and 19.2% of the latter evaluated their abilities as "good"). Formerly the students had no experience of using foreign sources in their work. Nowadays, according to the survey, 39.6% of the students of the Humanities and 28.1% of the students of Natural Sciences are able to do it (10.9% of the first group and 5.8% of the second one are quite good at it).

In our opinion, the data on the development of classroom work skills provide a convincing demonstration of the *growth of the general level of classroom and cognitive activity* of SSU students for the last two decades. This is also testimony to the fact that universities have raised the requirements towards their students. According to the data at our disposal, this tendency is typical for other universities of our country as well.

But the most important for us is *the students' better understanding of the role and value of higher education as well as the change of its functional meaning in the present conditions.* Thus, 76% of the students of the Humanities and 73.8% of the students of Natural Sciences confirmed the fact that the main aim of their acquiring higher education was to develop their own personality. This meshes perfectly other goals: to master a profession (63.3% of the students of the Humanities and 66.6% of the students of Natural Sciences), to secure a good career (50.2% of the students of the Humanities and 46.5% of the students of Natural Sciences).

University leaders of classroom and cognitive activity have also changed. In the 80ies among the Humanities those were History and Philology students. In late 90ies Psychology, Sociology and Law students took the lead in such aspect as the general level of classroom and cognitive activity (according to the aggregate indicator). It goes without saying that the determination of leadership is rather conventional and does not in the least mean that the situation at some faculties became worse than it used to be. New *prestigious courses* simply became symbols of our time and therefore grew more interesting for the students. That is why the second place in the ability to use foreign sources was taken by the students of Sociology. This is a result of their deeper learning foreign languages according to a special program and due to the position of the Chair that widely uses foreign sources in the teaching process.

In general, the survey has proved that *the level of classroom and cognitive activity of SSU students has not only dropped in comparison to the data of early 80ies, but has even increased.* And uncertain prospects of professional career growing on in our society during the years of reforms instead of reducing this activity - on the contrary – they helped it to grow.

The survey of 1981 found a direct, though not explicitly pronounced, relationship between the professional orientation of the students and their level of classroom and cognitive activity. The deliberate wish to work in the specified field and at a chosen profession was to some extent a stimulus to obtain "good" classroom work results. In late 90ies another stimulus came up: uncertainty in the professional career made some students get interested in the fields beyond their syllabus. It is quite appropriate to say that some young people have acquired more activity raising the degree of development of their intellectual and communicative work. In its turn this proves the fact that the students are better prepared for the future which is uncertain for each individual, especially in the time of changes.

We are reminded that a great uncertainty of professional career of specialists was much spoken about in the 70ies and 80ies. Books were full of data showing a very unfavourable tendency – the lack of balance between the professional structure of university and college graduates and the structure of jobs available for them. According to the data of the National survey in 1985-1987, less than half graduates working in national economy and science were employed in the field of their training.[2] Only half of the young people were employed in the field they were qualified in technical and vocational schools and institutions of higher education. 27% of young people had to take a job that required a qualification lower than the one they got during their studies. According to the data obtained by a research performed at SSU in 1981, only 18.7% of the students while entering the university expected to get a job according to the chosen profession. The other entrants just liked the chosen field of science. The situation remained the same in 1997-1998: one-fifth (18%) of entrants thought about a particular profession; 45.8% of the students of the Humanities and 51.4% of the students of Natural Sciences just liked the chosen sphere of knowledge.

80% of the students of the Humanities and 81.3% of students of Natural Sciences like to study at *their faculty*. The leaders according to this indicator are the students of Law (the index is + 0.88), Psychology (+ 0.83), Public and Municipal Administration (+ 0.78), English and German Philology (+ 0.71), Sociology and Social Work (+ 0.69). 67.5% of students of the Humanities and 46.2% of the students of Natural Sciences would choose their institution and course if they had a chance to do it again. The leaders according to the stability of choice are again the students of Law (90.5% positive answers), Public and Municipal Administration (82.4%) and Psychology (80.9%). The research has revealed a paradox: the better, in the students' opinion, are the possibilities to get a job according to the obtained qualification and to be promoted, the less represented is the aspect of "self-development". The most evident example make the students of Law against the students of Russian Philology and History. While for the former their personal development is of less importance, for the latter (the students of Russian Philology and History) it is of greater importance. However, there is another variant of the 'career vs intellectual development' relations: future "go-getters" (in the positive sense of the word) never forget about their personality development. This is relative to those who are going to become officials – the students of Public and Municipal Administration and of Social work.

Another aspect of the analysis is also important: *the indicators of classroom work results (the marks) directly depend on all the other indicators of classroom and cognitive activity.* The research data prove the fact that A-students (honours students) and C-students (those getting satisfactory marks) have different personal and creative potentials. The first group is more organised, their classroom work skills are better developed. Thus, while 74% of A-students of the Humanities know how to use the data obtained from different sources quite well (what means a well developed logical thinking and a good command of the material), the corresponding figure for C-students is only 20%. Almost 40% A-students of Natural Sciences understand the lecture material at once. For C-students this indicator is not available. 80% of A-students and 40% of C-students of Natural Sciences are interested in their studies (for the students of the Humanities the corresponding figures are 92.6% and 61%, respectively). In general, A-students feel better at the University. They have a positive attitude. 70% A-students of Natural Sciences think that most of the teachers respect the students; among the C-students this number is 46.7% only. 45% of A-students of Natural Sciences consider most of the teachers to be "interesting as persons". Half of the C-students think the same. The situation with the students of the Humanities is similar.

A-students have a more stable professional orientation. Thus, 55% A-students of Natural Sciences would enter the same university and the same faculty if they had to do it again,

---

[2] Sbytov V. F. and others. Social development of Soviet scientific intelligentsia. Kiev: Visha Shkola. 1988. P. 16.

among the C-students this number is 36.7%. For the students of the Humanities the corresponding figures are 79.3% and 50%, respectively. More A-students have definite professional plans. Only 17.5% A-students of Natural Sciences have no idea about where they are going to work. 65% of them want to work according to the acquired qualification (at the same time 27% of them would like to set to research work). Nearly half of the C-students have no definite plans for their future. The situation with students of the Humanities is similar. Most of A- and B-students have definite professional plans: 65.4% of A-students (compared to 29.4% of C-students) would like to work according to the acquired qualification. The latter group has a more manifested material interest: 11.2% while choosing a new job would be primarily guided by the wage and 11. 8% would like to start business.

Thus, the research of classroom and cognitive activity of students in the 80ies and 90ies proves the fact that its level has raised during this period. At the same time the experience of our university shows that the potentials of its further growth remain quite substantial. The research of the processes taking place in institutions of higher education, done with the help of sociological methods is meant to facilitate the use of these potentials in a more efficient way. The most topical field is to explore the level of realisation of professional intentions and plans of the graduates and their degree of adaptation to complicated life conditions. The students' evaluation of their professional training, critical understanding of their first steps in real life would help to adjust the arrangement of training process for the next generations of students so as to make them better prepared not only for today's life but for the future as well.

In: *Topics in Cognitive Psychology*
Serge P. Shohov (Editor) pp. 19-58

ISBN 1-59033-836-7.
© 2003 Nova Science Publishers, Inc.

Chapter 3

CONFIRMATORY FACTOR ANALYSIS OF THE WECHSLER ADULT INTELLIGENCE SCALE-III (WAIS-III): 1-, 2-, AND 4-FACTOR MODELS

John R. Reddon, Carlos G. de Brito and Katherine A. Nicholls[*]

Clinical Diagnostics and Research Centre
Alberta Hospital Edmonton
Alberta, Canada

ABSTRACT

The factor structure of the WAIS-III in the 13 normative age samples was examined using principal components analysis for 1-factor (general), 2-factor (Verbal and Performance), and 4-factor (Verbal Comprehension, Perceptual Organization, Working Memory, and Processing Speed) solutions. For the 2-factor and 4-factor solutions an orthogonal procrustes rotation was used to rotate the loadings to the least squares best fit of the hypothesis matrix. Congruence coefficients and root mean square differences were used to assess consistency of the subtest loadings across age groups and goodness of fit with the hypothesized structure. In addition, the putative factor structures for the 1-, 2-, and 4-factor solutions were used to evaluate the predictability of subtests within and between factors. Results indicate that users of the WAIS-III need to be extremely cautious attributing deficits or strengths in specific abilities beyond a generalized measure of intelligence in which verbal abilities are central.

* * *

With the outbreak of the first world war in 1914, the U.S. military was faced with the problem of how to allocate personnel into different types of service and of how to select individuals most suitable for officer ranks (Kaufman, 2000). Even though the U.S. did not enter the war until 1917, did not see active combat until July of 1918, and the war was over in

[*] Address: Clinical Diagnostics and Research Centre, Alberta Hospital Edmonton, 17480 - Fort Road, Box 307, Edmonton, Alberta T5J 2J7 Canada.

November of 1918, about 1,000,000 recruits were assessed under the leadership of Yerkes. Yerkes was well prepared for this task given that he was an experimental psychologist with considerable intelligence test construction experience (Yerkes & Anderson, 1915; Yerkes & Bridges, 1914; Yerkes & Forster, 1915, 1923). The Army Alpha and Beta tests were administered in group format to recruits proficient in English and to those lacking in English proficiency, respectively (Yerkes, 1921; Yoakum & Yerkes, 1920). Wechsler received his M.A. at Columbia University in 1917 and then obtained a job scoring the Army Alpha. He also administered the Stanford-Binet in individual format to recruits who had done poorly on the Army Alpha or Beta (Kaufman, 2000). After the war, Wechsler completed his Ph.D. at Columbia in 1925 and worked at the Bellevue hospital in New York up until 1932. For the remainder of his career he had a faculty position at Columbia, was involved in private practice, and was involved in the ongoing development of intelligence scales.

The Wechsler-Bellevue Intelligence Scale (W-B; Wechsler, 1939) was designed for individual administration for ages 7 to 59. It was derived from the Verbal (Information, Comprehension, Similarities, Arithmetic, and Vocabulary) and non-Verbal (Picture Arrangement, Picture Completion, Object Assembly, Block Design, and Digit Symbol-Coding) subtests in the Army Alpha and the Army Beta, respectively, as well as the Digit Span task of the Stanford-Binet (Frank, 1983). The W-BII, an alternate form of the W-B, was introduced by Wechsler (1946). Wechsler's contribution with the W-B and W-BII was to combine the Verbal and non-Verbal (Performance) subtests into a Full Scale and to convert raw scores to standard scores using normative data (Frank, 1983; Thurstone, 1925). The Wechsler Intelligence Scale for Children (WISC; Wechlser, 1949) for ages 6 to 16 and the Wechsler Preschool and Primary Scales of Intelligence (WPPSI; Wechsler, 1967) for ages 3 to 7 were downward extensions of the W-B. The Wechsler Adult Intelligence Scale (WAIS; Wechsler, 1955), WAIS-R (Wechsler, 1981), and WAIS-III (Wechsler, 1997a, 1997b) were revisions of the W-B. A short screening test for the WAIS-III, the Wechsler Abbreviated Scale of Intelligence (WASI; Psychological Corporation, 1999), was also recently introduced based on four of the WAIS-III subtests (Vocabulary, Block Design, Similarities, and Matrix Reasoning). The WISC was revised with the introduction of the WISC-R (Wechsler, 1974) and WISC-III (Wechsler, 1991) and the WPPSI was revised with the introduction of the WPPSI-R (Wechsler, 1989) and WPPSI-III (Wechsler, 2002a, 2002b).

About 34% and 20%, respectively, of the assessments undertaken by clinical psychologists and neuropsychologists are of intelligence (Camara, Nathan, & Puente, 2000). The Wechsler tests have been ranked in the top 10 to 20 tests in terms of the frequency of use (Camara et al., 2000). On the WAIS-III, the Vocabulary, Similarities, Arithmetic, Digit Span, Information, and Comprehension subtests are used to compute Verbal IQ (VIQ). Picture Completion, Digit-Symbol Coding, Block Design, Matrix Reasoning, and Picture Arrangement are used to compute Performance IQ (PIQ). The subtests constituting VIQ and PIQ are also used to compute Full Scale IQ (FSIQ). Four factor indices are computed by replacing Picture Arrangement and Comprehension with Letter-Number Sequencing and Symbol Search. Object Assembly is an optional subtest that is not typically included in the computation of FSIQ, VIQ, PIQ, or the 4-factor index scores. In the 4-factor solution, VIQ subdivides into a Verbal Comprehension factor and a Working Memory factor. Vocabulary, Similarities, and Information comprise the Verbal Comprehension factor. Arithmetic, Digit Span, and Letter-Number Sequencing comprise the Working Memory factor. As well, in the 4-factor solution, PIQ subdivides into Perceptual Organization and Processing Speed factors.

Picture Completion, Block Design, and Matrix Reasoning comprise the Perceptual Organization factor. Digit Symbol-Coding and Symbol Search comprise the Processing Speed factor.

The nature and the structure of intelligence is an ongoing and controversial issue in the field of abilities. Interestingly, Thurstone's (1935) first book on factor analysis was entitled "The Vectors of the Mind."

While insight has been provided from many factor analytic studies conducted on Wechsler's intelligence scales (Bowden, Carstairs, & Shores, 1999; Enns & Reddon, 1998; Hill, Reddon, & Jackson, 1985; Leckliter, Matarazzo, & Silverstein, 1986), the putative factor structure of the recently revised WAIS-III has received limited evaluation. Such studies are important as they provide insight into the dimensional structure and interpretative basis.

The purpose of the current study was to provide a detailed examination of the factor structure of the WAIS-III for 1-, 2-, and 4-factor solutions using confirmatory factor analysis across the 13 age groups and for the average age group for the normative data reported by Wechsler (1997a). Resulting factor structures were compared across age groups and evaluated for correspondence with the hypothesized structure. Reliabilities of the factors and the predictability of subtests within and between factors were also evaluated.

METHOD

Data from the WAIS-III standardization sample of 2,450 individuals between the ages of 16-85 years were used for this study (Wechsler, 1997a). Wechsler reported 14 correlation matrices: 1 correlation matrix for every age group and 1 average correlation matrix across the 13 normative age groups. The subtests comprising VIQ and PIQ were used for the 1-factor and 2-factor solutions. For the 2-factor solution, the Verbal factor was defined by the six VIQ subtests and the Performance factor was defined by the five PIQ subtests. For the 4-factor solution, the four factors were defined by the subtests constituting these factor indices. The Verbal Comprehension, Perceptual Organization, and Working Memory factors are each comprised of three subtests whereas the Processing Speed factor is comprised of two subtests.

Principal components analysis (Joliffe, 1986) of the correlation matrices with a confirmatory orthogonal procrustes rotation (Cliff, 1966; Shönemann, 1966) was used to construct the 2- and 4-factor solutions, and the first and largest factor from the unrotated solution was used to construct the 1-factor solution. Root mean square differences and congruence coefficients were used to evaluate the consistency of factor loadings across age groups and to assess goodness of fit with the hypothesized structure. Calculation of the reliability of weighted composites (Mosier, 1943) with the factor score coefficients as weights and the reported subtest reliabilities (Wechsler, 1997a) was used to estimate the reliability of the factors (cf. Enns & Reddon, 1998). The putative factor structures for the 1-, 2-, and 4-factor solutions were also used to evaluate the predictability of subtests within and between factors.

RESULTS

1-Factor Solution (General Factor)

The 11 subtests (6 Verbal, 5 Performance) involved in the computation of FSIQ were subjected to a prediction analysis where each subtest was predicted from the remaining subtests (see Table 1). The squared multiple correlation (SMC) indicates the extent to which any particular subtest can be predicted from the remaining 10 subtests. SMCs denote the proportion of explained variance and can range from 0 to 1, where 0 indicates complete independence and 1 indicates complete dependence. These 11 subtests were also subjected to a principal component analysis and the loadings for the first unrotated principal component (i.e., the general factor, abbreviated as g) across age groups are presented in Table 2. The loadings are correlations of the subtests with the factor score and can therefore range from -1 to +1. The consistency in loadings across age groups was evaluated using congruence coefficients and root mean square differences (see Table 3). The congruence coefficient is the cosine of the angle in degrees of the loadings between age groups. Congruence coefficients can range between -1 and +1 and have an interpretation much like a correlation coefficient (i.e., 0 indicates orthogonality or independence and 1 indicates perfect congruence). The root mean square difference is the square root of the average squared differences between loadings. For this index larger values indicate greater dissimilarity.

Prediction Analysis (FSIQ Subtests)

The mean SMCs across the 13 age groups were quite similar to the SMCs in the 16-89 combined age group (i.e., the largest discrepancy was .04; see Table 1). Using the mean SMCs across age groups as an estimate of the overall effect, Vocabulary (.75), Information (.69), Similarities (.66), Comprehension (.66), and Arithmetic (.58) have the highest mean SMCs whereas Digit Symbol-Coding (.33), Digit Span (.36), Picture Completion (.42), and Picture Arrangement (.45) have the lowest mean SMCs. The five subtests with the highest mean SMCs were all Verbal subtests. In general, the six Verbal subtests (mean of mean SMCs across the 13 age groups $M_M = .62$) were on average more predictable than the five Performance subtests ($M_M = .45$). In terms of variability across age groups, Vocabulary, Information, and Block Design had the least variability (range .13, .13, and .15, respectively), whereas Picture Completion, Matrix Reasoning, and Similarities were most variable (range .33, .29, .27, respectively). These prediction analysis results indicate that Verbal abilities and particularly Vocabulary are pivotal to Wechler's conception of intelligence as expressed in the WAIS-III.

Table 1. Squared Multiple Correlations for each Subtest by Age Group for the WAIS-III

Subtest	16-17	18-19	20-24	25-29	30-34	35-44	45-54	55-64	65-69	70-74	75-79	80-84	85-89	16-89	M	SD	Range
Verbal																	
Vocabulary	.70	.74	.74	.79	.76	.76	.72	.77	.80	.74	.72	.78	.67	.73	.75	.04	.13
Similarities	.48	.65	.67	.64	.69	.64	.69	.68	.75	.70	.73	.70	.60	.65	.66	.07	.27
Arithmetic	.52	.65	.64	.64	.66	.58	.56	.60	.67	.56	.44	.53	.45	.56	.58	.08	.23
Digit Span	.29	.42	.46	.44	.35	.31	.26	.39	.40	.31	.45	.34	.26	.32	.36	.07	.20
Information	.61	.67	.67	.70	.70	.68	.68	.71	.74	.68	.73	.69	.67	.68	.69	.03	.13
Comprehension	.56	.64	.64	.67	.67	.67	.66	.69	.76	.67	.66	.63	.60	.63	.66	.05	.20
Performance																	
Picture Completion	.38	.24	.38	.38	.44	.40	.46	.44	.57	.49	.38	.44	.45	.40	.42	.08	.33
Digit Symbol-Coding	.30	.29	.26	.25	.23	.30	.36	.33	.45	.32	.37	.43	.44	.29	.33	.07	.22
Block Design	.50	.54	.55	.52	.51	.54	.58	.44	.58	.54	.43	.50	.45	.49	.51	.05	.15
Matrix Reasoning	.47	.51	.60	.53	.55	.57	.62	.63	.58	.54	.34	.52	.37	.51	.53	.09	.29
Picture Arrangement	.29	.42	.41	.46	.55	.42	.50	.50	.48	.45	.37	.47	.51	.42	.45	.07	.26
Sum	5.10	5.77	6.03	6.03	6.11	5.88	6.09	6.19	6.77	6.00	5.63	6.02	5.49	5.69	5.93	.39	1.67

Note. All 11 subtests were predicted with the remaining 10 subtests. 16-89 pooled age group excluded from computation of *M*, *SD*, and *range*.

Table 2. Loadings of Subtests on the First Principal Component by Age Group for the WAIS-III

Subtest	16-17	18-19	20-24	25-29	30-34	35-44	45-54	55-64	65-69	70-74	75-79	80-84	85-89	16-89	M	SD	Range
									Age Group								
Verbal																	
Vocabulary	.84	.86	.84	.87	.87	.86	.85	.86	.88	.86	.83	.86	.80	.85	.85	.02	.08
Similarities	.72	.83	.80	.80	.82	.81	.83	.84	.88	.83	.88	.84	.80	.82	.82	.04	.16
Arithmetic	.73	.82	.81	.83	.81	.78	.78	.79	.83	.75	.68	.76	.66	.78	.77	.05	.17
Digit Span	.56	.65	.62	.70	.57	.56	.53	.65	.61	.50	.68	.51	.51	.59	.59	.07	.20
Information	.80	.81	.81	.82	.84	.82	.83	.85	.83	.84	.84	.79	.83	.83	.82	.02	.06
Comprehension	.76	.81	.77	.83	.82	.82	.82	.84	.86	.84	.79	.80	.76	.81	.81	.03	.10
Performance																	
Picture Completion	.61	.52	.64	.59	.67	.64	.72	.70	.77	.72	.62	.67	.68	.66	.66	.07	.25
Digit Symbol-Coding	.57	.57	.50	.53	.49	.55	.60	.60	.70	.60	.61	.65	.68	.59	.59	.06	.21
Block Design	.72	.74	.76	.72	.74	.71	.78	.68	.75	.75	.66	.66	.71	.72	.72	.04	.12
Matrix Reasoning	.72	.74	.79	.76	.75	.78	.82	.82	.79	.76	.61	.74	.63	.75	.75	.06	.21
Picture Arrangement	.57	.67	.65	.72	.76	.71	.73	.74	.71	.71	.65	.72	.74	.70	.70	.05	.19
Variance	5.33	5.97	5.94	6.17	6.15	5.98	6.34	6.45	6.82	6.18	5.72	5.94	5.62	6.06	6.05	.38	1.49
% Total Variance	48.5	54.3	54.0	56.1	55.9	54.3	57.7	58.7	62.0	56.2	52.0	54.0	51.1	55.1	55.0	3.45	13.5
Reliability	.97	.98	.98	.98	.98	.98	.98	.98	.98	.98	.97	.98	.97	.98	.98	.04	.01
Congruence	.99	.99	.99	.99	.99	.99	.99	.99	.99	.99	.99	.99	.99	.99	.99	.00	.00
RMSD	.32	.29	.29	.28	.28	.29	.27	.25	.23	.28	.30	.29	.30	.28	.28	.02	.09

Note. RMSD denotes root mean square difference. 16-89 pooled age group excluded from computation of *M*, *SD*, and *range*.

Table 3. Congruence Coefficients (Below Diagonal) and Root Mean Square Differences (Above Diagonal) for the First Unrotated Principal Component by Age Group for the WAIS-III

Age Group	16-17	18-19	20-24	25-29	30-34	35-44	45-54	55-64	65-69	70-74	75-79	80-84	85-89	16-89
16-17		.07	.06	.08	.08	.06	.08	.09	.10	.07	.08	.07	.08	.06
18-19	1.00		.05	.03	.06	.05	.08	.07	.09	.08	.08	.08	.10	.05
20-24	1.00	1.00		.04	.05	.04	.06	.06	.08	.06	.09	.07	.10	.04
25-29	1.00	1.00	1.00		.05	.05	.07	.05	.08	.08	.08	.08	.10	.05
30-34	1.00	1.00	1.00	1.00		.03	.05	.05	.08	.05	.09	.06	.09	.04
35-44	1.00	1.00	1.00	1.00	1.00		.04	.04	.07	.04	.08	.04	.08	.02
45-54	1.00	1.00	1.00	1.00	1.00	1.00		.05	.05	.02	.10	.05	.08	.04
55-64	1.00	.99	1.00	1.00	1.00	1.00	1.00		.05	.05	.08	.06	.09	.04
65-69	1.00	1.00	1.00	1.00	1.00	1.00	1.00	1.00		.06	.10	.06	.10	.06
70-74	1.00	1.00	1.00	1.00	1.00	1.00	1.00	1.00	1.00		.09	.04	.06	.03
75-79	.99	.99	.99	.99	.99	.99	.99	1.00	.99	.99		.08	.07	.07
80-84	1.00	.99	1.00	.99	1.00	1.00	1.00	1.00	1.00	1.00	.99		.06	.04
85-89	.99	.99	.99	.99	.99	1.00	1.00	.99	1.00	1.00	.99	1.00		.07
16-89	1.00	1.00	1.00	1.00	1.00	1.00	1.00	1.00	1.00	1.00	1.00	1.00	1.00	1.00

Note. Excluding the 16-89 age group, congruence coefficients ranged between .9909 and .9996 ($M = .9965$, $SD = .0022$) and root mean square differences ranged between .0242 and .1047 ($M = .0677$, $SD = .0192$).

General Factor Loadings

Across the 13 age groups the first unrotated principal component accounts for between 48.5% and 62.0% ($M = 55.0\%$) of the total variance of the correlation matrix among the 11 subtests (see Table 2). Consequently, in general and in any particular age group, about half the total variance in the correlation matrix was accounted for by g. The reliability estimates for the first unrotated factor were obtained using the factor score coefficients as weights with the reliability estimates for the subtests reported by Wechsler (1997a, p. 50) to obtain the reliability of a weighted composite (cf. Mosier, 1943). Across the 13 age groups the factor reliability estimates were distributed in the interval .97 to .98 and were comparable to the reliability estimates reported by Wechsler (1997a) for FSIQ. Therefore, the general factor is almost perfectly reliable.

Using the mean loadings across age groups as an estimate overall effect, the lowest two loadings on the general factor were associated with one of the Verbal subtests (.59, Digit Span) and one of the Performance subtests (.59, Digit Symbol-Coding). For the remaining five Verbal subtests the mean loadings ranged from .77 to .85 with Vocabulary obtaining the highest loading. For the remaining four Performance subtests the mean loadings ranged from .66 (Picture Completion) to .75 (Matrix Reasoning). In other words, excluding Digit Span, on average all other Verbal subtests loaded higher on the general factor than did any of the Performance subtests. In terms of variability of the loadings across age groups, Information (range .06), Vocabulary (range .08), and Block Design (range .12) were most consistent, whereas, Picture Completion (range .25), Digit Symbol-Coding (range .21), and Matrix Reasoning (range .21) were least consistent. Consequently, the results reported in Table 2 corroborate the results reported in Table 1. Verbal abilities and in particular Vocabulary are central to Wechsler's conception of intelligence as operationalized in the WAIS-III.

General Factor Congruence Coefficients and Root Mean Square Differences

Congruence coefficients and root mean square differences were used to evaluate the consistency of g loadings (Table 2) across age groups and are presented in Table 3. To four decimal places and excluding the 16-89 pooled age group, the congruence coefficients ranged between .9909 to .9996 with a mean of .9965 and the root mean square differences ranged between .0242 and .1047 with a mean of .0677. These results in association with the range of .0242 to .1047 for the root mean square differences (i.e., the square root of the average squared difference of loadings between age groups) indicate that the general factor of the WAIS-III is equivalent across age groups. Congruence coefficients and root mean square differences of the loadings in Table 2 with a vector of 1's are reported at the bottom of Table 2. A vector of 1's is what would be obtained if all subtests on the general factor were weighted equally and obtained a loading of 1.0 on the general factor. Across the 13 age groups the congruence coefficients were all .99 which indicates that there is little angular separation from a vector of 1's. In terms of the magnitude of discrepancy from the vector of 1's, the root mean square differences ranged between .23 and .32 ($M = .28$) across age groups. Consequently, the average difference from a loading of 1 across all subtests and age groups is .28.

2-Factor Solution (Verbal and Performance Factors)

The 11 subtests used in the computation of FSIQ are subdivided into 6 Verbal subtests and 5 Performance subtests and are used to compute Verbal IQ and Performance IQ, respectively. A prediction analysis was undertaken whereby each Verbal subtest was predicted from the remaining 5 Verbal subtests and each of the 5 Performance subtests was predicted from all 6 Verbal subtests. Similarly, each of the 5 Performance subtests was predicted from the remaining 4 Performance subtests and each of the 6 Verbal subtests was predicted from all 5 Performance subtests. The prediction analysis results are presented in Table 4. For the factor analysis, a binary hypothesis matrix (0 absent, 1 present) was constructed with one column for the Verbal factor (1's for the Verbal subtests and 0's for the Performance subtests) and one column for the Performance factor (1's for the Performance subtests and 0's for the Verbal subtests). In each of the 13 age groups as well as the pooled 16-89 age group the first two unrotated principal components were rotated orthogonally with an orthogonal procrustes rotation (Cliff, 1966; Shönemann, 1966) to the least squares best fit of the hypothesis matrix. The loadings for the Verbal factor are presented in Table 5 and the loadings for the Performance factor are presented in Table 6. Loadings set to 1 in the hypothesis matrix are underlined and loadings set to 0 are not underlined. Congruence coefficients and root mean square differences between age groups are presented in Tables 7 and 8 for the Verbal and Performance factors, respectively. Congruence coefficients and root mean square differences are presented for the Verbal and Performance factors with the corresponding column of the binary hypothesis matrix at the bottom of Tables 5 and 6, respectively. In addition, the root mean square differences are partitioned at the bottom of Tables 5 and 6 into the hypothesized (i.e., set equal to 1) and non-hypothesized (i.e., set equal to 0) components so that the degree of fit for these two components could be evaluated.

Prediction Analysis (VIQ and PIQ Subtests)

For the results of the prediction analysis for both the Verbal and Performance subtests of the WAIS-III, presented in Table 4, the top half of the table contains the SMCs for predicting each of the six Verbal subtests and the five Performance subtests from the Verbal subtests. The bottom half of the table contains the SMCs for predicting the Performance subtests and the Verbal subtests from the Performance subtests. Using the mean across the 13 age groups as an estimate of the overall effect, the results of this analysis indicate that the six Verbal subtests (M_M = .59; Vocabulary, Similarities, Arithmetic, Digit Span, Information, and Comprehension) are more predictable from the five remaining Verbal subtests than are the five Performance subtests (M_M = .36; Picture Completion, Digit Symbol-Coding, Block Design, Matrix Reasoning, and Picture Arrangement). In terms of the consistency of prediction with the Verbal subtests across age groups, gauged by the range, Vocabulary (.13), Information (.14), and Digit Span (.16) were most consistent and Picture Completion (.30), Matrix Reasoning (.29), and Arithmetic (.27) were least consistent. Across the 13 age groups, prediction with the Performance subtests of the Verbal subtests (M_M = .41) and Performance subtests (M_M = .38) were comparable. Consistency of prediction with the Performance subtests, gauged by the range, was most consistent for Block Design (.15), Information (.18), and Vocabulary (.21) and least consistent for Arithmetic (.35), Similarities (.28), and Picture Completion (.28). The prediction analysis results for the Verbal and Performance subtests indicate that the Verbal subtests have more in common with each other than they do with the

Performance subtests but that the Performance subtests have about as much in common with each other as they do with the Verbal subtests. In other words, for the 11 subtests constituting FSIQ as well as VIQ and PIQ, the Verbal subtests are somewhat more specific but also more pervasive than the Performance subtests.

Verbal Factor Loadings

Across the 13 age groups the Verbal factor accounted for between 34.7 and 41.4% (M = 38.5%) of the variance in the correlation matrix among the 11 subtests. The reliability estimates for this factor ranged from .93 to .95 across age groups (M = .94). The Verbal subtest with the lowest mean loading was Digit Span (.46). The next lowest Verbal subtest mean loading on this factor was Arithmetic (.63). The mean loadings of the remaining four Verbal subtests were all high (range .79 to .83). The mean loadings of the five Performance subtests on the Verbal factor ranged between .28 and .50. The Performance subtest with the lowest mean loading was Digit Symbol-Coding (.28) which was followed by Picture Completion (.36), Block Design (.39), Matrix Reasoning (.47), and Picture Arrangement (.50). With the exception of the Verbal subtest Digit Span (.46), all five other Verbal subtests had higher mean loadings on the Verbal factor than any of the five Performance subtests.

Performance Factor Loadings

The variance accounted for by the Performance factor was lower in all 13 age groups than for the Verbal factor, ranging between 22.5 and 29.1% (M = 25.4%) which is due in part to fewer subtests constituting the Performance factor than the Verbal factor (i.e., 5 versus 6). Across the 13 age groups, the reliability estimates for the Performance factor (range .87 to .92) were comparable to the Verbal factor (range .93 to .95) reliability estimates. The Performance subtest with the lowest mean loading on the Performance factor was Picture Arrangement (.49) which was the Performance subtest with the highest mean loading on the Verbal factor (.50). All four other Performance subtests had higher mean loadings on the Performance factor (range .61 to .68) than on the Verbal factor (range .28 to .47). However, the loadings of the Performance subtests on the Performance factor tended to be lower than the loadings of the Verbal subtests on the Verbal factor. Of the six Verbal subtests, Arithmetic (.49) and Digit Span (.39) had the highest mean loadings on the Performance factor. However, neither of these two subtests loaded higher on the Performance factor than on the Verbal factor. For the other four Verbal subtests (Vocabulary, Similarities, Information, and Comprehension) their mean loadings on the Performance factor were also less than their mean loadings on the Verbal factor.

Verbal Factor Congruence Coefficients and Root Mean Square Differences

The bottom of Table 5 contains the congruence coefficients and root mean square differences across age groups with the column of the binary hypothesis matrix constituting the Verbal factor. These congruence coefficients ranged between .72 and .93 (M = .86) and the root mean square differences ranged between .28 and .52 (M = .37) across the 13 age groups. Separating the root mean square differences with the column of the hypothesis matrix constituting the Verbal factor into hypothesized (Verbal) and non-hypothesized (Performance) components resulted in a bit better fit for the six Verbal subtests (M = .32) than the five Performance subtests (M = .42) across the 13 age groups. Excluding the 16-89 pooled age group, the between sample congruence coefficients (see Table 7) ranged between .8465 and .9966 with a mean of .9609. The root mean square differences ranged between .0565 and .3342 ($M = .1620$) across the 13 age groups. Consequently, for the Verbal factor compared to the first unrotated principal component, the between sample congruence coefficients ($M = .9609$ versus .9965) and the root mean square differences ($M = .1620$ versus .0677) indicated less consistency across samples.

Performance Factor Congruence Coefficients and Root Mean Square Differences

The congruence coefficients and root mean square differences of the Performance factor with the column of the binary hypothesis matrix constituting the Performance factor are reported at the bottom of Table 6. Across the 13 age groups, the congruence coefficients ranged between .63 and .91 ($M = .81$) and the root mean square differences ranged between .30 and .53 ($M = .39$). Consequently, with respect to the hypothesis matrix and in terms of the congruence coefficients and root mean square differences, the fit of the Performance factor ($M = .81, .39$, respectively) is comparable to the fit of the Verbal factor ($M = .86, .37$, respectively). Separating the root mean square differences into hypothesized (Performance) and non-hypothesized (Verbal) components resulted in equivalent fit for the five Performance subtests ($M = .41$) and six Verbal subtests ($M = .37$) across the 13 age groups. The between sample congruence coefficients reported in Table 8 ranged between .6375 and .9941 ($M = .8999$) across the 13 age groups and the root mean square differences across the 13 age groups ranged between .0659 and .4570 ($M = .2193$). The between sample congruences ($M = .8999$) and root mean square differences ($M = .2193$) for the Performance factor are comparable to what was obtained for the Verbal factor (.9609 and .1620, respectively). Concordant with what was found with respect to the Verbal factor relative to the first unrotated component, the Performance factor was also less consistent across samples than the first unrotated principal component (congruence coefficients: $M = .8999$ versus .9965; root mean square differences: $M = .2193$ versus .0677).

4-Factor Solution (Verbal Comprehension, Perceptual Organization, Working Memory, and Processing Speed Factors)

The 11 subtests involved in the 4-factor solution are somewhat different than the 11 subtests involved in the 1-factor and 2-factor solutions. The Picture Arrangement and Comprehension subtests, which are involved in the 1- and 2-factor solutions, are not included in the 4-factor solution. The Symbol Search and Letter-Number Sequencing subtests, which are included in the 4-factor solution, are not included in either the 1-factor or 2-factor solutions. Despite these disparities, the Verbal factor in the 2-factor solution subdivides in the 4-factor solution into the Verbal Comprehension and Working Memory factors, and the Performance factor in the 2-factor solution subdivides in the 4-factor solution into the Perceptual Organization and Processing Speed factors. The results of the prediction analysis for the Verbal Comprehension, Perceptual Organization, Working Memory, and Processing Speed factors of the WAIS-III are presented in Table 9. Prediction with the three subtests of the Verbal Comprehension factor appears in the top portion of the table, and is followed by the prediction with the three subtests of the Perceptual Organization factor, then the three subtests of the Working Memory factor, and finally the two subtests of the Processing Speed factor. For the factor analysis, a binary hypothesis matrix (0 absent, 1 present) was constructed with one column for the Verbal Comprehension subtests (1's for the Verbal Comprehension subtests and 0's for all other subtests), one column for the Perceptual Organization subtests (1's for the Perceptual Organization subtests and 0's for all other subtests), one column for the Working Memory subtests (1's for the Working Memory subtests and 0's for all other subtests), and one column for the Processing Speed subtests (1's for the Processing Speed subtests and 0's for all other subtests). In each of the 13 age groups as well as the pooled 16-89 age group the first four unrotated principal components were rotated orthogonally with an orthogonal procrustes rotation (Cliff, 1966; Shönemann, 1966) to the least squares best fit of the hypothesis matrix. The loadings for the Verbal Comprehension, Perceptual Organization, Working Memory, and Processing Speed factors are presented in Tables 10, 11, 12, and 13, respectively. In Tables 10 to 13, loadings set to 1 in the hypothesis matrix are underlined and loadings set to 0 not underlined. At the bottom of Tables 10 to 13 the congruence coefficients and root mean square differences with the column of the hypothesis matrix constituting the respective factor are reported as an assessment of goodness of fit with the hypothesized structure. In addition, the root mean square differences with the respective column of the hypothesis matrix are separated into hypothesized (i.e., set equal to 1) and non-hypothesized components (i.e., set equal to 0). Congruence coefficients and root mean square differences between age groups are presented in Tables 14 to 17 for the Verbal Comprehension, Perceptual Organization, Working Memory, and Processing Speed factors, respectively.

Prediction Analysis (Verbal Comprehension, Perceptual Organization, Working Memory, and Processing Speed Subtests)

Using the mean across age groups as an estimate of overall effect, the mean of the mean SMCs (.64) for the Verbal Comprehension subtests was larger than the mean of the mean SMCs for the subtests on the other three factors (.31, .32, and .25, respectively, for Perceptual Organization, Working Memory, and Processing Speed). Consequently, the three Verbal Comprehension subtests (Vocabulary, Similarities, and Information) are each better predicted by the Verbal Comprehension subtests than are the subtests from the other three factors. The Perceptual Organization and Working Memory subtests were predicted equally as well and the Processing Speed subtests were predicted almost as well.

For the prediction involving the three subtests (Picture Completion, Block Design, and Matrix Reasoning) on the Perceptual Organization factor, the mean of the mean SMCs across age groups were .38, .38, .30, and .31, respectively, for the Verbal Comprehension, Perceptual Organization, Working Memory, and Processing Speed subtests. Consequently, the Verbal Comprehension subtests were predicted as well from the Perceptual Organization subtests as were the Perceptual Organization subtests. In addition, the Working Memory (M_M = .30) and Processing Speed (M_M = .31) subtests were predicted almost as well from the Perceptual Organization subtests as were either the Verbal Comprehension and Perceptual Organization subtests.

Table 4. Squared Multiple Correlations for Predicting each of the WAIS-III Verbal and Performance Subtests Separately by Verbal Subtests and Performance Subtests by Age Group

Subtest	16-17	18-19	20-24	25-29	30-34	35-44	45-54	55-64	65-69	70-74	75-79	80-84	85-89	16-89	M	SD	Range
												Age Group					
Verbal						*Prediction with Verbal Subtests*											
Vocabulary	.69	.73	.74	.78	.75	.75	.72	.75	.79	.73	.71	.77	.66	.73	.74	.04	.13
Similarities	.46	.63	.65	.64	.67	.62	.64	.66	.72	.67	.70	.68	.55	.64	.64	.07	.26
Arithmetic	.44	.59	.56	.59	.55	.50	.50	.56	.63	.50	.43	.51	.36	.51	.52	.07	.27
Digit Span	.24	.37	.39	.40	.31	.29	.25	.38	.38	.28	.38	.26	.24	.30	.32	.06	.16
Information	.60	.64	.65	.69	.69	.66	.66	.70	.74	.67	.72	.67	.60	.67	.67	.04	.14
Comprehension	.55	.63	.63	.66	.65	.66	.65	.68	.72	.66	.64	.60	.57	.63	.64	.04	.17
Performance																	
Picture Completion	.24	.19	.29	.22	.33	.26	.36	.34	.49	.39	.28	.27	.36	.28	.31	.08	.30
Digit Symbol-Coding	.27	.27	.23	.22	.22	.23	.26	.28	.39	.26	.31	.31	.36	.25	.28	.05	.17
Block Design	.36	.47	.48	.40	.41	.37	.49	.32	.45	.41	.28	.32	.35	.37	.39	.07	.21
Matrix Reasoning	.36	.44	.51	.44	.52	.47	.55	.53	.51	.46	.26	.39	.30	.43	.44	.09	.29
Picture Arrangement	.21	.36	.33	.38	.47	.39	.36	.43	.37	.40	.32	.35	.44	.35	.37	.06	.26
Verbal						*Prediction With Performance Subtests*											
Vocabulary	.40	.45	.41	.44	.51	.46	.49	.51	.54	.48	.33	.42	.35	.44	.45	.06	.21
Similarities	.29	.44	.38	.36	.46	.42	.54	.50	.57	.51	.46	.42	.43	.43	.44	.08	.28
Arithmetic	.40	.52	.55	.49	.57	.46	.45	.44	.51	.42	.22	.34	.35	.43	.44	.10	.35
Digit Span	.22	.33	.38	.35	.28	.21	.17	.26	.26	.18	.32	.21	.16	.23	.26	.07	.22
Information	.37	.43	.39	.40	.48	.41	.49	.50	.42	.47	.37	.32	.50	.41	.43	.06	.18
Comprehension	.30	.42	.35	.41	.46	.42	.44	.46	.54	.48	.29	.39	.34	.39	.41	.07	.25
Performance																	
Picture	.34	.21	.36	.36	.40	.38	.43	.41	.49	.44	.34	.42	.37	.38	.38	.07	.28

| | | | | | | | Age Group | | | | | | | | | | |
Subtest	16-17	18-19	20-24	25-29	30-34	35-44	45-54	55-64	65-69	70-74	75-79	80-84	85-89	16-89	M	SD	Range
Picture Completion																	
Digit Symbol-Coding	.16	.19	.18	.20	.14	.24	.31	.27	.38	.28	.28	.35	.36	.24	.26	.08	.24
Block Design	.45	.42	.48	.47	.46	.50	.51	.42	.55	.52	.40	.44	.41	.46	.46	.05	.15
Matrix Reasoning	.42	.45	.53	.47	.38	.49	.53	.56	.51	.45	.29	.46	.32	.44	.45	.08	.27
Picture Arrangement	.25	.31	.32	.38	.44	.31	.49	.43	.45	.36	.29	.42	.42	.36	.37	.07	.24

Note. Prediction with Verbal subtests involved predicting each Verbal subtest with the remaining five Verbal subtests and predicting each Performance subtest with all six Verbal subtests. Similarly, prediction with Performance subtests involved predicting each Verbal subtest with all five Performance subtests and predicting each Performance subtest with the remaining four Performance subtests. 16-89 pooled age group excluded from computation of M, SD, and range.

Table 5. Loadings on the Verbal Factor from 2-Factor Orthogonal Procrustes Rotated Solution by Age Group for the WAIS-III

| | | | | | | | Age Group | | | | | | | | | | |
Subtest	16-17	18-19	20-24	25-29	30-34	35-44	45-54	55-64	65-69	70-74	75-79	80-84	85-89	16-89	M	SD	Range
Verbal																	
Vocabulary	.87	.87	.85	.89	.85	.84	.82	.84	.81	.71	.86	.85	.79	.87	.83	.05	.18
Similarities	.80	.82	.84	.84	.86	.82	.79	.79	.76	.53	.81	.78	.79	.83	.79	.08	.33
Arithmetic	.61	.58	.57	.70	.50	.63	.65	.72	.76	.79	.71	.74	.25	.61	.63	.14	.54
Digit Span	.22	.28	.20	.58	.14	.47	.57	.68	.75	.86	.54	.58	.12	.35	.46	.24	.74
Information	.82	.88	.85	.85	.80	.87	.81	.81	.86	.69	.87	.83	.77	.86	.82	.05	.19
Comprehension	.80	.84	.87	.82	.81	.81	.79	.81	.74	.65	.86	.77	.79	.85	.80	.06	.22
Performance																	
Picture Completion	.27	.31	.40	.16	.58	.26	.37	.33	.43	.29	.28	.27	.72	.36	.36	.15	.56
Digit Symbol-Coding	.41	.31	.12	.31	.18	.17	.12	.30	.40	.40	.27	.31	.37	.22	.28	.10	.29
Block Design	.39	.50	.52	.36	.55	.30	.48	.24	.34	.39	.31	.20	.49	.39	.39	.11	.35
Matrix Reasoning	.43	.46	.51	.46	.49	.49	.56	.52	.52	.61	.32	.40	.38	.47	.47	.08	.29
Picture Arrangement	.32	.63	.62	.48	.78	.61	.36	.49	.30	.46	.39	.43	.64	.51	.50	.15	.48

	16-17	18-19	20-24	25-29	30-34	35-44	45-54	55-64	65-69	70-74	75-79	80-84	85-89	16-89	M	SD	Range
Variance	3.81	4.38	4.35	4.43	4.55	4.20	4.15	4.38	4.48	4.03	4.19	4.06	3.98	4.22	4.23	.22	.74
% Total Variance	34.7	39.8	39.5	40.2	41.4	38.1	37.8	39.8	40.8	36.6	38.1	36.9	36.2	38.4	38.5	1.99	6.7
Reliability	.93	.94	.95	.95	.94	.94	.93	.94	.95	.95	.95	.95	.93	.94	.94	.01	.02
Congruence	.86	.83	.82	.91	.76	.88	.89	.90	.90	.86	.93	.92	.72	.87	.86	.06	.21
RMSD Overall	.38	.41	.43	.31	.49	.35	.34	.32	.32	.38	.28	.29	.52	.37	.37	.07	.24
RMSD Hypothesized	.39	.36	.39	.24	.43	.30	.28	.23	.22	.31	.25	.26	.51	.33	.32	.09	.29
RMSD Non-hypothesized	.37	.46	.47	.37	.55	.40	.41	.39	.40	.44	.32	.33	.54	.40	.42	.07	.23

Note. RMSD denotes root mean square difference. Hypothesized subtests were set equal to 1 in the hypothesis matrix and are underlined. Subtests set equal to 0 in the hypothesis matrix are not underlined and are termed non-hypothesized. 16-89 pooled age group excluded from computation of M, SD, and *range*.

Table 6. Loadings on the Performance Factor from 2-Factor Orthogonal Procrustes Rotated Solution by Age Group for the WAIS-III

						Age Group											
Subtest	16-17	18-19	20-24	25-29	30-34	35-44	45-54	55-64	65-69	70-74	75-79	80-84	85-89	16-89	M	SD	Range
Verbal																	
Vocabulary	.23	.25	.26	.24	.28	.31	.34	.32	.40	.49	.22	.32	.28	.25	.30	.08	.27
Similarities	.12	.25	.20	.20	.20	.25	.35	.36	.45	.66	.37	.38	.27	.26	.31	.14	.54
Arithmetic	.41	.61	.61	.45	.70	.46	.43	.35	.38	.23	.17	.29	.78	.49	.45	.18	.61
Digit Span	.64	.75	.79	.39	.81	.31	.13	.19	.05	-.24	.42	.09	.70	.51	.39	.33	1.05
Information	.24	.15	.20	.23	.31	.20	.33	.34	.26	.48	.22	.22	.36	.22	.27	.09	.33
Comprehension	.19	.20	.10	.27	.27	.29	.33	.33	.45	.53	.16	.32	.21	.21	.28	.12	.43
Performance																	
Picture Completion	.66	.47	.55	.79	.33	.73	.67	.72	.70	.76	.69	.73	.16	.63	.61	.19	.63
Digit Symbol-Coding	.39	.55	.70	.47	.61	.70	.79	.60	.62	.47	.68	.65	.65	.70	.61	.11	.40
Block Design	.68	.58	.59	.74	.50	.79	.65	.80	.78	.70	.72	.81	.54	.69	.68	.10	.31
Matrix Reasoning	.62	.65	.64	.66	.61	.64	.62	.67	.61	.47	.60	.69	.55	.63	.62	.06	.22
Picture Arrangement	.53	.27	.25	.57	.20	.37	.71	.57	.76	.56	.58	.62	.39	.48	.49	.18	.56

																M	SD	Range
Variance	2.48	2.48	2.73	2.78	2.59	2.78	3.03	2.90	3.21	3.12	2.61	2.96	2.61	2.71	2.79	2.79	.24	.73
% Total Variance	22.5	22.5	24.8	25.3	23.6	25.3	27.6	26.3	29.1	28.4	23.7	26.9	23.7	24.7	25.4	25.4	2.18	6.60
Reliability	.88	.89	.91	.92	.91	.90	.87	.90	.90	.91	.88	.90	.87	.89	.89	.90	.02	.05
Congruence	.82	.72	.88	.73	.63	.87	.88	.88	.87	.75	.90	.91	.63	.85	.81	.81	.10	.28
RMSD Overall	.39	.47	.34	.46	.53	.35	.32	.33	.34	.45	.31	.30	.53	.36	.39	.39	.08	.23
RMSD Hypothesized	.43	.51	.37	.48	.57	.38	.32	.34	.31	.43	.35	.31	.57	.38	.41	.41	.09	.26
RMSD Non-hypothesized	.35	.43	.31	.44	.49	.31	.33	.32	.36	.46	.28	.29	.49	.35	.37	.37	.08	.21

Note. RMSD denotes root mean square difference. Hypothesized subtests were set equal to 1 in the hypothesis matrix and are underlined. Subtests set equal to 0 in the hypothesis matrix are not underlined and are termed non-hypothesized. 16-89 pooled age group excluded from computation of M, SD, and range.

Table 7. Congruence Coefficients (Below Diagonal) and Root Mean Square Differences (Above Diagonal) for the Verbal Factor from 2-Factor Confirmatory Rotation by Age Group for the WAIS-III

							Age Group							
Age Group	16-17	18-19	20-24	25-29	30-34	35-44	45-54	55-64	65-69	70-74	75-79	80-84	85-89	16-89
16-17		.11	.14	.13	.19	.14	.15	.16	.18	.24	.12	.14	.21	.10
18-19	.99		.07	.13	.12	.10	.14	.16	.20	.24	.14	.16	.18	.06
20-24	.97	.99		.17	.08	.12	.15	.19	.23	.27	.17	.19	.17	.08
25-29	.98	.98	.96		.22	.08	.11	.08	.12	.17	.07	.07	.27	.10
30-34	.96	.98	.99	.94		.17	.20	.23	.27	.31	.22	.24	.12	.14
35-44	.97	.99	.98	.99	.96		.11	.09	.16	.20	.10	.10	.23	.06
45-54	.97	.97	.97	.99	.95	.98		.11	.12	.17	.11	.12	.25	.10
55-64	.97	.97	.95	.99	.93	.99	.99		.09	.13	.09	.06	.27	.12
65-69	.96	.95	.93	.98	.91	.97	.98	.99		.12	.12	.10	.29	.16
70-74	.92	.92	.90	.96	.88	.95	.96	.98	.98		.19	.16	.33	.22
75-79	.98	.98	.96	.99	.94	.99	.98	.99	.98	.95		.06	.26	.10
80-84	.97	.97	.95	.99	.93	.99	.98	1.00	.99	.97	1.00		.27	.12
85-89	.94	.96	.96	.91	.98	.93	.92	.90	.89	.85	.91	.90		.19
16-89	.99	.99	.99	.99	.98	.99	.99	.98	.97	.94	.99	.98	.95	

Note. Excluding the 16-89 age group, congruence coefficients ranged between .8465 and .9966 ($M = .9609$, $SD = .0315$) and root mean square differences ranged between .0565 and .3342 ($M = .1620$, $SD = .0653$).

Table 8. Congruence Coefficients (Below Diagonal) and Root Mean Square Differences (Above Diagonal) for the Performance Factor From 2-Factor Confirmatory Rotation by Age Group for the WAIS-III

Age Group														
Age Group	16-17	18-19	20-24	25-29	30-34	35-44	45-54	55-64	65-69	70-74	75-79	80-84	85-89	16-89
16-17		.14	.16	.10	.20	.16	.22	.18	.25	.36	.15	.22	.22	.11
18-19	.96		.07	.19	.09	.18	.27	.24	.30	.40	.21	.28	.14	.13
20-24	.95	.99		.20	.10	.19	.27	.26	.32	.42	.22	.29	.16	.13
25-29	.98	.93	.92		.25	.10	.15	.11	.17	.29	.13	.14	.26	.10
30-34	.92	.98	.98	.87		.23	.30	.29	.35	.44	.27	.33	.10	.18
35-44	.95	.93	.93	.98	.89		.14	.10	.17	.27	.13	.12	.25	.09
45-54	.91	.86	.86	.96	.83	.97		.09	.09	.22	.15	.09	.28	.15
55-64	.93	.88	.87	.98	.83	.98	.98		.09	.20	.12	.06	.29	.14
65-69	.89	.83	.81	.95	.78	.95	.99	.99		.17	.18	.08	.33	.20
70-74	.76	.68	.67	.85	.64	.86	.92	.93	.95		.28	.20	.42	.32
75-79	.95	.90	.91	.97	.84	.97	.96	.97	.95	.85		.13	.28	.11
80-84	.91	.85	.84	.96	.79	.97	.98	.99	.99	.93	.97		.36	.19
85-89	.89	.96	.95	.86	.98	.87	.85	.84	.80	.66	.84	.80		.23
16-89	.97	.97	.97	.98	.93	.98	.96	.96	.93	.81	.97	.95	.93	

Note. Excluding the 16-89 age group, congruence coefficients ranged between .6375 and .9941 ($M = .8999$, $SD = .0824$) and root mean square differences ranged between .0659 and .4570 ($M = .2193$, $SD = .0934$).

Table 9. Squared Multiple Correlations for Predicting each of the WAIS-III Verbal Comprehension, Perceptual Organization, Working Memory, and Processing Speed Subtests by the Subtests on Each Factor.

Subtest	16-17	18-19	20-24	25-29	30-34	35-44	45-54	55-64	65-69	70-74	75-79	80-84	85-89	16-89	M	SD	Range
							Age Group										
Prediction With Verbal Comprehension Subtests																	
Verbal Comprehension																	
Vocabulary	.59	.66	.71	.73	.70	.68	.67	.70	.76	.70	.67	.73	.60	.69	.68	.05	.17
Similarities	.43	.58	.61	.61	.64	.59	.61	.64	.68	.63	.67	.66	.53	.61	.61	.07	.25
Information	.56	.62	.61	.65	.67	.62	.60	.67	.69	.59	.67	.63	.53	.62	.62	.05	.16
Perceptual Organization																	
Picture Completion	.21	.17	.24	.17	.29	.25	.35	.31	.45	.38	.26	.25	.34	.27	.28	.08	.28
Block Design	.29	.35	.32	.28	.32	.26	.44	.27	.36	.37	.26	.26	.31	.31	.31	.05	.18
Matrix Reasoning	.29	.33	.33	.35	.34	.36	.52	.48	.43	.38	.21	.33	.24	.35	.35	.09	.31
Working Memory																	
Arithmetic	.38	.50	.42	.52	.46	.44	.45	.47	.57	.45	.37	.45	.30	.44	.44	.07	.27
Digit Span	.14	.25	.19	.33	.17	.19	.19	.30	.29	.21	.33	.20	.14	.21	.23	.07	.19
Letter-Number Sequencing	.14	.27	.15	.41	.31	.43	.24	.43	.45	.31	.32	.30	.10	.28	.30	.12	.35
Processing Speed																	
Digit Symbol-Coding	.21	.22	.12	.16	.14	.19	.17	.27	.36	.23	.24	.25	.28	.21	.22	.06	.24
Symbol Search	.23	.29	.26	.26	.20	.25	.28	.37	.40	.36	.25	.24	.31	.27	.28	.06	.20
Prediction With Perceptual Organization Subtests																	
Verbal Comprehension																	
Vocabulary	.32	.35	.38	.35	.43	.38	.48	.41	.48	.41	.25	.35	.31	.37	.38	.07	.23
Similarities	.28	.41	.32	.32	.35	.34	.54	.45	.54	.45	.38	.38	.38	.38	.40	.08	.26
Information	.33	.33	.32	.33	.39	.31	.48	.45	.39	.42	.28	.28	.39	.35	.36	.06	.20
Perceptual Organization																	
Picture	.27	.17	.30	.32	.35	.34	.37	.37	.43	.39	.25	.31	.23	.31	.32	.07	.26

	Age Group																
Subtest	16-17	18-19	20-24	25-29	30-34	35-44	45-54	55-64	65-69	70-74	75-79	80-84	85-89	16-89	M	SD	Range
Picture Completion																	
Block Design	.44	.40	.46	.45	.40	.47	.42	.41	.50	.47	.37	.41	.35	.43	.43	.04	.15
Matrix Reasoning	.36	.36	.49	.42	.31	.45	.49	.45	.48	.41	.26	.41	.29	.40	.40	.08	.23
Working Memory																	
Arithmetic	.31	.47	.54	.44	.54	.42	.45	.43	.48	.40	.19	.28	.25	.40	.40	.11	.35
Digit Span	.19	.31	.31	.32	.26	.16	.15	.25	.24	.14	.22	.10	.11	.20	.21	.08	.22
Letter-Number Sequencing	.17	.45	.30	.47	.33	.26	.29	.30	.25	.39	.25	.41	.09	.28	.30	.11	.38
Processing Speed																	
Digit Symbol-Coding	.16	.19	.18	.16	.14	.23	.31	.27	.37	.28	.25	.31	.33	.23	.24	.07	.23
Symbol Search	.28	.33	.40	.34	.31	.32	.42	.41	.49	.42	.30	.40	.41	.37	.37	.11	.21
Prediction With Working Memory Subtests																	
Verbal Comprehension																	
Vocabulary	.32	.48	.39	.56	.44	.39	.38	.51	.59	.42	.43	.42	.24	.41	.43	.09	.35
Similarities	.21	.40	.31	.42	.36	.43	.37	.42	.57	.27	.47	.42	.18	.36	.37	.11	.39
Information	.34	.40	.35	.54	.41	.45	.45	.49	.55	.44	.42	.42	.31	.42	.43	.07	.24
Perceptual Organization																	
Picture Completion	.13	.21	.25	.24	.26	.15	.30	.25	.30	.23	.16	.40	.09	.21	.23	.08	.31
Block Design	.28	.40	.46	.47	.37	.32	.40	.29	.36	.30	.27	.22	.20	.32	.33	.08	.27
Matrix Reasoning		.28	.48	.47	.50	.48	.40	.39	.44	.43	.45	.24	.30	.21	.37	.39	.10
Working Memory																	
Arithmetic	.34	.41	.39	.40	.41	.44	.27	.42	.41	.43	.32	.33	.26	.37	.37	.06	.18
Digit Span	.39	.49	.55	.42	.43	.36	.40	.42	.46	.26	.28	.35	.29	.39	.39	.08	.29
Letter-Number Sequencing	.47	.48	.52	.38	.47	.47	.41	.43	.42	.39	.23	.44	.32	.41	.42	.08	.29
Processing Speed																	

	Age Group																
Subtest	16-17	18-19	20-24	25-29	30-34	35-44	45-54	55-64	65-69	70-74	75-79	80-84	85-89	16-89	M	SD	Range
Digit Symbol-Coding	.23	.25	.22	.23	.20	.17	.29	.28	.37	.22	.37	.33	.32	.25	.27	.06	.20
Symbol Search	.29	.30	.37	.39	.27	.25	.39	.37	.43	.35	.42	.44	.24	.34	.35	.07	.20
Prediction With Processing Speed Subtests																	
Verbal Comprehension																	
Vocabulary	.25	.27	.23	.22	.21	.27	.26	.34	.38	.31	.19	.27	.21	.26	.26	.06	.19
Similarities	.16	.25	.20	.22	.16	.21	.22	.31	.41	.31	.29	.26	.29	.24	.25	.07	.25
Information	.19	.21	.21	.22	.20	.18	.20	.33	.29	.31	.19	.15	.28	.22	.23	.06	.18
Perceptual Organization																	
Picture Completion	.21	.17	.23	.16	.17	.23	.29	.29	.38	.33	.24	.31	.28	.25	.25	.07	.22
Block Design	.20	.25	.34	.25	.29	.28	.34	.28	.37	.34	.25	.32	.34	.29	.30	.05	.17
Matrix Reasoning	.16	.22	.27	.28	.16	.25	.29	.32	.37	.30	.15	.26	.20	.24	.25	.07	.22
Working Memory																	
Arithmetic	.28	.30	.33	.34	.26	.24	.32	.33	.41	.27	.19	.25	.25	.29	.29	.06	.22
Digit Span	.18	.18	.28	.22	.18	.13	.13	.20	.23	.12	.27	.21	.11	.18	.19	.05	.17
Letter-Number Sequencing	.15	.20	.23	.26	.21	.19	.29	.30	.30	.32	.38	.44	.23	.27	.27	.08	.29
Processing Speed																	
Digit Symbol-Coding	.41	.44	.37	.49	.28	.35	.49	.48	.53	.35	.41	.44	.50	.42	.43	.07	.25
Symbol Search	.41	.44	.37	.49	.28	.35	.49	.48	.53	.35	.41	.44	.50	.42	.43	.07	.25

Note. For predictions by subtests on each of the four factors, all subtests within that factor were predicted by the remaining subtests on that factor. Subtests on the other factors were predicted using all subtests belonging to the factor involved in the prediction. 16-89 pooled age group excluded from computation of *M*, *SD*, and *range*.

Table 10. Loadings on the Verbal Comprehension Factor from 4-Factor Orthogonal Procrustes Rotated Solution by Age Group for the WAIS III

Subtest	16-17	18-19	20-24	25-29	30-34	35-44	45-54	55-64	65-69	70-74	75-79	80-84	85-89	16-89	M	SD	Range
Verbal Comprehension																	
Vocabulary	.77	.79	.83	.79	.79	.81	.69	.78	.79	.80	.83	.79	.82	.82	.79	.04	.14
Similarities	.75	.76	.81	.80	.80	.81	.71	.79	.72	.83	.76	.76	.74	.79	.77	.04	.12
Information	.79	.80	.83	.81	.83	.80	.73	.79	.80	.72	.81	.80	.78	.82	.79	.32	.11
Perceptual Organization																	
Picture Completion	.09	.06	.16	.22	.21	.28	.16	.29	.50	.40	.46	.08	.53	.26	.26	.16	.47
Block Design	.30	.46	.31	.17	.30	.16	.58	.11	.20	.32	.21	.32	.27	.24	.29	.13	.47
Matrix Reasoning	.42	.32	.32	.27	.42	.31	.57	.46	.27	.27	.05	.46	.13	.31	.33	.14	.52
Working Memory																	
Arithmetic	.52	.53	.44	.55	.50	.38	.62	.43	.45	.39	.41	.63	.26	.47	.47	.10	.37
Digit Span	.01	.15	.16	.22	.05	.10	.16	.19	.12	.30	.33	.19	.27	.14	.17	.00	.32
Letter-Number Sequencing	.09	.11	.06	.27	.17	.39	.05	.32	.49	.06	.28	.16	.07	.21	.19	.14	.44
Processing Speed																	
Digit Symbol-Coding	.25	.20	.14	.14	.24	.16	.02	.23	.27	.21	.23	.16	.20	.22	.19	.07	.25
Symbol Search	.22	.27	.25	.25	.13	.27	.20	.30	.24	.27	.11	.08	.22	.23	.22	.07	.22
Variance	2.45	2.60	2.58	2.58	2.63	2.56	2.65	2.64	2.72	2.54	2.60	2.65	2.44	2.56	2.59	.08	.28
% Total Variance	22.2	23.6	23.5	23.4	23.9	23.2	24.1	24.0	24.7	23.1	23.6	24.1	22.2	23.3	23.5	.72	2.50
Reliability	.90	.91	.92	.91	.92	.92	.89	.91	.91	.90	.91	.92	.91	.91	.91	.01	.03
Congruence	.85	.84	.89	.86	.86	.87	.75	.84	.81	.85	.86	.83	.86	.88	.84	.03	.14
RMSD Overall	.27	.28	.24	.27	.27	.26	.36	.29	.32	.28	.27	.29	.26	.25	.28	.03	.12

	Age Group																
Subtest	16-17	18-19	20-24	25-29	30-34	35-44	45-54	55-64	65-69	70-74	75-79	80-84	85-89	16-89	M	SD	Range
RMSD Hypothesized	.23	.22	.17	.20	.19	.19	.29	.21	.23	.22	.20	.22	.22	.19	.21	.03	.12
RMSD Non-hypothesized	.29	.31	.26	.29	.29	.27	.38	.31	.34	.30	.29	.32	.28	.27	.30	.03	.12

Note. RMSD denotes root mean square difference. Hypothesized subtests were set equal to 1 in the hypothesis matrix and are underlined. Subtests set equal to 0 in the hypothesis matrix are not underlined and are termed non-hypothesized. 16-89 pooled age group excluded from computation of *M*, *SD*, and *range*.

Table 11. Loadings on the Perceptual Organization Factor from 4-Factor Orthogonal Procrustes Rotated Solution by Age Group for the WAIS-III

	Age Group																
Subtest	16-17	18-19	20-24	25-29	30-34	35-44	45-54	55-64	65-69	70-74	75-79	80-84	85-89	16-89	M	SD	Range
Verbal Comprehension																	
Vocabulary	.26	.21	.28	.21	.35	.30	.45	.21	.29	.27	.16	.26	.27	.24	.27	.07	.29
Similarities	.28	.30	.27	.20	.33	.21	.45	.34	.41	.36	.32	.31	.39	.31	.32	.07	.25
Information	.28	.32	.23	.25	.25	.24	.41	.31	.26	.36	.24	.30	.27	.25	.29	.05	.18
Perceptual Organization																	
Picture Completion	.80	.95	.79	.89	.88	.73	.92	.70	.61	.65	.63	.83	.28	.72	.74	.18	.67
Block Design	.75	.51	.68	.67	.70	.80	.31	.83	.78	.71	.76	.66	.72	.78	.68	.14	.52
Matrix Reasoning	.60	.37	.67	.59	.36	.72	.52	.62	.74	.66	.75	.56	.85	.68	.62	.14	.49
Working Memory																	
Arithmetic	.14	.32	.45	.35	.27	.42	.18	.39	.48	.36	.16	.17	.41	.34	.31	.12	.34
Digit Span	.28	.21	.15	.16	.23	.06	.07	.20	.20	-.21	.16	-.17	.01	.12	.10	.15	.49
Letter-Number Sequencing	.17	.40	.26	.44	.39	.16	.38	.13	-.02	.53	.20	.43	-.05	.24	.26	.18	.58

| | Age Group | | | | | | | | | | | | | | | | |
Subtest	16-17	18-19	20-24	25-29	30-34	35-44	45-54	55-64	65-69	70-74	75-79	80-84	85-89	16-89	M	SD	Range
Processing Speed																	
Digit Symbol-Coding	.09	.10	.12	.11	-.01	.20	.40	.17	.26	.22	.21	.34	.36	.16	.20	.12	.41
Symbol Search	.33	.33	.40	.32	.43	.35	.40	.41	.46	.44	.31	.47	.44	.37	.39	.06	.16
Variance	2.03	1.96	2.21	2.18	2.14	2.24	2.28	2.23	2.40	2.40	1.95	2.28	2.11	2.15	2.19	.15	.45
% Total Variance	18.5	17.8	20.1	19.9	19.5	20.4	20.7	20.3	21.8	21.7	17.7	20.7	19.2	19.6	19.9	1.30	4.10
Reliability	.86	.77	.84	.89	.82	.88	.79	.88	.88	.88	.85	.86	.83	.86	.85	.04	.12
Congruence	.87	.75	.83	.84	.76	.87	.67	.83	.79	.76	.88	.79	.73	.86	.80	.06	.21
RMSD Overall	.26	.34	.29	.28	.34	.26	.40	.29	.32	.35	.25	.33	.36	.27	.31	.05	.15
RMSD Hypothesized	.29	.46	.29	.31	.41	.25	.49	.29	.30	.33	.29	.33	.46	.28	.35	.08	.24
RMSD Non-hypothesized	.24	.29	.29	.27	.31	.26	.37	.29	.33	.36	.23	.32	.31	.27	.30	.04	.14

Note. RMSD denotes root mean square difference. Hypothesized subtests were set equal to 1 in the hypothesis matrix and are underlined. Subtests set equal to 0 in the hypothesis matrix are not underlined and are termed non-hypothesized. 16-89 pooled age group excluded from computation of *M*, *SD*, and *range*.

Table 12. Loadings on the Working Memory Factor from 4-Factor Orthogonal Procrustes Rotated Solution by Age Group for the WAIS-III

Subtest	Age Group														M	SD	Range
	16-17	18-19	20-24	25-29	30-34	35-44	45-54	55-64	65-69	70-74	75-79	80-84	85-89	16-89			
Verbal Comprehension																	
Vocabulary	.22	.31	.26	.42	.27	.24	.30	.37	.36	.33	.34	.34	.24	.30	.31	.06	.20
Similarities	.18	.30	.17	.29	.20	.30	.25	.25	.31	.07	.34	.31	.12	.23	.24	.08	.27
Information	.22	.18	.23	.32	.25	.34	.28	.32	.38	.35	.35	.34	.24	.28	.29	.06	.20
Perceptual Organization																	
Picture Completion	.06	-.03	.13	-.06	.13	.00	.19	.16	.05	.03	-.20	.46	-.08	.08	.06	.16	.66
Block Design	.28	.33	.38	.50	.21	.27	.24	.26	.22	.16	.22	-.11	.18	.24	.24	.14	.61
Matrix Reasoning	.25	.64	.35	.50	.55	.37	.20	.30	.38	.49	.50	.07	.25	.38	.37	.16	.57
Working Memory																	
Arithmetic	.62	.52	.56	.46	.62	.63	.41	.58	.54	.65	.69	.41	.65	.56	.56	.09	.28
Digit Span	.81	.84	.85	.83	.85	.86	.92	.87	.92	.80	.64	.78	.79	.87	.83	.07	.28
Letter-Number Sequencing	.86	.76	.86	.64	.71	.74	.78	.72	.65	.69	.49	.77	.76	.74	.73	.10	.37
Processing Speed																	
Digit Symbol-Coding	.23	.25	.20	.25	.23	.20	.28	.22	.26	.18	.29	.37	.34	.24	.25	.06	.19
Symbol Search	.25	.24	.32	.30	.24	.20	.29	.28	.32	.30	.44	.45	.20	.28	.29	.08	.25
Variance	2.17	2.41	2.35	2.34	2.28	2.23	2.14	2.23	2.29	2.17	2.09	2.27	2.02	2.19	2.23	.11	.39
% Total Variance	19.7	22.0	21.4	21.3	20.7	20.3	19.5	20.2	20.9	19.7	19.0	20.7	18.3	19.9	20.3	1.03	3.70
Reliability	.88	.90	.86	.87	.88	.89	.91	.88	.90	.91	.85	.87	.88	.88	.88	.02	.06
Congruence	.90	.79	.85	.73	.84	.86	.83	.84	.80	.84	.73	.75	.89	.85	.82	.06	.17
RMSD Overall	.23	.33	.27	.37	.29	.27	.29	.28	.31	.28	.36	.35	.24	.28	.30	.04	.14

| Subtest | Age Group | | | | | | | | | | | | | | | | |
	16-17	18-19	20-24	25-29	30-34	35-44	45-54	55-64	65-69	70-74	75-79	80-84	85-89	16-89	M	SD	Range
RMSD Hypothesized	.26	.32	.28	.39	.29	.27	.37	.30	.34	.29	.40	.39	.27	.30	.32	.05	.14
RMSD Non-hypothesized	.22	.33	.27	.36	.29	.26	.26	.28	.31	.28	.35	.33	.22	.27	.29	.04	.14

Note. RMSD denotes root mean square difference. Hypothesized subtests were set equal to 1 in the hypothesis matrix and are underlined. Subtests set equal to 0 in the hypothesis matrix are not underlined and are termed non-hypothesized. 16-89 pooled age group excluded from computation of *M*, *SD*, and *range*.

Table 13. Loadings on the Processing Speed Factor from 4-Factor Orthogonal Procrustes Rotated Solution by Age Group for the WAIS-III

| Subtest | Age Group | | | | | | | | | | | | | | | | |
	16-17	18-19	20-24	25-29	30-34	35-44	45-54	55-64	65-69	70-74	75-79	80-84	85-89	16-89	M	SD	Range
Verbal Comprehension																	
Vocabulary	.25	.22	.13	.14	.13	.22	.08	.25	.22	.17	.09	.16	.05	.18	.16	.07	.20
Similarities	.07	.11	.14	.15	.09	.16	.09	.14	.23	.20	.20	.18	.17	.16	.15	.05	.16
Information	.15	.15	.12	.10	.15	.05	.06	.14	.07	.10	.04	-.10	.21	.12	.10	.08	.31
Perceptual Organization																	
Picture Completion	.32	.20	.23	.14	.07	.26	.10	.23	.31	.32	.41	-.05	.56	.28	.24	.16	.61
Block Design	.06	.10	.12	.12	.29	.21	.45	.17	.28	.26	.20	.52	.24	.18	.23	.13	.46
Matrix Reasoning	.03	.12	.17	.17	.05	.08	.26	.18	.13	.08	-.09	.35	.00	.07	.12	.11	.44
Working Memory																	
Arithmetic	.23	.24	.15	.25	.21	.10	.37	.13	.16	.10	.00	.26	.09	.15	.18	.10	.37
Digit Span	.14	.12	.27	.13	.12	.18	.01	.05	.08	.21	.22	.38	.02	.12	.15	.10	.37
Letter-Number Sequencing	.11	.13	.11	.17	.14	.13	.20	.33	.35	.17	.51	.18	.44	.25	.23	.13	.40

							Age Group										
Subtest	16-17	18-19	20-24	25-29	30-34	35-44	45-54	55-64	65-69	70-74	75-79	80-84	85-89	16-89	M	SD	Range
Processing Speed																	
Digit Symbol-Coding	.85	.88	.92	.89	.86	.87	.77	.88	.83	.86	.78	.67	.70	.86	.83	.08	.25
Symbol Search	.76	.75	.65	.76	.71	.71	.73	.68	.67	.62	.70	.59	.73	.72	.70	.05	.17
Variance	1.57	1.57	1.52	1.61	1.47	1.50	1.59	1.58	1.58	1.46	1.66	1.50	1.66	1.54	1.56	.07	.20
% Total Variance	14.3	14.3	13.8	14.6	13.4	13.6	14.5	14.3	14.4	13.3	15.1	13.6	15.1	14.0	14.2	.60	1.80
Reliability	.80	.80	.80	.81	.84	.84	.83	.84	.81	.82	.85	.80	.82	.81	.82	.02	.05
Congruence	.90	.92	.90	.93	.92	.91	.84	.88	.84	.86	.81	.72	.78	.90	.86	.06	.21
RMSD Overall	.18	.17	.19	.16	.17	.18	.23	.20	.23	.22	.26	.30	.27	.19	.21	.04	.14
RMSD Hypothesized	.20	.20	.25	.18	.22	.23	.25	.24	.26	.29	.27	.38	.29	.22	.25	.05	.20
RMSD Non-hypothesized	.18	.16	.17	.16	.16	.17	.23	.19	.22	.19	.25	.28	.27	.18	.20	.04	.12

Note. RMSD denotes root mean square difference. Hypothesized subtests were set equal to 1 in the hypothesis matrix and are underlined. Subtests set equal to 0 in the hypothesis matrix are not underlined and are termed non-hypothesized. 16-89 pooled age group excluded from computation of *M*, *SD*, and *range*.

Table 14. Congruence Coefficients (Below Diagonal) and Root Mean Square Differences (Above Diagonal) for the Verbal Comprehension Factor from 4-Factor Confirmatory Rotation by Age Group for the WAIS-III

Age Group	16-17	18-19	20-24	25-29	30-34	35-44	45-54	55-64	65-69	70-74	75-79	80-84	85-89	16-89
16-17		.08	.08	.12	.06	.14	.14	.13	.19	.15	.20	.09	.20	.09
18-19	.99		.07	.12	.09	.15	.12	.15	.19	.13	.19	.09	.19	.10
20-24	.99	.99		.09	.08	.12	.14	.12	.18	.10	.16	.10	.15	.06
25-29	.97	.97	.98		.10	.08	.18	.08	.12	.11	.12	.11	.15	.05
30-34	.99	.98	.99	.98		.11	.14	.11	.15	.13	.17	.08	.17	.06
35-44	.96	.95	.97	.99	.98		.21	.07	.09	.14	.13	.15	.15	.07
45-54	.96	.97	.96	.93	.96	.91		.20	.24	.18	.25	.12	.24	.17
55-64	.96	.95	.97	.99	.98	.99	.92		.11	.13	.16	.14	.17	.08
65-69	.93	.92	.94	.97	.95	.98	.88	.98		.16	.12	.19	.16	.12
70-74	.95	.96	.98	.97	.96	.96	.93	.96	.95		.12	.16	.08	.09
75-79	.91	.92	.94	.97	.94	.96	.87	.95	.97	.97		.19	.10	.10
80-84	.98	.98	.98	.98	.99	.95	.97	.96	.92	.95	.92		.21	.10
85-89	.91	.92	.95	.95	.94	.95	.88	.94	.95	.99	.98	.91		.13
16-89	.98	.98	.99	.99	.99	.99	.94	.99	.97	.98	.97	.98	.96	

Note. Excluding the 16-89 age group, congruence coefficients ranged between .8651 and .9937 ($M = .9557$, $SD = .0281$) and root mean square differences ranged between .0568 and .2538 ($M = .1378$, $SD = .0446$).

Table 15. Congruence Coefficients (Below Diagonal) and Root Mean Square Differences (Above Diagonal) for the Perceptual Organization Factor from 4-Factor Confirmatory Rotation by Age Group for the WAIS-III

Age Group	16-17	18-19	20-24	25-29	30-34	35-44	45-54	55-64	65-69	70-74	75-79	80-84	85-89	16-89
16-17		.14	.11	.12	.12	.12	.21	.10	.16	.21	.09	.18	.24	.09
18-19	.94		.13	.09	.09	.19	.16	.17	.23	.20	.19	.17	.31	.16
20-24	.97	.95		.08	.13	.07	.20	.08	.13	.15	.12	.16	.21	.06
25-29	.96	.98	.98		.11	.12	.19	.13	.20	.16	.14	.15	.28	.10
30-34	.96	.98	.96	.97		.17	.20	.15	.22	.20	.18	.18	.30	.14
35-44	.96	.91	.99	.96	.92		.23	.08	.11	.16	.10	.16	.18	.05
45-54	.89	.93	.90	.91	.90	.87		.23	.25	.20	.22	.16	.30	.21
55-64	.97	.93	.98	.96	.94	.99	.87		.08	.18	.10	.18	.18	.05
65-69	.94	.87	.96	.91	.89	.97	.85	.98		.21	.14	.22	.13	.11
70-74	.89	.90	.94	.94	.91	.94	.90	.93	.89		.17	.10	.23	.14
75-79	.98	.90	.96	.95	.91	.97	.87	.98	.96	.93		.17	.18	.07
80-84	.92	.92	.94	.95	.92	.94	.94	.92	.88	.98	.93		.29	.18
85-89	.85	.74	.88	.81	.76	.92	.78	.92	.96	.87	.92	.84		.22
16-89	.98	.94	.99	.97	.95	.99	.89	.99	.97	.95	.99	.95	.91	

Note. Excluding the 16-89 age group, congruence coefficients ranged between .7364 and .9877 ($M = .9223$, $SD = .0517$) and root mean square differences ranged between .0617 and .3387 ($M = .1773$, $SD = .0617$).

Table 16. Congruence Coefficients (Below Diagonal) and Root Mean Square Differences (Above Diagonal) for the Working Memory Factor from 4-Factor Confirmatory Rotation by Age Group for the WAIS-III

Age Group	16-17	18-19	20-24	25-29	30-34	35-44	45-54	55-64	65-69	70-74	75-79	80-84	85-89	16-89
16-17		.14	.06	.16	.11	.08	.10	.08	.12	.12	.19	.22	.07	.07
18-19	.96		.12	.10	.08	.11	.16	.13	.12	.12	.16	.28	.15	.10
20-24	.99	.97		.13	.10	.09	.10	.08	.11	.12	.20	.22	.12	.07
25-29	.94	.98	.96		.13	.12	.16	.13	.11	.14	.15	.29	.17	.11
30-34	.97	.98	.98	.96		.08	.13	.09	.09	.07	.16	.23	.12	.06
35-44	.98	.97	.98	.96	.98		.12	.08	.07	.10	.15	.24	.09	.06
45-54	.98	.94	.98	.94	.96	.97		.07	.10	.15	.22	.16	.13	.08
55-64	.98	.96	.99	.96	.98	.99	.99		.06	.10	.17	.19	.11	.04
65-69	.97	.97	.97	.97	.98	.99	.98	.99		.10	.14	.21	.12	.05
70-74	.97	.97	.97	.95	.99	.98	.94	.98	.98		.14	.24	.11	.08
75-79	.91	.94	.91	.95	.94	.94	.88	.93	.95	.95		.29	.17	.16
80-84	.89	.82	.88	.80	.87	.86	.94	.91	.90	.86	.79		.28	.24
85-89	.99	.95	.97	.93	.96	.98	.96	.97	.96	.97	.93	.87		.17
16-89	.99	.98	.99	.97	.99	.99	.98	1.00	.99	.98	.94	.90	.98	

Note. Excluding the 16-89 age group, congruence coefficients ranged between .7889 and .9924 ($M = .9479$, $SD = .0441$) and root mean square differences ranged between .0588 and .3215 ($M = .1525$, $SD = .0664$).

Table 17. Congruence Coefficients (Below Diagonal) and Root Mean Square Differences (Above Diagonal) for the Processing Speed Factor from 4-Factor Confirmatory Rotation by Age Group for the WAIS-III

Age Group	16-17	18-19	20-24	25-29	30-34	35-44	45-54	55-64	65-69	70-74	75-79	80-84	85-89	16-89
16-17		.05	.09	.09	.11	.08	.18	.10	.12	.10	.17	.25	.17	.07
18-19	.99		.07	.04	.08	.07	.14	.08	.11	.10	.18	.21	.18	.06
20-24	.97	.98		.07	.10	.06	.16	.10	.12	.07	.17	.20	.19	.08
25-29	.97	.99	.98		.07	.08	.13	.08	.11	.10	.18	.19	.19	.07
30-34	.96	.98	.97	.98		.08	.11	.11	.12	.10	.18	.18	.19	.08
35-44	.98	.98	.99	.98	.97		.15	.08	.09	.05	.15	.19	.16	.05
45-54	.89	.93	.91	.95	.96	.92		.15	.14	.16	.23	.15	.21	.14
55-64	.96	.98	.96	.98	.96	.97	.93		.06	.09	.15	.21	.15	.05
65-69	.95	.96	.95	.96	.95	.97	.93	.99		.08	.12	.20	.12	.06
70-74	.96	.97	.98	.96	.96	.99	.91	.97	.98		.13	.19	.15	.06
75-79	.90	.89	.90	.89	.89	.93	.83	.93	.95	.94		.26	.11	.12
80-84	.78	.84	.86	.87	.88	.86	.92	.84	.86	.86	.76		.33	.26
85-89	.91	.89	.88	.88	.87	.91	.85	.93	.95	.93	.96	.71		.18
16-89	.98	.99	.98	.98	.97	.99	.93	.99	.99	.99	.95	.84	.94	

Note. Excluding the 16-89 age group, congruence coefficients ranged between .7056 and .9939 ($M = .9276$, $SD = .0575$) and root mean square differences ranged between .0422 and .3321 ($M = .1483$, $SD = .0715$).

For the prediction involving the three Working Memory subtests (Arithmetic, Digit-Span, and Letter-Number Sequencing), the average of the mean SMCs across age groups were .41, .32, .39, and .31, respectively, for the Verbal Comprehension, Perceptual Organization, Working Memory, and Processing Speed subtests. These results indicate that the Verbal Comprehension subtests (M_M = .41) were predicted as well from the Working Memory subtests as were the Working Memory subtests (M_M = .39). In addition, the Perceptual Organization (M_M = .32) and Processing Speed (M_M = .31) subtests were predicted almost as well from the Working Memory subtests as were either the Verbal Comprehension or Working Memory subtests.

For the prediction involving the two Processing Speed subtests (Digit Symbol-Coding and Symbol Search), the average mean SMCs were .25, .27, .25, and .43, respectively, for the Verbal Comprehension, Perceptual Organization, Working Memory, and Processing Speed subtests. These results indicate that the Processing Speed subtests were predicted better from the Processing Speed subtests than were the subtests on the other three factors. Additionally, subtests from the other three factors were on average predicted equivalently from the Processing Speed subtests (i.e., the range in average mean SMCs was .25 to .27).

In summary, the results from the prediction analysis using the subtests from the four factors indicate that of all four predictions involving the subtests from the four factors, Verbal Comprehension was the factor best predicted by its own subtests. The prediction for the Processing Speed subtests followed in terms of their uniqueness of predictability. For both the prediction with the Perceptual Organization and Working Memory subtests, the Verbal Comprehension subtests were equally as well predicted as were the subtests involved in the prediction and the subtests in the other two factors were almost as well predicted. Consequently, in terms of distinctive content variance, the Verbal Comprehension and Processing Speed subtests held up quite well but the subtests on the Perceptual Organization and Working Memory factors did not.

Verbal Comprehension Factor Loadings

Across the 13 age groups the Verbal Comprehension factor accounted for between 22.2% and 24.7% (M = 23.5) of the variance among the 11 subtests used in the computation of the 4 factors. Consequently, in any particular age group, about one quarter of the variance in the correlation matrix was associated with the Verbal Comprehension factor. Reliability estimates for this factor ranged from .89 to .92 across the 13 age groups (M = .91). The mean value of .91 is comparable to the mean values of .94 and .90 for the Verbal and Performance factors, respectively, from the 2-factor solution. Using the mean as an estimate of overall effect, the loadings of the three Verbal Comprehension subtests (range .77 to .79) on the Verbal Comprehension factor exceeded the loadings of the other eight subtests on this factor (range .17 to .47). For the eight subtests comprising the other three factors, the largest mean loading on the Verbal Comprehension factor was obtained by Arithmetic (.47). Excluding Arithmetic, the range in mean loadings from the remaining seven non-Verbal Comprehension subtests was .17 to .33.

Perceptual Organization Factor Loadings

Across the 13 age groups the Perceptual Organization factor accounted for between 17.7% and 21.8% of the variance among the 11 subtests. The mean across age groups (19.9%) was comparable to the mean across age groups for the Verbal Comprehension factor

(25.3%). Reliability estimates for the Perceptual Organization factor ranged between .77 and .89 across the 13 age groups with a mean of .85 which is comparable to what was obtained for the Verbal Comprehension factor (.91) as well as the Verbal (.94) and Performance (.90) factors from the 2-factor solution. The mean loadings of the three Perceptual Organization subtests (range .68 to .74) on the Perceptual Organization factor exceeded the mean loadings of the other eight subtests on this factor (range .10 to .39).

Working Memory Factor Loadings

The variance accounted for by the Working Memory factor ranged between 18.3% and 22.0% (M = 20.3%) across the 13 age groups. Reliability estimates for this factor ranged between .85 and .91 (M = .88) across the 13 age groups which is comparable to what was obtained for the Verbal (.94) and Performance (.90) factors from the 2-factor solution. For the Working Memory factor, the three subtests constituting this factor had mean loadings across age groups (range .56 to .87) that exceeded the mean loadings of the other eight subtests on this factor (range .08 to .38). For the three Working Memory subtests, the mean loading of Arithmetic (.56) was lower than both Letter-Number Sequencing (.74) and Digit Span (.87).

Processing Speed Factor Loadings

The Verbal Comprehension, Perceptual Organization, and Working Memory factors accounted for comparable amounts of variance, but the variance accounted for by the Processing Speed factor was somewhat less (range 13.4% to 15.1% across age groups M = 14.2%). Reliability estimates for the Processing Speed factor across age groups (range .80 to .85, M = .82) were comparable to what was obtained for the three other factors as well as what was obtained for the Verbal and Performance factors from the 2-factor solution. Across age groups the loadings of the two Processing Speed subtests (Symbol Search .70, Digit Symbol-Coding .78) exceeded the mean loadings of the nine other subtests (range .10 to .24) on the Processing Speed factor.

Verbal Comprehension Factor Congruence
Coefficients and Root Mean Square Differences

The bottom of Table 10 contains, across age groups, the congruence coefficients and root mean square differences of the Verbal Comprehension factor loadings with the column of the binary hypothesis matrix constituting the Verbal Comprehension factor. The congruence coefficients ranged from .75 to .89 (M = .84), and the root mean square differences ranged from .24 to .36 (M = .28) across the 13 age groups. These values are comparable to what was obtained for the Verbal factor from the 2-factor solution (i.e., congruence coefficients .72 to .93, M = .86; root mean square differences .28 to.52, M = .37). Separating the root mean square difference into hypothesized and non-hypothesized components resulted in a bit better fit for the three Verbal Comprehension subtests (M = .21) than the eight non-Verbal Comprehension subtests (M = .30) across age groups. The between sample congruence coefficients reported in Table 14 ranged between .8651 and .9937 across samples with a mean of .9557. The range as well as the mean are equivalent to the between sample congruence coefficients obtained for the Verbal factor from the 2-factor solution (range .8465 to .9966, M = .9609). In terms of the between sample root mean square differences for the Verbal Comprehension factor from the 4-factor solution, values ranged between .0568 and .2538 with a mean of .1378 which is comparable to the Verbal factor from the 2-factor solution (range .0565 to .3342, $M = .1620$).

Perceptual Organization Factor Congruence
Coefficients and Root Mean Square Differences

The congruence coefficients and root mean square differences across age groups with the column of the binary hypothesis matrix constituting the Perceptual Organization factor are presented at the bottom of Table 11. The congruence coefficients ranged between .67 and .88 ($M = .86$) which is comparable to the Performance factor from the 2-factor solution (.63 to .91, $M = .81$). The root mean square differences ranged between .25 to .40 ($M = .31$) which is comparable to the Performance factor from the 2-factor solution (.30 to .53, $M = .39$). Separating the root mean square differences into hypothesized and non-hypothesized components resulted in an equivalent fit for the three Perceptual Organization subtests ($M = .35$) and eight non-Perceptual Organization subtests ($M = .30$) across age groups. In terms of the between sample congruence coefficients for the Perceptual Organization factor the range was .7364 to .9877 ($M = .9223$) which is comparable to the Performance factor from the 2-factor solution (range .6375 to .9941, $M = .8999$). In terms of the between sample root mean square differences for the Perceptual Organization factor, the range was .0617 to .3387 with a mean of .1773 which is comparable to the Performance factor from the 2-factor solution (range .0659 to .4570, $M = .2193$).

Working Memory Factor Congruence Coefficients
and Root Mean Square Differences

The congruence coefficients and root mean square differences of the Working Memory factor with the column of the binary hypothesis matrix constituting this factor are presented at the bottom of Table 11. The congruence coefficients ranged between .73 and .90 ($M = .82$), and the root mean square differences ranged between .23 and .36 ($M = .30$). These results are similar to what was obtained for the Verbal factor from the 2-factor solution (i.e., congruence coefficients .72 to .92, $M = .86$, root mean square differences .28 to .52, $M = .37$). Separating the root mean square differences into hypothesized and non-hypothesized components resulted in an equivalent fit for the three Working Memory subtests ($M = .32$) and eight non-Working Memory subtests ($M = .29$) across age groups. The between sample congruence coefficients for the Working Memory factor, reported in Table 15, ranged between .7889 and .9924 ($M = .9609$). In terms of the Working Memory root mean square differences, the range was .0588 to .3215 with a mean of .1525 which is very close to what was obtained for the Verbal factor from the 2-factor solution (range .0565 to .3342, $M = .1620$).

Processing Speed Factor Congruence Coefficients
and Root Mean Square Differences

The congruence coefficients and root mean square differences across age groups of the Processing Speed factor with the column of the binary hypothesis matrix constituting this factor are reported at the bottom of Table 13. These congruence coefficients ranged between .72 and .93 ($M = .86$) and the root mean square differences ranged between .16 and .30 ($M = .21$) across the 13 age groups and are similar to what was obtained for the Performance factor from the 2-factor solution (i.e., congruence coefficients .63 to .91, $M = .81$, root mean square differences .30 to .53, $M = .39$). Separating the root mean square differences into the hypothesized and non-hypothesized components resulted in an equivalent fit for the two Processing Speed subtests ($M = .25$) and the nine non-Processing Speed subtests ($M = .20$) across age groups. In terms of the between sample congruence coefficients reported in Table 17, the values ranged between .7036 and .9939 with a mean of .9276. These values are comparable to what was obtained for the Performance factor from the 2-factor solution (range .6375 to .9941, $M = .8999$). The between sample root mean square differences reported in Table 17 for the Processing Speed factor, ranged between .0422 and .3321 with a mean of .1483 which is comparable to what was obtained for the Performance factor from the 2-factor solution (range .0659 to .4570, $M = .2193$).

DISCUSSION

The objective of the current study was to investigate the factor structure of the WAIS-III through an analysis of 1- (general factor), 2- (Verbal and Performance), and 4-factor (Verbal Comprehension, Perceptual Organization, Working Memory, and Processing Speed) solutions. For the three different factor analytic solutions, the focus of interpretation was the amount of variance accounted for, the reliability of the factors, the degree of fit with the hypothesized structure, and the consistency of loadings across age groups. Two measures of degree of fit with the hypothesized structure and consistency of loadings across age groups were used. The congruence coefficient assesses angular separation in degrees with the cosine and the root mean square difference measures magnitude of deviation. In addition, for each of the three different solutions (i.e., 1-, 2-, and 4-factor), the predictability of subtests within and between factors, across 13 age groups and the combined age group, were evaluated using the squared multiple correlation (SMC) as a measure of fit.

The average percentage variance accounted for, across the 13 age groups, was largest for the general factor from the 1-factor solution (55.0%) which was followed by the Verbal (38.5%) and Performance (25.4%) factors from the 2-factor solution, and the Verbal Comprehension (23.5%), Working Memory (20.3%), Perceptual Organization (19.9%), and Processing Speed (14.2%) factors from the 4-factor solution. The factor reliabilities, averaged across the 13 age groups, displayed a pattern which was similar to the factor variances. The largest mean reliability was for the general factor (.98). The mean reliabilities for the 2-factor solution were somewhat less but nevertheless comparable (.94 Verbal, .90 Performance). Subdividing the factors from the 2-factor solution into their associated factors for the 4-factor solution (Verbal: Verbal Comprehension .91, Working Memory .88; Performance: Perceptual Organization .85, Processing Speed .82) resulted in a slight decrement in average reliability. Consequently, variance accounted for and reliabilities, as one would expect, are related to the number of subtests comprising the factor (i.e., 11 g; 6 Verbal, 5 Performance; 3 Verbal Comprehension, 3 Working Memory, 3 Perceptual Organization, and 2 Processing Speed).

The highest mean factor loadings across age groups on the 1-factor solution were from five of the six Verbal subtests. Of the six Verbal subtests, Vocabulary had the highest loading and Digit Span had the lowest loading. Consequently, Vocabulary in particular and verbal abilities in general are central to the definition of general intelligence as measured by the WAIS-III. Consequently, Wechsler's strategy of combining verbal (Army Alpha) and non-verbal (Army Beta) tasks into an overall score did not result in equal weighting. The literacy aspect of the Army Alpha persists in the general intelligence measure (i.e., FSIQ) of the

WAIS-III. In other words, general intelligence on the WAIS-III is predominated by crystallized in contrast to fluid abilities (cf. Horn & Cattell, 1966).

With the 2-factor (Verbal and Performance) solution, the lowest average loadings across age groups on the Verbal factor by Verbal subtests were Digit Span (.46) and Arithmetic (.63), and, of the six Verbal subtests, these two subtests had the highest mean loadings on the Performance factor (Arithmetic .49, Digit Span .39). The range in mean loadings for the other four Verbal subtests on the Verbal factor was .79 to .83. For the Performance factor the mean loadings of four of the five Performance subtests were higher on the Performance factor than the Verbal factor (range .61 to .68) but were generally not as large as the loadings of the Verbal subtests on the Verbal factor. Picture Arrangement was the single Performance subtest which loaded higher on the Verbal factor (.50) than the Performance factor (.49). The pattern of loadings on the 2-factor solution indicates that the two factors are relatively distinct, although of the two factors the Verbal factor has stronger linkages with its defining subtests. The 2-factor solution is generally supportive of the distinction made in the Army Alpha and Beta between verbal and non-verbal material. Empirically, however, this distinction is less than perfect.

With the 4-factor solution, the mean loadings across age groups for the subtests defining these factors were for all four factors higher for the defining subtests than for the remaining subtests. For Verbal Comprehension the range in mean loadings for the three defining scales was .77 to .79 and the range in mean loadings for the other eight scales was .17 to .47 for Arithmetic. For the Perceptual Organization factor the range in mean loadings for the three defining subtests was .62 (Matrix Reasoning) to .74 (Picture Completion) and the range in mean loadings for the other eight subtests was .10 to .37 for Symbol Search. For the Working Memory factor the range in mean loadings for the three defining subtests was .56 (Arithmetic) to .83 (Digit Span) and for the 8 other subtests the range was .06 to .37 (Matrix Reasoning). For the Processing Speed factor the range in mean loadings was .70 to .83 and the range in mean loadings for the other nine subtests was .10 to .24. Consequently, of the four factors (Verbal Comprehension, Perceptual Organization, Working Memory, and Processing Speed) the Verbal Comprehension factor has stronger linkages with its defining subtests.

For the general factor loadings, across age groups, the congruence coefficients ranged between .99 and .99 ($M = .99$) and root mean square differences ranged between .23 and .32 ($M = .28$) with the hypothesized structure (i.e., a vector of 1's). Consequently, g shows negligible angular separation from a vector of 1's but the average discrepancy from a vector of 1's is substantial (i.e., .28). With the 2-factor solution, the congruence coefficients (.72 - .93, $M = .86$) and root mean square differences (.28 - .52, $M = .37$) for the Verbal factor with the hypothesized structure were comparable to what was obtained for the Performance factor (congruence coefficients: .63 - .91, $M = .81$; root mean square differences: .30 - .53, $M = .39$). Separating the root mean square differences into the hypothesized and non-hypothesized components, the Verbal factor fit a bit better than the Performance factor in terms of the hypothesized subtests ($M = .32$ versus .41, respectively). The Verbal factor, however, fit a bit better for the hypothesized in contrast to non-hypothesized subtests ($M = .32$ versus .42, respectively) whereas the Performance factor resulted in an equivalent fit for the hypothesized and non-hypothesized subtests ($M = .41$ versus .37, respectively). Non-hypothesized subtests fit equivalently for the Verbal and Performance factors. For the 4-factor solution, the congruence coefficients were comparable for each of the four factors (Verbal Comprehension

.75 - .89, M = .84; Perceptual Organization .67 - .88, M = .78; Working Memory .73 - .90, M = .82; Processing Speed .72 - .93, M = .86) but the root mean square differences were comparable for only three of the four factors (Verbal Comprehension .24 - .36, M = .28; Perceptual Organization .25 - .40, M = .31; Working Memory .23 - .36, M = .30) because Processing Speed fit somewhat better than the other three factors (Processing Speed .16 - .30, M = .21). Consequently, the congruence coefficients with the hypothesized structure indicate that the general factor fits better than any of the factors from the 2-factor or 4-factor solutions. The congruence coefficients for the factors from the 2-factor and 4-factor solution were comparable. However, the root mean square differences were higher, indicating poorer fit, for the 2-factor solution than the 1-factor or 4-factor solutions. Three of the 4-factor solution factors were comparable to the 1-factor solution in terms of root mean square differences but the Processing Speed factor was somewhat lower and hence better (.21 versus .28). Separating the root mean square differences into hypothesized and non-hypothesized components, in terms of the hypothesized component, Verbal Comprehension fit best (M = .21), followed by Processing Speed (M = .25), Working Memory (M = .32), and Perceptual Organization (M = .35). In terms of the non-hypothesized component the root mean square differences with the hypothesized structure was equivalent for Verbal Comprehension, Perceptual Organization, and Working Memory (M = .30, .30, and .29, respectively) but lower for Processing Speed (M = .20). Therefore, in terms of hypothesized structure, the 1-factor and 4-factor solutions are somewhat better than the 2-factor solution but within the 2-factor solution Verbal is better than Performance and within the 4-factor solution Verbal Comprehension and Processing Speed are better than either Perceptual Organization or Working Memory.

For the general factor, the between sample congruence coefficients (range: .9909 - .9996, M = .9965) were superior to what was obtained with the 2-factor (Verbal .8465 - .9966, M = .9609; Performance .6375 - .9941, M = .8999) and 4-factor (Verbal Comprehension .8651 - .9937, M = .9557; Perceptual Organization .7364 - .9877, M = .9223; Working Memory .7889 - .9924, M = .9609; Processing Speed .7036 - .9939, M = .9276) solutions, particularly in terms of the range, however, the mean values for the 1-factor, 2-factor, and 4-factor solutions were comparable. The mean between sample root mean square differences was smallest and best for g (.0677) and largest and poorest for the Performance factor (.2193) from the 2-factor solution. All other mean between sample root mean square differences were comparable (2-factor: Verbal .1620; 4-factor: Verbal Comprehension .1378, Perceptual Organization .1773, Working Memory .1525, Processing Speed .1483).

In terms of the prediction analysis, using SMCs as a measure of fit, the average predictability of the 11 subtests constituting the general factor was .54 across age groups. Separating this into the six Verbal and five Performance subtests resulted in an average predictability of .62 for the Verbal subtests and .45 for the Performance subtests. Of all 11 subtests Vocabulary had the highest average predictability (.75). Further, the average predictability of all Verbal subtests with the exception of Digit Span were higher than all five Performance subtests. Consequently, g as measured by the WAIS-III is predominated by crystallized abilities. On average across age groups, for the 2-factor solution the Verbal subtests predicted the Verbal subtests better than the Performance subtests (.59 versus .36) but the Performance subtests predicted the Verbal subtests as well as the Performance subtests (.41 versus .38). With the 4-factor solution, across age groups, only the Verbal Comprehension and Processing Speed subtests predicted their own subtests better than the subtests on any of the other three factors. Subtests on the Perceptual Organization factor and subtests on the Working Memory factor predicted subtests on the Verbal Comprehension factor as well as subtests on their own factor. Consequently, the prediction analysis results indicate that verbal abilities are paramount in the 1-factor, 2-factor, and 4-factor models. The only exception is one of the four factors from the 4-factor model (i.e., Processing Speed).

Overall, the results indicate that the variance accounted for and reliabilities decline going from the 1-, 2-, to 4-factor solutions. In terms of loadings, g was predominated by verbal abilities, in the 2-factor solution Picture Arrangement loaded on average higher on the Verbal factor than the Performance factor, and the 4-factor solution was univocal. Additionally, for both the 2-factor and 4-factor solutions the linkages of the Verbal subtests to the Verbal factors (i.e., 2-factor: Verbal and 4-factor: Verbal Comprehension) generally exceeded the magnitude of the linkages of the other subtests to their associated factors (i.e., 2-factor: Performance and 4-factor: Perceptual Organization, Working Memory, and Processing Speed). In terms of fit with the hypothesized structure, the congruence coefficients indicated that the 1-factor solution fit best but the 2-factor or 4-factor solutions were equivalent. In terms of root mean square differences with the hypothesized structure, the 1-factor and 4-factor solutions were equivalent and better than the 2-factor solution. The between sample congruence coefficients and root mean square differences were best for the 1-factor solution and worst for the Performance factor from the 2-factor solution. The prediction analysis results indicated that regardless of what solution was considered (i.e., 1-, 2-, or 4-factor), verbal abilities intruded significantly and substantially and were consequently paramount.

The intrusive nature of verbal abilities in nearly all aspects of the WAIS-III is likely due to the central importance of verbal abilities in human cognition, attention, consciousness, perception, memory, and information processing. It is also likely due to Yerkes' and subsequently Wechsler's focus on verbal and non-verbal tasks which would have applicability to broad segments of the population. Yerkes use of the Army Alpha for literate recruits and his use of the Army Beta for illiterate or English as a second language recruits can now be seen as somewhat artificial. Verbal abilities are not independent of non-verbal abilities except prior to the onset of language acquisition in children.

Constructs in general and factors in particular are subject to the fallacies of reification and nominalism (cf. Ford & Urban, 1998, chap. 1). Reification involves attributing a real existence to an abstraction and nominalism involves taking a subset of features of a model and generalizing to the entire model. For example, Working Memory is only a heuristic theory which is useful for understanding memory (Baddeley, 1999, chap. 3). In addition, Working Memory is functionally intertwined with Procedural as well as Declarative memory systems (cf. Carroll, 1993, p. 646). In the case of the WAIS-III, the Working Memory factor, defined by the Arithmetic, Digit Span, and Letter-Number-Sequencing subtests, is not a direct measure of this theoretical construct. Prior to the WAIS-III, this factor in the WAIS-R was based on Digit Span and Arithmetic and was labeled Freedom From Distractibility. One of the problems with the Arithmetic subtest is that it requires some basic math calculation knowledge and skill in addition to the attention and manipulation features of Working Memory. Consequently, scores on the Working Memory factor in the WAIS-III are likely invalid for individuals with various degrees of dyscalculia or anarithmetria. Unfortunately, the other two Working Memory subtests on the WAIS-III (Digit Span and Letter-Number Sequencing) involve numbers and are therefore impacted by numerical ability (Carroll, 1993, chap. 7). As well, the broader construct of Memory Span which involves Digit Span and

Letter-Number Sequencing is inadequately defined (Carroll, 1993, chap. 7). In the case of the Processing Speed factor on the WAIS-III the subtests constituting this factor (Digit-Symbol Coding and Symbol Search) are only putative indices of the construct and the factor confounds speed with level (i.e., task specific ability). Choice reaction time and inspection time measures with elementary cognitive tasks are likely better indices of Processing Speed. Unfortunately, reaction times may be attenuated by higher level cognitive processes (Grotzer & Perkins, 2000, p. 501). Furthermore, speed may have social value but does not determine level (Carroll, 1993, chap. 11).

Although the focus of the current research was the WAIS-III, the results are also relevant to the interpretation and use of the entire family of Wechsler's intelligence scales (i.e., WAIS-III, WASI, WISC-III, WPPSI-III, and their predecessors) because all of Wechsler's intelligence scales have a common heritage (i.e., the Army Alpha and Beta). The Army Alpha (VIQ) versus Army Beta (PIQ) distinction paramount in Wechsler's intelligence scales arose from the exigencies of World War I. Such a distinction is of historical significance but no longer tenable. Furthermore, the factor indices associated with these various intelligence scales are post hoc attempts to ascertain the meaning of test scores. Such attempts are imperfect approximations because the identified dimensions or factors were not defined a priori and measured explicitly. Users of Wechsler's intelligence scales, therefore, need to be extremely cautious attributing deficits or strengths in specific abilities beyond a generalized measure of intelligence in which verbal abilities are central.

REFERENCES

Baddeley, A. D. (1999). *Essentials of human memory*. East Sussex: Psychology Press.

Bowden, S. C., Carstairs, J. R., & Shores, A. E. (1999). Confirmatory factor analysis of combined Wechsler Adult Intelligence Scale-Revised and Wechsler Memory Scale-Revised scores in a healthy community sample. *Psychological Assessment. 11,* 339-344.

Camara, W. J., Nathan, J. S., & Puente, A. E. (2000). Psychological test usage: Implications in professional psychology. *Professional Psychology: Research and Practice, 31,* 141-154.

Carroll, J. B. (1993). *Human cognitive abilities: A survey of factor-analytic studies*. New York: Cambridge University Press.

Cliff, N. (1966). Orthogonal rotation to congruence. *Psychometrika, 31,* 33-42.

Enns, R. A., & Reddon, J. R. (1998). The factor structure of the Wechsler Adult Intelligence Scale-Revised: One or 2 but not three factors. *Journal of Clinical Psychology, 54,* 447-449.

Ford, D. H., & Urban, H. B. (1998). *Contemporary models of psychotherapy: A comparative analysis* (2nd. ed.). New York: Wiley.

Frank, G. (1983). *The Wechsler enterprise: An assessment of the development, structure, and use of the Wechsler tests of intelligence*. New York: Pergamon.

Grotzer, T. A., & Perkins, D. N. (2000). Teaching intelligence: A performance conception. In R. J. Sternberg (Ed.), *Handbook of intelligence* (pp. 492-515). New York: Cambridge University Press.

Hill, T. D., Reddon, J. R., & Jackson, D. N. (1985). The factor structure of the Wechsler subtests: A brief review. *Clinical Psychology Review, 5,* 287-306.

Horn, J. L., & Cattell, R. B. (1966). Refinement and test of the theory of fluid and crystallized intelligence. *Acata Psychologica, 26,* 107-129.

Joliffe, I. T. (1986). *Principal component analysis.* New York: Springer-Verlag.

Kaufman, A. S. (2000). Tests of intelligence. In R. J. Sternberg (Ed.), *Handbook of intelligence* (pp. 445-476). New York: Cambridge University Press.

Leckliter, I. N., Matarazzo, J. D., & Silverstein, A. B. (1986). A literature review of factor analytic studies of the WAIS-R. *Journal of Clinical Psychology, 42,* 333-342.

Mosier, C. I. (1943). On the reliability of a weighted composite. *Psychometrika, 8,* 161-168.

The Psychological Corporation. (1999). *Wechsler Abbreviated Scale of Intelligence manual.* San Antonio, TX: The Psychological Corporation.

Schönemann, P. H. (1966). The generalized solution of the orthogonalized procrustes problem. *Psychometrika, 31,* 1-10.

Thurstone, L. L. (1925). A method of scaling psychological and educational tests. *Journal of Educational Psychology, 16,* 433-451.

Thurstone, L. L. (1935). *The vectors of the mind.* Chicago: University of Chicago Press.

Wechsler, D. (1939). *Measurement of adult intelligence.* Baltimore, MD: Williams and Wilkins.

Wechsler, D. (1946). *Manual for the Wechsler-Bellevue Intelligence Scale, Form II.* San Antonio, TX: The Psychological Corporation.

Wechsler, D. (1949). *Manual for the Wechsler Adult Intelligence Scale for Children (WISC).* San Antonio, TX: The Psychological Corporation.

Wechsler, D. (1955). *Manual for the Wechsler Adult Intelligence Scale (WAIS).* San Antonio, TX: The Psychological Corporation.

Wechsler, D. (1967). *Manual for the Wechsler Preschool and Primary Scale of Intelligence (WPPSI).* San Antonio, TX: The Psychological Corporation.

Wechsler, D. (1974). *Manual for the Wechsler Intelligence Scale for Children - Revised (WISC-R).* San Antonio, TX: The Psychological Corporation.

Wechsler, D. (1981). *Manual for the Wechsler Adult Intelligence Scale - Revised (WAIS-R).* San Antonio, TX: The Psychological Corporation.

Wechsler, D. (1989). *Manual for the Wechsler Preschool and Primary Scale of Intelligence - Revised (WPPSI-R).* San Antonio, TX: The Psychological Corporation.

Wechsler, D. (1991). *Manual for the Wechsler Intelligence Scale - Third Edition (WISC-III).* San Antonio, TX: The Psychological Corporation.

Wechsler, D. (1997a). *WAIS-III: Technical manual.* Orlando, FL: Psychological Corporation.

Wechsler, D. (1997b). *WAIS-III: Administration and scoring manual.* Orlando, FL: Psychological Corporation.

Wechsler, D. (2002a). *Wechsler Preschool and Primary Scale of Intelligence - third edition (WPPSI-III) technical manual.* Orlando, FL: Psychological Corporation.

Wechsler, D. (2002b). *Wechsler Preschool and Primary Scale of Intelligence - third edition (WPPSI-III) examiner's manual.* Orlando, FL: Psychological Corporation.

Yoakum, L. S., & Yerkes, R. M. (Ed). (1920). *Army mental tests.* New York: H. Holt.

Yerkes, R. M. (Ed). (1921). Psychological examining in the United States Army. *Memoirs of the National Academy of Sciences, 15,* 1-890.

Yerkes, R. M., & Anderson, H. M. (1915). The importance of social status as indicated by the results of the point scale method of measuring mental capacity. *Journal of Educational Psychology, 6,* 137-150.

Yerkes, R. M., & Bridges, J. W. (1914). The point scale: A new method for measuring mental ability. *Boston Medical and Surgical Journal, 171,* 857-865.

Yerkes, R. M., & Forster, J. C. (1915). *A point scale for measuring mental ability.* Baltimore, MD: Warwick & York.

Yerkes, R. M., & Forster, J. C. (1923). *A point scale for measuring mental ability (1923 version).* Baltimore, MD: Warwick & York.

In: *Topics in Cognitive Psychology*
Serge P. Shohov (Editor) pp. 59-70

ISBN 1-59033-836-7.
© 2003 Nova Science Publishers, Inc.

Chapter 4

PROSPECTIVE MEMORY: WHY DO WE REMEMBER TO PERFORM INTENDED ACTIONS?

Matthias Kliegel [†]
University of Zurich, Switzerland

ABSTRACT

The present chapter targets the topic of remembering the delayed execution of an intention, i.e. prospective memory. After specifying the significance of this research area, a model of prospective remembering is described identifying four phases in the process of forming and executing a delayed intention. The main part of the chapter summarizes recent work of the author concerning the question whether and how the importance of an intention influences the delayed execution. Three studies with five experiments are integrated presenting evidence for the author's resource-allocation-conflict-hypothesis. In sum, data support the assumption that importance instructions may improve prospective memory if the prospective task requires the strategic allocation of attentional monitoring resources.

WHAT IS PROSPECTIVE MEMORY?

Please imagine someone asking you to specify the three most important memory problems you had in the last week. It is very likely that at least one of the problems you list concerns the delayed execution of an intended action, e.g., forgetting to give someone a call. This type of memory has been labelled *prospective memory* and interest in this rather new field of cognitive psychology is growing (e.g., Brandimonte, Einstein, & McDaniel, 1996).

Kliegel and Martin (2003) have summarized three reasons why research on prospective memory is highly relevant: Prospective memory is of great relevance for everyday life. Various studies have reported that 50-80% of all everyday memory problems are, at least in part, prospective memory problems (e.g., Crovitz & Daniel, 1984; Terry, 1998). Prospective

[†] *Correspondence:* Matthias Kliegel, Institute of Psychology, Department of Gerontopsychology, University of Zurich, Schaffhauserstr. 15, CH-8006 Zurich, Switzerland. e-mail: m.kliegel@psychologie.unizh.ch

memory is of enormous clinical relevance. Several authors have addressed the question of prospective memory problems in neuropsychological patients and reported differential effects in many clinical populations (e.g., Fortin, Godbout, & Braun, 2002). Current efforts in this context concern the mechanisms of these impairments (e.g., Kopp & Thöne-Otto, 2003) as well as possible strategies of rehabilitation (e.g., Thöne-Otto & Walter, 2003). Finally, prospective memory research is of tremendous theoretical relevance. Since the early studies on prospective memory researchers have been aiming to disentangle prospective memory from the traditional topic of memory research, i.e., the memory for previously learned information or *retrospective memory*. In addressing this issue, concepts of cognitive functioning in general are being advanced (e.g., Guynn, 2003; Guynn, McDaniel & Einstein, 2001; Einstein & McDaniel, 1996). In addition, one major focus of prospective memory research has been the life-span development of prospective remembering. Investigating age-effects and possible underlying mechanisms, the influence of executive functioning is currently being examined (e.g., Kliegel, Martin, McDaniel & Einstein, 2002; Kliegel, McDaniel, & Einstein, 2000; Kliegel, Ramuschkat, & Martin, 2003; Martin, Kliegel, & McDaniel, 2003).

To identify potential factors influencing prospective memory performance, Kliegel et al. (2002) proposed a process model of prospective memory that distinguishes four phases of prospective remembering (see Figure 1; cf. also Ellis, 1996). The authors classified prospective tasks according to variations in the intention formation phase (e.g., appraisal of importance or pleasantness), the intention retention phase (e.g., short- vs. long-term delay), the intention initiation phase (e.g., event- vs. time-based tasks), and the intention execution phase (e.g., short or long).

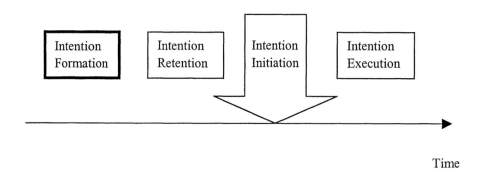

Time

Figure 1. A Process Model of Prospective Memory (after Kliegel et al., 2002)

A review by Kvavilashvili and Ellis (1996) suggested that most of the existing paradigms have investigated task-related aspects of the initiation and execution (e.g., Einstein & McDaniel, 1990, 1996) and the retention phases (e.g., Brandimonte & Passolunghi, 1994), but much less research has focused on how features of the formation phase affect prospective remembering (see also Kliegel et al., 2002; Kvavilashvili, 1992; McDaniel & Einstein, 2000). Hence, there is a lack of research on the influence of intention formation-related factors such as the perceived importance of carrying out an intention that is formed during encoding and its influence on prospective memory performance. Besides the lack of empirical research targeting encoding-related factors such as task importance, it seems intuitively plausible that performance in supposedly important prospective memory tasks should be better compared to tasks perceived to be less important. Consistent with this expectation, Winograd (1988) speculated that people tend to make inferences about the importance of a prospective memory task on the basis of whether or not we remember to perform the task.

Although the influence of motivation via perceived task importance has been explicitly proposed in several recent theoretical models framing prospective memory research (Ellis, 1996; Kliegel et al., 2002; Kvavilashvili & Ellis, 1996; McDaniel & Einstein, 2000) and matches our daily experience, there are only few empirical studies addressing this issue. Most of them, have shown that perceived task importance does improve prospective performance (Andrzejewski, Moore, Corvette, & Herrmann, 1991; Cicogna & Nigro, 1998; Ellis, 1988; Kvavilashvili, 1987, Exp 2; Meacham & Singer, 1977; Somerville, Wellman, & Cultice, 1983; but see Bakker, Schretlen, & Brandt, 2002). However, the conditions under which the motivation to perform the prospective memory task makes a difference in performance, and the mechanisms by which perceived task importance has an effect, are not well understood. Therefore, in recent years we have been addressing these questions and it is the aim of the present chapter to present our main hypothesis and summarize our key findings.

THE INFLUENCE OF TASK IMPORTANCE ON PROSPECTIVE REMEMBERING

Kliegel, Martin, McDaniel, and Einstein (2001) presented two experiments in which they initially investigated the effects of task importance on prospective memory performance testing their resource-allocation-conflict-hypothesis. In sum, their results demonstrate that motivation via perceived task importance has an effect on prospective memory performance in a well-established time-based prospective memory task (i.e., pressing a designated key every two minutes while working on a word rating task; cf. Einstein, Smith, McDaniel, & Shaw, 1997), but not on prospective remembering in a typical event-based prospective memory task (i.e., pressing a designated key whenever a target word had to be rated; cf. Einstein et al., 1997). With respect to the mechanisms underlying these findings, Kliegel et al. (2001) argue that the differential effects depend on the degree to which the prospective tasks require the strategic allocation of attentional resources.

In typical prospective memory tasks, e.g., pressing a designated key every two minutes while working on a word rating task, participants have to work on two tasks simultaneously: the ongoing task (e.g., working on a word rating task) and the prospective memory task (e.g., pressing a designated key every two minutes). However, both the prospective memory task and the ongoing task require the allocation of limited attentional processes, such as monitoring for the prospective memory cue (e.g., the two minutes interval) and monitoring the words to be rated in the ongoing task, respectively. If a prospective memory task is considered important, it should get more attentional resources than a task considered less important. However, the beneficial effects of additional monitoring should only occur in prospective tasks that actually rely on strategic attentional processes (e.g., active monitoring), and not on prospective tasks that rely on more automatic processes (we will elaborate on this below).

In the Kliegel et al. (2001) study, this hypothesis was confirmed for a typical time-based task in the course of which the participants had to regularly monitor the time in order to know when to initiate the intended action; this task is generally seen as highly attention-demanding (Martin & Schumann-Hengsteler, 2001; Einstein & McDaniel, 1996). In contrast, some event-based tasks such as Kliegel et al.'s event-based task in Experiment 2 (i.e., pressing a designated key whenever a target word had to be rated) are seen as more automatically cued by the prospective target and therefore as not relying on strategic monitoring processes. Here, in fact, task importance did not improve prospective memory performance. However, while failing to detect a direct effect of task importance on the performance in their simple event-based task, Kliegel et al. (2001) found an indirect monitoring-related effect of prospective task importance on cover task performance. In particular, when they added a digit detection task (i.e., participants heard a series of single digits aloud on a tape and were told to count all occurrences of the number 9 using a hand-held counter) to the general task demands, Kliegel et al. found that cover task performance was less accurate (subjects failed to complete trials) when the instructions emphasized the importance of the event-based prospective memory task than when the same prospective memory task was identified as less important. Although performance in their event-based prospective memory task still was not affected by the manipulation of the importance of the prospective task, under high general monitoring demands cover task performance was affected. Given that dividing attention interferes with monitoring and assuming that the mechanism underlying the effects of importance is an increase in strategic monitoring, it seems reasonable to hypothesize that this indirect importance effect was due to the additional monitoring evoked by the manipulation of the importance of the prospective task.

Linking these findings to recent theoretical developments in prospective memory research, the assumption of a monitoring effect underlying the effects of importance manipulations are consistent with predictions from the multiprocess framework of prospective memory proposed by McDaniel and Einstein (2000). They present two general views on how prospective remembering can be accomplished. Either one could strategically monitor the environment for the presence of the target event, or one could rely on anticipated environmental conditions more or less automatically re-instantiating the intended action. In reviewing the literature, McDaniel and Einstein suggest that the extent to which prospective remembering is supported by relatively automatic processes (vs. strategic, resource-demanding monitoring) mainly varies as a function of the characteristics of the task, the target cue, and the ongoing task. Under some conditions, prospective remembering does not require strategic rehearsal (see also Einstein, McDaniel, Manzi, Cochran, & Baker, 2000; but see Kliegel et al., 2000 for a more complex event-based paradigm). That is, when there is good encoding of the target cue-action association (see also Guynn et al., 2001; Guynn, McDaniel, & Einstein, 1998), when a salient target cue is used, or when the activities associated with the background task focus processing of the target event (see also Brandimonte & Passolunghi, 1994; McDaniel & Einstein, 1993; McDaniel, Guynn, & Einstein, 1997; Meier & Graf, 2000). Under these circumstances, McDaniel and Einstein (2000) argue, the role of attention-demanding strategic rehearsal in prospective remembering is minimized. In fact, Kliegel et al. (2001) using such an event-based paradigm (i.e., pressing a designated key whenever a target word had to be rated) demonstrated in their Experiment 2 that additional strategic monitoring due to importance did not improve prospective memory performance.

Extending these findings, most recently, Kliegel, Martin, McDaniel, and Einstein (in press) further tested this line of reasoning in two event-based tasks that differed in the extent to which the ongoing task encourages focal processing of the target event. In their previous research just described, there may have been other undetermined differences between the time- and event-based tasks used and these may have produced the differential effects of importance. In the first experiment, Kliegel et al. (in press) used conditions very similar to those in the event-based experiment of Kliegel et al. (2001), however, increasing the overall memory load by providing two prospective memory targets as well as increasing the experimental power by testing a larger group of subjects. As indicated earlier, in this task, the ongoing activity focuses processing of the target event, and therefore it was assumed that good prospective remembering can be accomplished through relatively automatic processes. One purpose of conducting this experiment was to examine if they could replicate their earlier finding of no importance effects on this type of task. Another purpose was to confirm the influence of adding a divided attention task on the importance-related performance in this rather simple prospective memory task. According to the views outlined above, to the extent that participants can rely on a relatively automatic retrieval process, dividing attention should have no or minimal effects on prospective memory performance. Also, in line with Kliegel et al. (2001), they expected to find poorer performance on the ongoing task when the instructions emphasized the importance of the prospective memory task and especially so with divided attention.

The results regarding prospective memory performance revealed no reliable main effects or interaction. In line with our prior findings, but in contrast to the assumption of a general importance effect in prospective memory, no effect of prospective memory importance was found for a standard event-based laboratory task. This was the case even though the difficulty of the prospective memory task was increased from that in Kliegel et al. (2001) by providing two prospective target words (instead of one). Hence, the results are in line with the idea that at least some event-based prospective memory tasks are mediated by relatively automatic processes, or at least require very little attention for successful performance. This is evidenced in the current study by the finding that prospective memory performance was largely unaffected even with the addition of a third task that increased the overall demands of the ongoing activities. To further examine the resource-allocation-conflict-hypothesis, as in Kliegel et al. (2001), ongoing task performance was also analyzed. Consistent with our hypothesis, particularly in the demanding background condition participants given high importance instructions made significantly more omissions in the ongoing task. Hence, although there was no importance effect on prospective memory performance, there still were traces of the assumed importance-related attention allocation policy evoked by the manipulation of the importance of the prospective memory task. In addition, regarding digit detection performance, results revealed a mean difference in numbers of errors that approaches statistical significance. Participants in the high importance condition, i.e., high importance of the prospective but not the ongoing task, made more errors than participants in the low importance condition. Thus, it seems that participants in the high importance condition took more attentional resources to concentrate on prospective memory performance and therefore made more errors in the digit detection task.

In Experiment 2, Kliegel et al. (in press) modified Kliegel et al.'s (2001) event-based paradigm to create an event-based prospective memory task that, according to McDaniel and Einstein's (2000) framework, would seem to depend on strategic monitoring for successful performance. Participants were asked to make the prospective response whenever they saw certain *target letters* in the words to be rated. This prospective memory task can be seen as more dependent on strategic monitoring processes because the activities associated with the ongoing task do not directly focus processing on the target event (letters instead of words). Thus, for this type of event-based prospective task they predicted an effect of task importance on prospective memory performance. Also, to the extent that importance instructions encourage participants to develop a strategic monitoring strategy, performance on the ongoing task should suffer with high-importance instructions and especially so in the highly demanding condition.

Here, in contrast to Kliegel et al.'s (2001) event-based task as well as in contrast to the findings from Kliegel et al.'s (in press) Experiment 1 the present results revealed a significant main effect for task importance indicating better prospective memory performance in the high importance condition. In addition, there was no significant main effect for background task, but there was a significant interaction indicating a greater importance effect in the demanding background task groups. Also with respect to performance in the ongoing word rating task, consistent with our assumptions, we found evidence of the assumed importance-related attention allocation evoked by the manipulation of the importance of the prospective memory task. Participants who received the high prospective memory importance instruction made more omissions in the word rating ongoing task. Finally, as with the word rating task, participants who focused their attention on the prospective memory task made more omissions in the digit-detection task.

In sum, results of the Kliegel et al. (in press) study showed that perceived task importance had a positive effect on the performance in the monitoring-demanding event-based prospective memory task, but not on the performance in the event-based task relying on rather automatic processing. Analyses of performance in the ongoing task were consistent with the interpretation that these differential effects were due to attentional trade-off processes between the prospective task and the background activity. In the monitoring-demanding event-based prospective memory task (Kliegel et al.'s, in press, Experiment 2), participants who perceived the prospective task to be of high importance were both better in the prospective task and worse in the ongoing task. Thus, participants in the high importance condition seemed to allocate fewer attentional resources to the ongoing task. Moreover, even in Kliegel at al.'s (in press) Experiment 1, despite the lack of an importance effect on prospective memory performance evidence of a trade-off in attention allocation between the prospective memory and the ongoing task was found. Here, in the demanding background task condition, participants who focused their attention on the prospective memory task also made more omissions in the ongoing word rating task.

Finally, in their discussion, Kliegel et al. (in press) acknowledge an additional alternative interpretation of their results that concerns the way importance was manipulated. In most of the prospective memory literature on importance, researchers stressed or did not stress the importance of the prospective intention and did not vary their instructions for the ongoing task. In contrast, in the previously summarized research (Kliegel et al., 2001, in press) the relative task importance between the prospective and the ongoing task was manipulated; in order to ensure that all participants would draw the same consequences regarding ongoing task importance. However, it seems possible that participants in fact did "translate" the relative importance instruction in favor of the prospective task into an instruction not to attend carefully to the ongoing task and that this is responsible for the obtained decrements in importance-related ongoing task performance. This interpretation can not be ruled out completely with the just described data – at least when only considering the experiments producing an importance effect (i.e., Experiment 1 in Kliegel et al., 2001, and Experiment 2 in Kliegel et al., in press). However, this alternative interpretation would have predicted different results than were obtained in the other two Experiments (i.e., Experiment 2 in the Kliegel et al., 2001, and Experiment 1 in the Kliegel et al., in press, study). If, in fact, Kliegel et al. (in press) argue, participants receiving instructions emphasizing the importance of the prospective memory task were only following an "instruction" not to attend carefully to the ongoing task, one would particularly expect a significant main effect of importance on ongoing task performance also in both Experiments revealing no importance effect in both studies – which was not the case. The interaction between task importance and background load, obtained in both studies, is at least consistent with the assumed importance-related attention allocation evoked by the manipulation of the importance of the prospective memory task. However, further research is needed to link the present findings to other importance manipulations used in the literature.

Therefore, Kliegel and Martin (2003) have manipulated importance in another way by providing more or less mandatory task instructions investigating whether the general effects associated with the resource-allocation-conflict-hypothesis could also be found using a different procedure and importance manipulation. It was an additional aim of this study to further examine the hypothesis concerning the underlying mechanisms of these effects. In consequence, a different (time-based) prospective memory paradigm also previously used in our lab (e.g., Martin & Schumann-Hengsteler, 2001) was administered. In this task, as the ongoing cover activity participants were playing a well-known logical deduction game (so called "Mastermind" – for more detailed information see Martin & Schumann-Hengsteler, 2001). There were two important differences to the previously described paradigm. First, the time characteristics of the cover activity were significantly different from the word rating task insofar as each single cover task trial lasted much longer (several minutes) and its duration depended on the participant's performance (in contrast to fixed 5-second trials in the word rating task). Thus, quickly checking the time for one or two seconds or performing the prospective action (i.e., changing a game protocol sheet every 3 minutes which lasts about 2 to 3 seconds) should not take too much time and, thus, distract attention from the cover task. Second, the prospective task itself was an action compatible with the cover activity. This is in contrast to pressing the target key whenever the target word appeared in the previous experiments, an action explicitly incompatible with appropriate cover task performance, i.e., rating the target word using the number keys. Moreover, the prospective time interval was longer (every 3 minutes vs. every 2 minutes), thus allowing less frequent time monitoring in the present procedure. In contrast to the previous study, we therefore assumed that in the present time-based task prospective time monitoring as well as prospective memory performance were less likely to affect attentional resources allocated to cover task performance. Hence, in line with the resource-allocation-conflict-hypothesis, we expected an effect of importance on prospective memory performance, but not on cover task performance.

As indicated, in the Kliegel and Martin (2003) study, we used a new way to manipulate the participants' motivation to perform well in the prospective memory task. In contrast to directly labeling the prospective memory task as more or less important, we varied the significance of the prospective memory task by either directly instructing the participants to follow the prospective instruction as an integrated and obligatory part of the entire procedure or by giving a prospective instruction telling the participants that besides the main (cover) activity we had a "secondary interest" together with an explanation why we were interested in these data. Contrasting these types of instruction does not only allow examining motivational effects from the perspective of a different manipulation. Moreover, comparing these instructions, for the first time, we systematically investigated two typical methods widely and interchangeably used in the literature (cf. Kliegel et al., 2000; 2001; 2002; Maylor, 1993, 1996 as examples of the integrated instruction-type and Einstein & McDaniel, 1990; Einstein, Holland, McDaniel, & Guynn, 1992; Einstein, McDaniel, Richardson, Guynn, & Cunfer, 1995; Kvavilashvili, 1987 as examples of the "secondary interest" type). However, no explicit hypotheses have been developed whether using these types of introducing the prospective memory task leads to differential task representations, motivation, and, as a consequence, task performance. From previous research, it is not clear whether one would expect to find better performance with one or the other type of instruction.

In the literature on prospective memory in children, it has recently been shown that providing an explanation reliably enhances prospective memory performance (Kvavilashvili, Messer, & Ebdon, 2001). However, giving the instruction for the prospective memory task by labeling the task as of "secondary interest" might result in the perception that the prospective task is less important than the cover task (i.e., the "primary interest"). Thus, a "secondary interest"-instruction, even when accompanied by an explanation, might lead to a lower perceived significance of the prospective memory task. This, in turn, would increase the likelihood of attentional trade-off processes to the disadvantage of the prospective task at least in maximum performance situations when limited attentional resources have to be split between cover task and prospective task. As a consequence, presenting the prospective memory task in the same rather obligatory way as the cover task (using an integrated instruction-style that introduces the prospective task as a part of the entire procedure) might lead to a comparable perceived significance of both cover and prospective memory task and, thus, to a higher perceived significance than when applying a "secondary interest" instruction. This might result in a higher motivation to actually perform the task as well as possible; in accord with the resource-allocation-conflict-hypothesis at least in case of maximum performance situations with limited attentional resources. Varying the amount of cognitive resources required through the manipulation of cover task complexity, we therefore expected strong motivational effects in the high complexity situation.

There were 52 participants, 27 women and 25 men, all of them university undergraduate or graduate students, with an average age of 25.2 years ($SD = 4.2$). The study followed a 2 (high vs. low complexity of the cover task) x 2 (integrated instruction vs. "secondary interest" instruction plus explanation) between-subject design.

Results regarding ongoing task performance revealed a significant main effect for cover task complexity. Significantly more Mastermind problems were solved in the low complexity versus the high complexity condition. The cover task was not affected by the prospective task being either of high or low significance, since there was no difference between subjects in the two prospective memory conditions with respect to performance level in both cover task conditions. Moreover, there was no significant interaction.

Examining prospective memory performance, there was no significant main effect of cover task complexity or salience of the prospective memory task. However, a reliable interaction between cover task complexity and significance of the prospective memory task on prospective memory task performance was revealed. Whereas prospective memory performance remained at about the same level in both low complexity conditions as well as the high complexity / high significance condition, there was a significant drop in prospective memory performance in the high complexity / low significance group. Here, the prospective memory performance was only about half of the performance in the three other conditions.

In sum, applying a different kind of manipulation of participants' motivation to perform a prospective memory task, in the present study the results confirm an influence of motivation on prospective performance. This is in line with our previous work on prospective memory (e.g., Kliegel et al., 2001, in press), but in contrast to findings from the retrospective memory literature (e.g., Nilsson, 1987). However, results also reveal that this effect only emerges under high cognitive resource demands. Hence, the present findings suggest that under specific circumstances motivational factors can affect prospective memory performance. In line with Kliegel et al. (2001, in press) and McDaniel and Einstein (2000), also in this study it seems that the crucial factor was the dual-task nature of prospective memory tasks. The significant interaction between task complexity and instruction format that was mainly due to a motivation effect in the high complexity background condition is consistent with the assumption that motivation has not a general effect on prospective memory performance. Rather, the results are in line with the hypothesis that motivation affects performance through selective allocation of attentional resources (only) in maximum performance situations with limited attentional resources.

Our results have some further theoretical and methodological implications. In contrast to Kliegel et al.'s (2001) Experiment 1, the present study reports a time-based paradigm that was not generally affected by the manipulation of participants' motivation. Thus, in line with Park, Hertzog, Kidder, Morell, and Mayhorn (1997), this finding underlines that not time-based or event-based tasks per se are more or less resource-demanding or difficult. The results rather support the conclusion that the demands of a prospective memory task depend on the characteristics of the presented cover activity as well as of the instructed prospective action itself. As discussed above, the time characteristics of the cover activity as well as the compatible nature of the prospective action of the present paradigm were designed as a task less depending on attentional trade-off processes than the time-based task applied in Kliegel et al. (2001). Accordingly, and in line with the outlined resource-allocation-conflict-hypothesis, in the time-based task only a combination of both high complexity and low motivation did affect prospective memory performance.

Finally, the findings concerning the two contrasted types of instruction suggest important methodological consequences for prospective memory research. Direct, integrated instructions and "secondary interest" instructions have been widely and interchangeably used. However, the present results demonstrate that both instructions lead to differences in the ensuing prospective memory performance – at least in case of maximum performance situations with limited attentional resources. Although explicating a reason to perform the prospective action has been shown as benefiting prospective memory performance in children (Kvavilashvili et al., 2001), introducing prospective memory as a second, and thus less significant, part of the experimental procedure seems to lead to a lower motivation to allocate attentional resources to this secondary interest. This seems at least to be true when the available attentional resources are limited. As a consequence, we propose to introduce the prospective memory task as a genuine and integrated part of the entire session, and not to downgrade the prospective action.

REFERENCES

Andrzejewski, S.J., Moore, C.M., Corvette, M., & Herrmann, D. (1991). Prospective memory skill. *Bulletin of the Psychonomic Society, 29,* 304-306.

Bakker, A., Schretlen, D.J., & Brandt, J. (2002). Testing prospective memory: Does the value of a borrowed item help people remember to get it back? *Clinical Neuropsychologist, 16,* 64-66.

Brandimonte, M.A., Einstein, G.O., & McDaniel, M.A. (Eds.) (1996). *Prospective memory: Theory and applications.* Mahwah, NJ: Erlbaum.

Brandimonte, M.A. & Passolunghi, M.C. (1994). The effect of cue-familiarity, cue-distinctiveness, and retention interval on prospective remembering. *The Quarterly Journal of Experimental Psychology, 47A,* 565-588.

Cicogna, P.C. & Nigro, G. (1998). Influence of importance of intention on prospective memory performance. *Perceptual and Motor Skills, 87,* 1387-1392.

Crovitz, H. F. & Daniel, W. F. (1984). Measurements of everyday memory: Toward the prevention of forgetting. *Bulletin of the Psychonomic Society, 22,* 413-414.

Einstein, G.O., Holland, L.J., McDaniel, M.A. & Guynn, M.J. (1992). Age-related deficits in prospective memory: The influence of task complexity. *Psychology and Aging, 7,* 471-478.

Einstein, G.O. & McDaniel, M.A. (1990). Normal aging and prospective memory. *Journal of Experimental Psychology: Learning, Memory, and Cognition, 16,* 717-726.

Einstein, G.O. & McDaniel, M.A. (1996). Retrieval processes in prospective memory: Theoretical approaches and some new findings. In M. Brandimonte, G.O. Einstein, & M.A. McDaniel (Eds.), *Prospective memory: Theory and applications* (pp. 115-142). Mahwah, NJ: Erlbaum.

Einstein, G.O., McDaniel, M.A., Manzi, M., Cochran, B., & Baker, M. (2000). Prospective memory and aging: Forgetting intentions over short delays. *Psychology and Aging, 15,* 671-683.

Einstein, G.O., McDaniel, M.A., Richardson, S.L., Guynn, M.J., & Cunfer, A.R. (1995). Aging and prospective memory: Examining the influences of self-initiated retrieval processes. *Journal of Experimental Psychology: Learning, Memory, and Cognition, 21,* 996-1007.

Einstein, G.O., Smith, R.E., McDaniel, M.A., & Shaw, P. (1997). Aging and prospective memory: The influence of increased task demands at encoding and retrieval. *Psychology and Aging, 12,* 479-488.

Ellis, J.A. (1988). Memory for future intentions: Investigating pulses and steps. In M.M. Gruneberg, P.E. Morris, & R.N. Sykes (Eds.), *Practical aspects of memory: Current research and issues: vol. 1* (pp. 371-376). Chichester: Wiley.

Ellis, J.A. (1996). Prospective memory or the realization of delayed intentions: A conceptual framework for research. In M. Brandimonte, G.O. Einstein, & M.A. McDaniel (Eds.), *Prospective memory: Theory and applications* (pp. 1-22). Mahwah, NJ: Erlbaum.

Fortin, S., Godbout, L., & Braun, C.M.J. (2002). Strategic sequence planning and prospective memory impairments in frontally lessoned head trauma patients performing activities of daily living. *Brain and Cognition, 48,* 361-365.

Guynn, M.J. (2003). A two-process model of strategic monitoring in event-based prospective memory: Activation/Retrieval Mode and Checking. *International Journal of Psychology.*

Guynn, M.J., McDaniel. M.A., & Einstein, G.O. (1998). Prospective memory: When reminders fail. *Memory and Cognition, 26,* 287-298.

Guynn, M.J., McDaniel. M.A., & Einstein, G.O. (2001). Remembering to perform actions: A different type of memory? In H.D. Zimmer, R.L. Cohen, M.J. Guynn, J. Engelkamp, R. Kormi-Nouri & M.A. Foley (Eds.), *Memory for action: A distinct form of episodic memory?* (pp. 25-48). New York: Oxford University Press.

Kliegel, M. & Martin, M. (2003). Mechanisms underlying motivational effects in prospective remembering. In S.P. Shohov (Ed.), *Advances in psychology research* (pp. 3-14). Huntington, NY: Nova Science Publishers.

Kliegel, M. & Martin, M. (2003). Prospective memory research: Why is it relevant? *International Journal of Psychology.*

Kliegel, M., Martin, M., McDaniel, M.A., & Einstein, G.O. (2001). Varying the importance of a prospective memory task: Differential effects across time- and event-based prospective memory. *Memory, 9,* 1-11.

Kliegel, M., Martin, M., McDaniel, M.A., & Einstein, G.O. (2002). Complex prospective memory and executive control of working memory: A process model. *Psychologische Beiträge, 44,* 303-318.

Kliegel, M., Martin, M., McDaniel, M.A. & Einstein, G.O. (2003). Importance effects on performance in even-based prospective memory tasks. *Memory.*

Kliegel, M., McDaniel, M.A., & Einstein, G.O. (2000). Plan formation, retention, and execution in prospective memory: A new paradigm and age-related effects. *Memory and Cognition, 28,* 1041-1049.

Kliegel, M., Ramuschkat, G., & Martin, M. (2003). Exekutive Funktionen und prospektive Gedächtnisleistung im Alter – Eine differentielle Analyse von ereignis- und zeitbasierter prospektiver Gedächtnisleistung. *Zeitschrift für Gerontologie und Geriatrie, 36,* 35-41.

Kopp, U.A. & Thöne-Otto, A.I.T. (2003). Disentangling executive functions and memory processes in event based prospective remembering after brain damage: A neuropsychological study. *International Journal of Psychology.*

Kvavilashvili, L. (1987). Remembering intention as a distinct form of memory. *British Journal of Psychology, 78,* 507-518.

Kvavilashvili, L. (1992). Remembering intentions: A critical review of existing experimental paradigms. *Applied Cognitive Psychology, 6,* 507-524.

Kvavilashvili, L. & Ellis, J. (1996). Varieties of intention: Some distinctions and classifications. In M. Brandimonte, G.O. Einstein, & M.A. McDaniel (Eds.), *Prospective memory: Theory and applications* (pp. 23-51). Mahwah, NJ: Erlbaum.

Kvavilashvili, L., Messer, D.J., & Ebdon, P. (2001). Prospective memory in children: The effects of age and task interruption. *Developmental Psychology, 37,* 418-430.

Martin, M., Kliegel, M., & McDaniel, M. (2003). The involvement of executive functions in prospective memory performance of adults. *International Journal of Psychology, 38,* 195-206.

Martin, M., & Schumann-Hengsteler, R. (2001). The influence of task demands on time-based prospective memory performance in young and old adults. *International Journal of Behavioral Development, 25,* 386-391.

Maylor, E.A. (1993). Aging and forgetting in prospective and retrospective memory tasks. *Psychology and Aging, 8,* 420-428.

Maylor, E.A. (1996). Age-related impairment in an event-based prospective memory task. *Psychology and Aging, 11,* 74-78.

McDaniel, M.A., Guynn, M.J., & Einstein, G.O. (1997, November). *Prospective memory: Two views and some new data.* Paper presented at the meeting of the Psychonomic Society, Philadelphia, PA.

McDaniel, M.A., & Einstein, G.O. (1993). The importance of cue familiarity and cue distinctiveness in prospective memory. *Memory, 1,* 23-41.

McDaniel, M.A. & Einstein, G.O. (2000). Strategic and automatic processes in prospective memory retrieval: A multiprocess framework. *Applied Cognitive Psychology, 14,* S127-S144.

Meacham, J.A. & Singer, J. (1977). Incentive effects in prospective remembering. *The Journal of Psychology, 97,* 191-197.

Meier, B. & Graf, P. (2000). Transfer appropriate processing for prospective memory tests. *Applied Cognitive Psychology, 14,* S11-S27.

Nilsson, L.G. (1987). Motivated memory: Dissociation between performance data and subjective reports. *Psychological Research, 49,* 183-188.

Park, D.C., Hertzog, C., Kidder, D.P., Morell, R.W., & Mayhorn, C.B. (1997). Effect of age on event-based and time-based prospective memory. *Psychology and Aging, 12,* 314-327.

Somerville, S.C., Wellmann, H.M., & Cultice, J.C. (1983). Young children's deliberate reminding. *Journal of Genetic Psychology, 143,* 87-96.

Terry, W. S. (1988). Everyday forgetting: Data from a diary study. *Psychological Reports, 62,* 299-303.

Thöne-Otto, A.I.T. & Walter, K. (2003). How to design an electronic memory aid for brain injured patients? Considerations on the basis of a model of prospective memory. *International Journal of Psychology,* 38, 236-244.

Winograd, E. (1988). Some observations on prospective remembering. In M. M. Gruneberg, P.M. Morris, & R. N. Sykes (Eds.), *Practical aspects of memory* (Vol. 1), (pp. 348-353). Chichester, England: Wiley.

In: *Topics in Cognitive Psychology*
Serge P. Shohov (Editor) pp. 71-100

ISBN 1-59033-836-7.
© 2003 Nova Science Publishers, Inc.

Chapter 5

GIFTED BRAIN AND TWINNING: INTEGRATIVE REVIEW OF THE RECENT LITERATURE

*Andrew A. Fingelkurts and Alexander A. Fingelkurts**
BM-Science Brain & Mind Technologies Research Centre,
Espoo, Finland
Human Brain Research Group, Human Physiology Department,
Biological Faculty, Moscow State University,
Russian Federation

ABSTRACT

In this review, on the basis of literature and data on the strong connection between high intelligence in pre/adolescents and high testosterone level in the prenatal fetus development and also on the increased concentration of testosterone in the amniotic liquid in the case of monozygotic male-twins pregnancy, the hypothesis of biologically conditioned intellectual giftedness in the monozygotic male-twins is suggested. Taking into consideration new experimental data and results of other investigators it is assumed that the high involvement of the right frontal cortical area in the ongoing information brain processing may serve as a physiological marker of intellectual giftedness. The prenatal developmental peculiarities and unfavorable psychosocial factors during postnatal twins' development are discussed as the reasons for the phenomenological absence of talented male-twins in human history.

Keywords: Intelligence, Giftedness, Twins, Left-handedness, Cerebral lateralization, EEG.

* Correspondance: BM-Science Brain & Mind Technologies Research Centre, P.O. Box 77, FI-02601 Espoo, Finland. E-mail: Andrew.Fingelkurts@bm-science.com; http://www.bm-science.com/team/fingelkurts.html; 358 - 40 - 8350344 (mobile)

1. INTRODUCTION

A long history of anatomical, morpho-functional, biochemical, neurophysiological and psychophysiological investigations of the human brain hemisphere's asymmetry proves the existence of a special bilateral principle in the development of such important brain functions like perception, attention, memory and speech.

Recent studies in neuroscience show that interhemispheric asymmetry (particularly in the frontal areas) carries the essential contribution also in the manifestation of high intelligence in humans (see the reviews O'Boyle et al., 1995, Fingelkurts & Fingelkurts, 2002).

The evaluation of functional states (FS) of the frontal cortical areas is significant, because it has been shown that the synthesis of two types of information – current and retrieval – which create the basis for the emergence of subjective feelings (Ivanizky, 1997), takes place in the frontal cortex (Crick & Koch, 1995; Goldman-Rakic, 1996). It has been well documented through experiments using EEG, PET and fMRI that frontal cortical areas play the main role in the mechanisms which provide and regulate working memory[1] (Stuss et al., 1982; Goldman-Rakic, 1996), and conscious perception (Crick & Koch, 1995). It is supposed that information stored in the temporal and parietal cortex, is reread on the neurons of the frontal cortex (Goldman-Rakic, 1996). And at last it has been shown that a "general intelligence" or *g* may in large part be a reflection of frontal functions (Duncan et. al., 1996; Thompson et al., 2001).

Our research (Fingelkurts & Fingelkurts, 1995; Kaplan et al., 1997; Fingelkurts et al., 1998) demonstrates the minimal involvement of the left frontal cortical area of human brain during the process of operational synchronization in *various* FS (from rest conditions to different cognitive tasks). Moreover, applying other methods and approaches has also demonstrated increased involvement of the right frontal cortex in comparison with the left frontal area that remained uninvolved in the ongoing informative-analytical activity of the brain (Kaplan et al., 1998; Fingelkurts Al., 1998; Fingelkurts An., 1998; Fingelkurts et al., 2000).

At the same time, the majority of investigations with rest conditions (Kiroi et al., 1996) and memory testing in humans (Kiroi et al., 1988; Pavlova & Romanenko, 1988) reveal the dominance of the left frontal cortex over the right one. These findings are normally associated with the dominance of the left hemisphere as a feature of the human species (Dobrohotova & Bragina, 1994; Annett, 1999). However, our data contradicts these findings. Probably, this discrepancy is due to the fact that all subjects in our research were MZ male-twins (Fingelkurts An., 1998; Fingelkurts Al., 1998).

Based on the findings that: 1) there is literature data that enhanced involvement of the right hemisphere in ongoing informational processing of the brain is a marker of extremely high intelligence (see the review, O'Boyle et al., 1995), 2) an increased level of testosterone leads to the faster maturation and cognitive development of the right brain hemisphere only (Geschwind & Behan, 1982), we hypothesize the following (this hypothesis has been suggested in 1998 and briefly discussed in *Questions of Psychology*, 2000): male-twins during prenatal development have an increased exposure to testosterone that leads to a more complicated (see details further) development of the right hemisphere which becomes

---

[1] Do not mix with short-term memory, which is the storage of newly obtained experience. Working memory is the active part of the constant memory, but it may include as well the signs of "old" memory.

dominant. These peculiarities of male-twins development result in potential giftedness. However, male-twins rarely realize this potential due to unfavorable socio-psychological conditions during postnatal development. Some of these suggestions are supported by external evidence, and perhaps some will turn out to be false, but meanwhile our hypothesis at least provides explanation for basic but widely scattered findings in physiological and psychological literature about androgens, intelligence, handedness, hemisphere specialization and twins. The synthesis of these findings reveals the many converging lines of evidence that support suggested hypothesis.

2. INTELLECTUAL GIFTEDNESS

How is giftedness defined? There is no one agreed-upon definition of giftedness or talent that dominates the field (Robinson & Clinkenbeard, 1998). Most definitions are psychologically based or educationally driven. We define giftedness as higher than average efficiency of neurological brain functioning (for details see Fingelkurts & Fingelkurts, 2002). Such a definition covers all areas of giftedness: general intellectual ability, specific academic aptitude, creative or productive thinking, leadership ability, visual and performing arts, and psychomotor ability (Ross, 1993). The effectiveness of human brain activity is determined by the number of neurons and the density of neuronal networks, which were organized during the prenatal period and which were active during crucial periods (first 4 years of life) of human development (Kimura, 1994; Rakic et al., 1994; Clinton, 1996; Newman, 1997). Experimentally it has been proven that nearly all aspects of nervous system organization (including cell growth, size regulation, cells' number, form, and neuron network density) are strongly influenced by androgens during prenatal development and immediately after the birth[2] (Levy & Gur, 1980; Geschwind & Behan, 1982; Geschwind & Galaburda, 1987; Galaburda et al., 1987; Sholl & Kim, 1990; Dempster, 1991; Snyder et al., 1995; Collaer & Hines, 1995).

Thus, the prenatal level of androgens might be the essential link in the organization of the gifted brain.

3. EVIDENCE FROM ENDOCRINOLOGY: PRENATAL LEVELS OF TESTOSTERONE

According to Geschwind and Behan, if the fetus gets an increased dosage of testosterone during the crucial period of prenatal development or if it is more sensitive to this hormone, then the brain of such a fetus starts to develop the right nondominant hemisphere more

---

[2] Although it is obvious that the human brain undergoes several growth spurts, there are periods of development during which the brain is particularly sensitive to certain types of experience (Johnson, 2001). For present discussion it is important that disturbances of the prenatal cerebral cortex development can result in a variety of minor malformations (Sarnat, 1987). These minor neocortical malformations have a direct effect on behavior (Rosen et al., 1995). The mechanism by which these small neocortical anomalies affect behavior remains unknown, but it was shown that these anomalies lead to profound and sometimes pervasive reorganization of the brain (Innocenti & Berbel, 1991). These findings support the idea that early neocortical anomalies have profound effect on cortical connectivity and these widespread changes in connectivity may have wide-ranging behavioral effects (Rosen et al., 1995).

intensively (Geschwind & Behan, 1982); but in ordinary conditions the left hemisphere develops faster and stronger (Thatcher et al., 1987). Selected influence of testosterone on the right hemisphere is explained by a significantly higher average concentration of androgen receptors (AR) in the right hemisphere compared to the left (Diamond, 1991). At the cortical level, the right frontal area is in many of those areas, which significantly overloads the left cortical areas by numbers of AR's (Sholl & Kim, 1990). This irregularity in AR density across the human brain is shown only in males. Evidently, the described particular development of morpho-functional brain organization must strongly influence the human cognitive abilities (Hellige, 1993; Halpern, 2000). This data is in agreement with the results of the research of Levy and Gur, which show that an increased level of embryonic sex hormones leads to the faster maturation and cognitive development of the right brain hemisphere (Levy & Gur, 1980).

From animals studies it is well known that testosterone can affect the central nervous system either directly as testosterone or through its metabolites estradiol and dihydrotestosterone (Pomeranez et al., 1985). Ironically estradiol and estrogen in females never reaches the brain. "High levels of alpha fetoprotein in the neonatal serum bind these estrogens and prevent their access to the brain. By contrast, in males the conversion of testosterone to estrogens takes place within the developing brain itself" (Small & Hoffman, 1994, p. 307-308). Injections of testosterone or its metabolites in the brain attenuate the reactive astrocytic response to penetrating wounds to the cortex and hippocampal structures (Garcia-Estrada et al., 1993). Recently it was also shown that circulating androgens in the developmental brain are responsible for male/female differences in brain structures, as well as for sex differences in the behavioral consequences of these brain differences (Rosen et al., 1999). It is assumed that "exposure to the [high levels of] testosterone might enhance the process of normal plasticity, thereby encouraging extraordinary restructuring of connectivity" (Rosen et al., 1999, p. 32).

Studies of the developing human fetal brain also support the hypothesis that testosterone in utero may lead to a more rapid growth of the right hemisphere (De Lacoste et al., 1991). It was shown that on the average, volumetric asymmetries (particularly frontal cortex) in the male brain favor the right hemisphere; in females the left hemisphere is slightly larger than its right counterpart.

Moreover, high levels of testosterone establish the special relation between the two brain hemispheres of the embryo (Galaburda et al., 1987; Geschwind & Galaburda, 1987; Collaer & Hines, 1995). This means an extremely high coordination and distribution of the brain cortical resources within and between the hemispheres (Alexander et al., 1996). These processes most likely result from an unusually strong developed corpus callosum (Habib et al., 1991). These findings together are supposed to be the causes for intellectual giftedness. (Benbow, 1986; O'Boyle et al., 1995; Alexander et al., 1996; Fingelkurts & Fingelkurts, 2000; 2002).

4. EVIDENCE FROM MORPHOLOGY: BRAIN SIZE/HEAD SIZE

It has been long known that testosterone influences brain size (see above) and the size of the skull (Verdonck et al., 1998). If so, than there should be some differences between males and females. Data from longitudinal study on head size of about 16800 newborns recorded over 112 years (1874–1985) clearly indicated that the boys had bigger head size ($p<0.01$) when compared with the girls (see Fig. 11 in Halberg et al., 2000). However the difference in body size was not found. Resent studies on the brain size in large sample of subjects also indicated that brain volume is bigger in males when compared with females (for the collection of different studies see Posthuma, 2002).

5. EVIDENCE FROM ANATOMY: CORPUS CALLOSUM STUDIES

The corpus callosum (CC) is a white matter structure that connects right and left brain hemispheres through fibers of different sizes (Highley et al., 1999). In most cases a larger CC implies a larger number of callosum fibers. Also the maximal fiber diameters tended to be higher in larger brains (Olivares et al., 2001). If androgens influences the development of various brain structures than there might be some differences between males and females. Differences due to sex have been reported for posterior portions of CC – isthmus size (Steinmetz et al., 1992; Clarke & Zaidel, 1994) and shape (De Lacoste-Utamsing & Holloway, 1982), the angle of the CC (Oka et al., 1999), and for anterior regions of CC and especially the genu (Witelson, 1989) showing a trend for a male advantage. Also it was shown that there is a pathway-specific decrease in interhemispheric connectivity with increasing lateralization (Aboitiz et al., 1992). Hence, abnormal growth of the right hemisphere as a result of increased levels of testosterone results in a more symmetric brain (Geschwind & Behan, 1982) and possibly is the reason for an unusually strong developed CC (Habib et al., 1991) in such subjects. In line with this supposition is recent research where it was shown that CC is larger in males than in females and is responsive to steroid hormone manipulations during development (Bimonte et al., 2000).

It is interesting that sex differences of CC also interacted with handedness (Clarke & Zaidel, 1994). Area of the midsagittal section of the CC (particularly in the isthmus) was found to be greater in non-consistent-right-handed men than in consistent-right-handed men (Witelson, 1989; Witelson & Golsmith, 1991). This finding supports a relationship between CC anatomy and functional asymmetry. The lack of such a relationship among women suggests that anatomical variation of CC in relation to lateralization is influenced by androgens (Witelson & Nowakowsli, 1991). The CC morphology, which varied with hand preference, may be related to individual differences in the pattern of hemispheric functional specialization, which in its turn depends on the prenatal levels of testosterone.

6. EVIDENCE FROM BEHAVIORAL GENETICS:
BIGGER BRAINS ARE SMARTER

Positive correlations between head size and psychometric intelligence have been observed (Jensen, 1994). Since head size includes both brain volume and thickness of the skull, the accurate measure of the brain size and its correlation with intelligence is of special interest. The resent study published in Nature Neuroscience (Thompson et al., 2001) reported high heritability of grey matter volume in several cortical regions. It is worth to note that the highest heritability (ranging from 95-100%) was shown for frontal regions. It was also shown that grey matter substantially correlated with general intelligence or 'g' (Thompson et al.,

2001). However this and other studies of brain volume and intelligence did not have enough statistical power to decompose the observed correlation into genetic and environmental components. The freshest research by Posthuma and colleagues (2002), also published in Nature Neuroscience overcame these problems. Using a dataset of 135 individuals the correlation between brain volume and *g* was decomposed into genetic and environmental components. It was shown that the correlation between both grey and white matter volume and *g* is completely due to genetic factors (Posthuma et al, 2002). Thus, bigger brains are smarter. Here it is worth to note, that although intelligence shows very high heritability, it is still very complex trait, which is influenced by a number of quantitative trait loci – QTL (Plomin & Crabbe, 2000). Majority of such QTLs are very sensitive to different factors during early prenatal development[3], where the increased levels of testosterone may be one of these factors.

7. EVIDENCE FROM COGNITIVE RESEARCH: TESTOSTERONE AND FUNCTIONAL BRAIN SPECIALIZATION

Recent research has shown that testosterone (and estrogen) continue to play critical roles in cognitive abilities even throughout the human life span (Halpern & Tan, 2001). For example, the spatial skills of normal males fluctuate in accordance with daily variations (Moffat & Hampson, 1996) and seasonal variations (Kimura & Hampson, 1994) in testosterone levels. It has been also shown the cognitive consequences of testosterone replacement therapies: testosterone treatment in men with naturally low levels improved both their spatial and verbal performance (Cherrier, 1999). Additional support for the role of testosterone levels in cognitive functioning comes from unique studies with female-to-male transsexuals, who were given high doses of testosterone in preparation for sex-change therapy (Van Goozen et al., 1995).

These findings (when the hormonal levels have been controlled experimentally) support the idea that testosterone may influence brain functional specialization and cognitive functioning, and thus participate in development of a "gifted brain".

8. EVIDENCE FROM BEHAVIORAL STUDIES: GIFTEDNESS AND RIGHT HEMISPHERE DOMINANCE

It has been suggested that the left hemisphere in humans has a very strong potential to manifest its dominant abilities (Annett, 1997). At the same time, in order to give equal opportunity in the dominant competition, – there must be special conditions allowing the forming of the morpho-functional peculiarities of the right hemisphere (Bogdanov, 1997). The increased levels of prenatal testosterone may play the role of such conditions (Fingelkurts & Fingelkurts, 2000).

---

[3] One must note that heritability for general intelligence increases from infancy (20%) to late adulthood (86%) (see Fig. 12.1 in Posthuma, 2002, p. 180), what leaves a room for influences of non-genetic (biological) factors during early (prenatal) brain development.

Taking into consideration all that is mentioned above, it is possible to conclude that the brain of a gifted person is organized differently than the brain of people with average abilities (Alexander et al., 1996; Halpern et al., 1998). This hypothesis is confirmed by the longitudinal investigation of O'Boyle' group (O'Boyle et al., 1995). Using various experimental methods this group has shown that increased involvement of the right brain hemisphere (and a special level of coordination of information resources between the right and the left hemispheres) in the process of insurance of higher psychic functions is directly related with intellectual giftedness and may serve as a physiological basis of giftedness (Alexander et al., 1996). In contrast, in subjects with learning disorders, the left-brain hemisphere is involved in basic information processing more than in normal subjects (Obrzut et al., 1980).

The authors have used the operational notion of giftedness. All intellectually gifted subjects had maximally high scores of common test SAT (Scholastic Aptitude Test). Extremely high scores were observed in SAT-M (Mathematical part). Scores in SAT-V (Verbal part) were slightly lower. Nevertheless, these SAT-V scores significantly exceed the analogous scores of subjects with average abilities, and females too (O'Boyle et al., 1995). "This highly selected talented [subjects] performs as well as college-bound high school seniors on tests used for college admission, despite the fact that they have not taken the advanced course work that is provided in high school" (Halpern et al., 1998, p. 91). This means that their high scores do not indicate that they are exceptionally good at the recall of factual knowledge, "[…] instead, they are 'creating' or 'discovering' new knowledge on their own" (Halpern et al., 1998, p. 91).

These findings are consistent with the concept of "general intelligence" or g, according to which people performing better on one task will tend also to perform better on another (Deary, 2001a).

For reasoning of the current paper it is important that g may reflect the function of some particular information processing system, contributing in part to the organization of many different activities and hence producing some positive correlation between them (Duncan et. al., 1996; Deary, 2001b). Moreover, it was postulated that in large part g reflects the action control functions of the brain's frontal lobes (Duncan et. al., 1996; Thompson et al., 2001). In our investigations it has been shown that behavioral functions (attention, memory encoding and retrieval) reflected in g arise from joint or cooperative activity in a variety of distinct frontal systems, i.e., through a so-called "operational synchrony" of different neuronal systems (Fingelkurts, 1998; Fingelkurts et. al., 1998; 2000; see also the review Fingelkurts & Fingelkurts, 2001).

9. Evidence from Electrophysiological Studies: Giftedness and Right Frontal Cortex Dominance

Is there a clearer physiological marker of right hemisphere dominance in gifted subjects? The electroencephalogram (EEG) is one of the instruments that reveal brain activity on the neuronal level (O'Boyle et al., 1991). Yet, regarding the study of gifted subjects, researchers, using EEG during several neurophysiological methods have shown that stronger involvement of the right frontal cortical area in ongoing activity in comparison with the left was observed in all experiments with gifted subjects (O'Boyle et al., 1995). Moreover, even in the frame of this gifted subjects' group, the connection between involvement of the right hemisphere and SAT scores was detected: the more pronounced the involvement of the right hemisphere in the current informational processing in the talented subject, the higher the intellectual abilities (as detected by SAT [SAT-mathematics + SAT-verbal]) were.

Here we need to say a few words about right frontal activity in general so that, in the discussion that follows, we can avoid the confusions that may have resulted. We are aware that increased involvement of the right frontal cortex might occur for a number of reasons, only some of which are related to giftedness. However, in this paper it is argued that right frontal cortical involvement in *any* brain activity (even in those cases when left frontal cortical involvement should be observed) and right brain hemisphere dominance in general is the biological predisposition to intellectual precocity (Fingelkurts & Fingelkurts, 2002).

One may suppose that detected dominance of the right hemisphere in experiments described above reflects the increase of emotional tension. It is well known that the right hemisphere is more "emotional" than the left. But in that case, the increased level of 'false alarms' and 'signal omits' must be detected. This is traditionally associated with the leading role of the right hemisphere in the genesis of errors during perceptive activity under the influence of emotional tension (Windmann & Kruger, 1998). However, this interpretation can be rejected on the basis of results obtained in the study (O'Boyle et al., 1995).

Thus, it has been shown that there is an increased involvement of the right hemisphere (and particularly its frontal cortical area) in the ongoing activity of subjects with high intelligence (Fox et al., 1988; O'Boyle et al., 1995; Haier & Benbow, 1995). EEG analysis also reveals increased involvement of the right frontal cortical areas (O'Boyle et al., 1995) during ongoing brain activity in the number of experimental tasks. Therefore, frontal asymmetry with the dominant right cortical area is supposed to be the physiological marker of a "gifted brain" (Fox et al., 1988; O'Boyle et al., 1991; Bell & Fox, 1992; O'Boyle et al., 1995; Fingelkurts & Fingelkurts, 2000; 2002).

10. Evidence from Functional Specialization of Frontal Cortex

The functional meaning of the involvement of the right frontal cortical area in the ongoing activity of gifted individuals is not fully understood, although it is in agreement with neurophysiological data about the connection of the frontal areas with the higher mental functions and intelligence (Pribram & Luria, 1973; Chen & Buckley, 1988; Ivanizkiy, 1997; Diamond, 1991; Crick & Koch, 1995; Goldman-Rakic, 1996; Duncan et al., 2000).

However, one may argue that despite impairments in "planning", "problem-solving", etc., frontal patients have supposedly intact intelligence. Duncan et al., (1996) have shown in their works that this conventional view is misleading. The simple tasks they have introduced suggest a close link between Spearman's *g* and frontal lobe functions. In patients with severe frontal difficulties, the tendency to neglect a task requirement (even though it has been understand and remembered) is extreme and relates closely to *g* (Duncan et al., 1996).

Along these lines the recent study at the single-cell level found the existence of large, spindle-shaped neurons in the anterior brain cortex (Nemchinsky et al., 1999). These neurons exist only in primates: the density is highest in humans, next – highest in chimpanzees, lower in other apes. It is supposed that these neurons possibly participate in the integration of sensory and cognitive information and are responsible for higher mental activity.

Moreover, according to previous studies, the right frontal area is primarily responsible for nonverbal image thinking, formation of associations using nonlinear principle, unconsciousness functions, and for higher emotions (Nakamura et al., 1999; Sidorova, 2000). These are the exact functions necessary for the realization of the creative process and of scientific insight. It is generally accepted that the new ideas and artistic images are not the result of someone observations and reflection, – they come to the mental sight at once in complete internal integrity. The reports of highly creative people about their thought processes suggest that a great part of their cognitive work goes on "underneath", beyond the conscious control of the person (Ghiselin, 1952; Dorfman et al., 1996; Monsay, 1997). For example Einstein described his thinking in the way that words for him do not play any role, but there is some kind of associative play of more or less clear images (Hadamard, 1949). Many scientific discoveries have come to their creators' as momentary intuitive knowledge (e.g. the discovery of periodic system of elements by D.I. Mendeleev or the structure of benzol ring – by F.A. Kekulé), which were only systematically proven after the fact. Perhaps the unconscious nature of these early stages in the creative process serves to protect the birth of a hypothesis and new ideas from the conservatism of consciousness. A similar phenomenon can be observed, for example, in the reports of split-brain patients when information presented to the right hemisphere (Koriat & Levy-Sadot, 1999; Koriat, 2000).

11. PREDICTION 1: TESTOSTERONE LEVELS SHOULD INFLUENCE THE EXPRESSION OF GENES FOR COGNITIVE ABILITY

One prediction of suggested in the present review hypothesis is that increased levels of testosterone during prenatal development should influence the expression of candidate genes for intelligence. Since increased levels of testosterone in utero may lead to a more rapid growth of neurons in the developing human fetal brain (see above), it should influence substances which are responsible for that. Such substances (endophenotypes of cognitive abilities[4], for discussion see De Geus & Boomsma, 2002) are nerve growth factor, NMDA and some others, which influence neuronal plasticity directly. The production of these substances is dependent on expression of particular genes (nerve growth factor beta polypeptide marker – NGFB, NMDA receptor genes and others), which are associated with intelligence. Thus, the evidence for IQ and NGFB association was provided in the IQ-QTL (Quantitative Trait loci) Project (Petrill et al., 1996). Morley and Montgomery (2001) in their extensive review showed that very promising candidate gene associated with cognitive ability is NMDA receptor genes. It was also shown (Tang et al., 1999) that overexpression of NMDA receptor gene in the forebrain results in a superior ability in learning and memory traits which are generally considered a central part of intelligence[5] (Posthuma, 2002).

---

[4] Biological, neurophysiological, electrophysiological and behavioral indices of the pathways that connect genes and cognitive ability are called *endophenotypes* of cognitive ability.

[5] Working memory had the highest phenotypic and highest genetic correlation with brain volumes (Posthuma et al., 2002), which are correlated with IQ. Also, working memory has often localized in the frontal lobes. These findings may not be surprising since working memory is considered a major component of general intelligence (Posthuma, 2002).

12. Prediction 2: Patients with Left Frontal Cortex Damage Should Exhibit Talents

The other prediction of suggested in the present paper hypothesis is that patients with left frontal cortex damage should exhibit right frontal dominance and hence be talented to some extent. It was shown that patients with the left-sided lobe variant of frontotemporal dementia (FTD) showed the emergence of visual and musical talents (Miller et al., 2000). Evidently, these studies are consistent with the idea that for facilitation of new skills and talents the dominance of right frontal area is very important (Fingelkurts & Fingelkurts, 2000; 2002).

13. Prediction 3: Gifted Individuals Should Have Right Hemisphere Dominance

Another prediction of the current hypothesis is that exceptional intellectuals should have a more complicated right brain hemisphere (particularly frontal cortex). Albert Einstein is one of the intellectual giants of recorded history. An intriguing case study has been conducted by Anderson, who studied Albert Einstein's brain (Anderson & Harvey, 1996). In contrast to a control group of autopsied men, the right frontal cortex of Einstein's brain possesses a significantly greater neuronal density. Data about the greater size of specific gyral regions in the right frontal cortex of Einstein's brain were also found in another resent research (Witelson et al., 1999, see Table on p. 2152). Note that in the control group there is slight tendency to left frontal dominance. Thus, it has been suggested that dendritic arborization of frontal areas is correlated with g and giftedness (Anderson, 1993).

Moreover, it was shown that reversed hemisphere dominance (right) is related with musical talent and left-handedness (Hassler & Gupta, 1993). In line with these findings is evidence that Einstein was left-handed (at least non-consistent-right-handed) (Winokur, 1984). Also Einstein's corpus callosum area tended to be larger than its predicted value when hand preference and age were taken into consideration (Witelson et al., 1999, see Table on p. 2152). Thus these findings are in an agreement with the idea that right frontal cortex plays a considerable role in gifted brain.

14. Prediction 4: Among Gifted Individuals There Should Be an Increased Number of Left-Handers

Since handedness is the most obvious index of cerebral dominance, one should expect an increased number of left-handed or at least non-consistent-right-handed (right hemisphere dominance) individuals among gifted individuals. The convergence evidence from multiple paradigms shows that males are more commonly found among extremely gifted young people (Benbow, 1988; Benbow & Lyubinski, 1993; O'Boyle et al., 1995). Also the proportion of left-handers in this extremely precocious group is about double what have been expected from the proportion of left-handers in the population (Halpern et al., 1998). These authors possibly for the first time studied the relationship between handedness and intelligence in a highly selected group of adults. They showed that left-handedness (right hemisphere dominance) "[…] is at a higher rate among the most intellectually gifted than among adults of average intelligence […]" (Halpern et al., 1998, p. 96). Resent data also supports these findings (for the review see Halpern, 2000).

15. PREDICTION 5: THERE MUST BE SEX DIFFERENCES IN COGNITIVE ABILITIES

Although most psychologists agree that there are no meaningful sex differences in general intelligence (Halpern, 2000), it should be mentioned that such differences were found for extremely gifted subjects. In 1980 Benbow and Stanley made a report (based on observation of 9,927 12- and 14-year-olds) stating that males are more successful in mathematics than females (Benbow & Stanley, 1980). This finding may be explained in a biological and/or socio-psychological way. The socio-psychological explanation has been more popular, but detailed investigations have not supported this point of view (Benbow, 1988). Simultaneously, scientists have come to the conclusion that males are more intellectually gifted than females in some parameters of intelligence (McGlone, 1980; Benbow, 1986; Hellige, 1993; O'Boyle et al., 1995) including verbal reasoning (Halpern et al., 1998). During the analysis of recent findings (over a million gifted adolescents), a biological explanation (Benbow, 1986; Benbow, 1988; Jensen, 1998) of the ontogenesis of the cognitive abilities origin was formed (Thatcher et al., 1987; Reed et al., 1991). Hemispheric volume is considered as an important factor. Thus, it has been shown that hemispheric volumes are higher in men than in women (Gur et al., 1999). It has been assumed that greater hemispheric volumes in the male brain are due to the early effects of testosterone. And if the prenatal levels of testosterone are increased then it results in the right hemisphere dominance (Geschwind & Galaburda, 1987). What are the special conditions of increased levels of testosterone?

16. PREDICTION 6: MONOZYGOTIC MALE-TWINS SHOULD HAVE INCREASED LEVELS OF TESTOSTERONE

It is important to consider the conditions of increased levels of testosterone during the crucial period (7-12 weeks of pregnancy) of the prenatal development (Geshwind & Behan, 1982). There are only a few explanations for increased levels of testosterone. The first explanation may be the innate hyperplasia of the cortex of the adrenals in the pregnant female. This situation leads to increased levels of prenatal testosterone in the fetus (Collaer & Hines, 1995; Berkow, 1997). Another explanation may be the occurrence of a male-twins pregnancy. It has been shown that various levels of hormones in early stages of embryonic prenatal development leads not only to gender formation (for discussion see Lippa, 2002), but also influence the development of the future cognitive and mental functions (Hines, 1982; Halpern & Tan, 2001). The influence of increased doses of androgens during the early stages of embryogenesis is well documented in animal experiments (Reinisch, 1974). The advantage of nonhuman research is that it allows to employ experimental methods that permit strong causal inferences (Halpern & Tan, 2001). These experiments demonstrated that when a female and male embryo are located in close proximity, increased levels of testosterone are detected in the blood and amniotic fluid of the female embryo (Vom Saal & Bronson, 1980). After birth, this female has a more aggressive character (Vom Saal et al., 1981), her sexual behavior would be less orientated on the males (Vom Saal & Bronson, 1980) and would be organized on the males type (Vom Saal et al., 1981). In cattle fraternal twins prenatal blood exchange between twins leads to sterility in the females – freemartin effect (for details see Segal, 2000).

Similarly, the male embryo, located near the female embryo, has increased estradiol levels in the blood and amniotic fluid. After birth this may results in a female sexual behavior (Vom Saal et al., 1983).

These findings have been clarified in humans. Thus, the evidence for the role of hormones has been shown by studying girls who were exposed to high levels of testosterone because their pregnant mother had congenital adrenal hyperplasia (Collaer & Hines, 1995). These girls had better spatial skills and are more likely to show aggressive behavior (very similar to boys) when compared with other girls. Investigations of different-sex dizygotic twins in humans have also shown that the female embryo in such pairs has the increased concentration of testosterone and in the future this girl displays masculine behavior. Similarly, the male embryo – consequently has the increased dose of estradiol that in the future leads to feminization of a boy (Vom Saal et al., 1983). Thus, according to data, if the twins are two male fetuses, then after starting to produce their own androgens in the 7th week of pregnancy they inevitably will be influenced by the increased levels of testosterone (Geschwind & Behan, 1982; Geschwind & Galaburda, 1987) not only in the amniotic fluid, but will take testosterone inside their bodies by means of feta-fetal (or transplacental) blood transfusion (Kaelber & Pough, 1969). Twin to twin transfusion is a significant clinical phenomenon (Segal, 2000). 70% of monozygotic (MZ) twins and 8% of dizygotic (DZ) twins have had in uterovascular connections (Hall, 1996). In the chronic form of twin-to-twin transfusion syndrome, one of the twins becomes anemic, hypovolemic and growth retarded and the other becomes plethoric, hypervolemic and often has congestive failure (Lopriore et al., 1995; Machin et al., 1996, for the review see Segal, 2000). Although the biological origins of two types of twins (MZ and DZ) may have a lot in common (Segal, 2000) and therefore DZ male-twins would also have higher levels of fetal testosterone, we prefer to limit the argument to MZ male-twins, since they have much more often the same placenta, chorion and amnion (Segal, 2000).

16.1. Evidence from Endocrinology of MZ Twins

The exact mechanism of the accumulation of increased levels of testosterone in embryonic target tissues has not been thoroughly studied. It is suggested that a critical factor is that during this period, embryonic production of testosterone is proportional with that of adult males (Wilson, 1999). Yet the volume of a fetus is significantly less than that of adult males. Thus, the surplus of androgens from each twin fetus enters the amniotic liquid and/or is transmitted through the placenta and the mother organism directly to the organism of the co-twin. Testosterone is a lipophilic hormone, and therefore is practically nonexistent in a free state in blood plasma. It is connected with special transport proteins and transported to target tissues. The brain is one of those organs which actively "need" androgens for its development. Transport proteins using the surplus of testosterone provide the locally increased concentration of testosterone in the embryonic male brain. Here in the male brain the enzyme aromatase converts testosterone to estrogens (Whitacre et al., 1999). The effect of such conditions on prenatal development may result in the right hemisphere dominance in male-twins, which gives them the potential for giftedness (Fingelkurts & Fingelkurts, 2000).

16.2. Evidence from Twins Research

The main group of subjects in our study consisted of MZ male-twins. For determination of twins type we used the Physical resemblance questionnaire (Nichols & Bilbro, 1966). In the introduction section it was mentioned that during several experimental conditions (waiting, encoding, retrieval and keeping information in mind) including rest conditions with eyes open and closed, it was demonstrated the increased involvement of the right frontal cortex in comparison with the left frontal cortex that remained uninvolved in the ongoing informative-analytical activity of the brain (Kaplan et al., 1998; Fingelkurts Al., 1998; Fingelkurts An., 1998; Fingelkurts et al., 2000).

Therefore it is possible to combine the findings described above and discuss them together. In that case, the fact of strong bilateral asymmetry (obtained in our work during testing of various brain functional states) of the frontal cortical areas with dominance of the right hemisphere becomes understandable. It is probable that this dominance is resulted from the joint prenatal life of the male-twins. Moreover, the investigations described above, allow us to hypothesize the biological potential for high intelligence in all MZ male-twins. Indeed, only gifted subjects showed the dominance of the right frontal area during the various experimental conditions (dichotic listening of the words and phonemes, finger typing with the right and left hand with simultaneous text reading, and perception of the chimeric-faces with EEG recording) (O'Boyle et al., 1991).

Our study included prolonged observation of twins' lives. Data showed that twin sets, which participated in our study, graduating from Moscow State University, earned the highest academic credits (4.9-5 credits based on 5-grade Russian system) and successfully completed their Ph.D. degrees. Also, twin pairs examined in our study had additional talents besides academic, e.g., dancing, painting and music. It should be mentioned here that male-twins in our study were a self-selected sample (they all entered to Moscow State University), so they are not representative of male-twins in general.

Our study included a very small sample size, only six pairs of MZ twins participated. This necessitated the review of other large-scale twins investigations that have revealed the dominance of the right frontal cortical area. Our analysis of an investigation of 2009 pairs of MZ twins of each sex (with retesting after 1.5 year) done by Van Baal et. al., (1996) revealed that in females the absolute and relative power of beta and alpha EEG rhythms of the left frontal area (in comparison with the right) are under strong genetic control; in the males, genetic control was detected for the right frontal area. This data is in line with our study. In another study, sex differences were detected in genetic influence on the coherency (COH) index of the frontal areas with other cortical zones: in females the COH focus was at the left frontal area, in the males – at the right (Van Baal et al., 1997). Thus, this analysis permits us to conclude that male and female pairs of MZ twins have different genetic determinants for the involvement of the right and left frontal areas in the ongoing brain activity. This is also in agreement with the reasoning of the present review.

17. PREDICTION 7: AMONG MZ TWINS THERE SHOULD BE AN INCREASED NUMBER OF LEFT-HANDERS

It is obvious that left-handedness reflects the dominance of the right hemisphere (for the review see Lippa, 2002). So, one of predictions of our hypothesis is that left-handedness should be more common in twins than in singletons (more pronounced in MZ twins than in DZ), and also more common in men than in women (Benbow et al., 2000). Although separate reports are controversial, analysis of available data together[6] shows that the percentage of left-handers is higher among the twin population than among single-born individuals (Dobrohotova & Bragina, 1994; Derom et al., 1996; Segal, 2000). Also systematic meta-analytic works of Annett support these findings (Annett, 1978; 1998). In one of her combined research, 45178 individuals participated (Davis & Annett, 1994). It was shown in this study that for each age group the proportion of left-handers was greater in males than females, and substantially greater in twins than in singletons. Recent meta-analysis of literature on twins data and their parents also showed prevalence of left-hand-claspers and left-arm-folders in twins (Reiss, 1999).

Annett suggests the right shift (RS) theory according to which normal human cerebral specialization (left hemisphere dominance and right-handedness) is caused by a gene with the instruction to impair the right hemisphere (Annett, 1978; Annett, 1997). On the basis of meta-analysis she noticed that expression of the rs+ gene is more effective in females than in males and less effective in twins than in single born children (Annett & Alexander, 1996). Moreover, it was shown that the suppression of the rs+ gene leads to high intelligence (Annett, 1999). This suggests that the expression of the rs+ gene might depend on factor(s) influencing cerebral maturation in early fetal life (Annett, 1996). Evidently, these studies are consistent with the idea of the present review that testosterone may be such a factor which suppress the rs+ gene expression.

18. PREDICTION 8: DERMATOGLYPHIC PATTERNS IN MZ TWINS SHOULD BE MORE COMPLICATED ON THE LEFT HAND

Analysis of the dermatoglyphic patterns of MZ twins are especially interesting since the morphology of the brain and ridge skin developed from the same embryonic tissue and for some time occur during the same prenatal developmental periods (Segal, 2000). Our analysis of dermatoglyphic data, which were collected by M.V. Volozcky (Volozcky, 1936) in 128 pairs of MZ and 106 pairs of DZ twins, shows that more complicated skin patterns in MZ

---

[6] Very large samples are needed to yield an adequately large sample size in the upper tails of distribution. Also large samples needed because of the low statistical power associated with the test of any hypothesis about handedness (Halpern et al., 1998). Note also, that extremely low rate of left-handedness (associated with writing) has been reported in some studies, but showed a high degree of left-handedness for activities against which there were no social sanctions (hammer and toothbrush use for example) (Teng et al., 1976, cited on Halpern et al, 1998).

twins are situated often on the left hand (which corresponds to the right hemisphere) in comparison with the single-born population. Determination of the sophisticated embryonic structure of the ectoderm results in the complicated structure of its derivates, particularly – the morphology of the brain and ridge skin (Gladkova, 1962; Bogdanov & Solonichenko, 1995). Consequently, on the level of the ridge skin it leads to complications of the dermatoglyphic patterns (in this study – the left hand). And on the level of the central nervous system it may be reflected in the complication of its macro- and microstructure (in this study – the right hemisphere) (Bogdanov, 1997). The connection between the central nervous system and dermatoglyphic patterns was shown even with EEG applications (Bogdanov et al., 1994). Also, there is literature data about the interrelation of skin patterns and nerve endings at the end of the fingers (Bonnevie, 1929). Thus, these findings support the idea of the present review that MZ male-twins may have dominant right hemisphere.

19. SUMMARIZING EVIDENCES AND PREDICTIONS

Taking together convergence lines of evidences and testified predictions that: 1) an increased dosage of testosterone during the crucial period of prenatal development results in the right brain hemisphere dominance (Geschwind & Behan, 1982), 2) the dominant right hemisphere and particularly frontal cortical area is supposed to be the physiological marker of a "gifted brain", 3) there is a close link between Spearman's g and frontal lobe functions which are necessary for the realization of the creative process and of scientific insight, 4) patients with the left-sided variant of frontotemporal dementia (FTD) showed the emergence of visual and musical talents (Miller et al., 2000), 5) the right frontal cortex of Einstein's brain possesses a significantly greater neuronal density if compared with a control group of autopsied men, 6) the population of gifted individuals exhibits the right hemisphere dominance, 7) there is a large number of left-handers among subjects with high intelligence and among the twin population, 8) even in adults the average level of testosterone is significantly higher in blood plasma if they are left-handed, ambidextrous and right-handed with the family left-handedness (when compared with right-handers with the family right-handedness) (Tan, 1991), 9) left-handed individuals have a more strongly developed corpus callosum (Habib et al., 1991; Moffat et al., 1997), which probably compensates for the unusual dominance of the right hemisphere, 10) monozygotic male-twins have increased levels of testosterone, and the right frontal dominance in MZ male-twins may be a result of the joint prenatal life of the male-twins, 11) more complicated skin patterns in MZ twins are situated often on the left hand (what corresponds to the right hemisphere) when compared with the single-born population, we may propose that the subjects' samples in all these cases overlap for the following common reason – *increased levels of testosterone in the crucial period of the prenatal development.*

Thus, it is possible to suppose the biological potential for intellectual giftedness in all MZ male-twins. Also we may stipulate that at least some of famous gifted males where conceived as twins. In that case prenatal twins' conditions provided the appropriate biological basis for the development of giftedness. It should be mentioned that the peculiarities of prenatal development of the MZ twins equally fair the males and females. But for reasoning of present review, because of described peculiarities of the males' organism (testosterone), only MZ male-twins are of the interest.

But an obvious question arises about the extremely small number (except sport, for details see Segal, 2000) of "bright" and gifted twin pairs (even males) in the human history.

20. WHY TALENTED TWINS APPEARED VERY RARELY IN HUMAN HISTORY?

At first sight, this fact seems to undermine the theoretical underpinning of the present review. However, there are two factors at least, which lead to the extremely small number of talented twins in the human history. First, only one from the embryonic MZ twins' pair is usually born or one of the twins died very early in the life (recall Elvis Presley's early loss of his twin brother Jesse, see Segal, 2000), second, the existence of unfavorable conditions of the joint postnatal twins' development, which preclude further development of potential brain giftedness.

20.1. Unfavorable Prenatal Conditions of MZ Twins

To analyze this, the authors addressed the twins' investigation of Charles Boklage (East Carolina University School). Of 325 examined twins pregnancies, only 19 resulted in the birth of twins. In 125 cases, only one from the twin-pair was born. In 181 cases both fetuses were lost during pregnancy (Boklage C.E., quotes on Segal, 2000). This means that in only 6% of pregnancies when twins were fertilized two babies are born. Thus, many single-born babies actually start their lives as part of a twin-set! What are the difficulties of the twins' pregnancy?

Examinations of twins placentas, have led researches to conclude that if a zygote is divided during the first four days after fertilization, then the twins will have different placentas, chorions and amnions (for the review see Segal, 2000). Such twins have the best odds of surviving the pregnancy, and in the future those co-twins will have more differences than similarities. Dichorionic MZ twins had the lowest incidence of preterm birth, perinatal mortality, and birth weight discordance (Machin et al., 1995). If a zygote's division occurs between the fifth and eight days after fertilization, then the twins will have one placenta and chorion, but two amnions. In this case, one of the twins tends to receive more nutrition and develops healthier, as a result of the umbilical cord wrapping around the neck of the other co-twin. Twin-to-twin transfusion syndrome is very often usual in this case, and it leads to a high risk of perinatal morbility and mortality (Feidstein et al., 2000). Even if both twins are born successfully, the second twin frequently dies during the first few years of life (Hall & Lopez-Rangel, 1996; Segal, 2000).

A zygote's splitting between 8 and 12 days after fertilization results in the twins having common placenta, chorion and amnion. This results in an inevitable competition for space and nutrition, and the frequent pathology of the umbilical cord, often leading to the death of at least one of the co-twins (Machin et al., 1996). If such a pregnancy and birth are successful, then such twins will be very friendly and similar to each other (Sokol et al., 1995). However, the left-handed twin, who normally is born first, is usually the healthier of the two (Christian, 1979; Bishop, 1990).

Finally, the splitting of a zygote after the 12th day of fertilization leads to the occurrence of so-called "conjoined" twins. In that case, their bodies are already shared, but they frequently have distinctly different temperaments and habits (Segal, 2000). Interestingly, there is an excess of females among conjoined twins (James, 1995).

Another possible birth scenario is that one twin absorbs the body of the other twin – "vanishing syndrome" (Hall, 1996; Segal, 2000). Also there is the situation, when one twin fetus is reabsorbed by the mother organism. These situations also result in a singleton pregnancy (Segal, 2000).

As was described above, among gifted subjects the proportion with dominant left hand is higher than among subjects with averaged abilities (Geschwind & Behan, 1982; Benbow, 1986; O'Boyle & Benbow, 1990). But the percentage of left-handers is higher among the twin population than among single-born individuals (Dobrohotova & Bragina, 1994; Derom et al., 1996; Neimark, 1997). This has caused some researchers to postulate that some of single-born people with a dominant left hand (including "hidden" left-handed and non-right-handed) are survivors from a twin-set (Neimark, 1997). Perhaps such people exist among famous gifted males, but this hold needs experimental checking.

20.2. Unfavorable Socio-Psychological Postnatal Conditions of MZ Twins

Despite data, which support the biological basis (not only genetic) of high intelligence (Meehl, 1992; O'Boyle et al., 1995) it is impossible to derogate the "environmental" (socio-psychological) factors that provide necessary conditions for the optimal realization of the biological basis (Segal, 2000; Fingelkurts & Fingelkurts, 2002). Such psycho-social factors in the majority of cases are very unfavorable for twins.

Various factors of the psychological and mental development of MZ twins may preclude the prenatal development of biological basis for the high intelligence, and as a result, such intelligence can't be fully realized (Fingelkurts & Fingelkurts, 2000). Thus, it has been shown that in general young twins have IQ scores on average lower than genetically unrelated singletons on 4-7 points (Segal, 2000). However, no evidence of differences between adult twins and their non-twin singletons on cognitive performance was found (Posthuma et al., 2000).

One main factor is that as children the twins are constantly together. This leads to the emergence of two opposite streams of development (Segal, 2000). Their constant communication, their shared environment, and the attitudes that others have towards the twins, leads to the development of a unique form of self-perception in twins, i.e. "twins reaction" (Zazzo, 1960).

As a result, twins have many difficulties distinguishing the concept of "I" from the concept of "We". This means that twins first distinguish themselves from the external world as a pair and only later as individuals (for review see Talizina et al., 1991). In extreme cases, co-twins perceive the reflection of his/her brother/sister in the mirror as his/her own; they refer to themselves by one name, ascribe their own personalities and psychological characteristics to one another, and even confuse the life events of each other (Neimark, 1997). All this makes the psychological and cognitive development of the twins difficult and complicated.

Another aspect of "twins reaction" is the resulting divergence of similarity between co-twins by means of different social roles. Scientists have determined two manifestations of this phenomenon: "competition with each other" and "competition against each other" (Gruszewska, 1998). Moreover, one may determine different social roles, e.g., "minister of foreign affairs", who organizes communication and presentation of the pair with the external world, and "minister of internal life" – or the "conscience" of the pair (Von Bracken, 1934 and Stoltenber, 1929, cited on Segal, 2000). Usually these roles change from time to time as twins grow up (Williams & Medalie, 1994).

Language and speech are essential for cognitive changes during the ontogenesis. The majority of researchers conclude that the development of language and speech in the twins is delayed (see review by Talizina et al., 1991; Akerman, 1995; Segal, 2000). Twins usually start to speak later than single-born kids, and the lexical number of words is less than in single-born children (McEvoy & Dodd, 1992). These delays are determined in socialized speech (Talizina et al., 1991). Another significant delay is in the development of communicative speech (McEvoy & Dodd, 1992). There are several reasons for this. Firstly, the unfavorable prenatal conditions (see above) of twins seem to have a lasting effect on their later physical and mental development (Akerman & Fischbein, 1991). The second factor is unfavorable postnatal development of twins (Kantonistova, 1980; Akerman, 1995). Usually, a single-born child is constantly in the company of adults and he (or she) develops the language and speech skills in order to communicate with parents and other children (Talizina et al., 1991). However, twins don't feel this need because each has a constant partner of the same age and at the same stage of physical and mental development, and usually they find ways to communicate without using speech or normal language. (Bishop & Bishop, 1998; Segal, 2000).

In cases when only one of the twin-set is born (or twins were separated from the birth) negative factors of joint twins' development in the postnatal period weren't observed (Pedersen et al., 1988). Thus, it was shown that singleton twins (the loss of one twin at birth) performed better than ordinary twins (for the details see Segal, 2000). Also, a Minnesota study reported that twins reared apart (i.e. rearing as the singletons) have an above average IQ score (Bouchard, 1990, cited on Segal, 2000). These findings give strong support to our reasoning that among gifted males there may exist a high percentage of twins "by conception", because in such cases the biological basis for high intelligence was present, but the negative factors of joint twins' postnatal development were absent. However this point could only be proven through specially organized investigations.

21. NEGATIVE FACTORS ACCOMPANYING HIGH INTELLIGENCE

The owner of high intelligence (the functional marker of which is increased involvement of the right hemisphere in the ongoing brain informational activity, and physiological marker of which is the bilateral asymmetry with the right frontal area dominance) (O'Boyle et al., 1995), has a significant number of accompanying problems, – a so-called "physiological price"[7] (Fingelkurts & Fingelkurts, 2000). It has been demonstrated that increased levels of

---

[7] The physiological price – the volume of the physiological and psychological expenditures, which provide the normal vitality of the organism on the given level.

testosterone in the critical period of human prenatal development, leads not only to the development of the right hemisphere and as a consequence – to intellectual giftedness, also have a negative influence on the thymus gland. This leads to the increased risk of the immune disorders, such as allergic and autoimmune reactions (Geschwind & Behan, 1982; Benbow, 1986). For example, it was shown that there is a significant correlation between giftedness and myopia (Ashton, 1983). This data was confirmed in recent research. Approximately 10.000 gifted students were tested. The results of the study proved the relationships between myopia and giftedness (Lubinski & Humphreys, 1992). Also it was shown the positive correlation between giftedness and allergy. This positive correlation could be seen when a child reported being told by a physician that he or she had an allergy (Lubinski & Humphreys, 1992). One may argue that testosterone normally has an immunoprotective effect, so many autoimmune diseases are more prevalent in women than in men (Whitacre et al., 1999). Here it should be mentioned that sex hormones show a biphasic dose effect (Whitacre, 2001): for testosterone, normal concentrations protect, while high doses facilitate immune responses acting as triggers of autoimmune events. It is interesting that the autoimmune diseases are more prevalence in MZ twins (Jarvinen et al., 1992; Segal, 2000) and associated with non-right-handedness (McManus et al., 1993). Lastly, the comprehensive recent study clarify that left-handers have a higher incidence of autoimmune diseases (Morfit & Weekes, 2001).

Moreover, gifted people also frequently suffer from depression or depressive episodes (Post, 1994). This is in agreement with findings which showed the increased involvement exactly of the right frontal area in ongoing activity and decreased involvement of the left (the diagnostic criteria was EEG) in depressive subjects (Hitt et al., 1995). However, it has been shown that right frontal activation is related to coping strategies in men when depressed, while left frontal activation is related to coping strategies in females (Nolen-Hoeksema, 1987). For instance, highly defensive men are more likely to isolate themselves, whereas highly defensive women are likely to do opposite (Kline et al., 1998). These findings suggest that gifted individuals might prefer solitary activities, which on one hand may represent a defensive coping strategy, and which on the other hand, may also help them to be creative.

Several studies have attempted to prove that extremes in mood are linked with creativity (Jamison, 1989, 1995; Post, 1994). The highly creative people are also known to be difficult in interpersonal relationships, socially harsh, and abrasive (Lubinski, 2000). This supports Eysenck's view that the highly creative are, on average, high on trait psychoticism (Eysenck, 1995).

At the same time, described negative aspects of intellectual giftedness more often occur with left-handed individuals (Dobrohotova & Bragina, 1994). Furthermore, left-handers are more frequently present among schizophrenics and epileptics than among the healthy population (Nasrallah et. al., 1981 and Ginoyan, 1985, quotes on Dobrohotova & Bragina, 1994). Schizophrenia or schizophrenic features and epilepsy are also frequent among gifted people (Post F., 1994). It is interesting that postmortem studies of brain anatomy in schizophrenics, "schizoid" and "shizotypal" people, and individuals with Asperger's syndrome have found reduced cortical volumes of the left hemisphere (Chiron et al., 1995; Bullmore et al., 1995; Weinberger, 1995) and especially in the frontal cortex (McGuire & Frith, 1996; Ross & Pearlson, 1996). The same results were obtained in recent meta-analysis (Wright et al., 2000). Described factors provide further indirect support for the hypothesis that among the gifted males there should be a high percentage of left-handed (Geschwind &

Behan, 1982; Benbow, 1986; O'Boyle et al., 1995), who are possibly the surviving members of an embryonic twin pair (Fingelkurts & Fingelkurts, 2000).

However, it has been shown that children with high intelligence (and left-handers) are physically healthier than their coeval with averaged abilities (Lubinski & Humohreys, 1992). The left-handed individuals also experience very quick reversal of pathological states, and slighter reestablishment of brain functions after trauma and disorders (Dobrohotova & Bragina, 1994). Possibly the described peculiarities may be the consequences of the special brain organization (Bogdanov, 1997) and, in particular, the right hemisphere.

22. Conclusions

Generalizing the data described in the present paper, we conclude that the potential for giftedness is an innate biological feature. Development of a talent is a biosocial issue, and the realization of a talent is a psychobiological issue (Fingelkurts & Fingelkurts, 2002).

The suggested hypothesis regarding the possible link between high intelligence (the physiological marker of which may be the dominance of the right frontal cortical area in comparison with the left) of the MZ male-twins and a high level of testosterone in the prenatal period is speculative. Therefore, we recommend further study of this question. For example, it is possible to suggest following testing of the suggested hypothesis. If compare intelligence of singletons of both sexes with MZ twins, what the hypothesis predict? As we have mentioned above, female MZ twins would be subject to the same negative environmental and social factors that are identified for MZ males. Thus, on average, we should observe some intellectual deficit in female MZ twins compared with female singletons. For males, the MZ twins have a higher level of fetal testosterone which, according to the hypothesis, should boost their intellectual ability. Thus, the negative intellectual difference that should be found for females should be reduced on average for MZ males or even reversed, when comparing with singleton males. Here it is important to stress that during this testing one must control the birth weight of subjects. It was shown that birth weight is a very important factor and is related to cognitive development (Akerman, 1995). If these predictions turn out to be correct, then the suggested hypothesis regarding the possible link between high intelligence of the MZ male-twins and a high level of testosterone in the prenatal period receives considerable support, but if they turn out to be false, then the hypothesis either must be rejected or at least thoroughly modified.

Question about the more complicated organization of the right brain hemisphere in male-twins is significant. Moreover, most of the current knowledge about the functions of the right brain hemisphere has been obtained in pathological conditions (heart attacks, strokes, cancer and so on) (Bragina & Dobrohotova, 1988); at the same time gifted intellectuals (or the male-twins) can be the healthy natural model for studying the morpho-functional peculiarities of the right brain hemisphere. Finally, the study of the intellectually gifted is a unique opportunity for the intensive investigation of the human potential in general.

The position presented in the present article should be seen as a working hypothesis that is worth attention, although some of its tenets are still open to debate and further investigation.

ACKNOWLEDGEMENTS

The authors would like to thank Dr. Inna Ravich-Scherbo, Prof. Nancy Segal, Prof. Alexander Kaplan, for the manuscript critical reading, which allowed for the improvement of the quality of the text. Authors also thankful to a number of anonymous referees for their helpful comments. This work was partly supported by CIMO Foundation, Finland and RFFI, Russia.

REFERENCES

Aboitiz, F., Scheibel, A.B., Fisher R.S., & Zaidel, E. (1992) Individual differences in brain asymmetries and fiber composition in the human corpus callosum. *Brain Res.* **598**, 154-161.

Akerman, B.A. (1995) Eight-year follow-up of cognitive development in 33 twin pairs. *Acta Genet. Med. Gemellol. (Roma)* **44(3-4)**, 179-188.

Akerman, B.A. & Fischbein, S. (1991) Twins: are they at risk? A longitudinal study of twins and nontwins from birth to 18 years of age. *Acta Genet. Med. Gemellol. (Roma)* **40(1)**, 29-40.

Alexander, J.E., O'Boyle, M.W., & Benbow, C.P. (1996) Developmentally advanced EEG alpha power in gifted male and female adolescents. *Int. J. Psychophysiol.* **23**, 25-31.

Anderson, B. (1993) Evidence from the rat for a general factor that underlies cognitive performance that relates to brain size: intelligence? *Neurosci. Lett.* **153**, 98-102.

Anderson, B. & Harvey, T. (1996) Alterations in cortical thickness and neuronal density in the frontal cortex of Albert Einstein. *Neurosci. Lett.* **210**, 161-164.

Annett, M. (1978) *A Single Gene Explanation of Right and Left-handedness and Brainedness.* Coventry: Lanchester Polytechnic.

Annett, M. (1996) In defense of the right shift theory. *Percept. Motor Skills* **82**, 115-137.

Annett, M. (1997) Schizophrenia and autism considered as the products of an agnosic right shift gene. *Cog. Neuropsychol.* **2(3)**, 195-240.

Annett, M. (1998) Handedness and cerebral dominance: The right shift theory. *J. Neuropsych.* **10**, 459-469.

Annett, M. (1999) Handedness and lexical skills in undergraduates. *Cortex.* **35**, 357-372.

Annett, M. & Alexander, M.P. (1996) Atypical cerebral dominance: predictions and tests of the right shift theory. *Neuropsychologia.* **34**, 1215-1227.

Ashton, G.C. (1983) Myopia and cognitive ability. *Behav. Genetics.* **13**, 526.

Bell, M.A. & Fox, N.A. (1992) The relations between frontal and brain electrical activity and cognitive development during infancy. *Child. Dev.* **63**, 1142-1163.

Benbow, C.P. (1986) Physiological correlates of extreme intellectual precocity. *Neuropsychologia.* **24**, 719-725.

Benbow, C.P. (1988) Sex differences in mathematical reasoning ability in intellectually talented preadolescents: their nature, effects and possible causes. *Brain Behav. Sci.* **11**, 169-232.

Benbow, C.P. & Stanley, J.C. (1980) Sex differences in mathematical ability: fact or artifact? *Science* **210**, 1262-1264.

Berkow, R. (ed.) (1997) *Practical Medicine Manual: Diagnosis and Therapy*. I. pp. 742-744. Moscow: Mir. (in Russian).

Bimonte, H.A., Fitch, R.H., & Denenberg, V.H. (2000) Neonatal estrogen blockade prevents normal callosal responsiveness to estradiol in adulthood. *Brain Res. Dev. Brain Res.* **122(2)**, 149-155.

Bishop, D.V.M. (1990) *Handedness and Developmental Disorder*. L: Mac Keith Press.

Bishop, D.V. & Bishop, S.J. (1998) "Twin language": a risk factor for language impairment? *J. Speech Lang. Hear. Res.* **41(1)**, 150-160.

Bogdanov, N.N. (1997) Dermatoglyphic patterns of left-handed. *Voprosi Psihologii (Questions of Psychology)* **2**, 76-87. (in Russian).

Bogdanov, N.N. & Solonichenko, V.G. (1995) The Williams syndrome as a genetically determined model of the right brain dominance. *Physiologicheskii Gyrnal (Physiol. J.)* **81(8)**, 81-84. (in Russian).

Bogdanov, N.N., Gorbachevskaya, N.L., Solonichenko, V.G., Iznak, A.F., Yakupova, L.P., Yakupova, L.P., Kogushko, L.F., & Pankratova, E.A. (1994) The EEG peculiarities of 6-8 years old girls with different dermatoglyphic patterns on hands. *Dokl. Acad. Nauk. (Proc. Acad. Science. Russia)*. **338(3)**, 420-424. (in Russian).

Bonnevie, K. (1929) Zur Mechanik der Papillarmusterbildung. I. Die Epidermis als formativer Faktor in der Entwickluhg der Fingerbeeren und der Papillarmuster. *Arch. Entwickl. Organ.* **117**, 384-420.

Bragina, N.N. & Dobrohotova, T.A. (1998) *Functional Asymmetry of Humans*. Moscow. (in Russian).

Bullmore, E., Brammer, M., Harvey, I., Murray, R., & Ron, M. (1995) Cerebral hemisphere asymmetry revisited: effects of handedness, gender and schizophrenia measured by radius of gyration of magnetic resonance images. *Psychol. Med.* **25**, 349-363.

Chen, A.C. & Buckley, K.C. (1988) Neural perspectives of cerebral correlates of giftedness. *Int. J. Neurosci.* **41**, 115-125.

Cherrier, M.M. (1999) Androgens, ageing, behavior and cognition: complex interactions and novel areas of inquiry. *New Zealand J. Psychol.* **28(1)**, 4-9.

Chiron, C., LeBoyer, M., Leon, F., Jambaque, I., Nuttin, C., & Syrota, A. (1955) Spect of the brain in childhood autism – evidence for a lack of normal hemispheric asymmetry. *Develop. Med. Child. Neurol.* **37**, 849-860.

Christian, J.C., Hunter, D.S., Evans, M.M., & Standeford, F.M. (1979) Association of handedness and birth order in monozygotic twins. *Acta Genet. Med. Gemellol (Roma)* **28(1)**, 67-68.

Clarck, J.M. & Zaidel, E. (1994) Anatomical-behavioral relationships: Corpus callosum morphometry and hemispheric specialization. *Beh. Brain Res.* **64**, 185-202.

Clinton, H.R. (1996) *It Takes a Village*. New York: Touchstone.

Collaer, M.L. & Hines, M. (1995) Human behavioral sex differences: A role for gonadal hormones during early development? *Psychol. Bull.* **26**, 243-248.

Crick, F. & Koch, Ch. (1995) Are we aware of neural activity in primary visual cortex? *Nature* **375(11)**, 121-123.

Davis, A. & Annett, M. (1994) Handedness as a function of twinning. Age and sex. *Cortex* **30**, 105-111.

Deary, I.J. (2001a) Human intelligence differences: towards a combined experimental-differential approach. *Trends Cog. Sci.* **5(4)**, 164-170.

Deary, I.J. (2001b) Human intelligence differences: a recent history. *Trends Cog. Sci.* **5(3)**, 127-130.

De Geus, E.J.C. & Boomsma, D.I. (2002) A genetic neuroscience approach to human cognition. *European Psychologist* **6(4)**, 241-253.

De Lacoste, M.C., Horvath, D.S., & Woodward, D.J. (1991) Possible sex differences in the developing human fetal brain. *Clin. Exp. Neuropsychol.* **13**, 831-846.

De Lacoste-Utamsing, C. & Holloway, R.L. (1982) Sexual dimorphism in the human corpus callosum. *Science* **216**, 1431-1432.

Dempster, F.N. (1991) Inhibitory processes: a neglected dimension of intelligence. *Intelligence* **15**, 157-173.

Derom, C., Thiery, E., Vlietinck, R., Loos, R., & Derom, R. (1996) Handedness in twin according to zygosity and chorion type: a preliminary report. *Behav. Genet.* **26(4)**, 407-408.

Diamond, M.C. (1991) Hormonal effects on the development or cerebral lateralization. *Psychoneuroendocrinology* **16(1-3)**, 121-129.

Dobrohotova, T.A. & Bragina N.N. (1994) *The Left-handers*. Moscow: Kniga. (in Russian).

Dorfman, J., Shames, V.A., & Kihlstrom, J.F. (1996) Intuition, incubation, and insight: Implicit cognition in problem solving. In: *Implicit Cognition* (Underwood, G., ed) pp. 257-296. Oxford, England: Oxford University Press.

Duncan, J., Emslie, H., & Williams, P. (1996) Intelligence and the frontal lobe: the organization of goal-directed behavior. *Cog. Psychol.* **30**, 257-303.

Duncan, J., Seitz, R.J., Kolodny, J., Bor, D., Herzog, H., Ahmed, A., Newell, F.N., & Emslie, H. (2000) A neural basis for general intelligence. *Science* **289**, 457-460.

Eysenck, H.J. (1995) *Genius*. Cambridge: Cambridge University Press.

Feldstein, V.A., Machin, G.A., Albanese, C.T., Sandberg, P., Farrell, J.A., Farmer, D.L., & Harrison, M.R. (2000) Twin-twin transfusion syndrome: the 'select' procedure. *Fet. Diagn. Ther.* **15(5)**, 257-261.

Fingelkurts, Al.A. (1998) *Some Regularities of Human EEG Spectral Patterns Dynamics During Cognitive Activity*. Ph.D. Dissertation. MSU, Moscow. (in Russian).

Fingelkurts, An.A. (1998) *Time-spatial Organization of Human EEG Segments' Structure*. Ph.D. Dissertation. MSU, Moscow. (in Russian).

Fingelkurts, An.A., & Fingelkurts, Al.A. (1995) *Microstructural Analysis of Active Human Brain EEG: General Characteristics and Peculiarities of "Change-point" Approach*. Masters Degree work. MSU, Moscow. (in Russian).

Fingelkurts, An.A. & Fingelkurts, Al.A. (2000) Hemispheric laterality, high intelligence and twins. *Vopr. Psihol. (Questions of Psychology)* **5**, 111-121. (in Russian).

Fingelkurts An.A. & Finglekurts, Al.A. (2001) Operational architectonics of the human brain biopotential field: Towards solving the mind-brain problem. *Brain and Mind*, **2(3)**, 261-296.

Fingelkurts, An.A. & Fingelkurts, Al.A. (2002) Exploring giftedness. Chapter 8. In: *Advances in Psychology Research* (Shohov, S.P., ed.), Vol. 9. pp. 137-155. Nova Science Publishers, Inc.

Fingelkurts, An.A., Fingelkurts, Al.A., Ivachko, R.M., & Kaplan, A.Ya. (1998) EEG analysis of operational synchrony between human brain cortical areas during memory task performance. *Vestn. Mosk. Univer. (Bull. of Moscow Univ.)*. *Series Biology* **1**, 3-11. (in Russian).

Fingelkurts, An.A., Fingelkurts, Al.A., Borisov, S.V., Ivashko, R.M., & Kaplan, A.Ya. (2000) Spatial structures of human multichannel EEG quasi-stationary segments during memory task. *Vestnik Moskovskogo Universiteta (Bull. of Moscow Univ.). Series Biology* **3**, 3-10. (in Russian).

Fox, N.A., Sutton, D.B., Aaron, N., & Levav, M. (1988) EEG asymmetry and negative emotionality in 14-month-old infants. *Psychophysiology* **25**, 446-447.

Galaburda, A.M., Corsiglia, C., Rosen, C., & Sherman, C. (1987) Planum temporale asymmetry, reappraisal since Geschwind and Levitsky. *Neuropsychologia* **25**, 853-868.

Garcia-Estrada, J., Del Rio, J.A., Luquin, S., Soriano, E., Gaecia-Segura, L.M. (1993) Gonadal hormones down-regulate reactive gliosis and astrocyte proliferation after a penetrating brain injury. *Brain Res.* **628**, 271-278.

Geschwind, N. & Behan, P. (1982) Left-handedness: association with immune disease, migraine, and developmental learning disorder. *Proc. National Acad. Sci. USA* **79**, 5097-5100.

Geschwind, N. & Galaburda, A.M. (1987) *Cerebral Lateralization.* Cambridge, MA: MIT Press.

Ghiselin, B. (1952) *The Creative Process.* Berkley/Los Angeles: University of California Press.

Gladkova, T.D. (1962) The phenomenon of symmetry and asymmetry in humans on the basis of dermatoglific patterns. *Voprosi Antropologii (Questions of Antrop.)* **10**, 44-54. (in Russian).

Goldman-Rakic, P.S. (1996) Regional and cellular fractionation of working memory. *Proc. Natl. Acad. Sci. USA* **26**, 13473-80.

Gruszewska, S.A. (1998) Interpersonal conflicts in the relationship of twins. *Acta Genet. Med. Gemellol. (Roma)* **47(3-4)**, 153-160.

Gur, R.C., Turetsky, B.I., Matsui, M., Yan, M., Bilker, W., Hughett, P., & Gur, R.E. (1999) Sex differences in brain gray and white matter in healthy young adults: Correlations with cognitive performance. *J. Neudocsi.* **19(10)**, 4065-4072.

Innocenti, G.M. & Berbel, P. (1991) Analysis of an experimental cortical network: I) Architectonics of visual areas 17 and 18 after neonatal injections of ibotenic acid; similarities with human microgyria. *J. Neur. Transplant.* **2**, 1-28.

Ivanitsky, A.M. (1997) Informational synthesis in crucial cortical area as the brain base of the subjective experience. *Gyrnal Vischei Nervnoi Deyatelnosty. (J. of Higher Nervous Activity)* **47(2)**, 10-21. (Translated from Original Russian Version: p. 209-225).

Habib, M., Gayraud, D., Oliva, A., Regis, J., et al. (1991) Effects of handedness and sex on the morphology of the corpus callosum: a study with brain magnetic resonance imaging. *Brain Cog.* **16**, 41-61.

Hadamard, J. (1949) *The Psychology of Invention in the Mathematical field.* New Jersey: Princeton University Press.

Haier, R.J. & Benbow, C.P. (1995) Sex differences in lateralization in temporal lobe glucose metabolism during mathematical reasoning. *Dev. Neurobiol.* **11**, 405-414.

Hall, J.G. (1996) Twinning: mechanisms and genetic implications. *Cur. Opinion Gen. Devel.* **6**, 343-347.

Hall, J.G. & Lopez-Rangel E. (1996) Twins and twinning. In: *Principles and Practice of Medical Genetics* (Emery, A.E., & Rimoin, D.L., eds) edn.3. New York: Churchill Livingston.

Halberg, F., Cornelissen, G., Katinas, G., Watanabe, Y., Otsuka, K., Maggioni, C., Perfetto, F., Tarquini, R., Schwartzkopff, O., & Bakken, E.E. (2000) Feedsidewards: Intermodulation (strictly) among time structures, chronomes, in and around us, and cosmo-vasculo-neuroimmunity: About ten-yearly changes: What Galileo missed and Schwabe found. In: *Neuroimmunomodulation: Perspectives at the New Millennium* (Conti A et al., eds). Annals of the New York Academy of Sciences, V. **917**, pp. 348-375.

Halpern, D. (2000) *Sex Differences in Cognitive Abilities*. (3rd ed.). Mahwah, NJ: Erlbaum.

Halpern, D. & Tan, U. (2001) Stereotypes and Steroids: using a psychobiosocial model to understand cognitive sex differences. *Brain Cog.* **45**, 392-414.

Halpern, D., Haviland, M.G., & Killian, C.D. (1998) Handedness and sex differences in intelligence: Evidence from the medical college admission test. *Brain Cog.* **38**, 87-101.

Hellige, J.B. (1993) *Hemispheric Asymmetry*. Cambridge, MA: Harvard University Press.

Highley, J.R., Esiri, M.M., McDonald, B., Cortina-Borja, M., Herron, B.M., & Crow, T.J. (1999) The size and fiber composition of the corpus callosum with respect to gender and schizophrenia: A postmortem study. *Brain* **122**, 99-100.

Hines, M. (1982) Prenatal gonadal hormones and sex differences in human behavior. *Psychol. Bull.* **92**, 56-80.

Hitt, S.K., Allen, J.J.B., & Duke, L.M. (1995) Stability of resting frontal alpha asymmetry in major depression. *Psychophysiology* **32**, 40.

Hassler, M. & Gupta, D. (1993) Functional brain organization, handedness, and immune vulnerability in musicians and non-musicians. *Neuropsychologia* **31(7)**, 655-660.

James, W.H. (1995) Twinning and neural tube defects. *Am. J. Hum. Genet.* **57**, 194.

Jamison, K.R. (1989) Mood disorders and patterns of creativity in British writers and artists. *Psychiatry* **52**, 125-34.

Jamison, K.R. (1995) Manic-depressive illness and creativity. *Sci. Am.* **272(2)**, 62-67.

Jarvinen, P., Kaprio, J., Makitalo, R., Kaskenvuop, M., & Aho, K. (1992) Systemic lupus erythematosus and related systemic disease in a national twin cohort: An increased prevalence of disease in MZ twins and concordance of disease features. *J. Int. Med.* **231**, 67-72.

Jensen, A.R. (1994) Psychometric g related to differences in head size. *Person Indiv. Diff.* **17**, 597-606.

Jensen, A.R. (1998) *The g Factor*. Westport, CT: Praeger.

Johnson, M.H. (2001) Functional brain development in humans. *Nature Rev. Neurosci.* **2**, 475-483.

Kaelber, C.T. & Pugh, T.E. (1969) Influence of intrauterine relations on the intelligence of twins. *N. Engl. J. Med.* **280**, 1030-1034.

Kantonistova, N.S. (1980) Study of imtellectual activity in twins. I. Developmental features. *Genetika* **16(1)**, 165-175.

Kaplan, A.Ya., Darkhovsky, B.S., Fingelkurts, Al.A., & Fingelkurts, An.A. (1997) Topological mapping of the process of change-point synchronization in the multichannel EEG in humans. *Gurnal Vischei Nervnoi Deyatelnosty (J. of High Nervous Activity)* **45(1)**, 32-37. (in Russian).

Kaplan, A.Ya., Fingelkurts, An.A., Fingelkurts, Al.A., & Ivashko, R.M. (1998) Nonrandom consistency of the sharp reorganizations of EEG basic rhythms. *Gurnal Vischei Nervnoi Deyatelnosty (J. of High Nervous Activity)* **48(5)**, 816-826. (in Russian).

Kimura, D. (1994) Body asymmetry and intellectual pattern. *Personal. Ind. Diff.* **17**, 53-60.

Kimura, D. & Hampson, E. (1994) Cognitive pattern in men and women is influenced by fluctuations in sex hormones. *Curr. Direct. Psychol. Sci.* **3**, 57-61.

Kiroi, V.N., Voi'nov, V.B., Mamin, P.A., & Hachaturyan, E.V. (1988) Spatial synchronization of bioelectrical brain activity during cognitive loading. *Fisiologiya Cheloveka (Human Physiology J.)* **14(2)**, 326. (in Russian).

Kiroi, V.N., Koshel'kova, N.A., & Voi'nov, V.B., 1996. Interrelation of values of local and distant synchronization of brain biopotentials during rest condition. *Fisiologiya Cheloveka (Human Physiology J.)* **22(3)**, 18-21. (in Russian).

Kline, J.P., Allen, J.J.B., & Schwartz, G.E. (1998) Is left-frontal brain activation in defensiveness gender specific? *J. Abnorm. Psychol.* **107**, 149-153.

Koriat, A. (2000) The feeling of knowing: Some metatheoretical implications for consciousness and control. *Conscious. Cog.* **9**, 149-171.

Koriat, A., & Levy-Sadot, R. (1999) Processes underlying metacognitive judgments: Information-based and experience-based monitoring of one's own knowledge. In: *Dual Process Theories in Social Psychology* (Chaiken, S. & Trope, Y., eds) pp. 483-502. New York: Guilford.

Levy, J. & Gur, R.C. (19800 Individual differences in psychoneurological organization. In: *Neuropsychology of Left-handedness* (Herron, J., ed) pp.142-152. New York: Academic.

Lippa, R.A. (2002). *Gender, Nature, and Nurture.* Mahwah, NJ: Lawrence Erlbaum Associates, Inc., Publishers.

Lopriore, E., Vandenbussche, F.P.H.A., Tiersma, S.M.E., De Beaufort, A.J., & Leeuw, P.J. (1995) Twin-to-twin transfusion syndrome. *J. Pediatr.* **127**, 675-680.

Lubinski, D. (2000) Scientific and social significance of assessing individual differences: "Sinking Shafts at a few Critical Points". *Annu. Rev. Psychol.* **51**, 405-444.

Lubinski, D., & Humphreys, L. (1992) Some bodily and medical correlates of mathematical giftedness and commensurate levels of socioeconomic status. *Intelligence* **16**, 99-115.

Machin, G., Bamforth, F., Innes, M., & McNichol, K. (1995) Some perinatal characteristics of monozygotic twins who are dichorionic. *Am. J. Med. Genet.* **55(1)**, 71-76.

Machin, G., Still, K., & Lalani, T. (1996) Correlations of placental vascular anatomy and clinical outcomes in 69 monochorionic twin pregnancies. *Am. J. Med. Genet.* **61**, 229-236.

McEvoy, S. & Dodd, B. (1992) The communication abilities of 2- to 4-year-old twins. *Eur. J. Disord. Commun.* **27(1)**, 73-87.

McGlone, J. (1980) Sex differences in human brain activity: a critical review. *Behav. Brain Sci.* **3**, 215-263.

McGuire, P.K., & Frith, C.D. (1996) Disordered functional connectivity in schizophrenia. *Psychol. Med.* **26**, 663-667.

McManus, E.C., Bryden, M.P., & Bulmer-Fleming, M.B. (1993) Handedness and autoimmune desease. *Lancet* **341**, 891-892.

Meehl, P.E. (1992) Factors and taxa, traits and types, differences of degree and differences in kind. *J. Personality* **60**, 117-174.

Miller, B.L., Boone, K., Cummings, J.L., Read, S.L., & Mishkin, F. (2000) Functional correlates of musical and visual ability in frontotemporal dementia. *British J. Psychiatry* **176**, 458-463.

Moffat, S.D. & Hampson, E. (1996) A curvilinear relationship between testosterone and spatial cognition in humans: Possible influence of hand preference. *Psychoneuroendocrinology* **21**, 323-337.

Moffat, S.D., Hampson, E., Wickett, J.C., Vernon, P.A., & Lee, D.H. (1997) Testosterone is correlated with regional morphology of the human corpus callosum. *Brain Res.* **767(2)**, 297-304.

Monsay, E.H. (1997) Intuition in the development of scientific theory and practice. In: *Intuition: The Inside Story* (Davis-Floyd, R. & Aarvidson, P.S., eds) pp. 103-120. New York: Routledge.

Morfit, N.S. & Weekes, N.Y. (2001) Handedness and immune function. *Brain Cog.* **46**, 209-213.

Morley, K.I. & Montgomery, G.W. (2001) The genetics of cognitive processes: candidate genes in humans and animals. *Behav Genet.* **31(6)**, 511-531.

Nakamura, K., Kawashima, R., Ito, K., Sugiura, M., Kato, T., Nakamura, A., Hatano, K., Nagumo, S., Kubota, K., Fukuda, H., & Kojima, S. (1999) Activation of the right inferior frontal cortex during assessment of facial emotion. *J. Neurophysiol.* **82(3)**, 1610-1614.

Neimark, J. (1997) Twins: Nature's clones. *Psychol. Today* **30(4)**, 36-69.

Newman, F. (1997) Brain research has implications for education: 1st grade too late? *State Educ. Leader* **15**, 1-2.

Nichols, R.C., & Bilbro, W.C., Jr. (1966) The diagnosis of twin zygosity. *Acta Genet. Stat. Med.* **16**, 265-275.

Nimchinsky, E.A., Gilissen, E., Allman, J.M., Perl, D.P., Erwin, J.M., & Hof, P.R. (1999). A neuronal morphologic type unique to humans and great apes. *Proc. Nat. Acad. Sci. USA.* **96**, 5268-5273.

Nolen-Hoeksema, S. (1987) Sex differences in unipolar depression: evidence and theory. *Psychol. Bull.* **101**, 259-282

O'Boyle, M.W. & Benbow, C.P. (1990) Handedness and its relationship to ability and talent. In: *Left-handedness: Behavioral Implications and Anomalies* (Coren, S. ed) pp. 343-372. Amsterdam: North Holland.

O'Boyle, M.W., Alexander, J.E., & Benbow, C.P. (1991) Enhanced RH activation in the mathematically precocious: a preliminary EEG investigation. *Brain Cog.* **17**, 138-153.

O'Boyle, M.W., Benbow, C.P., & Alexander, J.E. (1995) Sex differences, hemispheric laterality, and associated brain activity in the intellectually gifted. *Develop. Neuropsychol.* **11(4)**, 415-443.

Obrzut, J.E., Hynd, G.W., Obrzut, A., & Leitgeb, J.L. (1980) Time sharing and dichotic listening asymmetry in normal and learning disabled children. *Brain and Language* **11**, 181-194.

Oka, S., Miyamoto, O., Janjua, N.A., Honjo-Fujiwara, N., Ohkawa, M., Nagao, S., Kondo, H., Minami, T., Toyoshima, T., & Itano, T. (1999) Re-evaluation of sexual dimorphism in human corpus callosum. *Neuroreport* **10**, 937-940.

Olivares, R., Montiel, J., & Aboitiz, F. (2001) Species differences and similarities in the fine structure of the mammalian corpus callosum. *Brain Behav. Evol.* **57**, 98-105.

Pavlova, L.P. & Romanenko, A.F. (1988) *System Approach to Psychophysiological Investigation of Human Brain*. Leningrad. (in Russian).

Pedersen, N.L., Plomin, R., McClearn, G.E., & Friberg, L. (1988) Neuroticism, extraversion, and related traits in adult twins reared apart and reared together. *J. Pers. Soc. Psychol.* **55**, 950-957.

Petrill, S.A., Plomin, R., McClearn, G.E., Smith, D.L., Vignetti, S., Chorney, M.J., Chorney, K., Thompson, L.A., Detterman, D.K., Benbow, C., Lubinski, D., Daniels, J., Owen, M., & McGuffin, P. (1996) DNA markers associated with general and specific cognitive abilities. *Intelligence* **23(3)**, 191-203.

Plomin, R. & Crabbe, J. (2000) DNA. *Psychol Bull.* **126(6),** 806-828.

Pomerantz, S.M., Fox, T.O., Sholl, S.A., Vito, C.C., & Goy, R.W. (1985) Androgen and estrogen receptors in fetal rhesus monkey brain and anterior pituitary. *Endocrinology* **116**, 83-89.

Post, F. (1994) Creativity and psychopathology: a study of 291 world-famous men. *British J. of Psychiatry* **165**, 22-24.

Posthuma, D. (2002). *Genetic Variation and Cognitive Ability*. Ph.D. Dissertation. Vrije University, PrintPartners Ipskamp, Enschede/Amsterdam.

Posthuma, D., De Geus, E.J., Bleichrodt, N., & Boomsma, D.I. (2000) Twin-singelton differences in intelligence? *Twin Res.* **3(2)**, 83-87.

Posthuma, D., De Geus, E.J., Baare, W.F., Hulshoff Pol, H.E., Kahn, R.S., & Boomsma, D.I. (2002) The association between brain volume and intelligence is of genetic origin. *Nature Neurosci.* **5(2)**, 83-84.

Pribram, K. & Luria, A.R. (1973) *Psychophysiology of the Frontal Lobes*. New York: Academic.

RaKic, P., Bourgeosis J-P., & Goldman-Rakic, P.C. (1994) Synaptic development of the cerebral cortex: implications for learning, memory, and mental illness. In: *Prog. Brain. Res.* (Van Pelt, J., Corner, M.A., Uylings, H.B.M., & Lopes da Silva, F.H., eds) **102**, 227-243.

Reed, T., Carmelli, D., & Rosenman, R.H. (1991) Effects of placentation on selected type A behaviors in adults males in the National Heart, Lung and Blood Institute (NHLBI) Twin Study. *Behavior. Genetics.* **21**, 9-19.

Reinisch, J.M. (1974) Fetal hormones, the brain, and human sex differences: a heuristic, integrative, review of the recent literature. *Arch. Sex. Behav.* **3**, 51-90.

Reiss, M. (1999) The genetics of hand-clasping – a review and a family study. *Ann. Hum. Biol.* **26**, 39-48.

Robinson, A. & Clinkenbeard, P.R. (1998) Giftedness: an exceptionality examined. *Annu. Rev. Psychol.* **49**, 117-139.

Ross, C.A., & Pearlson, G.D. (1996) Schizophrenia, the heteromodal association neocortex and development: potential for a neurogenetic approach. *Trends in Neurosci.* **19**, 171-176.

Ross, P. (1993) *National Excellence: A Case for Developing America's Talent*. Washington, DC: Off. Educ. Res. Improve., US Off.Educ.

Rosen, G.D., Herman, A.E., & Galaburda, A.M. (1999) Sex differences in the effects of early neocortical injury on neuronal size distribution of the medial geniculate nucleus in the rat are mediated by perinatal gonadal steroids. *Cereb. Cortex* **9**, 27-34.

Rosen, G.D., Waters, S.N., Galaburda, A.M., & Denenberg, V.H. (1995) Behavioral consequences of neonatal injury of the neocortex. *Brain Res.* **681**, 177-189.

Sarnat, H.B. (1987) Disturbances of late neuronal migration in the perinatal period. *AJDC* **141**, 969-980.

Segal, N.L. (2000) *Entwined Lives: Twins and What They Tell Us About Human Behavior.* A Plume Book.

Sidorova, O.A. (2000) Characteristics of the perception and imagination of emotions in patients with focal brain pathology. *Ross. Fisiol. Gyrnal Im. M. Sechenova. (Russ. Physiol. J. M. Sechenova.)* **86(5)**, 541-547. (in Russian).

Sholl, S.A. & Kim, K.L. (1990) Androgen receptors are differentially distributed between right and left cerebral hemispheres of the fetal male rhesus monkey. *Brain Res.* **516(1)**, 122-126.

Sokol, D.K., Moore, C.A., Rose, R.J., Williams, C.J., Reed, T. & Christian, J.C. (1995) Intra-pair differences in personality and cognitive ability among young monozygotic twins distinguished by chorion type. *Behav. Genet.* **25**, 457-466.

Small, S.L. & Hoffman, G.E. (1994) Neuroanatomical lateralization of language: Sexual dimorphism and the ethology of neural computation. *Brain Cog.* **26**, 300-311.

Snyder, P.J., Bilder, R.M., Wu, H., Bogerts, B., & Lieberman, J.A. (1995) Cerebellar volume asymmetries are related to handedness: A quantitative MRI. *Neuropsychologia.* **33**, 407-419.

Steinmetz, H., Jancke, L., Kleinschmidt, A., Schlaug, G., Volkmann, J., & Huang, Y. (1992) Sex but no hand difference in the isthmus of the corpus callosum. *Neurol.* **42**, 749-752.

Stuss, D.T., Kaplan, E.F., Benson, D.F., Weir, W.S., Chiulli, S., & Sarazin, F.F. (1982) Evidence for the involvement of the orbito-frontal cortex in memory functions: an interference effect. *J. Comp. Physiol. Psychol.* **96**, 913-925.

Talizina, N.F., Krivzova, S.V., & Muhamatulina, E.V. (1991) *The Nature of Individual Differences: The Experience from Twins Approach.* Moscow. (in Russian).

Tan, U. (1991) Serum testosterone levels in male and female subjects with standard and anomalous dominance. *Int. J. Neurosci.* **58(3-4)**, 211-214.

Tang, Y.P., Shimizu, E., Dube, G.R., Rampon, C., Kerchner, G.A., Zhuo, M., Liu, G., & Tsien, J.Z. (1999) Genetic enhancement of learning and memory in mice. *Nature* **401(6748)**, 63-69.

Thatcher, R.W., Walker, R., & Guidice, S. (1987) Human cerebral hemispheres develop at different rates and ages. *Science* **236**, 1110-1113.

Thompson, P.M., Cannon, T.D., Narr, K.L., van Erp, T., Poutanen, V.P., Huttunen, M., Lonnqvist, J., Standertskjold-Nordenstam, C.G., Kaprio, J., Khaledy, M., Dail, R., Zoumalan, C.I., & Toga, A.W. (2001) Genetic influences on brain structure. *Nature Neurosci.* **4(12)**, 1253-1258.

Van Baal, G., De Geus, E., & Boomsma, D. (1996) Genetic architecture of EEG power spectra in early life. *Electroencephalogr. and Clin. Neurophysiol.* **98(6)**, 1-13.

Van Baal, G., De Geus, E., & Boomsma, D. (1997) Genetic influences on EEG coherence in 5-year-old twins. In: *A Genetic Perspective on the Developing Brain: Electrophysiological Indices of Neural Functioning in Five to Seven Year Old Twins* (Van Baal, G.C.M. ed) pp. 80-104. Print Partners Ipskamp, Enschede, The Netherlands.

Van Goozen, S.H.M., Cohen-Kettenis, P.T., Gooren, L.J.G., Frijda, N.H., & Van De Poll, A. (1995) Gender differences in behavior: Activating effects of cross-sex hormones. *Psychoneuroendocrinology* **20(4)**, 343-363.

Verdonck, A., De Ridder, L., Kuhn, R., Darras, V., Carels, C., & de Zegher, F. (1998) Effect of testosterone replacement after neonatal castration on craniofacial growth in rats. *Arch Oral Biol.* **43(7)**, 551-557.

Volozkoy, M.V. (1936) To the question about the genetics of finger papillary pictures. *Trydi Medico-geneticheskogo Instityta (Proc. Medico-Genetic. Inst.)* Moscow-Leningrad, **4**, 404-439. (in Russian).

Vom Saal, F.S. & Bronson, F.H. (1980) Sexual characteristics of adult female are correlated with their blood testosterone levels during prenatal development. *Science* **208**, 597-599.

Vom Saal, F.S., Pryor, S., & Bronson, F.H. (1981) Effects of prior intrauterine position and housing on estrous cycle length in adolescent mice. *J. Reprod. Fert.* **62**, 33-37.

Vom Saal, F.S., Grant, W.M., McMullen, C.W., & Laves, K.S. (1983) High fetal estrogen concentrations: correlation with increased adult sexual activity and decreased aggression in male mice. *Science* **220**, 1306-1309.

Weinberger, D.R. (1995) Schizophrenia: from neuropathology to neurodevelopment. *Lancet* **346**, 55-57.

Williams, R.L. & Medalie, J.H. (1994) Twins: double pleasure or double trouble? *Am. Fam. Physician.* **49(4)**, 869-876.

Wilson, J.D. (1999) The role of androgens in male gender role behavior. *Endocrine Rev.* **20**, 726-737.

Windmann, S. & Kruger, T. (1998) Subconscious detection of threat as reflected by an enhanced response bias. *Conscious. Cog.* **7(4)**, 603-633.

Winokur, M. (1984) *Einstein: A Portrait.* Corte Madera, CA: Pomegranate Artbooks.

Witelson, S.F. (1989) Hand and sex differences in the isthmus and genu of the human corpus callosum. A postmortem morphological study. *Brain* **112**, 799-835.

Witelson, S.F. & Goldsmith, C.H. (1991) The relationship of hand preference to anatomy of the corpus callosum in men. *Brain Res.* **545(1-2)**, 175-182.

Witelson, S.F. & Nowakowski, R.S. (1991) Left out axons make men right: a hypothesis for the origin of handedness and functional asymmetry. *Neuropsychologia* **29(4)**, 327-333.

Witelson, S.F., Kigar, D.L., Harvey, T. (1999) The exceptional brain of Albert Einstein. *The Lancet* **353**, 2149-2153.

Whitacre, C.C. (2001) Sex differences in autoimmune disease. *Nature Immunol.* **2(6)**, 777-780.

Whitacre, C.C., Reingold, S.C., O'Looney, P.A., Blankenhorn, E., Brinley, F., et al. (1999) Sex differences in autoimmune disease: Focus on multiple sclerosis. *Science.* www.sciencemag.org/feature/data983519.shl

Wright, I.C., Rabe-Hesketh, S., Woodruff, P.W.R., David, A.S., Murray, R.M., & Bullmore, E.T. (2000) Meta-analysis of regional brain volumes in schizophrenia. *Am. J. Psychiatry* **157(1)**, 16-25.

Zazzo, R. (1960) *Le Jumeaux: Le Couple et la Personne.* Paris.

In: *Topics in Cognitive Psychology*
Serge P. Shohov (Editor) pp. 101-116

ISBN 1-59033-836-7.
© 2003 Nova Science Publishers, Inc.

Chapter 6

DEVELOPING AUTOBIOGRAPHICAL MEMORY IN THE CULTURAL CONTEXTS OF PARENT-CHILD REMINISCING

Qi Wang and Erin L. Spillane
Cornell University

ABSTRACT

Family socialization practices, especially parent-child conversational interactions, play a paramount role in mediating children's acquisition of culture-appropriate modes of thinking, remembering, feeling, and behaving. Current research has revealed divergent family sociolinguistic environments in European American and East Asian cultures, reflecting different orientations that focus on either autonomy or relatedness. In this article, we draw upon empirical evidence on parent-child reminiscing in European American and East Asian families to analyze cultural variation in the cognitive, social, and emotional aspects of sharing memory narratives. We will demonstrate that parents in these cultures show different patterns and tendencies when conversing with their children about the shared past. Such differences, in turn, appear to have long-term consequences on the development of autobiographical memory.

INTRODUCTION

Social interaction within the family is always influenced by the whole of the culture of the group and takes place within a definite framework furnished by the control culture.
— W. Waller, 1938, p. 18

Sociocultural theorists emphasize the importance of social-cultural contexts in which cognitive changes occur (Gauvain, 2001; Rogoff, 1990; Sigel, 2002; Vygotsky, 1978; Wertsch, 1991). According to Vygotsky (1978), cognitive development entails a process of formal or informal learning through the face-to-face guidance, encouragement, and support of more competent members of the society, such as parents, older siblings, and teachers. As a result, within *a Zone of Proximal Development* (ZPD), children internalize culturally-valued skills, knowledge, and concepts into their own repertoire of thinking. Rogoff (1990) further proposes a metaphorical concept of "children as apprentices." She contends that apprenticeships in adult-guided participation "provide the beginner with access to both overt aspects of the skill and the more hidden inner processes of thought" (p. 40). During such joint activities, children play an active role by making use of opportunities presented to them and trying out newly acquired skills, strategies, and cognitive tools (Gauvain, 2001, Goodnow, 2000; Valsiner, 2000).

As researchers persist in analyses of the intricacies of cognitive development, one form of social interaction has drawn wide attention, that is the parent-child reminiscing of the shared past (e.g., Fivush, 1994; Hudson, 1990; Nelson, 1993, 1996; Pillemer & White, 1989; Tessler & Nelson, 1994). Joint conversations about shared experiences, in which parents play a guiding role to structure the discussion and to scaffold the child's active participation, appear to be a common practice in the family. Research on this form of interaction has shown its importance in providing children with the necessary organizational framework around which to structure their personal memories (Harley & Reese, 1999; Leichtman, Pillemer, Wang, Koreishi, & Han, 2000; Peterson & McCabe, 1994; Reese, Haden, & Fivush, 1993). From parents' modeling of conversational styles and ways of thinking and talking about the past, children learn to create narratives about their own experiences and to further ascribe emotional meaning and personal significance to these experiences. Many researchers thus claim that children acquire autobiographical memory – distinct, long-lasting memory of significant personal experiences from an individual's life – through learning to converse about their experiences with significant others (Fivush, Haden, & Adam, 1995; Nelson, 1993; Pillemer & White, 1989; Tessler & Nelson, 1994).

Much of the work on parent-child reminiscing and its long-term effects on children's autobiographical memory has mainly focused on European and Euro-American populations. On the other hand, recent studies have revealed systematic cross-cultural differences in the style and content of autobiographical memory in both adults and children. It is found that European and Euro-American adults on average can recall events they experienced at about age 3.5 (Pillemer & White, 1989), which is more than six months earlier than native Koreans and Chinese and overseas Asians (MacDonald, Uesiliana, & Hayne, 2000; Mullen, 1994; Wang, 2001a). In addition, memories reported by Euro-American adults tend to be voluminous, detailed, emotionally elaborate, focusing on one's own roles, predilections, and opinions. In contrast, memories of Chinese are often brief, emotionally neutral, centering on collective activities, significant others, and daily routines (Wang, 2001a; Wang & Conway, submitted). Even at preschool age, Euro-American children tend to have autobiographical accounts that are more elaborate, more specific, more self-focused, and less socially oriented than do their Korean and Chinese peers (Han, Leichtman, & Wang, 1998; Wang & Leichtman, 2000). Given the prime importance of sharing memory narrative for the development of autobiographical memory, these cross-cultural findings challenge researchers to reexamine family reminiscing activities in a larger cultural context.

Does parent-child reminiscing take place in different fashions across cultures that lead to the varied modes of remembering in adults and children? Culture, as a process of symbolic mediation (Bruner, 1990; Vaslner, 2000; Vygotsky, 1978, Wang & Brockmeier, 2002), manifests itself in the actions, thoughts, emotions, beliefs, and moral values of individuals, as well as in the surrounding social institutions, including the family. Family reminiscing activities are thus bound to reflect the values and orientations of the larger society, thereby resulting in different narrative environments in which young children learn to construct stories of themselves and gradually take over their parents' values and styles. Of particular interest to researchers has been the variations in family reminiscing in cultures characterized as independently versus interdependently oriented (Markus & Kitayama, 1991; Shweder, Goodnow, Hatano, LeVine, Markus, & Miller, 1998; Wang, in press-a). Interdependently oriented cultures, such as those of East Asia, place a great emphasis on interpersonal harmony, social obligation, and conformity to authority. Independently oriented cultures, such as of the United States, value qualities associated with autonomy, self-expression, and personal uniqueness.

Drawing upon empirical findings with European American and East Asian (particularly Chinese) families, we analyze here, in turn, the cognitive, social, and emotional aspects of cultural differences in parent-child reminiscing, and discuss their implications for the development of autobiographical memory. We will demonstrate that family memory sharing often takes different forms and contents in these cultures, reflecting the prevailing cultural orientations towards individual autonomy versus interpersonal relatedness. Our central theme is: Parent-child reminiscing constitutes an important cultural context in which autobiographical memory develops in culturally favored fashions.

"WHAT DID YOU REMEMBER?": NARRATIVE STYLES IN PARENT-CHILD REMINISCING

Sociointeractionist approaches to memory development view the emergence of autobiographical memory as a direct result of children's developing narrative skills that take place in collaboration with significant adults and in order to structure memory for personally meaningful events (Fivush et al., 1995; Fivush & Schwarzmueller, 1998; Nelson, 1996; Pillemer & White, 1989). Specifically, early parent-child conversations about shared experiences teach children appropriate forms of personal reminiscing (i.e., what to remember, how to remember, and why to remember it), reinstate past experiences through linguistic representation, and highlight the social function of memory sharing (Fivush & Hudson, 1990; Nelson, 1993; Tessler & Nelson, 1994). Thus, children develop, through such joint endeavors, the knowledge and ability to discuss the past in a socially acceptable manner and to also build an organized personal history from a growing foundation of autobiographical memories. Studies conducted in European and Euro-American cultures have demonstrated that children participate in memory conversations with adults early in life, and by age 3 to 4 – the average onset of autobiographical memory in Euro-American adults – children begin to contribute independently to discussions about the shared past (Fivush & Hamond, 1990; Harley & Reese, 1999).

Studies have further uncovered important factors such as the amount and style of parent-child memory talk in shaping children's subsequent remembering (Harley & Reese, 1999; Leichtman et al., 2000; Peterson & McCabe, 1994; Reese et al., 1993; Tessler & Nelson, 1994). Of particular importance, two contrasting styles of parent-child reminiscing appear to affect children's developing autobiographical memories over time. *High-elaborative* parents frequently hold lengthy and embellished discussions with their children about past events. They collaboratively recreate stories with their children and encourage them to provide detailed accounts of the past. When children falter, these parents often provide new information to scaffold the child's response, in an effort to keep the conversation going. In contrast, *low-elaborative* parents in general talk less with their children about shared past experiences. When conversing about the past, these parents often ask questions that tend to elicit brief responses from the child. They provide few details or embellishments and often allow the conversation to change course or end with little further prompting. Consequently, children who engage in rich, embellished reminiscing with their parents often come to discuss the past in a more elaborate, detailed manner and retain more memory information over time. Thus, the volume and stylistic differences in early parent-child narrative interactions appear to be a defining feature in the structure and content of children's own autobiographical memories later on.

Recent cross-cultural studies of parent-child memory-sharing in European American and East Asian cultures have revealed different conversational amounts and styles that mirror those between high-elaborative and low-elaborative mothers described in previous studies with Euro-American samples (e.g. Fivush, 1994; Harley & Reese, 1999; Reese et al., 1993). For example, Mullen and Yi (1995) conducted a one-day observation of conversational interactions between Euro-American and Korean mothers and their 3-year-old children. Mother and child each wore a vest containing a small tape-recorder during the day that recorded all naturally occurring conversations between them. Compared with Korean mother-child pairs, American pairs engaged in conversations about past events nearly three times as often.

In another study, Wang, Leichtman, and Davies (2000) asked Euro-American and Chinese mothers to talk with their 3-year-old children about two specific recent events they both participated in. Mother and child discussed the events alone in a quiet place in the home and their conversations were tape-recorded. It was found that American mothers showed a high-elaborative conversational style where they dwelled upon specific episodes, supplemented children's responses with rich and embellished information, and invited children to co-construct stories of the shared past. Chinese mothers, in contrast, showed a relatively low-elaborative conversational style in which they frequently posed and repeated factual questions, provided little detail or embellishment to assist the child's participation, and often tried to elicit correct answers in a way that emulated a memory test. The following two conversational excerpts help to illustrate these differences (Wang et al., 2000).[1]

American Mother-Daughter Pair

M   Sara, do you remember, um, on Fourth of July... What did we do on the Fourth of July? We went down to Grandma and Grampie's. What did we all go do? What did we watch?

C   Um, I don't know.

M   A parade. Do you remember the parade on the Fourth of July?

C   I know! A boy... he was, um, just walking... he gave me a flag.

M   At the parade?

---

[1] The conversational excerpts included in this article were collected in the cited empirical studies. They were not presented in previously published papers except otherwise noted.

C   Yeah. And Alex didn't get any 'cause he was... Alex was too, too young.
M   And he gave one to you?
C   Yeah.
....

Chinese Mother-Daughter Pair

M   Last time, mom promised to take you to the zoo during the recess. When mom took
     you to the zoo, what did you see there?
C   Tigers.
M   Tigers. What else?
C   And lions.
M   Lions. What else?
C   And ......
....

These examples demonstrate that memory conversations differed in the degree of elaboration and scaffolding that mothers provided to their children. For Euro-American mothers, joint reminiscing with their children created an opportunity for them to collaboratively reconstruct elaborate stories about shared experiences. Therefore, these mothers often provided abundant support whenever necessary to facilitate their children's participation. For Chinese mothers, in contrast, the conversations provided a forum for their children's memory performance. These mothers tended to play a directive role, attempting to elicit memory from their children while not providing embellished information or following up on children's responses. Similar to these findings, Choi (1992) found that Korean mothers were often more directive and less supportive than Canadian mothers when conversing about the past with their young children.

Intriguingly, children as young as age 3 appeared to have already adopted their mothers' style of conversation when talking about the shared past (Wang, 2001b; Wang et al., 2000). Compared with their Chinese peers, Euro-American children used a more elaborative conversational style where they frequently volunteered new and descriptive information about the events under discussion, assuming a cooperative partnership with their mothers during the conversation. In contrast, Chinese children often simply replied to their mother's inquiries, especially repeated prompts, with either short answers or no new information. They also tended to play a passive role when responding to their mothers' inquires.

The stylistic differences in early parent-child reminiscing across cultures are further echoed in children's independent autobiographical reports (Han, Leichtman, & Wang, 1998; Wang, submitted). For example, in Han, Leichtman, and Wang's (1998) study where Euro-American and native Korean and Chinese 4- and 6-year-olds recounted their past experiences (e.g., their last birthday) with a familiar adult interviewer, American children provided more elaborate and detailed memory narratives compared with their Asian peers. They produced lengthier propositions (subject-verb constructions) and used more descriptives (words that provide descriptive texture to the narrative, such as adjectives, adverbs, and modifiers) when talking about their experiences. American children also made more references to specific past events than did Asians who talked more frequently about daily routines or script events. In general, in comparison with the "fleshed-out" accounts of the American children, the Asian children's narratives contained more "bare-bones" accounts of their activities (Han et al, 1998).

Notably, these stylistic differences between personal memories of Euro-American and Asian children further extend into adulthood. That is, Euro-American adults often report autobiographical memories that are more voluminous, detailed, and specific when compared with those of Asians. In addition, European and Euro-American adults are able to access their earliest childhood memories from an age, on average, more than six months younger than native Koreans and Chinese and overseas Asians (MacDonald et al., 2000; Mullen, 1994; Wang, 2001a, 2003).

The parallels in narrative styles between early parent-child reminiscing and later on autobiographical memories in children and adults suggest that early social-linguistic environments are an important source from which children learn to remember personal experiences (Fivush et al., 1995; Nelson, 1996; Pillemer & White, 1989). More importantly, parents in different cultures tend to employ different conversational styles that instill different ways of autobiographical remembering in their children. Growing up in different narrative environments, children gradually internalize these different styles from their parents in talking about and remembering personal experiences, which further influence the structure and long-term accessibility of their memories.

In extending the sociointeractionist theory of memory development, the cross-cultural data indicate that the structural organization of family reminiscing activities is not merely a product of dyadic interactions confined within an immediate social setting. Instead, it takes shape in a culturally situated context comprising culturally prescribed role-negotiation between parents and children (e.g., hierarchical or equal), parent's implicit and explicit child-rearing goals (e.g., to establish autonomy or relatedness), and general cultural beliefs about personal remembering (e.g., the function of memory). This leads to our consideration of the social aspects of sharing memory narrative.

"WHAT DID YOU LIKE BEST?": INDIVIDUAL VS. SOCIAL ORIENTATIONS IN PARENT-CHILD REMINISCING

Parent-child reminiscing is an important medium of socialization. Many researchers maintain that joint narrative construction of past events helps children construct the system of meaning-making, gain knowledge about self and others, and apprehend social messages (Fivush, 1994; Middleton & Edwards, 1990; Miller et al., 1992; Nelson, 1996). For instance, Middleton and Edwards (1990) describe family conversations about shared experiences as a rich learning environment "in which the parent takes pains to elicit perceptions, memories and judgements from the children, to examine and elaborate upon them, to contextualize and assign significance to them, in terms of a shared past in which personal identity, family relationships and the landmarks of development can be reconstructed" (p. 41). Even more so, we argue that family narrative practices are interwoven into the larger fabric of the culture, a fabric in where culture-specific values, beliefs, and ideologies are institutionalized in various material and symbolic ways that create and reconsolidate different genres of autobiographical memory (Wang & Brockmeier, 2002).

An important dimension of culture is the orientations towards autonomy versus relatedness, which have profound and overarching effects on individuals' cognition, emotion, and social behavior. These varied orientations result from and are further reflected in the structural organization of a society, its moral, religious and philosophical traditions, and its prevailing notions of selfhood (Fiske, Kitayama, Markus, & Nisbett, 1998; Geertz, 1973; Markus & Kitayama, 1991; Triandis, 1989). Accordingly, autobiographical memory takes on different genres and consists of different themes as a function of the dominant orientations in a particular culture. In European American culture that highly values autonomy and individuality, the past is often remembered as if it were a drama, where the rememberer plays the protagonist who is the focus of the plot and determines the storylines. A different genre of autobiographical memory is observed in many East Asian cultures that emphasize interrelatedness and group solidarity. As reflected in autobiographical writings as well as empirical data, individuals in these cultures tend to remember their life stories with a heightened sensitivity to significant others with whom they share the spotlight (Mullen, 1994; Pillemer, 1998; Wang, 2001a; Wang & Brockmeier, 2002).

The different genres of autobiographical memory associated with autonomous and relational orientations are reflected in the social content of sharing memory narratives between Euro-American and Asian parents and their children (Miller, Fung, & Mintz, 1996; Miller, Wiley, Fung, & Liang, 1997; Mullen & Yi, 1995; Wang, 2001b; Wang et al., 2000). Memory talk between American parents and children often takes a child-centered approach, where the child remains the focal point of the conversation and the mother frequently refers to the child's interests, preferences, opinions, and personal attributes. These features are illustrated in the following conversation between an American mother and her 3-year-old son (Wang et al., 2000).

M   Do you remember when we went to the circus?
C   Um, we got cotton-candy there.
M   What else?
C   Horses and baby horses, dragons and everything.
M   And how'd you like that?
C   The horse, horse baby.
M   You liked the baby horse, the little tiny one.
C   Yep.
M   What part did you love the least?
C   We made Gram a big, big present. It had some letters in it.
......

In contrast, memory talk in Korean (Mullen & Yi, 1995) and Chinese (Miller et al., 1996, 1997; Wang, 2001b) families often take a mother-centered, hierarchically organized approach in which mothers set the direction of the conversation, emphasize interpersonal relations, and frequently talk about moral rules and behavioral expectations with their children. The following conversational excerpt between a Chinese mother and her 3-year-old son illustrates such an approach (Wang et al., 2000).

.....
M   Did you sing "Happy-New-Year"?
C   Yes.
M   Mama heard Beibei sing "Happy-New-Year", right?
C   um.

M   So Mama wished Beibei grow up happily in the new year, right?
C   Right.
M   You will be one-year older. Beibei should be more obedient to the teachers in the new year, right?
C   Right.
M   And with the little friends …
C   Be nice to each other.
M   Correct.

Like their mothers, American youngsters talked more frequently about their personal preferences and judgements than did their Chinese peers who made more spontaneous references to significant others as opposed to themselves and to rules and disciplines during memory sharing (Wang, 2001b; Wang et al., 2000). Joint reminiscing appears to serve different functions in the two cultural contexts. American parents use memory conversations as a means of reinstating a sense of self, encouraging autonomy, and enhancing self-assertiveness in their young children. In contrast, Chinese and Korean parents tend to use such conversations with their young children to convey social norms and to instill culturally valued qualities such as compliance to authority, appropriate conduct, humility, and a sense of belonging. Thus, personal storytelling as a routine family socialization practice in both Euro-American and Asian cultures is already functionally differentiated by 2 to 3 years of age.

The content differences in early parent-child reminiscing show direct outcomes in children's independent memory reports. In the study by Han et al. (1998) discussed earlier, Euro-American children, compared with their Chinese and Korean peers, showed greater usage of internal state language, which included talks about inner emotional and cognitive processes and personal preferences and evaluations. Particularly, American children mentioned more than twice as many preferences and evaluations as Asian children did, which furthers the notion that Asian children were less practiced than Americans in formulating and focusing on their own subjective judgments. On the other hand, both Chinese and Korean children spoke more of other people relative to themselves than did Americans, which reflects the emphasis on social relationships, knowledge of other people, and attention to obligations to others during Asian family narrative practices.

To further capture the social characteristics of children's personal narratives, Wang and Leichtman (2000) asked Chinese and Euro-American kindergartners to recount instances in which they felt a particular emotion such as happiness, fear, or anger. Content analyses revealed that, compared with American children, Chinese children showed a greater tendency to introduce social interactions and positive interpersonal relations, a greater concern with moral correctness and authority, and less of a tendency to express individual judgments, opinions, or self-determination in their memory narratives.

Together, these findings indicate that before the onset of formal schooling, Euro-American and Asian children already learn to remember and talk about their personal experiences in culturally canonical forms modeled by their parents during early memory conversations. As Pillemer (1998) points out, "Parents' implicit or explicit communicative goals influence which functions will assume center stage in the child's own memory operations" (p. 129). Parent-child reminiscing serves socialization purposes that align with the dominant cultural orientations in the society. The low-elaborative, interdependently oriented conversations between East Asian parents and children are well suited to the goal of imparting to children social norms and behavioral expectations to build affiliation with significant others. The highly elaborative, independently oriented conversations between Euro-American parents and children facilitate the development of children's autonomy and an individual-unique autobiographical history. Thus, early narrative environments constitute resources from which children develop culturally desirable qualities and actively construct culture-specific genres of life stories.

"WHY DID YOU GET UPSET?": EMOTIONAL CONTENT OF PARENT-CHILD REMINISCING

The schematic knowledge of situational antecedents of emotions, i.e., emotion situation knowledge (Denham, Zoller, & Couchoud, 1994), is closely associated with both conceptual representations of emotions and autobiographical memories of emotional experiences (Conway & Bekerian, 1987; Stein & Liwag, 1997). It operates on the interpretation of emotional meanings of specific situations and on the anticipation and experience of emotions within these situations. Only after the emotional meaning of an event is fully "appraised" by referring to stored emotion situation knowledge can the event information be well integrated into existing knowledge structures, allowing it to be effectively processed and stored. Thus, much like other scripts (Schank, 1982), such knowledge may serve the functions of processing, representing, and organizing autobiographical memories of personally significant emotional events. This notion agrees with Tomkins's (1979) proposal that personal experiences are organized by ideo-affective construals or scripts that individuals develop for interpreting and responding to families of magnified and co-assembled affect scenes.

Building upon these theoretical views, Wang (2001b) proposes that emotion situation knowledge comprises an important mechanism for the emergence and development of autobiographical memory. The current literature shows that the age trend in children's acquisition of emotion situation knowledge parallels the age trend in children's development of autobiographical memory. Specifically, by age 4, and sometimes as young as age 2, children can give what would be considered by adults the appropriate emotional response to a situation; and children show an increasing ability to understand situations eliciting various emotions across preschool years (e.g., Borke, 1971; Lewis & Michalson, 1983; Shantz, 1975). Correspondingly, by 3 to 4 years of age, children become increasingly independent in providing personal memories with a canonical structure and specific details, and memories of preschoolers show an age-related increase in complexity and elaboration (Fivush & Hamond, 1990; Pillemer & White, 1989). The acquisition of emotion situation knowledge allows children to understand the personal meaning of past events and to organize memories in a structured fashion, thereby facilitating retention of and access to the event information over the long term.

Family discussions about emotions provide an important channel through which children form their theory of emotions. Studies conducted in Western cultures have found that from as early as 18 months of age, children begin to participate in family discourse about feeling states (Bretherton & Beeghly, 1982; Bretherton, Fritz, Zahn-Waxler, & Ridgeway, 1986; Denham et al., 1994; Stein & Liwag, 1997). At around 28 months, many children begin to discuss a wide range of emotions experienced by both themselves and others, and are able to provide causal explanations of their emotional reactions. By the end of preschool years, children's ability to verbally reflect on emotional situations has gained in accuracy, clarity, and complexity. Early exposures to family emotional discussions show direct, long-term consequences on children's developing emotion situation knowledge (Dunn, Bretherton, & Munn, 1987; Dunn, Brown, & Beardsall, 1991).

Furthermore, emotion talk in the family is often observed in the context of memory sharing, where parents and children discuss feeling states engendered in past events as well as the causes and consequences of the feeling states. Parent-child reminiscing of past emotions not only teaches children about appropriate emotional reactions within particular situations, but also makes salient the personal significance of the events under discussion and, therefore, shows why they are memorable. In addition, emotional aspects of memory conversations provide a rich evaluative framework, intensify self-awareness during reminiscing, and further build the critical link between autobiographical memories and self-concept (Fivush, 1993; Stein & Liwag, 1997). Hence, emotional memory sharing is crucial for children's acquisition of emotion knowledge and for their development of autobiographical memory.

Cultures hold different beliefs about emotion and emotion sharing, which are mirrored in divergent socialization goals and practices. In European American culture that emphasizes self-expression and individuality, talking about emotions is regarded as a direct expression of the self and an affirmation of the importance of the individual. Parents are often eager to "help children convey or articulate their own emotions and feelings so that ultimately they can 'get their needs met'" (Chao, 1995, p.339). In contrast, in Chinese culture that emphasizes social harmony and group interests, emotion tends to be viewed as destructive or even dangerous to ongoing relationships. Explicit communication of emotions is often treated as superfluous or even improper. Children are encouraged to develop the ability to infer others' feeling states without being told while restraining their own emotions through psychological discipline (Bond, 1991; Chao, 1995; Chen, Hastings, Rubin, Chen, Cen & Stewart, 1998).

Such divergent beliefs and practices pertinent to emotion are reflected in the emotional content of parent-child reminiscing in the two cultures. In a recent study, Wang (2001b) asked Euro-American and Chinese mothers to discuss with their 3-year-olds four specific one-point-in-time events in which they both participated and during which the child experienced happiness, sadness, fear or anger. Mothers selected the emotional events and, during a one-week period, talked with their children at home about the events at any time they chose on one or several occasions. As predicted, the two cultural groups differed in their ways of integrating emotions into ongoing conversations, consonant with their respective cultural values and socialization goals. American mother-child conversations exhibited an "emotion-explaining" style, in which mothers and children provided rich causal explanations for the antecedents of emotions. Mothers frequently talked about the causes and consequences of feeling states, providing elaborate explanations as to why and how an emotion was experienced. Such emotional discourse, as shown in the following conversational excerpt of an American mother-son pair, highlights the personal importance of emotion and facilitates the development of children's emotional understanding.

....

M Olivia's package. And why did it make you angry that she got a package?

C Because she wanted to have it, and pull it, and didn't want me to play with it, and didn't let me... and Olivia let me go on my head.

M And Olivia wouldn't let you help open it, or play with it? And what did you do when you got angry?

C I didn't.

M What did you do when you got angry?

C Because, Oh, yeah. I jumped on my bed.

......

Conversely, Chinese mother-child conversations showed an "emotion-criticizing" style that focused on imparting proper behavior in the child and gave few causal explanations for the emotion itself. Although mothers attributed emotions to the child and other people involved in the memory event, they rarely went further to discuss the causes and consequences of the emotions and often gave moral judgments about the incorrectness of children's emotional experience or behavior. As illustrated in the following conversational excerpt between a Chinese mother and her 3-year-old son, such emotional discourse puts social constraints on children's emotions and commits children to behavioral standards rather than helping them develop emotion situation knowledge.

.....

M Is it right to hit people? Mom is asking you, is it right to hit people? Is it?

C He kicked the ball so hard. I couldn't catch it.

M That make it ok for you to hit him?

C I couldn't catch the ball.

M Were you angry?

C I was angry.

M How could you hit Grandma when she asked you to stop? How could you hit Grandma?

......

Given these cultural differences in early emotion socialization, one would expect that American children acquire emotion situation knowledge earlier than their Chinese peers. This question was investigated in a subsequent study with Euro-American and Chinese 3- to 6-year-old children (Wang, in press-b). In this study, children were presented with 20 short stories and were asked about the feeling states of a story protagonist with whom they shared the same age, gender, and ethnicity, within situations that children in both cultures were likely to experience in daily life. Children's mothers and a second group of adults read the same stories and judged the story protagonist's emotions as the children had done. Based on the overall number of concordant judgements between children and adults, the data showed that, compared with their Chinese peers, American children not only had a better grasp of emotion knowledge but also made more rapid progress in such knowledge across the preschool years.

Together, these findings indicate that emotional memory sharing between parents and children manifests in nuanced versions across cultures in transmitting to children culture-specific knowledge about emotion and ways of personal reminiscing. For Euro-American parents, emotions constitute an important aspect of the child's self and therefore need to be fully explained and elaborated upon in order to facilitate the child's emotional understanding and individuality. Their rich emotional explanations may contribute to the early acquisition of emotion knowledge in American children. Such knowledge, in turn, helps children understand emotional meanings of past events and efficiently organize their personal memories for later retrieval. Indeed, American children as young as age two and a half are capable of forming coherent and meaningful representations of events that are personally significant and precipitate emotions (Liwag & Stein, 1995; Stein & Liwag, 1997; Stein, Trabasso, & Liwag, 1993). In contrast, for Chinese parents, emotions are consequences of children's social acts and therefore are instrumental for reinforcing in the child proper behavioral conduct and a sense of connectedness. Their didactic conversations about emotional events may inhibit the child's development of emotional understanding and, in turn, their remembering of significant personal experiences over the long term.

Thus, current cross-cultural data suggest the impact of divergent early cultural-familial contexts on children's development of emotion knowledge and the possible influence of such knowledge on personal remembering. Furthermore, they have important implications for the findings that European and Euro-American adults are able to recall childhood memories that are earlier-dated and more emotionally elaborate than those of Asians (MacDonald et al., 2000; Mullen, 1994; Wang, 2001a; Wang & Conway, submitted). To corroborate these findings, Wang and colleagues are currently launching a longitudinal cross-cultural study that intends to establish the developmental connection between emotion situation knowledge and autobiographical memory and to further substantiate the importance of culturally-situated early narrative environments in which children are raised.

CONCLUSION: AUTOBIOGRAPHICAL REMEMBERING AS CULTURAL PRACTICE

The emerging segment of sociointeractionist research reveals diverse family narrative environments across cultures, which reflect varied cultural orientations focusing on individual autonomy or on interpersonal relatedness (Miller et al., 1996, 1997; Mullen & Yi, 1995; Wang et al., 2000; Wang, 2001b). During memory conversations, European American parents often play a supportive role, encouraging the child to provide memory information, discussing the causes and consequences of emotions, and focusing on the feelings, predilections, and opinions of the child who was cast as the central character of the story. In contrast, East Asians parents tend to play a central and directive role in posing memory questions and emphasizing moral rules and behavioral expectations to the child. These early differences in the structural organization and semantic content of parent-child reminiscing in Euro-American and Asian families, in turn, show long-term consequences on children's developing autobiographical memory.

By taking different cognitive styles and socioemotional contents, parent-child reminiscing in Euro-American and East Asian cultures further maintain important functional variations (Wang, in press-a; Wang & Brockmeier, 2002). Instead of serving the purpose of helping children build individuality and construct a unique autobiographical history, as is often occasioned in Euro-American middle-class families, family discussions about the shared past in East Asian cultures primarily serve to establish a sense of belonging and proper behavioral conduct in children. Thus, within a larger cultural milieu (that promotes an orientation towards autonomy or relatedness), families preserve sociolinguistic environments in which children learn to co-narrate and, in this way, formulate stories of themselves. In doing so, they gradually acquire not only their parents' narrative repertoire but also their values and beliefs. As the data reveal, independent autobiographical accounts provided by children and adults in these cultures exhibit stylistic and content differences that reflect the dominant mode of narrative expression modeled in family reminiscing early on as well as the value systems characteristic of the surrounding culture.

Patently, the development of autobiographical memory is not an isolated individual product; nor is it solely constrained by the individual's immediate social environment. Family beliefs, customs, and practices of narrative discourse are deeply shaped by and inextricably intermingled within a multitude of social relations and societal institutions with organized material and symbolic systems of beliefs and values. Parent-child reminiscing, therefor, comprises culture-specific forms of social participation through which autobiographical memory takes shape and is further given culture-unique meaning and significance. Ultimately, culturally promoted practices of narrative interaction between parents and children assume an important forum of intergenerational transmission of, among others, genres of autobiographical remembering, which, in turn, actively reinforce, and are also reinforced by, culturally prevailing orientations towards autonomy or relatedness. As such, autobiographical remembering is, indeed, a cultural practice.

REFERENCES

Bond, M. H. (1991). *Beyond the Chinese Face*. Hong Kong: Oxford University Press.

Borke, H. (1971). Interpersonal perception of young children: Egocentrism or empathy. *Developmental Psychology, 5,* 263-269.

Bretherton, I. & Beeghly, M. (1982). Talking about internal states: The acquisition of an explicit theory of mind. *Developmental Psychology, 18,* 906-921.

Bretherton, I., Fritz, J., Zahn-Waxler, C., & Ridgeway, D. (1986). Learning to talk about emotions: A functionalist perspective. *Child Development, 57,* 529-548.

Bruner, J. (1990). *Acts of Meaning*. Cambridge, MA: Harvard University Press.

Chao, R. K. (1995). Chinese and European American cultural models of the self reflected in mothers' childrearing beliefs. *Ethos, 23, 3,* 328-354.

Chen, X., Hastings, P. D., Rubin, K. H., Chen, H., Cen, G., & Stewart, S. L. (1998). Child-rearing attitudes and behavioral inhibition in Chinese and Canadian toddlers: A cross-cultural study. *Developmental Psychology, 34, 4,* 677-686.

Choi, S. H. (1992). Communicative socialization processes: Korea and Canada. In S. Iwasaki, Y. Kashima, & K. Leung (Eds.), *Innovations in cross-cultural psychology* (pp. 103-122). Amsterdam: Swets & Zeitlinger.

Conway, M. A., & Bekerian, D. A. (1987). Situational knowledge and emotions. *Cognition and Emotion, 1, 2,* 145-191.

Denham, S. A., Zoller, D., & Couchoud, E. A. (1994). Socialization of preschoolers' emotion understanding. *Developmental Psychology, 30, 6,* 928-936.

Dunn, J., Bretherton, I., & Munn, P. (1987). Conversations about feeling states between mothers and their young children. *Developmental Psychology, 23, 1,* 132-139.

Dunn, J., Brown, J., & Beardsall, L. (1991). Family talk about feeling states and children's later understanding of others' emotions. *Developmental Psychology, 27, 3,* 448-455.

Fiske, A. P., Kitayama, S., Markus, H. R., & Nisbett, R. E. (1998). The cultural matrix of social psychology. In D. T. Gilbert, S. T. Fiske, & G. Lindzey (Eds.), *The handbook of social psychology*, vol. 2 (4th ed.) (pp. 915-981). Boston, MA: Mcgraw-Hill.

Fivush, R. (1993). Emotional content of parent-child conversations about the past. In C. A. Nelson (Ed.), Memory and affect in development. *Minnesota Symposia on Child Psychology, 26,* 39-77. Hillsdale, NJ: Erlbaum.

Fivush, R. (1994). Constructing narrative, emotions, and self in parent-child conversations about the past. In U. Neisser & R. Fivush (Eds), *The remembering self: construction and accuracy in the self-narrative* (pp. 136-157). New York: Cambridge University Press.

Fivush, R., Haden, C., & Adam, S. (1995). Structure and coherence of preschoolers' personal narratives over time: Implications for childhood amnesia. *Journal of experimental child psychology, 60,* 32-56.

Fivush, R. & Hamond, N. R. (1990). Autobiographical memory across the preschool years: Toward reconceptualizing childhood amnesia. In R. Fivush & J. Hudson (Eds.), *Knowing and remembering in young children* (pp. 223-248). New York: Cambridge University Press.

Fivush, R. & Hudson, J. (1990). (Eds.). *Knowing and remembering in young children.* New York: Cambridge Unviersity Press.

Fivush, R. & Schwarzmueller, A. (1998). Children remember childhood: Implications for childhood amnesia. *Applied Cognitive Psychology, 12,* 455-473.

Gauvain, M. (2001). Cultural tools, social interaction and the development of thinking. *Human Development, 44,* 126-143.

Geertz, C. (1973). *The interpretation of cultures.* New York: Basic Books.

Goodnow, J. J. (2000). Combing analyses of culture and cognition: Essay review of mind, culture, and activity. *Human Development, 43,* 115-125.

Han, J. J., Leichtman, M. D. & Wang, Q. (1998). Autobiographical memory in Korean, Chinese, and American children. *Developmental Psychology, 34, 4,* 701-713.

Harley, K. & Reese, E. (1999). Origins of autobiographical memory. *Developmental Psychology, 35, 5,* 1338-1348.

Hudson, J. A. (1990). The emergence of autobiographical memory in mother-child conversation. In R. Fivush & J. A. Hudson (Eds.), *Knowing and remembering in young children* (pp. 166-196). NY: Cambridge University Press.

Leichtman, M. D., Pillemer, D. B., Wang, Q., Koreishi, A. & Han, J. J. (2000). When Baby Maisy came to school: Mothers' interview styles and preschoolers' event memories. *Cognitive Development, 15,* 1-16.

Lewis, M. & Michalson, L. (1983). *Children's emotions and moods: Developmental theory and measurement.* New York, NY: Plenum Press.

Liwag, M. D., & Stein, N. L. (1995). Children's memory for emotional events: The importance of emotion-related retrieval cues. *Journal of Experimental Child Psychology, 60,* 2-31.

MacDonald, S., Uesiliana, K., Hayne, H. (2000). Cross-cultural and gender differences in childhood amnesia. *Memory, 8, 6,* 365-376.

Markus, H.R. & Kitayama, S. (1991). Culture and the self: Implications for cognition, emotion, and motivation. *Psychological Review, 98, 2,* 224-253.

Middleton, D. & Edwards, D. (1990). Conversational remembering: A social psychological approach. In D. Middleton and D. Edwards (Eds.), *Collective remembering* (pp. 23-45). CA: Sage Publications Inc.

Miller, P. J., Mintz, J., Hoogstra, L., Fung, H. & Potts, R. (1992). The narrated self: Young children's construction of self in relation to others in conversational stories of personal experience. *Merrill-Palmer Quarterly, 38, 1*, 45-67.

Miller, P. J., Fung, H. & Mintz, J. (1996). Self-construction through narrative practices: A Chinese and American comparison of early socialization. *Ethos, 24, 2*, 237-280.

Miller, P. J., Wiley, A. R., Fung, H. & Liang, C. H. (1997). Personal storytelling as a medium of socialization in Chinese and American families. *Child Development, 68*, 3, 557-568.

Mullen, M. K. (1994). Earliest recollections of childhood: A demographic analysis. *Cognition, 52, 1*, 55-79.

Mullen, M. K. & Yi, S. (1995). The cultural context of talk about the past: Implications for the development of autobiographical memory. *Cognitive Development, 10*, 407-419.

Nelson, K. (1993). Explaining the emergence of autobiographical memory in early childhood. In A. F. Collins, S. E. Gathercole, M. A., Conway, & P. E. Morris, (Eds.), *Theories of memory* (pp. 355-385). Hillsdale, NJ: Lawrence Erlbaum Associates, Inc.

Nelson, K. (1996). *Language in cognitive development: The emergence of the mediated mind.* New York: Cambridge University Press.

Peterson, C. & McCabe, A. (1994). A social interactionist account of developing decontextualized narrative skill. *Developmental Psychology, 30*, 937-948.

Pillemer, D. B. (1998). *Momentous events, vivid memories.* Cambridge, MA: Harvard University Press.

Pillemer, D. B. & White, S. H. (1989). Childhood events recalled by children and adults. In H.W. Reese (Ed.), *Advances in child development and behavior (Vol. 21)* (pp. 297-340). New York: Academic Press.

Reese, E., Haden, C. A., & Fivush, R. (1993). Mother-child conversations about the past: Relationships of style and memory over time. *Cognitive Development, 8*, 403-430.

Rogoff, B. (1990). *Apprenticeship in thinking: Cognitive development in social context.* Now York: Oxford.

Schank, R. (1982). *Dynamic memory: A theory of learning in computers and people.* Cambridge, MA: Harvard University Press.

Shantz, C. U. (1975). The development of social cognition. In E. M. Hetherington (Ed.), *Review of child development research.* Chicago: University of Chicago Press.

Shweder, R. A., Goodnow, J., Hatano, G., LeVine, R., Markus, H., & Miller, P. (1998). The cultural psychology of development: One mind, many mentalities. In W. Damon (Ed.), *The handbook of child psychology*, vol. 1 (5th ed., pp. 865-937). New York: Wiley.

Sigel, I. (2002). The psychological distancing model: A study of the socialization of cognition. *Culture and Psychology, 8, 2*, 189-214.

Stein, N. L., & Liwag, M. D. (1997). Children's understanding, evaluation, and memory for emotional events. In P. W. van den Broek, P. J. Bauer, & T. Bourg (Eds.), *Developmental spans in event comprehension and representation* (pp. 199-235). Mahwah, NJ: Lawrence Erlbaum Associates.

Stein, N. L., Trabasso, T., & Liwag, M. (1993). The representation and organization of emotional experience: Unfolding the emotion episode. In M. Lewis & J. M. Haviland (Eds.), *Handbook of emotions.* New York: The Guilford Press.

Tessler, M. & Nelson, K. (1994). Making memories: The influence of joint encoding on later recall by young children. *Consciousness and Cognition, 3,* 307-326.

Tomkins, S. S. (1979). Script theory: Differential magnification of affects. In C. B. Keasey (Ed.), *Nebraska Symposium on Motivation, 26,* 201-236. Lincoln: University of Nebraska Press.

Triandis, H.C. (1989). The self and social behavior in differing cultural contexts. *Psychological Review, 96, 3,* 506-520.

Valsiner, J. (2000). *Culture and Human Development.* Sage Publications.

Vygotsky, L. (1978). *Mind in Society.* Cambridge, MA: Harvard University Press.

Waller, W. (1938). *The family: A dynamic interpretation.* New York: The Dryden Press, Inc.

Wang, Q. (2001a). Cultural effects on adults' earliest childhood recollection and self-description: Implications for the relation between memory and the self. *Journal of Personality and Social Psychology, 81, 2,* 220-233.

Wang, Q. (2001b). "Did you have fun?": American and Chinese mother-child conversations about shared emotional experiences. *Cognitive Development, 16,* 693-715.

Wang, Q. (2002). Infantile amnesia reconsidered: A cross-cultural analysis. *Memory, 11, 1, 65-80.*

Wang, Q. (submitted). *The emergence of cultural self-construct: Autobiographical memory and self-description in American and Chinese children.*

Wang, Q. (in press-a). The cultural context of parent-child reminiscing: A functional analysis. In M. W. Pratt & B. Fiese (Eds.), *Family stories and the life course: Across time and generations.* Lawrence Erlbaum Associates.

Wang, Q. (in press-b). Emotion situation knowledge in American and Chinese preschool children and adults. *Cognition & Emotion.*

Wang, Q. & Brockmeier, J. (2002). Autobiographical remembering as cultural practice: Understanding the interplay between memory, self and culture. *Culture & Psychology, 8,* 45-64.

Wang, Q. & Conway, M. A. (submitted). *The stories we keep: Autobiographical memory in American and Chinese middle-aged adults.*

Wang, Q. & Leichtman, M. D. (2000). Same beginnings, different stories: A comparison of American and Chinese children's narratives. *Child Development, 71, 5,* 1329-1346.

Wang, Q., Leichtman, M. D., & Davies, K. (2000). Sharing memories and telling stories: American and Chinese mothers and their 3-year-olds. *Memory, 8, 3,* 159-177.

Wertsch, J. V. (1991). *Voices of the mind: A sociocultural approach to mediated action.* Cambridge: Harvard University Press.

In: *Topics in Cognitive Psychology*
Serge P. Shohov (Editor) pp. 117-133

ISBN 1-59033-836-7.
© 2003 Nova Science Publishers, Inc.

Chapter 7

THOUGHT SUPPRESSION IN PHOBIA:
SUCCESS AND STRATEGIES·

Lydia Fehm[*]
Dresden University of Technology
Department of Clinical Psychology and Psychotherapy

ABSTRACT

Many studies show that intended thought suppression often paradoxically leads to higher frequencies of unwanted thoughts. This effect has been linked to the development and/or maintenance of anxiety disorders. So far, the empirical evidence for thought suppression playing a major role in maintaining those disorders is inconsistent. One important issue is whether the ability to suppress unwanted thoughts is generally impaired or specifically for thoughts related to the disorder.

In a clinical study patients with agoraphobia and patients with social phobia were compared with a control group without mental disorders. All participants were instructed to suppress two target thoughts related to the respective central fear of the two disorders and one non-specific item. During the suppression period, all occurrences of unwanted thoughts had to be signaled. Agoraphobics showed a rather specific deficit in thought suppression, while social phobics seem to be characterized by a general impairment of mental control, affecting specific as well as non-specific stimuli. Strategies used during the suppression task did not differ between target thoughts nor groups. Interestingly, the majority of participants reported the use of more than one strategy to accomplish the task.

Key Words: Thought Control, Cognitive Processes, Agoraphobia, Social phobia

---

[*] This article includes results previously published in Fehm, L. & Margraf, J. (2002). Thought suppression: Specificity in agoraphobia versus broad impairment in social phobia? *Behaviour Research and Therapy, 40(1),* 57-66.

[*] Contact address: Chemnitzer Str. 46; D – 01187 Dresden, Germany; Phone: +49 - 351 - 4633 6989; Fax: +49 - 351 - 4633 6984; email: Lydia.Fehm@mailbox.tu-dresden.de

INTRODUCTION

Investigations of thought suppression and its strategies have found broad interest during the last years. The outset for investigating the effects of intended thought suppression can be traced back to 1987, when Daniel M. Wegner and his group published their article describing two studies (Wegner, Schneider, Carter & White, 1987). Participants were assigned to two experimental conditions: One group was instructed to suppress thoughts of a presented stimulus, a second group was to express stimulus thoughts (thoughts of a white bear, which lead to the expression "white-bear-studies"). In a second period, the conditions were interchanged between groups. Wegner and his group found that the instruction to suppress a thought was not only difficult to accomplish but moreover produced the opposite effect, resulting in an increased frequency of the formerly suppressed thought. The group described two possible paradoxical effects of thought suppression: first the augmentend frequency of the to be suppressed target thought already during the suppression period, which was named *immediate enhancement effect*, and second the so called *rebound effect*, which describes the elevated frequency of thoughts after withdrawal of the suppression instruction compared to a condition without former suppression instruction.

Since then many studies have investigated thought suppression, with variations in instructions for the expression period, in the method of thought sampling, and with different stimuli to suppress (ranging from personally irrelevant material like a white bear to recollections of personally relevant events in the past and from single words to stories or films). With regard to the rebound effect, these studies produced mixed results: Some authors found the rebound effect for personally non-relevant material (Clark, Ball & Pape, 1991; Rutledge, Hollenberg & Hancock, 1993; Kelly & Kahn, 1994, Study 2; Rutledge, Hancock & Rutledge, 1996; Wegner & Gold, 1995; Wegner et al., 1987; Wegner, Schneider, Knutson & McMahon, 1991; Wenzlaff, Wegner & Klein, 1991), while others found an increase in thought frequency only for personally relevant material (Smári, Birgisdóttir & Brynjólfsdóttir, 1995). Some authors found no rebound effect at all, but could demonstrate an immediate enhancement effect (Merckelbach, Muris, van den Hout & de Jong, 1991; Muris, Merckelbach & de Jong, 1993; Salkovskis & Campbell, 1994). Finally, some studies found neither of the two possible paradoxical effects of thought suppression (Kelly & Kahn, 1994, Study 1; Muris, Merckelbach, van den Hout & de Jong, 1992; Muris, Merckelbach, Horselenberg, Sijsenaar & Leeuw, 1997; Muris, de Jongh, Merckelbach, Postema & Vet, 1998; Salkovskis & Campbell, 1994; Smári, Sigurjónsdóttir & Sæmundsdóttir, 1994). As mere reviewing of the studies yielded no conclusive over-all picture concerning the significance of enhancement- and/or rebound-effects, Abramowitz, Tolin and Street (2001) conducted a meta-analysis to determine the strength of those effects with the help of statistical analyses. They found rather stable evidence for the rebound effect with a small to moderate effect size. The size of the effect was further affected by the method of measuring thought suppression and the nature of the target thought. It has to be noted that the meta-analysis was limited to studies including a non-suppression condition. As a consequence, just about half of the studies conducted with clinical or analogue populations was included.

The results first presented by Wegner stimulated not only research using the thought suppression paradigm but also influenced models of the development and especially the maintenance of mental disorders. As unwanted thoughts are the core features of generalized anxiety disorder (GAD; see DSM-IV, APA, 1994; Wells, 1995) and obsessive-compulsive disorder (OCD; e.g. Salkovskis, 1996; Clark & Purdon, 1993, 1995) paradoxical effects of thought suppression were discussed primarily for those. For these disorders prolonged efforts to suppress or control their unwanted thoughts (worries or intrusions) are assumed which leads to the unwanted effect of an increased frequency of the disturbing thoughts. When the person tries harder to suppress, the paradoxical effect will equally strengthen which constitutes a circulus vitiosus.

The possible role within the etiological and nosological model has now been investigated with a range of disorders, comprising GAD, OCD, post-traumatic stress disorder / acute stress disorder (PTSD / ASD), depression, addiction and phobias. Impaired mental control in clinical samples has been demonstrated at least partly for GAD (Becker, Rinck, Roth & Margraf, 1998), OCD (e.g. Janeck & Calamari, 1999; Tolin, Abramowitz, Przeworski & Foa, 2001), and PTSD / ASD (e.g. Harvey & Bryant, 1998; Shipherd & Beck, 1998).

For simple phobia, Muris et al. (1998) reported that dental phobics showed higher levels of intrusive and negative thinking during dental treatment than non-phobics. They also demonstrated that dental phobics engaged a lot more in thought suppression during dental treatment than a control group. They conclude that their results are "...consistent with the notion that thought suppression plays a role in psychopathological conditions such as the anxiety disorders" (p. 285) as previously formulated by Wegner (1989). In a second study the authors modified their assumptions. Their study of thought suppression in spider phobics (Muris et al., 1997) found only minimal effects of thought suppression increasing the frequency of spider-related thoughts. They argue that these results contradictive to their earlier statement may be explained with spider phobics coping with their fears predominantly in a behavioural way, so that effects in cognitive variables would be small. This is plausible, as a spider is a very concrete object of fear. But what would happen in phobic patients with more vague objects of fear, or with a wide variety of stimuli which evoke fear, as is the case with social phobia and agoraphobia?

The present study provides data investigating these phobias. A second aspect is of relevance: Is the cognitive mechanism possibly identified in the study specific for a certain disorder or would it be a general attribute of all individuals suffering from anxiety disorders?

In our study, two clinical groups with social phobia respectively agoraphobia were compared with a control group. As specificity was to be addressed, participants had to suppress thoughts of a situation relevant for the respective disorder as well as a non-specific thought.

METHOD

Assessment

Interviews

All patients were interviewed individually with the help of a structured interview, using the ADIS-R (Anxiety Disorders Interview Schedule - Revised; DiNardo & Barlow, 1988) in its german version (DIPS; Diagnostisches Interview bei Psychischen Störungen; Margraf, Schneider & Ehlers, 1991). The DIPS uses DSM-III-R criteria and explores anxiety disorders, eating disorders, affective disorders and substance misuse. It also contains a screening for psychotic disorders. For the control group the short version of the DIPS (Mini-Dips; Margraf,

1994) was applied. Both instruments show good reliability and validity (e.g. Margraf, Schneider & Spoerkel, 1991; Ruhmland, Fehm, Junkers & Margraf, 1995). Clinicial participants were interviewed by their future therapists, who had extensive training with the interview and were supervised weekly. Members of the control group were interviewed via telephone by trained interviewers.

Questionnaires

As a measure of general psychopathology the Symptom Checklist 90 - Revised was used (SCL-90-R; Derogatis, Lipman & Covi, 1973; German: Franke, 1995). Additional measures for anxiety and depression were the Beck Anxiety Inventory (BAI; Beck, Brown, Epstein & Steer, 1988; German: Margraf & Ehlers, in press), the Beck Depression Inventory (BDI; Beck & Steer, 1987; German: Hautzinger, Bailer & Keller, 1994) and the Social Phobia and Social Interaction Scales (SPS/SIAS; Mattick & Clarke, 1998; German: Stangier, Heidenreich, Berardi, Golbs & Hoyer, 1999). Strategies of thought control used in everyday life were assessed by the Thought Control Questionnaire (TCQ; Wells & Davies, 1994; German: Fehm, 1994). Two worry-related questionnaires assessed frequency and topics of worry: the Penn State Worry Questionnaire (PSWQ; Meyer, Miller, Metzger & Borkovec, 1990; German: Stoeber, 1995) and the Worry Domains Questionnaire (WDQ; Tallis, Eysenck & Mathews, 1992; German: Stoeber, 1995). State anxiety before the experimental procedure was assessed by the State version of the State Trait Anxiety Inventory (STAI; Spielberger, Gorsuch & Lushene, 1970; German: Laux, Glanzmann, Schaffner & Spielberger, 1981).

Participants

The sample consisted of three groups, each comprising 30 participants. Groups 1 and 2 were patients applying for treatment at a german outpatient center. They had either the primary diagnosis of social phobia (SP; DSM-III-R: 300.23; APA, 1987) or agoraphobia with a history of panic disorder (AG; DSM-III-R: 300.21), respectively. Members of the control group had no actual mental disorder or any history of panic attacks or anxiety disorders. They were recruited via newspaper advertisements and received a small financial compensation for their participation.

The groups did not differ in sex ratio or age. The two clinical groups were comparable in regard to the severity of the main disorder and the number of comorbid diagnoses. The additional diagnoses were mostly depressive disorders and specific phobias. Table 1 summarizes information about the sample.

Table 1. Sociodemographic and Questionnaire Data for the Sample

	agoraphobic group ($n = 30$)	social phobic group ($n = 30$)	control group ($n = 30$)	Differences
Men / women	14 / 16	14 / 16	14 / 16	-
Age	36.2	31.06	32.86	$F(2, 87) = 2.14$; n.s.
	(8.82)	(9.64)	(10.64)	
severity rating (1 - 8)	5.86	5.66	-	$t(58) = .64$
	(1.04)	(1.37)		n.s.
number of additional diagnoses	1.4	1.6	-	$t(58) = -1.19$
	(.72)	(.99)		n.s.
SCL-90-R total	.89 [a]	.77 [a]	.26 [b]	$F(2, 86) = 10.52$; ***
	(.64)	(.59)	(.42)	
BAI	26.96 [a]	17.20 [b]	4.56 [c]	$F(2, 86) = 42.66$; ***
	(13.0)	(8.8)	(4.1)	
BDI	12.21 [a]	14.22 [a]	3.43 [b]	$F(2, 86) = 12.96$; ***
	(9.5)	(10.7)	(4.64)	
SPS	19.90 [a]	33.08 [b]	5.96 [c]	$F(2, 72) = 38.40$; ***
	(12.6)	(14.4)	(6.1)	
SIAS	19.45 [a]	46.04 [b]	11.93 [a]	$F(2, 72) = 48.22$; ***
	(14.6)	(14.9)	(9.2)	

Note: Standard deviations appear in parentheses.
Abbreviations: SCL: Symptom Checklist; BAI: Beck Anxiety Inventory; BDI: Beck Depression Inventory; SPS: Social Phobia Scale; SIAS: Social Interaction Anxiety Scale.
***: $p < .001$. Different superscripts across rows indicate significant differences between group means (post hoc Tukey b-comparisons, $p < .05$)

Differences between questionnaire scores follow the assumptions, e.g. AG-patients scoring highest on the bodily anxiety symptom measure, and SP-patients scoring highest on social phobia measures (see table 1). Patients groups did not differ in general symptom stress measured by the SCL-90-R.

Design and Procedure

All participants had to suppress three different target thoughts. Two were related to the central fear of the two relevant anxiety disorders and a third related to a common worry domain (possible financial problems). This yielded a 3 x 3-factorial design, with one group factor and a within-subjects factor (target thought).

The target thoughts were presented as sentences beginning with "I" to allow a high degree of identification with the material. They read as follows: "I could be completely helpless and faint in a threatening situation" (agoraphobic fear), "I could completely disgrace myself in a threatening situation" (social phobic fear) and "I could get into a financial strait without my fault" (financial worry, unrelated to anxiety symptoms). The order of presentation of the three target thoughts was counterbalanced. No effects related to order of presentation were found ($\chi^2 = 2.17$, $df = 4$, $p = .702$).

After assessing the diagnostic status with the help of the interview and questionnaires, the experimental protocol began. The participant first read the sentence to be suppressed and completed ratings asking for the vividness of the image, the unpleasantness, the relevance, the associated tension and the frequency of this fear in daily life. The degree of each aspect was assessed with 11-point rating scales (e.g. 0 = "not vivid at all" to 10 = "very vivid"). Questions for frequency were asked openly. After the ratings the person was instructed to suppress the thought during the following five minutes. Each occurrence of thoughts related to the fear to be suppressed had to be signaled by pressing the computer mouse. Before starting the suppression task, the experimenter left the room to prevent possible activation of social fears, which could affect participants' concentration on the suppression task. For the same reason no recording devices (video or audio) were used. As a third precaution the version of the paradigm eliciting the least state anxiety was chosen, as indicated by a earlier work by our group (Fehm, Dilcher, & Margraf, 2001). This study compared the versions of thinking aloud and thinking silently during the suppression task. Thinking aloud was associated with a significantly higher amount of anxiety and excitement and a stronger tendency to avoid the situation. Consequently the "think silent" version of the paradigm was selected for this study.

After five minutes the experimenter re-entered the room and handed a new sheet with questions assessing the difficulty of suppressing the target thought (rating 0 – 10) and the percentage of time devoted to the thought against the instruction during the experimental period (0 – 100). This procedure was repeated for the remaining two target thoughts. The success of thought suppression was measured by three variables for each target thought: the number of button presses ("button presses"), the rating of difficulty ("difficulty suppressing"), and the percentage rating ("percentage of time").

After completion of three suppression tasks, participants were asked about the strategies they had used to accomplish the task. This was done for all three targets, starting with the last one, expecting best recall here. Strategies were assessed only after completion of all suppression tasks to ensure that presenting stategies would not enhance their use during the task. Five strategies were presented, for which the extent of use had to be rated on a 11-point scale (0 = "not at all" to 10 "very strong") for each target thought: "Thinking of objects in the room", "Thinking of a certain person", "Choosing a task in mind (e.g. counting)", "Thinking of a pleasant event" and "Thinking of an unpleasant event". In addition, participants had the opportunity to write down up to three other strategies and rate their use.

RESULTS

Pre-Experimental Ratings

State anxiety was measured by the State trait anxiety inventory (STAI) before and after the experimental procedure. A group comparison revealed no pre-experimental group differences in state anxiety (Agoraphobics: $M = 41.1$, $SD = 3.94$; Social phobics: $M = 40.7$, $SD = 4.79$; Controls: $M = 43.7$, $SD = 9.34$; $F(2, 87) = 1.74$, n.s.). This was important to ensure so that different levels of anxiety already existing before the suppression task could be ruled out as a possible reason for different reactions to the task.

As a second step the characteristics of the to be suppressed material were analyzed (vividness, unpleasantness, relevance, frequency and tension). As the two anxiety-related target thoughts were designed to tap a central fear of each anxiety disorder respectively differences in the ratings between groups were expected. The respective target sentence was expected to show the highest distinctions for the related disorder group, e.g. agoraphobics were expected to rate "their" target thought as more vivid, more unpleasant and more frequent than the other two groups. The third target thought was designed to be of equal relevance for all groups, so no differences between groups should emerge. The pattern of results followed our expectations: agoraphobics showed the highest scores for the agoraphobia-related target thought. The pattern was repeated with social phobic individuals and the social-phobic material. The control group showed the lowest means for both targets. For the non-specific target thought, there were no group differences in any of the variables. Means, standard deviations and comparisons for all ratings are displayed in table 2.

Table 2. Descriptive Ratings of the Experimental Material
(Means and Standard Deviations) and Comparisons

Variable	agoraphobic group		social phobic group		control group		Differences
	M	SD	M	SD	M	SD	F
Vividness							
ago	8.16[a]	2.05	4.70[b]	3.75	2.50[c]	2.91	$F(2, 87) = 27.45$; ***
soc	7.06[a]	2.84	8.10[a]	2.32	3.80[b]	3.52	$F(2, 87) = 17.50$; ***
fin	3.63	3.03	4.73	2.77	4.16	3.09	$F(2, 87) = 1.02$; n.s.
Unpleasantness							
ago	8.70[a]	1.91	4.73[b]	3.45	2.83[c]	3.45	$F(2, 87) = 29.29$; ***
soc	7.53[a]	2.67	9.20[b]	1.15	3.43[c]	3.63	$F(2, 87) = 36.50$; ***
fin	5.33	3.86	5.53	3.31	5.06	3.21	$F(2, 87) = .13$; n.s.
Tension							
ago	7.40[a]	2.44	3.20[b]	2.88	2.40[b]	2.87	$F(2, 87) = 28.82$; ***
soc	6.36[a]	2.96	6.70[a]	2.61	2.60[b]	2.62	$F(2, 87) = 20.74$; ***
fin	3.30	3.04	4.36	3.28	3.56	2.77	$F(2, 87) = .99$; n.s.
Relevance							
ago	8.78[a]	1.43	3.53[b]	3.71	1.03[c]	1.99	$F(2, 87) = 71.10$; ***
soc	6.96[a]	2.63	8.06[a]	2.42	1.90[b]	2.41	$F(2, 87) = 52.33$; ***
fin	4.21	3.54	4.93	3.18	3.86	3.41	$F(2, 87) = .77$; n.s.
Frequency per day							
ago	6.08[a]	8.26	1.90[b]	4.57	0.16[b]	0.59	$F(2, 87) = 9.29$; ***
soc	3.33[a]	4.02	5.68[b]	10.44	0.43[a]	0.72	$F(2, 87) = 4.94$; **
fin	1.01	3.63	0.65	0.84	0.60	0.89	$F(2, 87) = .32$; n.s.

Note: ago: Agoraphobia-related sentence; soc: Social phobia-related sentence; fin: non-specific sentence
***: $p < .001$; **: $p < .01$
Different superscripts across rows indicate significant differences between group means (post hoc Tukey b-comparisons, $p < .05$)

Manipulation Check

To check if participants followed the instructions, two self-ratings were used: After each suppression period, the participants rated their effort to follow instructions correctly. After all three suppression periods they were again invited to retrospectively rate their motivation to comply for each of the three periods. Both ratings were delivered on a 11-point scale, with 10 being the highest expression of the variable. Ratings of effort to suppress for each of the three target thoughts were high: Agoraphobia-related thought: $M = 8.5$ ($SD = 2.2$), Social phobia-related thought: $M = 8.5$ ($SD = 2.1$), thought of financial threat: $M = 8.8$ ($SD = 1.8$). Ratings of motivation were somewhat lower, but still in a high range: Agoraphobia-related thought: $M = 7.7$ ($SD = 2.6$), Social phobia-related thought: $M = 7.4$ ($SD = 2.9$), thought of financial threat: $M = 7.8$ ($SD = 2.7$). Therefore, there were no signs to doubt participants' motivation to follow the instructions to suppress their thoughts as asked.

Group Differences in Thought Suppression

Three variables could be used to determine the success of thought suppression: The number of button presses during the task ("button presses") and ratings of the difficulty of suppression the target ("difficulty suppressing") and the percentage of the experimental time spent thinking about the forbidden target ("percentage of time"). Those variables were intercorrelated rather highly, but nevertheless seem to tap different aspects of thought suppression, as the correlation is far from perfect. Intercorrelations vary between .58 to .78 ($M = .67$).

Most of the participants were not completely able to fulfill the suppression instruction, thus replicating common findings. Only three participants of the agoraphobic group and four participants of the control group had no button press in any of the three target thoughts. As some authors exclude those subjects from data analysis (e.g. Becker et al.,1998) the scores for motivation to comply with instructions and for the effort to suppress were inspected. Those revealed no doubts, that these participants might have ignored the experimental instructions or were unwilling to follow them, so all participants were included in all analyses. Means and standard deviations for the three dependent variables across groups are displayed in table 3.

Table 3. Means and Standard Deviations of the Three Dependent Measures

Variable	agoraphobic group		social phobic group		control group	
	M	SD	M	SD	M	SD
number of button presses						
ago	6.80	8.25	7.55	11.20	1.70	2.16
soc	5.30	4.69	9.58	10.20	2.03	2.29
fin	3.20	4.59	7.44	6.99	2.33	2.35
difficulty suppressing (0 – 10)						
ago	5.13	2.52	3.70	2.87	1.43	1.63
soc	4.33	2.24	5.66	2.95	2.23	2.09
fin	2.16	2.21	3.83	2.58	2.70	2.64
percentage of time (0 – 100)						
ago	21.00	23.74	17.93	24.25	3.76	6.50
soc	17.66	16.03	24.10	25.40	4.93	6.41
fin	8.80	14.42	15.03	17.37	5.76	7.50

Note: ago: Agoraphobia-related stimulus; soc: Social phobia-related stimulus; fin: non-specific stimulus

First, all groups and all target thoughts were analyzed together for each of the three dependent measures with analyses of variance with one factor "group" and one repeated-measures factor "target thought". To determine the importance of possible differences, the effect size measure f was computed (cf. Cohen, 1988).

For all three variables a significant effect of group as well as a significant interaction was found ("button presses ": Group: $F(2, 86) = 8.98, p < .001, f = .38$; Interaction: $F(4, 172) = 2.56, p < .042, f = .13$; "difficulty suppressing": Group: $F(2, 87) = 13.35, p < .001, f = .40$; Interaction: $F(4, 174) = 10.42, p < .002, f = .33$; "percentage of time": Group: $F(2, 87) = 7.80, p < .002, f = .35$; Interaction: $F(4, 174) = 4.09, p < .004, f = .16$).

With respect to group and interaction effects reported above, the results indicated the existence of generally impaired mental control, reflected by a main effect of group as well as a specifically impaired control, reflected by a significant interaction of target thought and group. As both clinical groups were analyzed together this might have hidden different patterns of results existing in the groups. Therefore, further analyses contrasting each of the clinical groups separately to the control group were carried out.

Those results differed between the clinical groups: For the agoraphobic sample, again significant effects for group as well as a significant interaction emerged ("button presses ": Group: $F(1, 58) = 9.49, p < .004, f = .34$; Interaction: $F(2, 116) = 7.30, p < .002, f = .19$; "difficulty suppressing": Group: $F(1, 58) = 17.21, p < .001, f = .39$; Interaction: $F(2, 116) = 19.20, p < .001, f = .39$; "percentage of time": Group: $F(1, 58) = 13.14, p < .002, f = .39$; Interaction: $F(2, 116) = 9.29, p < .001, f = .21$). The effect sizes for the interactions ($.19 < f < .39$) were somewhat smaller than group effects ($.34 < f < .39$), but still in the moderate range.

A different pattern emerged comparing the social phobics with the control group. Strong effects for group differences emerged with effect sizes ranging between .43 and .45. Looking for interaction effects only one of the three dependent variables ("difficulty suppressing") yielded a significant difference, which was rather small ("button presses ": Group: $F(1, 57) = 16.43, p < .001, f = .44$; Interaction: $F(2, 114) = 1.09$, n.s.; "difficulty suppressing": Group: $F(1, 58) = 22.57, p < .001, f = .45$; Interaction: $F(2, 116) = 4.66, p < .02, f = .19$; "percentage of time": Group: $F(1, 58) = 15.36, p < .001, f = .43$; Interaction: $F(2, 116) = 2.98$, n.s.). For both comparisons, the clinical groups had higher indices of problems with thought suppression (see table 3).

Thus, the clinical groups seem to be differentially affected in their ability of mental control: Whereas patients with agoraphobia seem to be exclusively impaired while controlling thoughts related to their main fear, patients with social phobia exhibit problems in suppressing anxiety-related thoughts as well as thoughts without relation to their disorder.

Group Comparisons for the Non-Specific Thought

The target thoughts related to the central fears of an anxiety disorder were expected to show differences between groups. But the non-specific target thought of a financial strait should allow group comparisons as it was comparably relevant to all three groups and also comparable in all characteristics assessed during the pre-experimental ratings (e.g. vividness, unpleasantness, or frequency per day; see above).

However, inspection of the means (see table 3) showed differences between groups for the financial thought, with the social phobic group having higher scores than the other two groups. These differences were statistically significant for all three dependent measures ("button presses": $F (2, 86) = 8.82$, $p < .001$; "difficulty suppressing": $F(2, 87) = 3.51$, $p < .03$; "percentage of time": $F(2, 87) = 3.54$, $p < .03$).

Post hoc comparisons revealed that for all measures the social phobics differ significantly from at least one other group.

Expressions of Worry

As the three groups apparently differed in their ability of thought suppression, different measures of worry were compared between groups. The intensity and frequency of worry, measured by the Penn State Worry Questionnaire differed significantly between groups: Agoraphobic group: $M = 49.9$, $SD = 12.0$; Social phobic group: $M = 52.5$, $SD = 12.7$; Control group: $M = 34.5$, $SD = 11.9$; $F (2, 74) = 17.61$, $p < .001$. But post-hoc comparisons between groups revealed differences only between the clinical groups and the control group respectively, but no difference between the two clinical groups could be found.

Concerning different worry topics as measured by the Worry Domains Questionnaire, the domain of financial worry seemed of special interest: no group differences at all were found (Agoraphobic group: $M = 4.0$, $SD = 4.0$; Social phobic group: $M = 4.6$, $SD = 3.5$; Control group: $M = 4.8$, $SD = 3.9$; $F (2, 74) = .29$; n.s.), showing again the comparability for the groups.

Strategies of Thought Control

Strategies of thought control were assessed in two ways: First, by using the five categories of thought suppression strategies in daily life asked for in the Thought Control Questionnaire (TCQ; Wells & Davies, 1994). Second, by investigating participants′ control strategies directly after the experimental suppression task.

To assess thought control strategies in general the three groups were compared regarding their scores in the five subscales of the TCQ. Results are presented in table 4.

Table 4. Thought Control Strategies Used in General
(Means, Standard Deviations and Differences between Groups)

TCQ-subscale	agoraphobic group (n = 22)		social phobic group (n = 23)		control group (n = 30)		Differences
	M	SD	M	SD	M	SD	F
Distraction	14.68	3.41	14.47	3.13	16.87	4.12	$F(2, 72) = 3.58$ $p < .04$
Social Control	13.04	1.93	14.08	2.55	12.66	2.72	$F(2, 72) = 2.23$ n.s.
Worry	9.45	3.01	9.67	2.83	9.56	3.27	$F(2. 72) = .03$ n.s.
Punishment	11.04	2.96	10.87	3.24	9.46	3.44	$F(2. 72) = 1.92$ n.s.
Re-appraisal	12.95	3.57	13.78	3.20	13.50	4.96	$F(2. 72) = .24$ n.s.

Note: TCQ: Thought control questionnaire

Significant differences between groups emerge only for the subscale "Distraction", but post-hoc comparisons fail to show significant differences between two of the subgroups. It has to be concluded that the three groups use the strategies presented by the TCQ with nearly the same frequency.

As a second approach to assess strategies of mental control the use of strategies during the experimental task was analyzed. Five strategies of thought control had been presented after the suppression task: "Thinking of objects in the room", "thinking of a certain person", "choosing a task (e.g. counting)", "thinking of a pleasant event" and "thinking of an unpleasant event" and one open question. More than half of the participants answered to the open question (52.2% for the financial target thought, 55.6% for the agoraphobia-related target thought, 58.9% for the social phobia-related target thought). Their answers were categorized which yielded six further categories: "Planning" (e.g. planning the rest of the day), "daily life" (e.g. thinking of events of the day), "using relaxation techniques", "lyrics" (e.g. repeating a poem), "dreaming" and "thought stopping". For each target thought up to five answers could not be classified into one of the categories (e.g. "I thought about different things") and were not included in the analysis. Some of the answers could be classified according the five given answers, and were assigned to the appropriate category (e.g. "thinking of my children" was classified into "thinking of a certain person"). For the present analysis a strategy was included if the rating was three or higher on a 0 to 10 scale.

Among the strategies presented explicitly, "Thinking about things in the room", "Thinking about a certain person" and "Thinking about a pleasant event", were used most frequently (used by 56, 53 rsp. 46% of the participants, scores averaged over target thoughts). "Thinking of an unpleasant event" was by far the strategy used least frequently. Among the strategies noted in the open question, "Planning" was the most frequent (18%); rarely used were "Thought stopping" (around 2%), "Relaxation", "Dreaming" (each around 4%) and "Lyrics" (around 5%).

Comparisons of strategies used for the different target thoughts revealed no differences between target thoughts. When groups were compared with regard to their use of each strategy, likewise no differences could be found. Thus, the use of a certain strategy seems to be unrelated to diagnostic status or to the target of thought suppression.

Number of Strategies used during the Task

As previous studies reported the use of more than one strategy to accomplish thought suppression, the number of strategies used during one suppression period was computed. Table 5 shows the numbers of different strategies used in each of the suppression periods.

Table 5. Number of Different Strategies Used in Each Suppression Period

target thought	agoraphobia-related	social phobia-related	control
	(n / %)	(n / %)	(n / %)
Number of strategies			
0	1 / 1.1	5 / 5.6	7 / 7.8
1	23 / 25.6	16 / 17.8	18 / 20.0
2	20 / 22.2	33 / 36.7	35 / 38.9
3	33 / 36.7	25 / 27.8	19 / 21.1
4	12 / 13.3	10 / 11.1	9 / 10.0
5	1 / 1.1	1 / 1.1	2 / 2.2

The majority of participants reported more than one strategy, with five different strategies being the maximum. It also has to be noted that a small proportion of participants is classified as not having used a strategy at all. This group may include participants using strategies not presented in the list, and who did not answer the open question as well as participants being unwilling or unable to report about their strategies.

Associations of Strategies and Success of Thought Suppression

To explore whether any of the strategies would be of particular use for the task of thought suppression correlations between the strategies and the three facets of thought suppression were computed. Results are shown in table 6.

Table 6. Associations between Strategies and Success of Thought Suppression

variable	button presses (n = 89)		rating of difficulty (n = 90)		percent of target period (n = 90)	
Strategy	r	p	r	p	r	p
objects in the room	-.17	.11	-.01	.92	-.04	.75
certain person	.17	.10	.13	.21	.23	.03
task (e.g. counting)	.02	.83	.01	.90	-.04	.74
pleasant event	.31	.01	.24	.02	.26	.01
unpleasant event	.07	.52	.07	.50	.04	.69
making plans	-.24	.03	-.28	.01	-.24	.03
relaxation	.03	.82	-.15	.15	-.11	.29
lyrics	-.07	.53	-.08	.43	-.06	.56
thought stopping	.21	.05	.22	.04	.14	.20
dreaming	-.07	.88	.03	.76	-.04	.69
daily life	.02	.43	.08	.44	.06	.57

Note. For better readability significant associations are printed in italics.

"Thinking of a pleasant event" and "Planning" were linked significantly to the outcome of thought suppression for all three target thoughts. Interestingly, only "Planning" seemed to facilitate the task as indicated by negative correlations. Thinking of a pleasant event, in contrast, was associated with more button presses, higher ratings of the difficulty of suppression and a higher proportion of time spent thinking about the forbidden target thoughts.

As predicted by Wegners theory, thought stopping as a strategy was associated with negative success of thought suppression, although the association reached significance only for the agoraphobia-related target thought.

DISCUSSION

One major aim of the study was to establish whether phobic patients show specific, disorder-related impairments in controlling their thoughts, or if anxiety patients have general deficits in thought control. Results revealed different patterns for the two clinical groups assessed in this study: Patients with agoraphobia showed a circumscribed effect of impaired mental control being prominent mainly for the disorder-related target thought when compared to a control group. In contrast, social phobics seem to be generally impaired in controlling unwanted negative thoughts.

As a possible explanation for the results different levels of state anxiety caused by the experimental situation have to be considered. A socially anxious person might feel more pressure to perform well and so might exhibit a higher degree of anxiety, which in turn would affect efforts of mental control. As state anxiety was measured before the experimental procedure this possible mediating variable could be ruled out: No group differences emerged before the experimental investigation.

Thinking silent poses less stress on the participants and no recording devices were used. During the thought suppression task, the experimenter left the room, to prevent being regarded as a possible critical observer. Consequently, the impact of individual differences in susceptibility to critical evaluation on the results should be low. Rather it seems, that social anxiety itself may be associated with problems in mental control.

A second part of the study investigated the role of the strategies used for thought suppression. Two strategies showing significant associations were identified: Engaging in planning is associated with facilitated thought suppression and thinking of pleasant events is related to worse performance in the suppression task. The number of strategies used was unrelated to the success of thought suppression. As these are only correlational results recommendations of certain strategies should not be inferred - this would require an experimental design.

One might have noticed that the three dependent variables used as indicators for the success of thought suppression yielded slightly differing results. Only a few studies employed multiple measures of thought suppression (e.g. Muris et al., 1993; Smári et al., 1995; Muris et al., 1997; Tolin et al., 2001), and likewise reported asynchrony of measures. One plausible explanation is that these variables reflect different aspects of thought suppression. Maybe, some remarks made by participants during the suppression task can help to explain the differences: Some of them described the target thought as turning up "in the background". The thought was reported to be not really present, so no need to press the button was felt, but nevertheless it seemed difficult to suppress the thought completely. A second aspect may be data format, that the subjectively rated difficulty was assessed as a continuous variable, whereas a button press demands a decision if the threshold for pressing has been crossed. As to date, none of the variables can be validated by external measures (e.g. electrodermal activity or cerebral activation). Therefore it can not be deducted which measure is more valid. Thus it seems recommendable to use multiple indicators of thought suppression to tap all different aspects of the task and its success.

An important limitation of the study has to be noted: As the study took place in a natural clinical environment, it was felt that participants should not be involved in more than three suppression periods for reasons of possibly decreasing motivation with yet another task. A second reason was that the total time of the investigation should not be too long, as other investigations and assessments followed. Nevertheless it would have been interesting to include further target thoughts, e.g. a personal relevant but positively valent thought. This would allow to differentiate between disorder-related effects and effects resulting from emotionality more clearly. Likewise the inclusion of periods without suppression instruction would allow the determination of rebound effects, which is not possible with the design used in this study.

Future research should further address problems of measuring different facets of thought suppression as discussed above. To determine the role of thought suppression within the framework of mental disorders we need to know more about the relationship of thought suppression in an experimental setting and thought suppression in everyday life. A study by Fehm and Hoyer (submitted) showed no association between a measure of thought control strategies in daily life (Thought Control Questionnaire, TCQ; Wells & Davies, 1994) and the strategies used in an experimental suppression task. This may be the result of a different range of strategies being available during the experimental situation and in everyday life. But it could also point to the possibility that asking for the habitual use of thought suppression strategies provides only little predictive power for actual reactions to a suppression task.

REFERENCES

Abramowitz, J. S., Tolin, D. F., & Street, G. P. (2001). Paradoxical effects of thought suppression: A meta-analysis of controlled studies. *Clinical Psychology Review, 21*, 683-703.

American Psychiatric Association (Ed.) (1987). *Diagnostic and statistical manual of mental disorders (3rd ed. revised; DSM-III-R)*. Washington,DC: American Psychiatric Press.

American Psychiatric Association (Ed.) (1994). *Diagnostic and statistical manual of mental disorders (4th ed.)*. Washington, D.C.: American Psychiatric Press.

Beck, A. T., Brown, G., Epstein, N., & Steer, R. A. (1988). An inventory for measuring clinical anxiety: psychometric properties. *Journal of Consulting and Clinical Psychology, 56*, 893-897.

Beck, A. T., & Steer, R. A. (1987). *Beck Depression Inventory Manual*. San Antonio, TX: The Psychological Corporation.

Becker, E. S., Rinck, M., Roth, W. T., & Margraf, J. (1998). Don't worry and beware of white bears: Thought suppression in anxiety patients. *Journal of Anxiety Disorders, 12*, 39-55.

Clark, D. M., Ball, S., & Pape, D. (1991). An experimental investigation of thought suppression. *Behaviour Research and Therapy, 29*, 253-257.

Clark, D. A., & Purdon, C. (1993). New perspectives for a cognitive theory of obsessions. *Australian Psychologist, 28*, 161-167.

Clark, D. A., & Purdon, C. L. (1995). The Assessment of unwanted intrusive thoughts: A review and critique of the literature. *Behaviour Research and Therapy, 33*, 967-976.

Cohen, J. (1988). *Statistical power analysis for the behavioral sciences.* Hillsdale: Erlbaum.

Derogatis, L. R., Lipman, R. S., & Covi, L. (1973). The SCL-90-R: An outpatient psychiatric rating scale - preliminary report. *Psychopharmacology Bulletin, 9*, 13-28.

DiNardo, P. A., & Barlow, D. H. (1988). *Anxiety Disorders Interview Schedule - Revised (ADIS-R).* Albany, NY: Graywind Publications.

Fehm, L. (1994). *Thought Control Questionnaire (TCQ) - deutsche Übersetzung.* Unpublished manuscript, Dresden University of Technology.

Fehm, L., Dilcher, K., & Margraf, J. (2001). Die Unterdrückung unerwünschter Gedanken: Vergleich zweier Varianten eines Paradigmas [Suppression of unwanted thoughts: Comparing two versions of an experimental paradigm]. *Zeitschrift für Klinische Psychologie 30*, 189-193.

Fehm, L., & Hoyer, J. (2002). *Measuring thought control strategies: The Thought Control Questionnaire and a look beyond.* Manuscript submitted for publication.

Franke, G. H. (1995). *Die Symptom-Checkliste von Derogatis - Deutsche Version - Manual.* Göttingen: Beltz Test GmbH.

Harvey, A. G., & Bryant, R. A. (1998). The effect of attempted thought suppression in acute stress disorder. *Behaviour Research and Therapy, 36*, 583 - 590.

Hautzinger, M., Bailer, J., & Keller, F. (1994). *Beck-Depressions-Inventar (BDI).* Bern: Huber.

Janeck, A. S., & Calamari, J.E. (1999). Thought suppression in obsessive-compulsive disorder. *Cognitive Therapy and Research, 23*, 497-509.

Kelly, A. E., & Kahn, J. H. (1994). Effects of suppression of personal intrusive thoughts. *Journal of Personality and Social Psychology, 66*, 998-1006.

Laux, L, Glanzmann, P., Schaffner, P., & Spielberger, C. D. (1981). *Das State-Trait-Angstinventar. Theoretische Grundlagen und Handanweisung.* Weinheim: Beltz Test GmbH.

Margraf, J. (1994). *Diagnostisches Kurz-Interview bei psychischen Störungen (Mini-DIPS).* Göttingen: Hogrefe.

Margraf, J., & Ehlers, A. (in press). *Das Beck-Angst-Inventar (BAI).* Bern: Huber.

Margraf, J., Schneider, S., & Ehlers, A. (1991). *Diagnostisches Interview bei Psychischen Störungen (DIPS).* Berlin: Springer.

Margraf, J., Schneider, S., & Spoerkel, H. (1991). Therapiebezogene Diagnostik: Validität des Diagnostischen Interviews bei Psychischen Störungen. *Verhaltenstherapie, 1*, 110-119.

Mattick, R. P., & Clarke, J. C. (1998). Development and validation of measures of social phobia scutiny fear and social interaction anxiety. *Behaviour Research and Therapy, 36*, 455-470.

Merckelbach, H., Muris, P., van den Hout, M., & de Jong, P. (1991). Rebound effects of thought suppression: Instruction-dependent? *Behavioural Psychotherapy, 19*, 225-238.

Meyer, T. J., Miller, M. L., Metzger, R. L., & Borkovec, T. D. (1990). Development and validation of the Penn State Worry Questionnaire. *Behaviour Research and Therapy, 28*, 487-495.

Muris, P., de Jongh, A., Merckelbach, H., Postema, S., & Vet, M. (1998). Thought suppression in phobic and non-phobic dental patients. *Anxiety, Stress and Coping*, *11*, 275-287.

Muris, P., Merckelbach, H., Horselenberg, R., Sijsenaar, M., & Leeuw, I. (1997). Thought suppression in spider phobia. *Behaviour Research and Therapy*, *35*, 769-774.

Muris, P., Merckelbach, H., van den Hout, M., & de Jong, P. (1992). Suppression of emotional and neutral material. *Behaviour Research and Therapy*, *30*, 639-642.

Muris, P., Merckelbach, H., & de Jong, P. (1993). Verbalization and environmental cuing in thought suppression. *Behaviour Research and Therapy*, *31*, 609-612.

Ruhmland, M., Fehm, L., Junkers, C., & Margraf, J. (1995). Gütekriterien eines diagnostischen Kurzinterviews (Mini-DIPS) [Quality criteria of a diagnostic mini-interview (Mini-DIPS).] *Verhaltenstherapie*, *5 (Suppl 1)*, A 4.

Rutledge, P. C., Hancock, R. A., & Rutledge, J. H. (1996). Predictors of thought rebound. *Behaviour Research and Therapy*, *34*, 555-562.

Rutledge, P. C., Hollenberg, D., & Hancock, R. A. (1993). Individual differences in the Wegner rebound effect: evidence for a moderator variable in thought rebound following thought suppression. *Psychological Reports*, *72*, 867-880.

Salkovskis, P. M. (1996). Cognitive-behavioral approaches to the understanding of obsessional problems. In: R. Rapee (Ed.), *Current controversies in the anxiety disorders* (pp. 103-133). New York: Guilford Press.

Salkovskis, P. M., & Campbell, P. (1994). Thought suppression induces intrusion in naturally occurring negative intrusive thoughts. *Behaviour Research and Therapy*, *32*, 1-8.

Shipherd, J. C., & Beck, J.G. (1999). The effects of suppressing trauma-related thoughts on women with rape-related posttraumatic stress disorder. *Behaviour Research and Therapy*, *37*, 99-112.

Smári, J., Birgisdóttir, A. B., & Brynjólfsdóttir, B. (1995). Obsessive-compulsive symptoms and suppression of personally relevant unwanted thoughts. *Personality and Individual Differences*, *18*, 621-625.

Smári, J., Sigurjónsdóttir, H., & Sæmundsdóttir, I. (1994). Thought suppression and obsession-compulsion. *Psychological Reports*, *75*, 227-235.

Spielberger, C. D., Gorsuch, R. L., & Lushene, R. E. (1970). *Manual for the State-Trait Anxiety Inventory*. Palo Alto, CA: Consulting Psychologists Press.

Stangier, U., Heidenreich, T., Berardi, A., Golbs, U., & Hoyer, J. (1999). Die Erfassung sozialer Phobie durch die Social Interaction Anxiety Scale (SIAS) und die Social Phobia Scale (SPS) [Assessment of social phobia by the Social Interaction Anxiety Scale and the Social Phobia Scale]. *Zeitschrift für Klinische Psychologie*, *28*, 28-36.

Stoeber, J. (1995). Besorgnis: Ein Vergleich dreier Inventare zur Erfassung allgemeiner Sorgen. *Zeitschrift für Differentielle und Diagnostische Psychologie*, *16*, 50-63.

Tallis, F., Eysenck, M., & Mathews, A. (1992). A questionnaire for the measurement of nonpathological worry. *Journal of Personal and Individual Differences*, *13*, 161-168.

Tolin, D. F., Abramowitz, J. S., Przeworski, A., & Foa, E. B. (2002). Thought suppression in obsessive-compulsive disorder. *Behaviour Research and Therapy*, *40*, 1255-1274.

Wegner, D. M. (1989). *White bears and other unwanted thoughts: Suppression, obsession and the psychology of mental control*. New York: Viking.

Wegner, D. M., & Gold, D. B. (1995). Fanning old flames: Emotional and cognitive effects of suppressing thoughts of a past relationship. *Journal of Personality and Social Psychology*, *68*, 782-792.

Wegner, D. M., Schneider, D. J., Carter, S. R., & White, T. L. (1987). Paradoxical effects of thought suppression. *Journal of Personality and Social Psychology*, *53*, 5-13.

Wegner, D. M., Schneider, D. J., Knutson, B., & McMahon, S. R. (1991). Polluting the stream of consiousness: The effect of thought suppression on the mind's environment. *Cognitive Therapy and Research*, *15*, 141-152.

Wells, A. (1995). Meta-Cognition and worry: A cognitive model of Generalized Anxiety Disorder. *Behavioural and Cognitive Psychotherapy*, *23*, 301-320.

Wells, A., & Davies, M. I. (1994). The Thought Control Questionnaire: A measure of individual differences in the control of unwanted thoughts. *Behaviour Research and Therapy*, *32*, 871-878.

Wenzlaff, R. M., Wegner, D. M., & Klein, S. B. (1991). The role of thought suppression in the bonding of thought and mood. *Journal of Personality and Social Psychology*, *60*, 500-508.

ACKNOWLEDGEMENTS

The author would like to thank Dr. Eni S. Becker for helpful comments to a earlier version of the manuscript.

.

In: *Topics in Cognitive Psychology*
Serge P. Shohov (Editor) pp. 135-150

ISBN 1-59033-836-7.
© 2003 Nova Science Publishers, Inc.

Chapter 8

EFFECTS OF TRAINING ON THE TIMING OF SIMPLE REPETITIVE MOVEMENTS

Gisa Aschersleben[*]

Max-Planck Institut für Psychologische Forschung,
München, Deutschland

ABSTRACT

Most research on the important role of knowledge of results has been done on continuous spatiotemporal movements like in tracking tasks. However, few studies concentrate on the effects of training and feedback in discrete timing tasks. In the introduction, we shall give an overview of studies examing the timing of movements in different tasks like the coincidence-anticipation task and the synchronization task as well as the effects of training in these tasks. Then, a study is presented that analyzes the influence of knowledge of results on the timing of repetitive movements in a sensorimotor synchronization task. Informative feedback about the asynchrony between keypress and pacing signal is presented to test the hypothesis that the availability of augmented feedback is a precondition for learning in such timing tasks. The results obtained in the experiments clearly show that informative feedback is highly effective in reducing the (usually observed) anticipatory tendency, whereas no practice effects were obtained when subjects tapped without getting any feedback at all or with non-informative visual feedback. Furthermore, the presentation of a minimal information set (feedback on the achievement of a critical interval) proved to be rather effective. However, it was only after the presentation of complete information, that is, feedback on the size and direction of the asynchrony, that it disappeared completely. The results are interpreted as support for an account assuming that the timing of movements is controlled more effectively if attention is directed to the intended outcome rather than to its intrinsic (e.g. kinesthetic) feedback.

---

[*] Inquiries or requests for reprints should be sent to: Gisa Aschersleben, Max-Planck-Institut für psychologische Forschung, Postfach 340121, D-80098 München, Germany, Tel.: +int(89)38602-251; Fax: +int(89)38602-250, email: aschersleben@psy.mpg.de, http://www.mpipf-muenchen.mpg.de/~aschersleben

INTRODUCTION

It has now long been accepted that knowledge of results plays an important informational role in motor skill acquisition (e.g., Adams, 1971; Salmoni, Schmidt, & Walter, 1984; for a recent overview see Wulf & Shea, 2002). Most research has been done on continuous spatiotemporal movements like in tracking tasks. However, few studies concentrate on the role of knowledge of results in discrete timing tasks. Examples for such discrete timing tasks are the coincidence-anticipation task or the synchronization task. In the coincidence-anticipation task, the subject is instructed to intercept a moving stimulus with a motor response at a predetermined position. By comparing different movement types, Williams and Jasiewicz (2001) showed that a simple key press with a finger is superior to either an arm movement or whole-body movement responses. In line with this finding, Gagnon, Bard, and Fleury (1990) report that in children timing biases (temporal constant errors) increase with increased complexity of the motor response. Several studies examine the effects of practice on the timing of movements in the coincidence-anticipation task (e.g., Bard, Fleury, Carrière, & Bellec, 1981; Gagnon et al., 1990; Haywood, 1975; Magill, Chamberlin, & Hall, 1991). Only minimal practice effects have been observed in coincidence tasks involving a simple motor response (button-press; Bard et al., 1981). However, knowledge of results (KR) has been proven to be an important variable for the learning of this timing task. Although Magill et al. (1991) and Williams and Jasiewicz (2001) demonstrated that, verbal knowledge of results was redundant for learning an anticipation timing skill and concluded, that the coincidence-anticipation task provides enough information in itself to produce adequate performance, provided that visual feedback is available, other studies were able to demonstrate an influence of KR on temporal performance in adults (e.g., Del Rey & Liu, 1990) as well as in children (Gagnon, Fleury, & Bard, 1988; Ramella, 1984).

Another discrete timing task in which, however, the subject is required to time simple *repetitive* movements, is the sensorimotor synchronization task. Here, subjects are asked to synchronize their finger-taps with a sequence of periodically repeated clicks, that is, they have to time their actions in a way that they coincide with certain events. In tasks such as these it is usually observed that subjects are unable to synchronize their actions with the external event exactly – the tap leads the click by about 20 to 50 ms ("synchronization error" or "negative asynchrony"; see, e.g., Aschersleben & Prinz, 1995, 1997; Fraisse, 1980; Kolers & Brewster, 1985; Mates, Radil, & Pöppel, 1992; Repp, 2000; for a recent overview, see, Aschersleben, 2002). The actual size of the asynchrony depends to a great extent on the experimental conditions under study. Mainly, two types of manipulations have been studied: features of the sensory feedback of the tap and features of the pacing signal. For example, adding external auditory feedback leads to a decrease in asynchrony (e.g., Aschersleben & Prinz, 1995, 1997; Mates & Aschersleben, 2000; Mates et al., 1992) whereas eliminating tactile feedback by local anesthesia results in an increase in asynchrony (Aschersleben, Gehrke, & Prinz, 2001). Studies manipulating sensory feedback of the tap support accounts that stress the importance of sensory effects on the timing of movements (for an overview, see, Aschersleben, 2002). In addition, in a number of studies features of the pacing signal were manipulated like its modality (Kolers & Brewster, 1985; Müller, Aschersleben, Schmitz, Schnitzler, Freund & Prinz, 2003), its duration (Vos, Mates, & van Kruysbergen, 1995), the duration of the interstimulus interval (Gehrke, 1996; Peters, 1989; Pressing, 1998), and the structure of the interstimulus interval (Thaut, Rathbun, & Miller, 1997; Wohlschläger &

Koch, 2000). Vos and co-workers (1995), for example, systematically manipulated the duration of the pacing signal and report a decrease in asynchrony with increasing duration. Thaut et al. (1997) tested the idea that the asynchrony might be dependent on the fact that different to music (where the intervals between two beats are filled with a number of tones), the interval between successive stimuli in synchronization experiments is usually empty. They asked subjects not only to tap in synchrony with a simple metronome but to a piece of music as well and observed a reduction in the amount of asynchrony under the latter condition.

The size of the asynchrony depends to a great extent on individual factors as well. The mean asynchrony observed in a specific person can be very small, thus, close to zero (positive asynchrony are rarely observed). However, there are repeatedly persons showing negative asynchronies in the order of 100 ms without being aware of this huge anticipatory tendency. One important factor influencing the size of the negative asynchrony is musical experience. Musically untrained persons reveal an asynchrony that is, on average, 10 ms larger than the asynchrony of persons who indicate to play an instrument as a hobby (Aschersleben, 1994). Even more clearly is the influence of musical experience in highly trained musicians (students at a music academy; Ludwig, 1992) or professional musicians (e.g., pianists). Among those there are occasionally people who are able to tap in exact synchrony (see, e.g., Repp, 1999).

The aim of the present study was to analyze the influence of practice on the asynchrony systematically. Our hypothesis was that the availability of unequivocal feedback is the important factor that makes people learn to overcome the anticipatory error. In everyday life, people are highly capable of synchronizing their movements with the occurrence of a stimulus (e.g., in shooting or in playing an instrument in an orchestra). However, it takes them several years of practice (i.e., thousands of trials) to become an expert and, for example, to be able to play an instrument in an orchestra. If our hypothesis is valid, subjects should be unable to do so in our laboratory experiments unless they are presented with knowledge of results (KR), that is, with informative feedback about their performance. However, if we present KR in synchronization experiments subjects should learn to overcome their anticipatory tendency and, after some period of training, the asynchrony should disappear.

Recent studies have indicated that feedback is ineffective if it is redundant with the performer's intrinsic feedback (Magill et al., 1991; Vereijken & Whiting, 1990). Vereijken and Whiting (1990) demonstrated that augmented feedback about, for example, movement amplitude in a ski-simulator task produced no learning benefits compared with those of practice without feedback. Presumably, the feedback did not provide any information that performers could not pick up directly. Magill et al. (1991) found that providing learners with verbal knowledge of results during practice did not result in more effective performance or learning than practice without KR. Thus, if the feedback does not provide augmented information beyond what can be derived from the learner's intrinsic feedback, it does not seem to result in additional learning advantages. Concerning the feedback given in the present study one could also argue that it is redundant with the performers' tactile and kinesthetic feedback, as the latter already provides the temporal deviation of the onset of the keypress from the onset of the pacing signal. In that, one assumes that subjects are able to refer to the distal events (i.e., take into account any processing times) and their timing in the distal world (which grounds on the basic principle that our cognitive system subtracts the system's own-generated contributions through some form of inverse computation; Epstein, 1973).

On the other hand, there are models assuming that the anticipatory error in synchronization tasks results from differences in peripheral and/or central processing times between keypress and pacing signal (e.g., Aschersleben & Prinz, 1995; 1997; Aschersleben, Stenneken, Cole, & Prinz, 2002; Fraisse, 1980; Gehrke, 1996; Mates, 1994; Paillard, 1949; for an overview see Aschersleben, 2002). It can be argued that informative feedback about the asynchrony in synchronization experiments (and about performance in motor tasks in general) is a necessary precondition for the cognitive system to learn to take into account its own-generated contributions (i.e., processing times). A demonstration that practice with informative feedback results in a reduction of the anticipatory error would support such an account.

Studies on the effects of knowledge of results in repetitive timing tasks are rare (e.g., Gallego, Ankaoua, Camus, & Jacquemin, 1986; Nagasaki, 1990), and, to our knowledge, there is no study examining the effects of informative feedback on synchronization performance. Nagasaki (1990), for example, studied practice effects on rhythm and variable error in periodic finger tapping, however, instead of analyzing performance in the synchronization phase, he was only interested in the following continuation phase, in which the metronome was switched off and the subjects were required to continue tapping at the same rate. Subjects were given knowledge of results on constant and variable errors in the intertap intervals with the result that a considerable reduction of variability error in timing was achieved by practice.

In the present study we presented informative feedback about the asynchrony between keypress and pacing signal to test the hypothesis that this augmented feedback is the precondition for learning in synchronization experiments, that is, to show that only after the presentation of KR subjects can overcome the anticipatory error and learn to tap in synchrony with the pacing signal. In the first experiment, subjects were given a minimal amount of KR, that is, they were only informed, if they tapped too early or too late. The second experiment was a control experiment with two groups of subjects. One subject group received no KR at all, the other group of subjects received the same kind of visual feedback as subjects in the first experiment, however, "KR" was not informative. In the third experiment, full information about the size and the direction of the asynchrony was given.

EXPERIMENT 1

In the first experiment we examined whether informative feedback has any effect on synchronization performance at all. We started with the presentation of a minimal information set, that is, subjects were informed after each single tap whether they had reached a defined criterion of synchrony. Thus, a kind of "bandwidth-KR" was presented, meaning that KR was given when the error exceeded a tolerance limit about the timing goal. Previous research has shown that the size of the bandwidth, itself, has an effect on learning (Lee & Carnahan, 1990; Sherwood, 1988). Sherwood (1988) found that subjects' performance increased with an increased bandwidth. As a consequence, we decided to use a bandwidth of 30 ms, which corresponds to the standard deviation usually observed within trials. Moreover, because of great interindividual differences in the mean asynchrony we had to make this criterion dependent on subject's individual performance both in the beginning and during consecutive sessions.

Method

Subjects

The sample consisted of 10 right-handed subjects (5 females and 5 males, mean age 27 years) who reported no sensory defects. None of them was musically trained.

Apparatus and Stimuli

Seated at a table in a sound-absorbing room, the subject was asked to tap with the index finger on a silent electrical contact switch. A wooden box covered the response apparatus and the responding effector, eliminating visual feedback. The auditory pacing signal (400 Hz, 82 dB[A], duration 10 ms) was presented binaurally through headphones (AKG K240, 600 ohm). A visual warning signal was presented by a red/green LED. A green square (10 mm square, duration 200 ms; 200 ms asynchrony between tap onset and square onset) appeared on a computer screen (EIZO 9070S) that was located in front of the subject (distance 60 cm). To cover external sounds, white noise (53 dB[A]) was used under all conditions. The stimuli were produced by a personal computer (Hewlett-Packard Vectra QS/20) via a D/A converter and an amplifier (Sony TA-F170). The computer controlled the experimental procedure and registered the onset of keypresses (with a resolution of 1 ms).

Procedure

There were 10 experimental sessions run on five consecutive days; that is, subjects completed two sessions a day. In the first session, the control condition without any KR was administered to establish the baseline. Subjects were asked to synchronize their taps with the clicks without getting any information about their performance. In the following eight sessions, after each tap feedback was provided by presenting a green square on the computer screen whenever the asynchrony of the last tap had reached a defined criterion. As there are usually large interindividual differences the criterion was dependent on the subject's performance. To determine the criterion we used an interval with a width of 30 ms. The lower limit of this interval was defined by computing the mean asynchrony of the last eight trials of the preceding session. The upper limit was computed by adding 30 ms to the lower limit. Whenever the subject produced an asynchrony within this critical range, the tap was followed by the green square, which indicated that the last tap had been correct according to the criterion. Whenever the subject produced an asynchrony beyond this range, the tap was not followed by the green square. Subjects were instructed to use the feedback as additional information and to make the square appear as often as possible. To measure immediate retention effects no feedback was presented in the last session.

Each session comprised 24 trials of 36 signals (interstimulus interval 800 ms). A single trial contained the following sequence of events: First, a green light signaled that the trial could be started. After pressing a key on the keyboard, the subject was continuously exposed to white noise, and the sequence of the pacing signals was started. The subject's task was to start tapping within the first three signals and then to tap along with the signal with the index finger as precisely as possible. At the beginning of each session, the subjects ran through eight warm-up trials (first and last session without feedback, from the second to the eighth session with KR).

Results

Data analysis started with the seventh signal in each trial. The first taps were not included because a minimum of three to five signals was required to pick up the beat. Hence, the means and standard deviations reported below always refer to the taps matching the remaining 30 signals in each trial. The means and standard deviations of asynchronies between tap onsets and click onsets were computed per trial. Negative values indicate that taps come first.

Mean asynchronies per trial were entered into a repeated measurement analysis of variance (ANOVA) with two within-subject factors: *session* (10 sessions) and *trial* (24 trials). Only one source of variance was significant: the main effect of *session*, $F(9,81) = 11.38$, $p <$ .001.[1] As there was no main effect of trial and no interactions involving this factor ($F < 1.0$), further analyses considered the averages of the 24 trials per session. Figure 1 (left-hand panel) shows the mean asynchrony in the 10 sessions. We observed a continuous reduction in asynchrony from −58 ms in the control session to −15 ms in the last session with KR (ninth session). The remaining asynchrony in this session was significantly different from zero ($t(9)$ = 2.3, $p <$ .05). In the very last session where KR was no longer presented, the amount of asynchrony slightly increased again ($M = -20$ ms; $t(9) = 3.5$, $p <$ .01), however, it was far from falling back to the level obtained in the first (control) session. We will come back to the results of this immediate retention test in Experiment 3 in which a delayed retention test was applied.

We analyzed the standard deviations of the mean asynchronies in the same way as the asynchronies and again one source of variance reached significance: the main factor *session*, $F(9,81) = 10.36$, $p <$ .001. We observed a continuous reduction from 34 ms in the control session to 23 ms in the last session with KR (see Figure 1, right-hand panel). In the very last session where KR was no longer presented, the standard deviation tended to increase again ($M = 25$ ms).

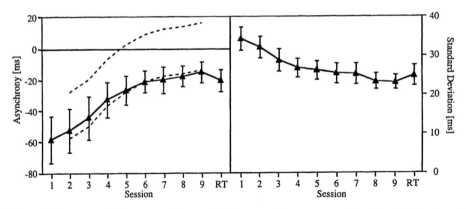

Figure 1: Averages and between-subject standard errors of the mean asynchronies (left-hand panel) and of the standard deviations of the mean asynchronies (right-hand panel) over 10 sessions (Experiment 1). Session 1 = control session without KR; RT = retention test without KR. Dashed lines show the mean limits of the critical interval.

---

[1] In order to avoid the risk of violating statistical assumptions in repeated-measures designs due to the inhomogeneity of the variance-covariance matrix, *p* values were corrected according to Geisser and Greenhouse (1958).

Discussion

In this first experiment with continuous feedback we were able to demonstrate an effect of practice on the amount of asynchrony: A significant reduction of the anticipatory error was observed when subjects were continuously exposed to informative feedback. Learning did not only show up in the asynchronies (constant error) but in the variable error (variability of the produced taps) as well. These results give a first indication that after the presentation of feedback subjects can – at least partly – overcome the anticipatory error and learn to tap more precisely.

However, two problems with the present results remain. First, the asynchrony did not disappear completely. One reason why the subjects did not reach zero asynchrony might be the kind of feedback we used. We presented a very small amount of information, that is, we only informed subjects whether they had reached a defined criterion or not. They never got any information about the size and the direction of their error. Another reason could be the instructions we gave to the subjects. They were instructed to synchronize click and tap *and* to use the green square as additional feedback. Some subjects were not able to follow both parts of the instructions, because making the green square appear on the screen meant that they had to tap too late, they reported. Experiment 3 addresses these two problems by using a completely different way to present KR and by changing the instructions.

The second problem concerns the interpretation of our data presented so far. We can in no way be sure that the informative feedback given to the subjects was the relevant factor that caused subjects to reduce their asynchrony over sessions. Perhaps, just tapping for a longer time leads to the same results. That is, until now we had confounded two factors, session and feedback, and do not know which was the effective one. To control for this, we conducted a control experiment in which subjects got no information about their performance at all. If we also observe a reduction in asynchrony over sessions we cannot maintain the interpretation that informative feedback was the relevant factor that caused learning in the first experiment.

EXPERIMENT 2

In Experiment 2, we had two groups of subjects tapping for 10 sessions without getting any information about their performance. To one group of subjects we presented no feedback signal at all (no feedback group: NF-group), and to the other group of subjects a non-informative visual signal was presented after each tap to control for the influence of the additional visual signal used in Experiment 1 (non-informative feedback group: NIF-group).

Method

Subjects

Eleven right-handed new subjects (6 females and 5 males, mean age 29 years) took part in the NF-group. In the NIF-group the sample consisted of 9 subjects (4 females and 5 males, mean age 28 years). None of the subjects reported sensory defects and none of them was musically trained.

Apparatus and Stimuli

The apparatus and stimuli were the same as in Experiment 1.

Procedure

For the subjects in the NF-group the experimental procedure was the same as in Experiment 1 with the exception that no feedback signal was presented at all, that is, subjects completed 10 identical (control) sessions. For the subjects in the NIF-group there was one control session without any feedback (session 1). During the following nine sessions the green square (see Experiment 1) was presented after each tap, irrespectively of the size of the asynchrony. To guarantee that the subjects looked at the screen during the whole experiment the color of the square randomly changed from green to blue (up to four times per trial). The secondary task of the subjects was to count these changes and to press a corresponding key on the keyboard after each trial.

Results

Mean asynchronies per trial were entered into two repeated measurement analyses of variance (ANOVA) with two within-subject factors: *session* (10 sessions) and *trial* (24 trials). No source of variance reached significance in either experiment ($p > .10$). The analyses of the standard deviations showed a slightly different picture. No source of variance reached significance for the NF-group ($F < 1$). For the NIF-group the factor session showed a significant effect [$F(9,72) = 6.44$, $p < .01$] indicating that there was a significant *increase* from the first to the second session, that is, when the secondary task was introduced (session 1: $M = 32$ ms. session 2: $M = 38$ ms). But within the following two sessions the original level was reached again (Scheffé test: Diffkrit = 6.57).

Discussion

We conducted this experiment with two control groups to test whether tapping over 10 sessions without getting any feedback or non-informative visual feedback reduces the anticipatory error. The answer is definitely no. In both groups there was not the slightest indication for a reduced amount of asynchrony (or of the standard deviation) after 10 sessions (i.e., after the production of about 10,000 taps). Furthermore, subjects usually were not aware of the fact that their taps were too early. But even if they were informed about the existence of that error – this was the case for several subjects in the NF-group – they were not able to learn to compensate for it during subsequent sessions. At the beginning of that experiment 7 out of 11 subjects knew that usually a negative asynchrony is observed in synchronization experiments. An ANOVA testing this group factor showed no difference between the two subjects groups ($F < 1.3$). Therefore, we have to conclude that the important factor that caused the significant changes in synchronization performance in Experiment 1 must have been the informative feedback.

EXPERIMENT 3

In Experiment 3 we come back to the idea that the kind of feedback we used in Experiment 1 was responsible for the remaining asynchrony in the last session. To test this consideration we presented the full information about the size and the direction of the error after each tap and, in addition, the mean values per trial after each trial. Furthermore, we changed the instructions and no longer insisted on the synchronization instruction because, as reported before, some subjects were not able to follow both parts of the instructions used in Experiment 1 (to synchronize tap and click *and* to use KR as additional feedback) because they were contradictory. Finally, we introduced a delayed retention test to determine the amount of learning over a longer period.

Method

Subjects

Nine right-handed new subjects (5 females and 4 males, mean age 25 years) who reported no sensory defects took part in the experiment. None of the subjects reported sensory defects and none of them was musically trained.

Apparatus and Stimuli

The apparatus and stimuli were the same as in Experiment 1 except for the stimulus we used to present the feedback. Instead of the green square a scale ranging from –100 ms to +100 ms was presented on the computer screen. After each tap a white bar (height 1 cm; duration 200 ms) indicated the size and the direction of the asynchrony produced by the last tap (see Figure 2).

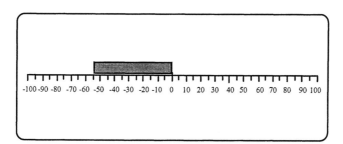

Figure 2: Illustration of the bar used in Experiment 3 to present knowledge of results (example of feedback presented after a tap that was produced 55 ms too early).

Procedure

The experimental procedure for the nine learning sessions (the first session again served as a control session without feedback) was the same as in Experiment 1 with the following exceptions: At the beginning of each trial we presented the scale on the computer screen. After each tap a white bar indicated the size and the direction of the last asynchrony. In addition, after each trial the mean asynchrony in that trial was presented on the screen. The subjects were instructed to reduce that error as much as possible. To measure the delayed retention effect we asked subjects to perfrom an additional control session (without giving feedback) two months later.

Results

The repeated measurement analysis of variance (ANOVA) with two within-subject factors *session* (10 sessions) and *trial* (24 trials) revealed one significant source of variance: the main effect of *session*, $F(9, 72) = 24.27, p < .001$. As there was no main effect of trial and no interactions involving this factor ($F < 1.0$), further analyses considered the averages of the 24 trials per session. Figure 3 (left-hand panel) shows the development of the mean asynchrony over 10 sessions. The remaining asynchrony in the last session ($M = -1.5$ ms) was no longer significantly different from zero ($t(8) = 1.76, p > .10$). In detail, eight out of nine subjects showed an asynchrony of less than 3 ms in the last session. To test the influence of informative feedback on the asynchrony in a direct comparison an additional analysis of variance was computed using the results of Experiment 2. This ANOVA with the between-subject factor *experiment* (the two subject groups in Experiment 2 were treated as two separate experiments) and the within-subject factor *session* revealed not only significant main factors but, more important, a highly significant interaction *experiment x session*, $F(9,162) = 7.01, p < .001$, indicating the differential influence of informative feedback on learning.

Because only 5 out of 9 subjects participated in the delayed retention test two months later, these results were analyzed separately. In the delayed retention test an increase in asynchrony was observed compared with the last session with feedback (session 10: $M = -2$ ms; retention test: $M = -19$ ms; $t(4) = 3.12, p < .05$).

The analysis of the standard deviation also revealed the factor *session* as being significant: $F(9, 72) = 7.14, p < .01$. In contrast to Experiment 1 there was an increase in the first session with KR (session 2: $M = 35$ ms) as compared to the control session (session 1: $M = 30$ ms) and only then a continuous reduction in the amount of the standard deviation (session 10: $M = 23$ ms; see Figure 3, right-hand panel).

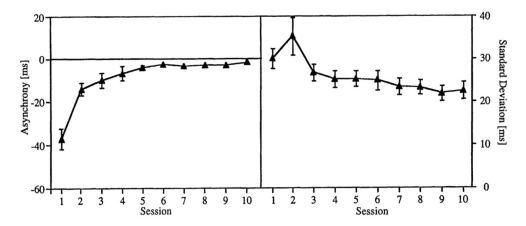

Figure 3: Averages and between-subject standard errors of the mean asynchronies (left-hand panel) and of the standard deviations of the mean asynchronies (right-hand panel) over 10 sessions (Experiment 3). Session 1 = control session without KR.

Discussion

First of all, this experiment can be regarded as a replication of the basic results obtained in Experiment 1. In both experiments with continuous feedback we were able to show an effect of practice: A significant reduction of the constant error (negative asynchrony) and the variable error (variability of the asynchrony) was observed when subjects were exposed to informative feedback. Furthermore, under conditions with full information about the asynchrony of the tap the anticipatory error disappeared completely. In the last session, the remaining asynchrony (−1.5 ms) was not significantly different from zero. The results of this experiment give further evidence for the idea that only after the presentation of informative feedback subjects can overcome the error. This interpretation is supported by the between-experiments analysis. The interaction between experiment and session was highly significant showing that simple practicing without feedback didn't have any effect at all while the presentation of informative feedback enables the subjects to learn to tap in synchrony with the pacing signal.

On the other hand, this synchronization task is not easy. First, subjects needed nine sessions with informative feedback to eliminate their synchronization error. Second, as suspected, subjects had problems handling this kind of feedback. This showed up in the tapping variability. In session 2 (the first session with KR) there was a clear increase in the standard deviations from 30 ms (in the first session) to 35 ms and only then a reduction (in session 3). Such an increase in variability was not observed in Experiment 1 and might be interpreted as a change in subjects' strategy. Because the task was much more difficult than that presented in the first experiment - subjects had a large amount of information to handle - they probably tried different strategies leading to an increase in variability. But within one session they settled on a strategy and performance became more stable again.

To study retention effects we asked subjects to do an additional control session two months later. In this delayed retention test we observed an increase in asynchrony as compared to the last session with feedback but it was still reduced as compared to the amount of asynchrony in the control session at the beginning. The same tendency was observed in Experiment 1 in an immediate retention test. These results indicate that the subjects had learned to tap more precisely and that this learning effect is a permanent one. However, the question remains why the asynchrony increased again. There are at least two possible anwers to this question. First, nine sessions might not be enough training to show permanent and stable changes in performance. Second, subjects may have fallen back into a different tapping strategy who on purpose had tapped "too late". These two points will be discussed in the General Discussion under the broader issue of action effect learning.

GENERAL DISCUSSION AND CONCLUSION

The aim of the present study was to analyze the influence of practice on the timing of simple movements in a synchronization task. The results obtained in the experiments clearly show that informative feedback is highly effective in reducing the synchronization error whereas there are no practice effects when subjects tap for 10 sessions without getting any feedback at all (Experiment 2, NF-group) or with non-informative visual feedback (Experiment 2, NIF-group). Even the presentation of a minimal information set (feedback on the achievement of a critical interval) proved to be rather effective (Experiment 1). Within nine sessions, subjects were able to reduce their asynchronies (from an average of 58 ms to 15 ms) when they received feedback directly after each tap on whether or not they had achieved a critical interval. However, it was only after the presentation of complete information, that is, feedback on the size and direction of the asynchrony, that it disappeared completely after 10 sessions (Experiment 3).

Furthermore, results demonstrate the limitations of the interval within which informative feedback can be integrated into structures controlling actions. In both experiments with informative feedback subjects lost the feeling of tapping in synchrony when they followed the KR instruction.[2] This observation is supported by the results of the immediate (Experiment 1) and the delayed (Experiment 3) retention tests. Subjects could not keep the level reached in the last session with KR but recurred to a different strategy. However, we still observed a reduction in asynchrony as compared to the first session. That is, the feedback not only had a temporary effect on performance, but in fact enhanced the learning of the task. Yet, a considerable performance decrement was seen when feedback was withdrawn. Similar effects in (delayed) retention have been reported by van der Linden, Cauraugh, and Greene (1993) and Winstein and co-workers (Winstein, Pohl, Cardinale, Green, Schlotz, & Waters, 1996), for example, who conclude that practice with concurrent feedback is beneficial for the immediate performance. However, for the learning of a sensorimotor skill feedback presented after task completion is superior (for an overview, see, Schmidt, 1991). The degrading effects of frequent and immediate feedback can be explained with the "guidance hypothesis" (Salmoni et al., 1984; Schmidt, 1991). According to this hypothesis, the learner develops a dependency on the feedback, thus, he or she is heavily "guided" by the feedback information. This dependency results in performance decrements when the feedback is not available anymore.

What can the results of the present study tell us about the control of movements in general? More than a century ago, James (1890) suggested that actions are controlled more effectively if attention is directed to the intended outcome of the action rather than to its intrinsic (e.g. kinesthetic) feedback. Experimental evidence for the negative effects of directing the performers' attention to their movements has been provided by Wulf and Weigelt (1997), who showed that giving learners body-related instructions reduced the learning of a ski-simulation task (for similar findings, see, Shea & Wulf, 1999). These results are in line with the "action effect hypothesis" proposed by Prinz (1997; see also Hommel, Müsseler, Aschersleben, & Prinz, 2001), according to which actions are planned and controlled by their intended action effects. By repeatedly performing a movement that produces perceivable external effects, actors may associate the responsible motor activity pattern with a code representing the to-be-expected action effects. Once formed, this link could be used to activate or select the motor pattern by activating the action-effect code.

In that context, feedback about the asynchrony given in the present study can be seen as a means to direct attention away from intrinsic kinesthetic and tactile feedback to the distal effects of the action (for a similar account see Wulf & Prinz, 2001). In the usual tapping task,

---

[2] Buekers, Magill, & Sneyers (1994) could show that it is possible to ignore the sensory feedback and to rely on informative feedback only. In their learning experiments subjects received (erroneous) informative feedback that was in conflict with their own sensory feedback. The results showed that if there was a conflict between two sources of feedback, then the externally presented verbal information took precedence over the sensory feedback, especially when subjects were uncertain about the validity of their own sensory feedback.

intrinsic feedback is the only source of action effect available to the subjects. However, when they are provided with informative feedback this might lead subjects to learn to take an external focus of attention and thus, relying their performance exclusively on the informative feedback. Such an interpretation is supported by a study in which the influence of KR on the production of short timing responses was examined. In a study with a deafferented patient, Fleury et al. (1994) could demonstrate the important contribution of proprioceptive afferents to timing regulations in the motor production of short durations. More importantly, the contribution of proprioceptive feedback could be rapidly compensated by knowledge of results, that is, the performance difference between normal subjects and the deafferented patient (who cannot rely on proprioception at all) disappeared.

REFERENCES

Adams, J. A. (1971). A closed-loop theory of motor learning. *Journal of Motor Behavior, 2*, 111-150.

Aschersleben, G. (1994). *Afferente Informationen und die Synchronisation von Ereignissen* [Afferent information and the synchronization of events]. Frankfurt: Lang.

Aschersleben, G. (2002). Temporal control of movements in sensorimotor synchronization. *Brain & Cognition, 48*, 66-79.

Aschersleben, G., & Prinz, W. (1995). Synchronizing actions with events: The role of sensory information. *Perception & Psychophysics, 57*, 305-317.

Aschersleben, G. & Prinz, W. (1997). Delayed auditory feedback in synchronization. *Journal of Motor Behavior, 29*, 35-46.

Aschersleben, G., Gehrke, J., & Prinz, W. (2001). Tapping with peripheral nerve block: A role for tactile feedback in the timing of movements. *Experimental Brain Research, 136*, 331-339.

Aschersleben, G., Stenneken, P., Cole, J., & Prinz, W. (2002). Timing mechanisms in sensori-motor synchronization. In W. Prinz & B. Hommel (Eds.), *Common mechanisms in perception and action: Attention and Performance, Vol. XIX* (pp. 227-244). Oxford: Oxford University Press.

Bard, C., Fleury, M., Carriere, L., & Bellec, J. (1981). Components of the coincidence-anticipation behavior of children aged from 6 to 11 years. *Perceptual & Motor Skills, 52*, 547-556.

Buekers, M. J., Magill, R. A., & Sneyers, K. M. (1994). Resolving the conflict between sensory feedback and knowledge of results, while learning a motor skill. *Journal of Motor Behavior, 26*, 27-35.

Del Rey, P. & Liu, X. (1990). The impact of knowledge of results with varying amounts of practice. *Journal of Human Movement Studies, 18*, 279-286.

Epstein, W. (1973). The process of "taking-into-account" in visual perception. *Perception, 2*, 267-285.

Fleury, M., Macar, F., Bard, C., Teasdale, N., Paillard, J., Lamarre, Y., & Forget, R. (1994). Production of a short timing responses: A comparative study with a deafferented patient. *Neuropsychologia, 32*, 1435-1440.

Fraisse, P. (1980). Les synchronisations sensori-motrices aux rythmes [The sensorimotor synchronization of rhythms]. In J. Requin (Ed.), *Anticipation et comportement* (pp. 233-257). Paris: Centre National.

Gagnon, M., Bard, C., & Fleury, M. (1990). Age, knowledge of results, stimulus speed, and direction as determinants of performance in a coincidence-anticipation task. In J. E. Clark & J. H. Humphrey (Eds.), *Advances in motor development research*, Vol. 3 (pp. 56-79). New York, NY: Ams Press.

Gagnon, M., Fleury, M., & Bard, C. (1988). Knowledge of results and spatial-temporal control in an anticipation-coincidence task among 6 to 10-yr-old children. *Canadian Journal of Psychology, 42*, 347-363.

Gallego, J., Ankaoua, J., Camus, J.-F., & Jacquemin, C. (1986). Synchronization and knowledge of results in a ventilatory motor task. *Perceptual & Motor Skills, 63*, 3-10.

Gehrke, J. (1996). *Afferente Informationsverarbeitung und die Synchronisation von Ereignissen* [Processing afferent information and the synchronization of events]. Dissertation at the Ludwig Maximilians University, Munich.

Geisser, S., & Greenhouse, S. W. (1958). An extension of Box's results on the use of F-distribution in multivariate analysis. *Annals of Mathematical Statistics, 29*, 885-891.

Haywood, K. M. (1975). Relative effects of three knowledge of results treatments on coincidence-anticipation performance. *Journal of Motor Behavior, 7*, 271-274.

Hommel, B., Müsseler, J., Aschersleben, G., & Prinz, W. (2001). The theory of event coding (TEC). A framework for perception and action planning. *Behavioral and Brain Sciences, 24*, 849-878.

James, W. (1890). *The principles of psychology.* New York: Holt.

Kolers, P. A., & Brewster, J. M. (1985). Rhythms and responses. *Journal of Experimental Psychology: Human Perception & Performance, 11*, 150-167.

Lee, T. D., & Carnahan, H. (1990). Bandwidth knowledge of results and motor learning: More than just a relative frequency effect. *Quarterly Journal of Experimental Psychology A, 42A*(4), 777-789.

Ludwig, C. (1992). *Experiment zur Synchronisation akustischer Führungssignale.* [Experiment on synchronization to auditory pacing signals]. Report at the Ludwig Maximilians University Munich.

Magill, R. A., Chamberlin, C. J., & Hall, K. G. (1991). Verbal knowledge of results as redundant information for learning an anticipation timing skill. *Human Movement Science, 10*, 485-507.

Mates, J. (1994). A model of synchronization of motor acts to a stimulus sequence. I. Timing and error corrections. *Biological Cybernetics, 70*, 463-473.

Mates, J. & Aschersleben, G. (2000). Sensorimotor synchronization: The influence of temporally displaced auditory feedback. *Acta Psychologica, 104*, 29-44.

Mates, J., Radil, T., & Pöppel, E. (1992). Cooperative tapping: time control under different feedback conditions. *Perception & Psychophysics, 52*, 691-704.

Müller, K., Aschersleben, G., Schmitz, F., Schnitzler, A., Freund, H.-J., & Prinz, W. (2003). *Modality-specific central control units in sensorimotor synchronization: a combined behavioral and magnetoencephalographic study.* Manuscript submitted for publication.

Nagasaki, H. (1990). Rhythm and variability of timing in periodic tapping. *Human Movement Science, 9*, 177-194.

Paillard, J. (1949). Quelques données psychophysiologiques relatives au déclenchement de la commande motrice [Some psychophysiological data relating to the triggering of motor commands]. *L'Année Psychologique, 48*, 28- 47.

Peters, M. (1989). The relationship between variability of intertap intervals and interval duration. *Psychological Research, 51*, 38-42.

Pressing, J. (1998). Error correction processes in temporal pattern production. *Journal of Mathematical Psychology, 42*, 63-101.

Prinz, W. (1997). Perception and action planning. *European Journal of Cognitive Psychology, 9*, 129-154.

Ramella, R. J. (1984). Effect of knowledge of results on anticipation timing by young children. *Perceptual & Motor Skills, 59*, 519-525.

Repp, B. H. (1999). Control of expressive and metronomic timing in pianists. *Journal of Motor Behavior, 31*, 145-164.

Repp, B. H. (2000). Compensation for subliminal timing perturbations in perceptual-motor synchronization. *Psychological Research, 63*, 106-128.

Salmoni, A. W., Schmidt, R. A., & Walter, C. B. (1984). Knowledge of results and motor learning: A review and critical appraisal. *Psychological Bulletin, 95*, 355-386.

Schmidt, R. A. (1991). Frequent augmented feedback can degrade learning: Evidence and interpretations. In J. Requin & G. E. Stelmach (Eds.), *Tutorials in motor neuroscience* (pp. 59-75). Dordrecht, Netherlands: Kluwer Academic Publishers.

Shea, C. H., & Wulf, G. (1999). Enhancing motor learning through external-focus instructions and feedback. *Human Movement Science, 18*, 553-571.

Sherwood, D. E. (1988). Effect of bandwith knowledge of results on movement consistency. *Perceptual and Motor Skills, 66*, 535-542.

Thaut, M. H., Rathbun, J. A., & Miller, R. A. (1997). Music versus metronome timekeeper in a rhythmic motor task. *International Journal of Arts Medicine, 5*, 4-12.

van der Linden, D. W., Cauraugh, J. H., & Greene, T. A. (1993). The effect of frequency of kinetic feedback on learning an isometric force production task in nondisabled subjects. *Physical Therapy, 73*, 79-87.

Vereijken, B., & Whiting, H. T. (1990). In defence of discovery learning. *Canadian Journal of Sport Sciences, 15*, 99-106.

Vos, P. G., Mates, J., & van Kruysbergen, N. W. (1995). The perceptual centre of a stimulus as the cue for synchronization to a metronome. *The Quarterly Journal of Experimental Psychology, 48*, 1024-1040.

Williams, L. R. T., & Jasiewicz, J. M. (2001). Knowledge of results, movement type, and sex in coincidence timing. *Perceptual & Motor Skills, 92*, 1057-1068.

Winstein, C. J., Pohl, P. S., Cardinale, C. Green, A., Schlotz, L., & Waters, C. S. (1996). Learning a partial-weight-bearing skill: Effectiveness of two froms of feedback. *Physical Therapy, 76*, 985-993.

Wohlschläger, A., & Koch, R. (2000). Synchronization error: An error in time perception. In P. Desain & L. Windsor (Eds.), *Rhythm perception and production* (pp. 115-127). Lisse: Swets & Zeitlinger.

Wulf, G., & Prinz, W. (2001). Directing attention to movement effects enhances learning: A review. *Psychonomic Bulletin & Review, 8*, 648-660.

Wulf, G., & Shea, C. H. (2002). Principles derived from the study of simple skills do not generalize to complex skill learning. *Psychonomic Bulletin & Review, 9*, 185-211.

Wulf, G. & Weigelt, C. (1997). Instructions in learning a complex motor skill: To tell or not to tell. *Research Quarterly for Exercise and Sport*, *68*, 362-367.

ACKNOWLEDGMENTS

We wish to thank Frank Miedreich for programming; Esther Löb and Renate Tschakert for collecting the data. Requests for reprints should be sent to Gisa Aschersleben, Max-Planck-Institut für Psychologische Forschung, Postfach 340121, D-80098 München, Germany. Email: aschersleben@psy.mpg.de URL: http://www.psy.mpg.de/~aschersleben

In: *Topics in Cognitive Psychology*
Serge P. Shohov (Editor) pp. 151-167

ISBN 1-59033-836-7.
© 2003 Nova Science Publishers, Inc.

Chapter 9

THE INFLUENCE OF VOCAL AND INSTRUMENTAL BACKGROUND MUSIC ON THE COGNITIVE PERFORMANCE OF INTROVERTS AND EXTRAVERTS

Adrian Furnham and Anna Stanley*
Department of Psychology
University College London, England

ABSTRACT

This study examined the effects of vocal and instrumental music upon the performance of introverts and extraverts on two different cognitive tasks. In the presence of either vocal or instrumental music or in silence, participants ($N = 87$) completed a reading comprehension and a phonological task. Following from Eysenck's theory of personality (1967), an interaction was predicted such that any background music would impair and enhance the performance of introverts and extraverts, respectively. A significant interaction was found only for the phonological task possibly because of ceiling effects on the reading comprehension task. As hypothesised, music impaired performance of introverts more than extraverts, but extraverts' performance was not enhanced by the music as predicted. A main effect of music was found for both of the tasks indicating performance was best when in silence and worst when vocal music was playing. The study also examined study habit preferences and found, as predicted, introverts reported preferring to study in environments free of distraction.

INTRODUCTION

Since the beginning of the 20th century researchers were interested in the possible benefits of music at work. During the 1940s and 1950s there was a flurry of interest as to whether music affected either morale (satisfaction) or productivity at work (Newman, Hunt

---

* Address correspondence to Prof. A Furnham, Department of Psychology, University College London, 26 Bedford Way, London WC1. E-mail: a.furnham@ucl.ac.uk.

and Rhodes, 1966) or both. Results showed that much depended on the type of music, as well as the particular task performed. In a review of the extensive work up to that point, Uhrbrock (1961) concludes the following:

1. Unqualified claims that increased production results from the introduction of music into the work situation are not proven.
2. The social implications of music in industry as an incentive system ultimately should be faced. A question may be asked, 'Is this a legitimate device that gives pleasure to workers and profit to employers?'
3. Feelings of euphoria during periods of music stimulation have a physiological basis, which is evidenced by changes in blood pressure that occur in some participants while listening to music.
4. Factory employees prefer working where music is played rather than where it is not played.
5. Not all workers like music while they work. From 1 to 10 percent are annoyed by it.
6. Quality of work can be adversely affected by the use of music in the work situation.
7. Instrumental, rather than vocal, music is preferred during working hours by the majority of workers.
8. There is a negative correlation between age and preference for work music.
9. At least three investigators have reported that young, inexperienced employees, engaged in doing simple, repetitive, monotonous tasks, increased their output when stimulated by music.
10. Evidence has been presented that demonstrates that experienced factory operators, whose work patterns were stabilized and who were performing complex tasks did not increase their production when music was played while they worked.
11. At times music has had an adverse effect on the output of individual employees, even though they reported that music was 'quite pleasant' (p.36).

Regarding the type of task in hand, music has been found to facilitate routine, monotonous tasks in an industrial setting (Smith, 1961; Fox, 1971; Wexley & Yukl, 1984), with fewer reported accidents (Hough, 1943) and an improvement in production quality (Kerr, 1945; Oldham, Cummings, Michel, Schmidtke & Zhou, 1995). For example, Fox and Embrey (1972) simulated a quality control function task where participants were required to examine small metal parts for objects for 30 minutes. They showed detection rates improved in the presence of music, particularly for the music selected by the participants themselves. The effect of music on more complex tasks has however yet to be fully determined, though it has repeatedly shown that noise leads to poorer performance on complex cognitive tasks (Loewen & Suedfeld, 1992). At present it is unclear if music has any effect at all on the performance of a *complex cognitive task*, though, there is little evidence to suggest this effect would be positive (Fox, 1971).

Many researchers (e.g. Burton, 1986; Kiger, 1989) have pointed out that improvement/impairment on a cognitive task depends on the type/style of music used as a background distracter (e.g. rock, classical, jazz), listener's preference (e.g. Parente, 1976; Burton, 1986), or familiarity (e.g. Hilliard & Tonin, 1979). Hilliard and Tonin (1979) found reading comprehension performance in the presence of familiar background music was significantly better than when the music was unfamiliar. Music can have different "informational load characteristics" (loudness, variety, tonal range, complexity) which alter the arousal invoked in the listener (Mehrabian, 1976). However, no researchers in this field have provided a clear operational definition of the meaning of high information load music. Kiger (1989) found participants who read in the presence of low-informational load music performed significantly better than did those in the presence of high informational load music. The consonant rhythms and melody of the low-informational load music was believed to have facilitated comprehension because it diverted less attention and allowed greater comprehension to the task.

Sogin (1988) examined the effect of different styles of background music (instrumental jazz, classical and popular) on college student's performance on a coding task. The style of music did *not* however have a significant effect on performance. The work of Geringer & Nelson (1979) and Wolfe (1983) offers an explanation for such a finding. When the music becomes a competing environmental stimulus in relation to another task, the music may be phased out of awareness or simply ignored. The person therefore attends to the primary task and tries to ignore the background sounds as much as possible. It appears the same position holds regardless of the style of music. Thus, it is not necessarily the genre of the music affecting performance, it is its propensity to produce arousal in the individual (thereby making it more difficult to ignore), whether it be via loudness, tonal range, complexity or variety (Mehrabian, 1976).

Over the past decade there was a flurry of research activity concerned with music and cognitive performance. Rauscher, Shaw and Ky (1993) demonstrated that specifically spatial-reasoning improved after exposure to a Mozart piano sonata. They hypothesised a direct neurophysiological primary effect to explain the phenomena. However, well over a dozen studies failed to replicate the effect, which is now dismissed as an anomaly (Steele, Bass & Crook, 1999). Strictly speaking the music was not a distracter but a mood-inducer but initially a specific process was described to explain how and why particular music has a particular effect on certain intellectual skills.

If it is the "arousing quality" of the music which is the key to it is distractibility, it follows that more easily aroused individuals will be differentially affected by the distraction than those that are less easily aroused. A series of studies by Furnham et al. (Furnham & Allass, 1999; Furnham & Bradley, 1997; Furnham, Trew & Sneade, 1999) and others (Belojevic et al, 2001) have examined this by focusing on the personality dimension of extroversion and Eysenck's (1967) theory. Eysenck (1967) describes and explains these differences between introverts and extraverts in terms of internal arousal, with introverts having a lower optimum cortical arousal level than extraverts. Hence, introverts and extraverts differ in the amount of externally derived stimulation they require to reach optimum point of arousal; introverts require less stimulation and are therefore, comfortable and attentive at much lower intensities of stimulation. If subjected to a stimulus that exceeds this threshold of excitation, the introvert will experience an inhibition of excitation and become over-stimulated environment and, hence, their performance will deteriorate. The extravert on the other hand, requires more stimulation and will therefore actively seek it in the environment. Such a proposal has been well-supported in the literature. Having examined the study habits of introverts and extraverts for example, Campbell and Hawley (1982) found that extraverts chose to study in the areas of the library where there was increased external stimulation, i.e. many other people and noise nearby, whereas introverts selected places away from any such distractions. It should be acknowledged, however, that in none of the above papers was the stimulation or arousal induced effect of any particular musical stimuli actually measured. In each instance it was judged arousing by the experimenters or a small group or else it fitted criteria supposedly arousing. This maybe seen as a criticism in these studies, specifically if they are interpreted in terms Yerke-Dodson laws.

Music at work has often been found to have a self-reported arousing effect on individuals (Smith & Morris, 1976; Fontaine & Schwalm, 1979). It follows therefore, that the potential distracting effects of specific music is expected to interact with the personality dimension of extroversion, which reflects individual levels of cortical arousal (Eysenck, 1967). Extraverts (low internal arousal) should perform better as their arousal would be increased to an optimum level. Introverts (high internal arousal) on the other hand, should perform more poorly as they would be over-stimulated. This is consistent with Vermolayeva-Tomina (1964) and the Russian theory of "negative induction". This suggests that in the highly aroused cortex (weak nervous system, introvert), attention to one stimulus decreases the sensitivity of the cortex to other stimulation. Vermolayeva-Tomina (1964) found those with a strong nervous system (extraverts) tended to learn more in distracting situations than those with a weak nervous system (introverts), and thus suggested that in the strong nervous system the absolute sensory threshold is lowered by concurrent stimulation in another modality, whereas in the weak nervous system, the absolute threshold is raised.

However, it should be acknowledged that it is quite possible that music (used as stimuli) could be extremely high in information load, arousal, distractibility (used here as synonyms) as to be supra-optimal for both introverts and extraverts. That is, the baseline arousal levels in a particular setting maybe so high that the music is "over" arousing even for extraverts. Equally, it maybe so low that it does not reach the optimal level for either introverts or extraverts. Certainly the theory asserts that the improvement among extraverts and the correspondent deterioration among introverts occurs only when the baseline and change arousal levels produce optimalization among extraverts and excess in introverts. Further some music like lullabies is designed specifically to reduce arousal and increase sleepiness.

Furnham and Bradley (1997) compared the performance of introverts and extraverts completing three cognitive tasks either in silence or in the presence of "pop music". Results showed a significant extroversion x background music interaction for two of the three tasks (reading comprehension and a memory test with delayed recall of 6 minutes). A significant interaction on a reading comprehension task was also found by Furnham, Gunter and Peterson (1994), this time with television as the distracting stimulus. All of these significant interactions indicated that extraverts performed better than introverts when in the presence of a distracter. A further study by Furnham and Allass (1999), varied the complexity of the musical distracter (simple/complex), predicting an interaction such that the musical distracter of increased complexity would result in an increase of extravert's and a decrease of introvert's, cognitive task performance due to the differential arousal levels of each. Such a significant interaction was obtained for three of the four cognitive tasks completed (both the immediate and the delayed memory tasks and an observation task). Results from these studies also appeared to indicate that the distraction effect was more pronounced on verbal than non-verbal tasks; and complex verbal tasks more than simple verbal tasks.

The majority of research in this area has focused on performance of tasks such as observation, memory and comprehension. The present study will ascertain if such an extroversion x musical distraction interaction extends to a different type of task: that of a phonological one. This will determine whether the effect is observed when both the stimulus (task) and the distracter (music) are in the same modality (audio). As well as this theoretical importance, this also has practical importance. For many occupations whereby listening is an essential component, (e.g. interpreters, telephonists, secretaries doing dictation), the effects of highly distracting environments on differing personality types may have strong implications for personnel selection. Previous research in the area suggests that performance of a complex task would be more negatively affected by the presence of a musical distracter, than performance of a simple task.

A second task used was that of a reading comprehension. This was selected not only because it has in the past been found to provide a strong interaction between extroversion and background music (e.g. Daoussis & McKelvie, 1986; Furnham, Trew & Sneade, 1999), but also because it will utilise many of the cognitive skills required for academic tasks (e.g. memory, concentration, interpretation and reading).

Further to the variation on the type of cognitive task used in the present study, it will also vary the musical distracter by comparing the distracting effect of vocal and non-vocal music. Vocals have been found to be particularly distracting (Belsham & Harman, 1977), possibly because their presence results in greater informational load of the music (Kiger, 1989). The idea that vocal music is more arousing and carries a greater information load that instrumental music needs to be demonstrated and is affect by many other factors such as the complexity and familiarly of the music. However, there is another reason why verbal music by be more distracting in this condition and this is due to the greater similarity of target and distractor stimuli (vocal music during a phonological task). According to Eysenck's (1967) theory, one would predict that introverts would find vocal music more distracting than non-vocal music as it has greater intrinsic potential to stimulate and arouse particularly if the music is familiar. Extraverts on the other hand, should benefit from the extra stimulation the vocals offer; therefore their performance should be greatest when exposed to this type of distracter.

In this study participants also completed a questionnaire on their study habits and musical preference. The questionnaire was devised to determine whether participants prefer to study with music on, whether they usually do this, the type of music they prefer to listen to when studying, the type of academic subject they usually study whilst listening to music, the volume of such music and so on. This was devised on the basis of previous research indicating factors such as these contribute to how distracted one is (e.g. Furnham & Bradley, 1997; Furnham, Trew & Sneade, 1999). It was assumed that many of these, e.g. how often one studies with music on, and whether this is preferred, will be predicted by the extroversion score. In the light of this previous research, extraverts should prefer to study with music on and should do so more often compared to introverts as they require more external stimulation than introverts to reach optimum functioning level (Eysenck 1967). Hence it may be that it is because extraverts are more *familiar* with studying to music that results in their better performance, rather than their different level of cortical arousal.

The hypothesis that extraverts will be more familiar with task-irrelevant sounds than introverts has interesting implications. There is a relevant literature on state-related learning which suggests affect can improve memory (Eich & Schooler, 2000). Thus, if extraverts are in a happier mood because of particular music it is possible their scores on memory based tests increase while the same music may have much less, even the opposite effect on introverts. Further, there is a literature on familiarity which suggests a mere exposure effect - such that the more frequent a person's exposure to a stimulus the more positive their attitude (Zajonc, 1984). Thus being in a more familiar setting (ie. doing cognitive tasks to music) extraverts maybe more comfortable and happy which may, in due course, effect the performance on those tasks.

The three main hypotheses are: first that the presence of background music will impair the cognitive test performance on both tests of introverts more than extraverts; Second that this effect will be magnified in the vocal music condition; Third that introverts will report preferences for low distraction environments when studying compared to extraverts.

METHOD

Participants

Eighty-seven participants from a mixed-comprehensive school in Dorset were selected to take part in the study. Fifty-seven of these were female and 30 were male, and were aged between 16 and 18 (mean=16.6 years, SD = 0.60). For all, English was their first language.

Materials

The NEO-5 factor inventory (Costa & McCrae, 1992) was used to measure not only the extroversion of each participant but also the other four personality factors of Costa & McCrae's "Big 5": conscientiousness, neuroticism, agreeableness and openness. This was used primarily to determine which of the participants were extraverts and which were introverts, but also enabled some exploratory analysis concerning whether musical distraction has a differing effect on performance of those high or low on other personality dimensions such as conscientiousness or neuroticism.

Participants completed a questionnaire on study habits and musical preference. This questionnaire was completed by all participants prior to the experiment enabling musical material to be selected on the basis of the most frequent preferences, i.e. genre and volume of music, hence increasing the ecological validity of the experiment. Participants were also asked to state their GCSE grades along with the two questionnaires in order to determine whether intelligence could be confounding any possible music x personality interaction.

The phonological task used consisted of a list of 75 words on an audiocassette, 38 of which were read by a female and 37 by a male. The words were selected at random from a newspaper with the only stipulation being that 25 of them had two syllables, 25 had three syllables, and the remaining 25 had four syllables. The number of each word (i.e. 1-75) was announced by a female voice before each word. The recording of the word list had a duration of 2 minutes and 30 seconds.

Participants had to identify and circle on an answer sheet the numbers of the words with *three* syllables. That is, they had only to indicate the presence of a 3 syllable word.

The reading comprehension consisted of a 400-word passage selected randomly from the "Financial Mail" section of the *Daily Mail* newspaper (14th September, 2000) and six multiple-choice questions about it (each with five alternative answers). The passage was selected on the basis that the vast majority of 16-18 year olds would be unlikely to have seen it before and is of a similar, mundane and neutral nature of the comprehensions used in academia, hence, again increasing the ecological validity of the task. Both the reading comprehension and the phonological tasks were piloted on a group of 10, 16-18 year olds, in order to ensure the tasks were of a suitable duration and difficulty. (Retrospectively, it would have been preferential to have a listening, rather than a reading comprehension task).

The music used in the study was selected on the basis of the preferences outlined by the participants in the study habits questionnaire, i.e. the most frequently preferred genre was selected. The following were the most frequently nominated: dance, soul, chart. On the basis of the preferences outlined, dance music was selected to be used in the study as more participants preferred to listen to it (25.3%) than any other genre of music. Two vocal and two non-vocal tracks within this genre were selected. These were matched as far as possible in terms of familiarity e.g. all appeared for equal duration and at a similar period in the U.K. chart (August-September, 2000). The tracks selected were as follows:

Vocal (always played in this order):
1) Spiller and Groovejet *"If this ain't love"*. Duration = 3 minutes, 45 seconds
2) Mel C *"I turn to you"*. Duration = 4 minutes

Non-vocal (always in this order):
1) Element 4 *"Big Brother TV theme"*. Duration = 3 minutes, 10 seconds
2) DaRude *"Sandstorm"*. Duration = 3 minutes, 5 seconds

Procedure

All participants were tested in their classes of between 8 and 12. The first stage of the study involved all participants completing the NEO-5 factor inventory and the study habits questionnaire. The results of these were analysed to determine the type of music to be used before the experimental procedure began.

Although different groups were tested in different classrooms (for the sake of convenience to the school), all windows, doors and curtains were kept closed to keep confounding distractions to a minimum. In all conditions, two audio cassette players were placed at the front of the classroom: one for the phonological word list to be played on and the other for the music. Participants were not exactly equi-distant from the speakers but efforts were made to ensure distances were roughly equal. The volume at which the cassettes were played remained constant throughout. The results of the study habits questionnaire revealed there was no significant difference between the number of participants preferring background music when studying to be at a high and those preferring it at a low volume, therefore the music was kept at a moderate volume throughout (which should be more distressing for introverted participants). Regrettably the decibel level was not recorded.

For the phonological task, the experimenter began by handing out a response sheet to each participant and reading aloud a list of standardised instructions outlining whether the participant was to circle or the numbers of words with three syllables. Having ensured all participants understood the task in hand; the experimenter began to play the music. At the moment the music began, (or immediately in the "silence" condition), the word list was played. The task ended when all the 75 words had been heard. Participants were then asked to indicate on a 10-point Likert scale at the bottom of their response sheet how distracted they were whilst doing the task (with 1 being "not distracted at all" and 10 being "very distracted").

For the reading comprehension task, the experimental procedure was similar, but this time, the participants were told they would have 6 minutes to read a passage and complete the multiple choice questions about it. The 6 minutes began at the moment the music started. As with the phonological tasks, upon completion of the tasks, participants were asked to indicate on the 10-point Likert scale how distracted they were. The duration of the whole experimental procedure was approximately 20 minutes. The order of the phonological reading tasks were counter-balanced.

In the reading comprehension task each of the six multiple-choice questions correctly answered was given 2 points. Just under 20% got a score of 8, while just under 60% got a score of 10 or less. In all 42.5% got the test totally correct. There was no difference between correct answers to the various questions. For the phonological task correct detection of a trisyllabic word received in 1 point. Any numbers of trisyllabic words not circled, resulted in deduction of one point. Hence, the maximum score was 25. The mean was 15.91 (SD = 5.87).

RESULTS

A. Main Analysis

Participants were classified as either introverted or extraverted on the basis of a median split of their extroversion scores on the NEO personality inventory. The median score was 31; therefore "introverts" were those scoring 31 or less ($n = 43$, mean score of group = 26.3, SD = 4.11) and "extraverts" were those scoring 32 or more ($n = 44$, mean score of 37.00, SD = 3.79). The terms "introvert" and "extravert" are more suited to describing subjects chosen from the extremes of the distribution of NEO extroversion scores but for convenience, they will be used here. The mean extroversion score for the participants was 31.50 (SD = 6.60), which is slightly above the British norm of 29.90 (SD = 6.57) for this age group (McCrae and Costa, 1985).

The mean score (and standard deviation) for introverts and extraverts in silent, instrumental and vocal conditions, for each of the tasks, can be seen in Table 1.

The data from each of the three tasks was analysed separately using 2 (introversion/extroversion) x 3 (silent/instrumental/vocal) between groups ANOVAs. For the reading comprehension task, there was a significant main effect of musical condition ($F_{(2,85)}$ = 7.90, p< 0.001), but no significant main effect of extroversion ($F_{(1,85)}$ = .10, ns) and no significant interaction between them ($F_{(2,85)}$ = 1.23, ns). For the phonological task, there was a main effect of musical condition ($F_{(2,85)}$ = 246.33, p<0.001), a main effect of extroversion $F_{(1,85)}$ = 59.32, p< 0.001) and a significant interaction between them ($F_{(2,85)}$ = 3.19, p< 0.05). Extraverts performed better than introverts in the presence of a musical distracter.

Despite the absence of a statistically significant interaction for the reading comprehension further ANOVAs were carried out using only the top and bottom quartiles of the extroversion scores ($n = 48$) and the extreme scores ($n = 28$). This did not however, alter the pattern of the results as the hypothesised interactions still failed to reach significance.

Table 1. The Mean Score and Associated Standard Deviations for Introverts and Extraverts in Silent, Instrumental and Vocal Conditions, for Each of the Tasks ($N = 87$)

Task		Introvert			Extravert		
		Silence	Instru-mental	Vocal	Silence	Instru-mental	Vocal
Reading compre-hension	Mean	11.53	9.14	10.15	11.20	10.00	9.50
	S.D.	1.12	2.68	1.52	1.03	2.14	1.71
	n	17	14	14	13	13	16
Phono-logical	Mean	21.5	13.25	7.87	23.18	17.20	12.78
	S.D.	3.42	2.14	1.30	1.33	0.83	1.09
	n	16	12	15	11	20	13

Table 1 shows that the reading comprehension test may have been too easy for these participants which may explain why there was no personality effect or significant interactions.

Paired t-test were conducted to determine whether the observed effects were due to some other difference between the two groups other than that associated with the differential arousal produced by the background music. There was no significant difference between the performance of introverts and extraverts in silence on any of the three tasks. Thus, it can be inferred any of the observed differences in task performance can be attributed to the effect of the musical distracter. Further paired t-tests were conducted to ascertain where the differences resulting in the main effect of music lay. The results can be seen in Table 2.

As can be seen in Table 2(a), the observed main effect of music for introverts in the comprehension task can be attributed to the difference between performance in silence and to music *per se* rather than the *type* of music playing. For both tasks, introverts performed better in silence than in the presence of music; the *type* of music made no difference. For introverts doing the phonology task, there was a significant difference between all three musical conditions. Introverts performed best in silence, followed by instrumental music, and least well when vocal music was playing.

As Table 2(b) indicates, performance of extraverts on the phonological task was significantly different in all three musical conditions. Performance was best when in silence, followed by instrumental music and worst when vocal music was playing. The effect of background music on the reading comprehension performance of extraverts was different however. There was a significant difference between vocal and silent conditions but not instrumental and silent or vocal and instrumental conditions. Thus, the *type* of music (i.e. whether it has vocals) not just the music *per se*, appeared to have a differential affect on performance of this task.

Table 2. The Results of Paired T-Tests Comparing the Effect of Musical Background on Performance of the Tasks for a) Introverts (n = 43) and b) Extraverts (n = 44)

a)   Introverts

Task	Conditions compared	df	t
Reading comprehension	Silence-vocal	12	2.64*
	Silence-instrumental	13	2.97*
	Vocal-instrumental	12	1.24
Complex phonological	Silence-vocal	14	13.9***
	Silence-instrumental	11	6.98***
	Vocal-instrumental	11	-9.61***

b)   Extraverts

Task	Conditions compared	df	t
Reading comprehension	Silence-vocal	9	3.21**
	Silence-instrumental	9	1.41
	Vocal-instrumental	14	-0.59
Complex phonological	Silence-vocal	8	11.66***
	Silence-instrumental	10	6.60***
	Vocal-instrumental	8	-3.42***

*** p<.001   ** p<.01   * p<.05

B. Reported Distraction

Simple regressions revealed that for both tasks, self-reports of how distracted participants reported to be, significantly predicted their performance. For the comprehension task, ($F_{(1,85)}$ = 5.15, p< 0.05), and for the phonological task ($F_{(1,85)}$ = 28.52, p< 0.001), the more distracted they reported to be, the less well they performed on the task. This can be seen as a manipulation check.

When the three tasks were collapsed, paired t-tests revealed all subjects reported they were more distracted by vocal music (t $_{(86)}$ = 10.73, p< 0.001) and instrumental music ($t_{(86)}$ = 11.02, p < 0.001) than when performing the task in silence. But for all participants there was no significant difference between vocal and instrumental music in terms of its capacity to distract.

Simple regressions were also used to determine whether any other factors such as school success or preference for background music on whilst usually studying, predicted task performance. In the absence of any IQ tests, subjects GCSE (General Certificate in Secondary Education equivalent to 10th grade) scores were taken as indices of school performance. For the comprehension task ($F_{(1,85)}$ = 3.48, ns), and the phonological task ($F_{(1,85)}$ = 1.08, ns), GCSE average did not significantly predict task performance. As to whether participants usually study with music on, performance on the comprehension task ($F_{(1,85)}$ = 1.07, ns), and on the phonological task ($F_{(1,85)}$ = 0.41, ns) was not significantly predicted by whether subjects usually study with music on. Thus, both school success and usual study habits can not be dismissed as confounding variables.

A simple regression however, did reveal that extroversion score significantly predicted preference for usual study with the music on ($F_{(1,85)} = 6.00$, $p < 0.05$). Those scoring high on extroversion (extraverts) preferred to study with background music significantly more than those scoring low on extroversion (introverts), ($t_{(86)} = 2.41$, $p < 0.05$). This would be predicted from the theory.

C. Study Habits

Results of the study habits questionnaire were subjected to a factor analysis, the results of which can be seen in Table 3.

As Table 3 shows, there are 5 interpretable factors: 1. *The presence of others;* whether there is a preference for working in groups or independently, 2. *The level of the distracter;* the familiarity of the music, or the volume at which it is played whilst studying. 3. *Background distractions;* whether music is preferred when studying or an environment free from distractions. 4. *Type of music;* which radio station is preferred, and whether listening to one's own collection is preferred to the radio. 5. *Character of music;* whether vocals are preferred, whether this depends on the task in hand etc.

Table 3. Varimax Rotated Factor Analysis of the Study Habits Questionnaire

Prefer to work independently	0.84				
More productive when study independently	0.84				
Concentrate better with another present	-0.68				
Don't like working in groups	0.67				
For complex tasks, I prefer silence		0.71			
Familiar music is more distracting		0.65			
Prefer the TV on whilst studying		-0.62			
Prefer music at a high volume		-0.55			
For simple tasks I prefer music on			0.73		
Prefer music on whilst studying			0.65		
Prefer distraction-free environment			-0.52		
Type of music preferred				0.70	
Prefer music to be at a low volume				0.65	
Prefer radio to my own collection				0.53	
Prefer music free from vocals					0.79
Type of music depends on task					0.70
Eigenvalue	4.20	1.87	1.49	1.24	1.14
Variance	26.23	11.68	9.33	7.76	7.13

Simple regressions were conducted to ascertain whether the five personality dimensions measured by the NEO-inventory (and gender) significantly predicted these five factors. Personality and gender only significantly predicted one of the five factors of the study habits questionnaire. This was the factor concerning the presence of others ($F_{(6,80)} = 4.35$, $p<.001$; Adj. $R^2 = 0.25$): preference for study independently, more productive when do so, dislike of working in groups etc. The significant personality dimensions were extroversion (Beta = -0.31, t = 2.72, $p<.01$) and conscientiousness (Beta = 0.31, t = 2.89, $p<.01$). Those scoring low on extroversion (introverts) and high on conscientiousness, prefer to work independently and believe they are more productive when they do so, do not like working in groups and feel they do not concentrate better with another person present. Gender did not significantly predict any of the five factors.

Further regressions were conducted to ascertain if the five personality dimension scores predicted several of the individual study habits questions, that may have affected the hypothesised interactions. On the question "I prefer to work in an environment free from distractions" there was a significant effect ($F_{(6.80)} = 2.45$, $p<.05$, Adj. $R^2 = 0.13$). There were two significant effects: Extraversion: Beta = -0.28, t = 2.32, $p<.05$; and Conscientiousness: Beta = .31, t = 2.78, $p<.01$. There was also a significant effect for the question "prefer to listen to the radio than my own collection whilst studying" ($F_{(6,80)} = 2.38$, $P<.05$, Adj. $R^2 = 0.13$). There was only one significant predictor: Extraversion: Beta = 0.29, t = 2.37, $p<.05$. Thus, those low on extroversion (introverts) and high on conscientiousness significantly preferred to work in an environment free from distractions. Those scoring high on extroversion (extraverts) significantly preferred to have background music on whilst studying, and prefer this to be the radio than their own music collection compared to introverts.

DISCUSSION

The aim of the experiment was to explore the effects vocal and instrumental music have upon the performance of introverts and extraverts on two different cognitive tasks. For all participants there was a significant main effect of music for each of the tasks, showing that all performed significantly better when in silence. Such findings support the work of Fendrick (1937), Fogelson (1973), and Furnham and Allass (1999); musical distraction can inhibit cognitive performance particularly on more complex tasks. Previous experiments used industrial tasks in industrial settings over a longer time span than the current study; hence direct comparisons cannot be drawn. Music in the workplace may be quite different in terms of choice, loudness and duration than in experimental settings, however, which do threaten generalizations to the world of work.

The results of this study yielded only one significant main effect of personality, with extraverts performing significantly better than introverts on the phonological task. The lack of significant main effects of personality on the reading comprehension is consistent with Furnham et al. (1994), Furnham and Bradley (1997) and Furnham and Allass (1999), who similarly found personality to have few significant effects on test performance. The reading comprehension task also failed to yield a significant extroversion x musical condition interaction. Although this does not lend support to Eysenck's theory of personality (1967), it does support the findings of Furnham et al. (1999) who also failed to find a significant interaction for a reading comprehension task. In this study this result may have been influenced by ceiling effects of the scores on this test. In other words, it was simply "too easy" for these participants and future researchers need to take this into account.

The phonological task however, did yield a significant interaction between extroversion and musical condition. Extraverts performed better on this task than introverts in the presence of music. For both groups of participants, performance was best in silence, followed by when instrumental music was playing and worst in the presence of vocal music. An extroversion x musical distraction interaction has not previously been examined with a phonological task. Results therefore, show that interactions observed with reading comprehension, memory and observation tasks (e.g. Furnham & Bradley, 1997; Furnham & Allass, 1999; Furnham & Strbac, 2002) can extend to a phonological task where both stimulus (task) and distraction (music) are presented in the same modality (audio). This finding also lends partial support to Eysenck's theory of personality (1967).

This support for Eysenck's theory is only partial because whilst introverts' performance was more detrimentally affected in the presence of music than extraverts', the performance of extraverts was not enhanced in the presence of music as hypothesised. Indeed few of the reviewed studies above found any sort of task improvement in the presence of music, except on tedious, low complexity tasks. The result was therefore, only in line with Eysenck's theory in that the performance of introverts was more affected by the music than the extraverts. Therefore, for those with a higher internal arousal (i.e. introverts), increased stimulation is more detrimental to performance than for those with a higher internal level of arousal (i.e. extraverts). Following from Eysenck's theory, the study suggested that the performance of extraverts in the presence of music would be *enhanced;* as extraverts require an increased amount of external stimulation to reach the optimum functioning level because they have a lower internal arousal baseline than introverts. The results of the present study do not support this claim however; for all tasks extraverts performed best in silence.

Regarding the effects of the *type* of music used as a distracter, vocal music was more detrimental to performance than instrumental. This would appear to support the work of Belsham and Harman (1977) who found vocals to be particularly distracting, but the present results only partially support this claim. For all participants' performance on the reading comprehension task, the different type of music (i.e. vocal or instrumental) did not significantly affect their task performance. This would imply that the type of task has an effect on whether the presence of vocals has a greater propensity to distract than the presence of music *per se*. Two possible explanations as to why the presence of vocals on the phonological task may have been more detrimental to cognitive performance than instrumental music are as follows. Firstly, as Belsham and Harman (1977) state, vocal music is more distracting than instrumental music, and it may have been more difficult to ignore the distracting vocal music than the less distracting instrumental music. Secondly, because the task required participants to attend to the nature of the words (i.e. the number of syllables), the presence of words in the distracting stimulus (i.e. the music) may have created greater interference than the presence of merely instrumental music, which was not directly interfering with the task itself.

Again, this result does not lend support to Eysenck's theory of personality (1967). If vocal music has a greater informational load than instrumental music as Kiger (1989) suggests, extraverts should have benefited from the greater stimulation it offered, therefore, their performance should have been greatest when exposed to this type of distracter. This was not the case however, as already noted, extraverts for all three tasks performed best in silence, and worst when vocal music was the distracting stimulus.

The results of the study habits questionnaire revealed there were differences between the study habits of introverts and extraverts, many of which do lend support to Eysenck's theory of personality (1967). Campbell and Hawley (1982) found introverts chose to study in areas of the library that were relatively free from distractions, whereas extraverts seek areas which are near to other students and increased distraction. The results here support such a finding with significantly more introverts preferring to work in an environment free from distraction (55.5%) than extraverts (30.9%). Further, significantly more extraverts prefer to study with background music on (69.5%) than introverts (53.3%). This in turn lends support both to previous findings of the same pattern of results (e.g. Furnham & Bradley, 1997; Furnham et al. 1999) and to Eysenck's theory of personality (1967). Eysenck proposed that due to the lower level of internal arousal, the extraverted individual will actively seek ways to increase it to an optimum functioning level; selecting environments with many distractions, or listening to music when studying are two methods the extraverts in the present study are clearly using.

Fogelson (1973) suggested that if one frequently listens to music whilst working, it has less of a distracting effect and is therefore, less likely to impair performance. The presence of the significant interaction for the complex phonological task used here, may therefore have been mediated by such a confound. It may be that the group of extraverts performed better than the introverts in the presence of music because they were significantly more likely to *usually* study in its presence. A simple regression however, found preference for usual study with music on did not significantly predict performance on any of the three tasks. Hence, this did not confound the results in the present study.

A further related point concerns the nature of the group-testing environment. Extraverts are likely to benefit from this form of testing more than introverts. This may have had an arousing effect on the participants, and so any effects on task performance would have included the effects of the arousing environment as well as the independent variable of the music. The fact that performance of the two groups when tasks were performed in silence was not significantly different however, suggests that group testing did not result in a difference of arousal for extraverts and introverts, therefore could not have been confounding the results.

One further possible explanation for the music x extroversion interaction, concerns the music selected. Hilliard and Tonin (1979) found familiar music to be less distracting than unfamiliar music, proposing that if it is well known, it is easier to disregard. As stated above, significantly more of the extraverted group of subjects (69.5%) than the introverted group (53.3%) listened to music whilst studying, therefore it is more likely that this group had heard the tracks used more frequently and were therefore, more familiar with them than the introverts. Such a claim is supported by the fact that significantly more extraverts (52.3%) than introverts (29%) prefer to listen to the radio than their own music collection when studying. As these tracks were in the UK chart at the time of the experiment, and were thus played on the radio frequently, the extraverted group were more likely to be familiar with them than the introverts who prefer to listen to their own music collection. Further, 80% of those extraverts preferring the radio listened to either *Radio One* or *Virgin FM*; both stations largely playing current chart music. Future study could eradicate this confounding variable by making use of novel musical stimuli. One of the aims of the present study however, was to utilise highly familiar tracks which students of this age would be likely to listen to when studying, hence increasing the ecological validity of the experiment.

It is possible that other personality or individual difference factors such as conscientiousness, neuroticism or intelligence, may come into play and have their own effect on performance which interacts with that produced by background music. The latter of these factors can be eradicated, as subject's GCSE scores were taken and found to have no effect on task performance. The NEO five-factor personality inventory measured the degree of conscientiousness and neuroticism in each subject's personality. Exploratory analyses were conducted, but neither of these variables was found to have any significant effect on the significant interaction for the complex phonological task or the other two tasks.

The findings of studies of this sort have important implications for the use of music in an academic setting though it should be acknowledged the area is complex with many dimensions to music distractors and potential tasks. Whilst previous work (e.g. Furnham and Allass, 1999) has suggested music can benefit some individuals (notably extraverts), the results here suggest that music is (nearly always) detrimental to the cognitive performance of all individuals regardless of extroversion score. The increasing availability and affordability of music through personal stereo systems such as the walkman, the Discman and more recently, the mini-disc player, is likely to increase the frequency with which music is listened to when students are studying. With over 60% of subjects in the present study reporting that they prefer to study with music on (rising to 77.3% when the task is simple), this is already an extremely important issue. It is clear that the effect of music on cognitive performance does depend on the type of task in hand, but for those wishing to maximise their work potential, study is optimum when done in silence. For those wishing to study with background music on however, instrumental music is less detrimental to performance than vocal, if the task is complex, and requires concentration. This detrimental effect is magnified for introverted individuals. The implications of this finding stretch beyond academia however, if introverts perform less well on certain tasks than extraverts in highly distracting environments/situations, there are fundamental implications for occupational psychology and personnel selection. Music is used in other settings (e.g. shops) to change mood aimed at increasing sales. That, however, is quite another research area.

REFERENCES

Banbury, S., & Berry, D. (1998). Disruption of office-related tasks by speech and office noise. *British Journal of Psychology*, **89**, 499-517.

Belojevic, G., Slepcevic, V., & Jakovljevic, B. (2001). Mental performance in noise: The role of introversion. *Journal of Environmental Psychology*, **21**, 209-213..

Belsham, R.L., & Harman, D.W. (1977). Effect of vocal vs. non-vocal music on visual recall. *Perceptual and Motor Skills*, **44**, 857-858.

Burton, L. (1986). Relationship between musical accompaniment and learning style in problem solving. *Perceptual and Motor Skills*, **62**, 48-49.

Campbell, J.B., & Hawley, C.W. (1982). Study habits and Eysenck's theory of Extroversion-Introversion. *Journal of Research in Personality*, **16**, 130-146.

Costa, P.T. Jr., & McCrae, R.R. (1992). *Revised NEO Personality Inventory (NEO-PI-R) and Five Factor Inventory (NEO-FFI) Professional Manual*. Odessa, FL: Psychological Assessment Resources, Inc.

Daoussis, L. & McKelvie, S.J. (1986). Musical preferences and effects of music on a reading comprehension test for extraverts and introverts. *Perceptual and Motor Skills*, **62**, 283-289.

Eich, E., & Schooler, J. (2000). Cognition/emotion interaction. In E. Eich and J. Kihlstrom (Eds). *Cognition and Emotion.* New York: Oxford University Press.

Eysenck, H. (1967). *The biological basis of personality.* Springfield, IL: Thomas.

Fendrick, P. (1937). The influence of music distraction upon reading efficiency. *Journal of Educational Research, 45,* 451-458.

Fogelson, S. (1973). Music as a distracter on reading test performance of eighth grade students. *Perceptual and Motor Skills, 62,* 48-49.

Fontaine, C.W., & Schwalm, N.D. (1979). Effects of familiarity of music on vigilant performance. *Performance and Motor Skills, 49,* 71-74.

Fox, J.G. (1971). Background music and Industrial efficiency: a review. *Applied Ergonomics, 22,* 70-73.

Fox, J., & Embrey, E. (1972). Music - an aid to productivity. *Applied Ergonomics, 3,* 202-205.

Furnham, A., & Allass, K. (1999). The influence of musical distraction of varying complexity on the cognitive performance of introverts and extraverts. *European Journal of Personality, 13,* 27-38.

Furnham, A., & Bradley, A. (1997). Music while you work: the differential distraction of background music on cognitive test performance of introverts and extraverts. *Applied Cognitive Psychology, 11,* 445-455.

Furnham, A., & Strbac, L. (2002). Music is distracting as noise: The differential distraction of background music and noise on the cognitive test performance of introverts and extraverts. *Ergonomics, 45,* 203-217.

Furnham, A., Gunter, B., & Peterson, E. (1994). Television distraction and the performance of introverts and extraverts. *Applied Cognitive Psychology, 8,* 705-711.

Furnham, A., Trew, S., & Sneade, I. (1999). The distracting effects of vocal and instrumental music on the cognitive task performance of introverts and extraverts. *Personality and Individual Differences, 27,* 381-392.

Geringer, J.M., & Nelson, J.K. (1979). Effects of background music on musical task performance and subsequent music preference. *Perceptual and Motor Skills, 49,* 39-45.

Hall, S. (1952). The effect of background music on the reading comprehension of 278 8th and 9th grade students. *Journal of Education Research, 45,* 451-458.

Hilliard, M.O., & Tonin, P. (1979). Effect of familiarity with background music on performance of simple and difficult reading comprehension tasks. *Perceptual and Motor Skills, 49,* 713-714.

Hough, E. (1943). Effect of music on accident reduction. *Journal of the Acoustical Society of America, 15,* 18.

Kerr, W.A. (1945). Experiments on the effects of music on factory production. *International Review of Applied Psychology, 5,* 40-45.

Kiger, D.M. (1989). Effects of music information load on a reading comprehension task. *Perceptual and Motor Skills, 69,* 531-534.

Kjellberg, A., Landstrom, U., Tesarz, M., Söderberg, L., & Akerlund, E. (1996). The effects of non-physical noise characteristics, ongoing task and noise sensitivity of annoyance and distraction due to noise at work. *Journal of Environmental Psychology, 16,* 123-136.

Loewen, L., & Suedfeld, P. (1992). Cognitive and arousal effects of masking office noise. *Environment and Behaviour, 24,* 381-395.

McCrae, R., & Costa, P. (1985). Comparison of EPA and Psychoticism scales with measures of the five-factor model of Personality. *Personality and Individual Differences, 6,* 587-597.

Mehrabian, A. (1976). *Public Places and Private Spaces.* New York: Basic Books.

Newman, R., Hunt, D. & Rhodes, F. (1966) Effect of music on employee attitude and productivity in a skate board factory. *Journal of Applied Psychology, 50,* 493-496

North, A., & Hargreaves, D. (1997). The musical milieu: Studies of listening in everyday life. *The Psychologist, 10,* 309-312.

North, A., & Hargreaves, D. (1996). The effects of music on responses to a dining area. *Journal of Environmental Psychology, 16,* 55-64.

Oldham, G.R., Cummings, A., Mischel, L.J., Schmidtke, J.M. & Zhou, J. (1995). Listen while you work? Quasi-experimental relations between personal-stereo headset use and employee work responses. *Journal of Applied Psychology, 80,* 547-564.

Parente, J. (1976). Music preference as a factor of musical distraction. *Perceptual and Motor Skills, 43,* 337-338.

Rauscher, F., Shaw, G., & Ky, K. (1993). Music and spatial task performance. *Nature, 365,* 611.

Rees, G., Frith, C.D., & Lavie, N. (1997). Modulating irrelevant motion perception by varying attentional load in an unrelated task. *Science, 278,* 1616-1619.

Smith, W.A. (1961). Effects of industrial music in a work situation requiring complex mental activity. *Psychological Reports, 8,* 159-162.

Smith, C.A. & Morris, L.W. (1976). Effects of stimulative and sedative music on cognitive and emotional components of Anxiety. *Psychological Reports, 38,* 1187-1193.

Sogin, D. (1988). Effect of three different musical styles of background music on coding by college-age students. *Perceptual and Motor Skills, 67,* 275-280.

Steele, K., Bass, K. & Crook, M. (1999). The mystery of the Mozart Effect. *Psychological Science, 10,* 366-369.

Toplyn, G., & Maguire, W. (1991). The differential effect of noise on creative task performance. *Creativity Research Journal, 4,* 337-347.

Uhrbrock, R. (1961) Music on the job: its influences on worker morale and productivity. *Personal Psychology, 14,* 9-38

Vermolayeva-Tomina, L.B. (1964). In Gray (Ed.), *Pavlov's Typology.* London: Pergamon Press.

Wexley, K.N., & Yukl, G.A. (1984). *Organizational Behavior and Personnel Psychology* (Rev.ed.). Homewood, Il: Irwin.

Wolfe, D. (1983). Effects of music loudness on task performance and self-report of college-aged students. *Journal of Research in Music Education, 31,* 191-201.

Zajonc, R. (1984). On primacy of affect. In K. Scherer, and P. Ekman (Eds). *Approaches to Emotion.* Hillsdale, New Jersey: LEA.

In: *Topics in Cognitive Psychology*
Serge P. Shohov (Editor) pp. 169-206

ISBN 1-59033-836-7.
© 2003 Nova Science Publishers, Inc.

Chapter 10

REVERSAL LEARNING IN CONCURRENT DISCRIMINATIONS IN RATS

*Esho Nakagawa**

Department of Psychology
Kagawa University, Japan

ABSTRACT

Six experiments examined effects of overtraining on reversal learning in concurrent discriminations in rats. In Experiment 1, rats were concurrently trained on two go/no-go successive discriminations to criterion or overtrained. They were then given reversal on either the two tasks (W) or on one out of them (P). Group W reversed faster than Group P after overtraining (i.e., the whole reversal versus partial reversal advantage effect), whereas Group P reversed faster than Group W after criterion (i.e., partial reversal versus whole reversal advantage effect). Experiment 2 was conducted to investigate the question of whether or not the whole reversal versus partial reversal advantage effect was caused by the effect of overtraining on extinction during reversal learning. In this experiment, rats were concurrently trained two simultaneous discriminations to criterion or overtrained. They were then given on extinction either the two tasks (W) or on one out of them (P). Finally, Group W was given a whole reversal, and Group p was given a partial reversal. Group W learned their reversal faster than Group P after overtraining, whereas Group P learned their reversal faster than Group W after criterion training. Experiments 3 and 4 were conducted to determine the source of the whole reversal versus partial reversal advantage effect. At the same time, these two experiments examined the difference in which overtraining had effects on reversal learning in concurrent and single discriminations. In Experiment 3, twenty-eight rats were concurrently trained on two simultaneous discriminations of the different sensory modality (i.e., smooth versus rough and vertical-horizontal stripes) to criterion or overtrained. They were then given reversal on either two tasks (W) or on one of them (P). The remaining 14 rats were trained on a simultaneous discrimination (i.e., smooth versus rough task) to criterion or overtrained, and then given reversal on the task (C). Group W reversed more rapidly than Group C, which in turn reversed more rapidly than Group P after overtraining, whereas Group P reversed more rapidly than Group W, which in turn reversed more rapidly than Group C in the absence of

---

* Contact address: Kagawa University, 1-1, Saiwai-Cho, Takamatsu, Kagawa, 760-8522, Japan; E-mail: esho @ ed.kagawa-u.ac.jp

overtraining. In Experiment 4, thirty-six rats were concurrently trained on two go/no-go successive discriminations to criterion or overtrained, and then given reversal on either the two tasks (W) or on one of them (P and S). The remaining 12 rats were trained on a go/no-go successive discrimination to criterion or overtrained, and then given reversal on the task (C). Group W took fewer days to criterion in reversal than Groups C and S, which in turn took fewer days than Group P after overtraining, whereas Group P took fewer days than Groups W, C, and S after criterion training. Experiments 5 and 6 were conducted to determine the source of the partial reversal versus whole reversal advantage effect seen in the absence of overtraining. In Experiment 5, rats were concurrently trained on two simultaneous discriminations to criterion, and then given reversal on either the two tasks (W) or on one of them (P and C). Group P, in which one of the two tasks were reversed but the other was not reversed, learned their reversal faster than Group C, in which one of the two tasks was reversed and added a new discrimination task instead of the other task. Group C learned their reversal faster than Group W. Experiment 6 replicated the results observed in Experiment5 in two go/no-go successive discriminations. These findings indicate that both a facilitation in the whole reversal condition and a retardation in the partial reversal condition make significant contribution to the whole reversal versus partial reversal advantage effect seen after overtraining, whereas a facilitation in the partial reversal condition and a retardation in the whole reversal condition to the partial reversal versus whole reversal advantage effect seen in the absence of overtraining. These findings of these six experiments in the present study make it clear that stimulus-stimulus associations (i.e., stimulus classes) between the discriminative stimuli are formed in concurrent discriminations after overtraining, but not after criterion training. Furthermore, these findings, especially, findings of Experiments 3 and 4 demonstrate that overtraining has different effects on reversal learning in concurrent and single discriminations.

There are many studies on stimulus class's formation in pigeons and rats. They make clear that both species have an ability to form stimulus classes or stimulus-stimulus associations between stimuli. Especially, some studies, using a whole versus partial reversal procedure, have reported that both species form stimulus classes between the discriminative stimuli that signal the same outcome during overtraining in two concurrent discriminations (Delius, Ameling, Lea, & Staddon, 1995;Nakagawa, 1978, 1986, 1992, 1999a, 1999b, 1999c, 1999d, 2000, 2001a, 2001b; Zentall, Steirn, Sherburne, & Urcuioli, 1991). In a concurrent discrimination, rats are given training in one discrimination task [a positive stimulus (A+)-a negative stimulus (C-)] on some trials and in the other discrimination [a positive stimulus (B+)-a negative stimulus (D-)] on the other trials in a random order in the same apparatus and within each session. The whole versus partial reversal procedure (i.e., the between-group whole versus partial reversal design) is a somewhat different design that has been used to examine emergent stimulus relations following the acquisition of conditional discriminations. If emergent relations between stimuli made them more similar to each other, it should be relatively difficult to associate them with incompatible response. Specifically, if training on conditional discriminations, one reverses the associations between one pair of them but not the other, learning should be relatively slow. In the whole versus partial reversal procedure, rats were trained to criterion or overtrained on two concurrent simple discriminations (A1+ vs. A2-; B1+ vs. B2-) in the Phase 1 training. After completing the Phase 1 training, they received either partial reversal (A1- vs. A2+; B1+ vs. B2-, or A1+ vs. A2-; B2+ vs. B1-) or whole reversal (A1- vs. A2+; B1- vs. B2+) in the Phase 2 reversal. If stimulus classes between stimuli make them more similar to each other, it should be relatively difficult to associate them with incompatible responses. That is, if rats formed stimulus classes between the discriminative stimuli, rats for which both discriminations were reversed should take fewer days to learn their reversal learning than those for which only one discrimination of the two tasks was reversed (i.e., whole reversal versus partial reversal advantage effect). (See also Nakagawa, 1978, 1986, 1992, 1998, 2001a; Zentall, Sherburne, Steirn, Randall, Roper, & Urcuioli, 1992; Zentall et al., 1991). The whole reversal versus partial reversal advantage effect indicates that rats form emergent stimulus relations between discriminative stimuli after the acquisition of conditional discriminations. This whole versus partial reversal procedure has a possibility to make it clear that rats form stimulus classes in concurrent discriminations.

Coate and Gardner (1965) and Liu and Zeiler (1968) have shown that following overtraining in concurrent discriminations, performance on the two discriminations is independent. On the other hand, Sasaki and Shinoda (1969), studying simultaneous discriminations in a Y maze, found that after overtraining a whole reversal condition (W), in which both discrimination tasks were reversed, produced more rapidly reversal than a partial reversal condition (P), in which only one of the two discriminations was reversed while the other was maintained as in original learning. Conversely, in the absence of overtraining, rats in the partial condition reversed more rapidly than did those in the whole condition. That is, Sasaki and Shinoda (1969) have shown the whole reversal versus partial reversal advantage effect after overtraining in two simultaneous concurrent discriminations in rats. Sanders (1971) found that children learned the whole reversal faster than the partial reversal, but that rats showed the opposite effect without overtraining. Nakagawa has also reported that rats learned whole reversal faster than the partial reversal after overtraining (i.e., the whole reversal versus partial reversal advantage effect), whereas they learned the partial reversal faster than the whole reversal after criterion training (i.e., the partial reversal versus whole reversal advantage effect) (1978, 1986, 1992, 1998, 2001a, 2001b).

In spite of the reliability of the whole reversal versus partial reversal advantage effect following overtraining and the partial reversal versus whole reversal advantage effct after criterion training in concurrent discriminations, the sources of these two advantage effect remains unclear. That is, it remains unclear whether the whole reversal versus the partial reversal advantage effects following overtraining are due to a facilitation of reversal in the whole condition, a retardation of reversal in the partial condition, or a combinations of these two effects. Furthermore, it remains unclear whether the partial reversal versus whole reversal advantage effect after criterion training is due to a facilitation of reversal in the partial, a retardation of reversal in the whole condition, or a combinations of these two effects.

The purpose of the present study was to determine the sources of both the whole reversal versus partial reversal advantage effect following overtraining (Experiments 3,4) and the partial reversal versus whole reversal advantage effect after criterion training (Experiments 5, 6) in concurrent discriminations in rats. At the same time, this present study was conducted to investigate the question of whether or not overtraining had different effects on reversal learning in concurrent and single discriminations in rats.

EXPERIMENT 1

The present experiment was conducted to replicate the effect of overtraining on the reversal using a go/no-go successive concurrent discrimination procedure to test the generality of the whole reversal versus partial reversal advantage effect observed in Sasaki and Shinoda (1969). Rats were trained with two go/no-go successive discrimination tasks to criterion or overtrained. After completing Phase 1 training, they transferred to either a whole reversal or a partial reversal. The expectation according to Sasaki and Shinoda's findings is that rats learn the whole reversal faster than the partial reversal after overtraining, but not after criterion training.

Method

Subjects

Thirty-two experimentally naive Sprague-Dawley rats (16 females, 16 males) were used. They were about 150 days old, with an average initial body weight of 254g for female rats and 345g for male ones. Rats were given handling for five min a day for 12 days. They were maintained on a daily 2-hr feeding schedule each day. The amount of food in the daily ration was gradually reduced until the body weight of each rat reached 80% of the baseline weight at the start of the experiment. Water was always available for rats in their individual home cage. The rats were maintained on a 6:18-hr light: dark cycle, with lights off at 11:00 p.m. Experimental sessions took place during the light phase of the cycle.

Apparatus

The apparatus (a straight runway) was the same as in Experiment 1 of Nakagawa (2002b). See also Figure 1 in Nakagawa (2002b). It consisted of a runway with a starting box and a goal box. A guillotine door was located at the front of the starting box. A piece of cardboard was placed at the entrance of the goal box to serve as a discriminandum. A gap over which rats had to jump was located 20 cm in front of the goal box. The apparatus was painted medium-gray inside and throughout the experiment by a 10-W fluorescent lamp suspended horizontally 45 cm above the top of the runway. Separate starting time and running time were obtained on each trial by means of two electrical digital timers. When the experimenter raised the guillotine door, a micro switch activated the first timer. When rats interrupted a photo beam cell 5 cm down the runway, this timer stopped, and at the same time the 57 cm further down the runway, the second timer stopped. A running time is the time between the interrupting of the first and the second photo beams.

Stimuli

The stimulus cards were 12-cm squares of cardboard. Each card was presented at the entrance of the goal box and served as an entrance door. They were arranged so that on rewarded trials the card serving as the correct door could be pushed down easily, thus permitting rats to gain entrance into the goal box, whereas on non-rewarded trials the card denoting the incorrect door was locked. For a white-black discrimination a white card and a black one were used. Vertically striped and horizontally striped cards were used for a vertical-horizontal stripe discrimination. Striped cards had alternating black and white lines 1 cm in width.

Procedure

Pretraining

Rats were given pretraining for eight days prior to the beginning of discrimination training. On Day 1 rats were allowed to explore the apparatus for two periods of seven and five min. From Day 2 to Day 4 they were trained to push down a stimulus card and enter the goal box to obtain food for ten daily trials. The gap between the runway and the goal box was not present for this stage of the experiment. From Day 5 to Day 8 they were trained to jump over the gap for ten trials a day. On the last day all rats jumped over the 15-cm gap. Medium-gray stimulus card was used during this period.

Phase 1 Discrimination Training (Original Learning)

Rats were trained concurrently to criterion in original learning for 12 trials a day, six on each of the two discriminations: white versus black and vertical versus horizontal stripes. Two rats in each group were trained with B+H+, two rats with B+V+, two rats with W+H+, and two rats with W+V+. The order of trials with the two tasks followed four predetermined random sequences. The order of rewarded trials and non-rewarded ones followed four predetermined random sequences. Rats were given three rewarded trials and three non-rewarded ones per day on each task. On rewarded trials rats were given two 45-mg milk pellets as a reward in the goal box. On non-rewarded trials they were retained for 60 sec. in the runway after the guillotine door was opened. Intertrial intervals ranged from four to eight min. The criterion in original learning was that the median of the running time on the rewarded trials was shorter than the shortest running time on the non-rewarded trials for each task for two successive days.

Half of the rats received the same training for a further 20 days after reaching the criterion (Group OT). The remaining rats received no further training on the original tasks once they had reached the criterion (Group NOT).

Phase 2 Reversal Learning

After completing the original learning, rats of each group were further divided into the two subgroups (W and P), matched with respect to the number of days to criterion. They were then trained under a given reversal condition until they achieved a criterion in reversal learning, which was the same as that in original learning. Group W was run under the whole reversal condition, in which the two discriminations were reversed. Group P was run under the partial reversal condition, in which only the vertical-horizontal stripe task was reversed, but the white-black task was not reversed. Other aspects of the procedure were the same as during the original training.

Results

Phase 1 Training

The mean number of days to reach criterion in Phase 1 of the experiment was as follows: 19.00 (SD = 5.34) on the black-white task (i.e., B-W) and 19.25 (SD = 4.92) on the horizontal-vertical stripe task (i.e., H-V) for Group W-NOT; 18.75 (SD = 6.80) on B-W task and 18.38 (SD = 7.24) on H-V task for Group W-OT; 19.00 (SD = 5.89) on B-W task and

20.00 (SD = 5.52) on H-V task for Group P-NOT; and 19.63 (SD = 8.47) on B-W task and 19.25 (SD = 8.64) on H-V task for Group P-OT. An ANOVA using group (W vs. P), degree of overtraining (NOT vs. OT), and task (W-B vs. V-H) revealed no significant main effects and no significant interactions, all Fs < 1.

Phase 2 Reversal Learning

The results for each group in Phase 2 reversal learning are illustrated in Figure 1. An ANOVA using group (W vs. P) and degree of overtraining (NOT vs. OT) was performed on the number of days to criterion on the vertical-horizontal stripe task. The analysis revealed a significant main effect of overtraining, F (1,28) = 8.82, p < .01, and a significant overtraining x group interaction, F (1,28) = 155.66, p < .001. Overtraining significantly facilitated reversal in Group W, F (1,28) = 119.30, p < .001, but significantly retarded reversal in Group P, F (1,28) = 45.18, p < .001. After overtraining Group W reversed more rapidly than Group P, F (1,28) = 74.17, p < .001, whereas Group P reversed more rapidly than Group W, F (1,28) = 81.58, p < .001 in the absence of overtraining.

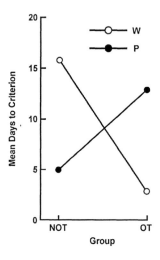

Figure 1. Mean days to criterion of each group in reversal learning as a function of overtraining trials. From "Cross-Modal Stimulus Class Formation in Rats as a Function of Overtraining." Esho Nakagawa, 2002c, In Serge P. Shohov. (Ed.), Advances in Psychology Research, 13, Chapter 9, pp.169-187. Copyright 2002 by NOVA Science Publisher Inc. Adapted with permission.

Overtraining significantly facilitated reversal on the white-black task in Group W [mean days to criterion was 2.75 (SD = 1.64) for the OT rats and 15.75 (SD = 2.44) for the NOT rats], F (1,14) = 136.87, p < .001.

Loss of Retention

In order to examine the degree of retention loss on the non-reversal task (i.e., the white-black task) of Group P, a special criterion was devised. The criterion was that the median of the running times on the rewarded trials was longer that every running time on the non-rewarded trials for the white-black task. Number of days to reach this criterion was taken as a measure of retention loss. For rats in Group P, only the vertical-horizontal stripe task out of the two discrimination tasks was reversed, whereas the other (i.e., the white-black task) was maintained as in original training. Thus, if performance on the two discriminations is independent, rats in Group P should make no error on the white-black task (i.e., the non-reversal task) trials. Consequently, the retention loss measure implies that performance on the two tasks is no longer independent, that is, degree of the development of associations between the discriminative stimuli that signal either reward, or non-reward, in the two discrimination tasks. The means and SDs of retention loss days in the white-black task were as follows: 8.38 (SD=2.56) for Group P-OT and 2.08 (SD=1.15) for Group P-NOT. Overtraining significantly increased the number of retention loss days in the white-black task, t (14) = 5.94, p < .001.

Discussion

Overtraining did facilitate reversal learning in Group W (a positive ORE) but retarded reversal learning in Group P (a negative ORE). Furthermore, Group W took significantly fewer days to criterion than Group P did under overtraining condition (i.e., whole reversal versus partial reversal advantage effect), whereas in the absence of overtraining, Group P took significantly fewer days to criterion than did Group W (i.e., partial reversal versus whole reversal advantage effect). These findings are consistent with the findings of Nakagawa (1978, 1986, 1992, 1998) with rats and Nakagawa (1980a, 1980b, 1981, 1985) with younger children. In addition, rats in Group P-OT showed greater retention loss of the original white-black discrimination than Group P-NOT. This additional finding is of interest since it indicates that following overtraining, performance on the two discriminations is no longer independent. Such an outcome can be understood if overtraining results in the development of associations between the discriminative stimuli that signal either reward, or non-reward, in the two tasks.

These findings are not readily explained by extant theories of discrimination learning: acquired cue distinctive theory (Lawrence, 1949, 1950), response of discrimination theory (Reid, 1953; Pubols, 1956), selective attention theory (Mackintosh, 1965a), analyzer hierarchy theory (Sutherland & Mackintosh, 1971), and response strategy or response pattern theory (Mandler, 1966, 1968; Mandler & Hooper, 1967; Hall, 1973a, 1973b, 1974). All these theories predict that overtraining should produce comparable positive OREs in Groups W and P, but this result was not observed. Nakagawa (1986, 1992, 1998, 1999a, 1999b, 1999c, 1999d, 2000, 2001a, 2001b) has argued that both the whole reversal versus partial reversal advantage effect and the pattern of OREs can be explained in terms of associations between the discriminative stimuli established during overtraining. According to Nakagawa, during the original training rats learn a connection between positive stimuli and an approach response as well as a connection between a negative stimulus and an avoidance response for each discrimination task. During overtraining they also form associations between the discriminative stimuli with the same response assignment. Thus, rats learn to associate the two positive stimuli as well as to associate the negative stimuli of the two independent discriminations. The associations between the two positive stimuli and between the two negative stimuli are called "cue-associations". The cue associations produce "an acquired equivalence" effect, whereby stimuli associated with the same consequence show enhanced generalization; that is, cue-associations mediate the transfer of appropriate responding from one positive (or negative) stimulus to the other positive (or negative) stimulus in reversal learning.

As a result of these cue-associations, the reversal of the one discrimination after overtraining in the whole condition should exert a synergistic influence upon the reversal of the other discrimination. Each reinforcement of the new positive stimulus in one discrimination should not only enhance the strength of the approach response to this stimulus but also augment the same response to the new positive stimulus in the other discrimination via the cue-association between the positive stimuli formed during overtraining. Correspondingly, the consequences of non-reinforcement of the new negative stimulus should also transfer between discriminations. Furthermore, in agreement with the present data, the cue-associations view predicts a large positive ORE in the whole condition because in the absence of overtraining there are no cue-associations present to mediate the synergistic interaction between the two discriminations.

A parallel explanation can be given for the retarded reversal observed in the partial condition after overtraining. In the presence of cue-associations, continued training with the non-reversed discrimination during the reversal stages will lead to interference with the development of an approach response to the new positive stimulus and of an avoidance response to the new negative stimulus of the reversed discrimination. Consequently, Group P should exhibit a negative ORE.

These findings also give support to a stimulus association theory advocated by Edward, Jagielo, Zentall, and Hogan (1982), Hall, Ray, and Bonardi (1993), Urcuioli, Zentall, Jackson-Smith, and Steirn (1989), and Zentall et al. (1991, 1992). According to this theory, a stimulus class consists of arbitrary stimuli, related to each other, through their association with the same outcome in rats, that is, rats form stimulus classes on a basis of reinforcement concordance. This whole reversal versus partial reversal advantage effect is consistent with the expectation from the discrimination theory advocated by Zentall et al. (1991) and Zentall (1998) that faster whole reversal than partial reversal is based on the difference in detectability of change in reinforcement across phases, between whole and partial reversals. These findings indicate that the discriminative stimuli become functionally equivalent during overtraining and that rats establish stimulus classes formation between discriminative stimuli that are associated with the same response during overtraining in two concurrent discriminations learning. See also Experiment 1 of Nakagawa (2002b).

The finding that Group P reversed more rapidly than Group W after criterion training (partial reversal versus whole reversal advantage effect) is caused by independence of performance on the two discriminations because Group P had only two, rather than four, associations to relearn.

EXPERIMENT 2

Experiment 1, studying go/no-go successive concurrent discriminations in a straight runway, makes it clear that, after overtraining a whole reversal learning group (Group W), in which both discrimination tasks are reversed, learns the reversal faster than a partial reversal learning group (Group P), in which only one of the two discrimination tasks is reversed while the other is maintained as in original training. Conversely, in the absence of overtraining Group P learns the reversal task faster than Group W. Furthermore, Sanders (1971) found that children learned the whole reversal faster than the partial reversal, but that rats showed the opposite effect under conditions that involved no overtraining. Nakagawa (1980a, 1980b, 1981, 1985) also found that younger children learned the whole reversal more rapidly than the partial reversal after overtraining but not after criterion training.

Sasaki and Shinoda (1969) proposed that the effect of overtraining on the reversal of concurrent discriminations (i.e., the whole reversal versus partial reversal advantage effect) occurred because of the influence of overtraining on extinction during the reversal learning phase.

The present experiment was conducted to investigate the question of whether or not the difference in the effects of overtraining on reversal learning between Group W and Group P was caused by its effect on extinction during reversal learning. According to Sasaki and Shinoda's view, overtraining should facilitate extinction in Group W but should delay extinction in Group P. Overtraining should neither facilitate nor delay reversal learning after extinction in either Group W or Group P.

Method

Subjects

Thirty-two experimentally naive male Sprague-Dawley rats were used. Their ages were about 180 days, with an initial average body weight of 457 g. Rats were given handling for five min a day for 12 days. All details of the feeding schedule and handling were the same as in Experiment 1. The rats were maintained on a 6:18-hr light: dark cycle, with lights off at 11:00 p.m.

Apparatus

The apparatus (a modified Y maze) was the same as in Experiment 1 of Nakagawa (1986). See also Figure 1 of Nakagawa (1986). The starting box measured 15 cm in height, 12 cm in width, and 25 cm in length. The distance from the starting box to the bifurcation was 65 cm. The arms of the Y maze were 85 cm in length. At the end of each arm was a goal box. Each goal box was 15 cm in height, 12 cm in width, and 25 cm in length. A guillotine door was located at the front of the starting box. At the entrance of the goal box a piece of cardboard was placed which served as a discriminandum. A gap over which rats had to jump (15 cm in depth, 12 cm in width, and 15 cm in length) was located 20 cm in front of the goal box. The apparatus was painted medium gray inside and lit throughout the experiment by two 10-W fluorescent lamps suspended horizontally 45 cm above the top of both the arms.

Stimuli

Stimulus cards were 12-cm squares of cardboard. Each square was presented at the entrance of each goal box and served as an entrance door. They were arranged so that the card serving as the correct door could be pushed down easily, thus permitting rats to gain entrance into the goal box, while the card denoting the incorrect door was locked. The same stimuli as in Experiment 1 were used for the white-black and the horizontal-vertical stripe discriminations.

Procedure

Pretraining

Rats were given pretraining for eight days prior to the beginning of discrimination training. On Day 1, rats were allowed to explore the apparatus for two periods of seven and five min. From Day 2 to Day 4, they were trained to push down a stimulus card and enter the goal box to obtain food for 10 daily trials. The gap was not present for this stage of the experiment. From Day 5 to Day 8, they were trained to jump over the gap for ten trials a day. On the last day, all rats jumped over the 15-cm gap. They were given the same number of trials on each arm during pretraining. Medium-gray stimulus cards were used during this period.

Phase 1 Discrimination Training (Original Learning)

Rats were concurrently trained to a criterion of original learning for 20 trials a day on the two discrimination tasks: white versus black and vertical versus horizontal stripes. A self-correction method was used, in which, if rats made an error, they were allowed to return to the choice point and select the correct stimulus. There was complete counter-balancing of the stimuli. That is, two rats of each group were trained on B+ H+, two rats on B+ V+, two rats on W+ H+, and two rats on W+ V+. The order of the trials of the two tasks followed four predetermined random sequences. The position of a positive stimulus also followed four predetermined random sequences. Rats were given two 45-mg milk pellets when they made the correct response. Intertrial intervals ranged from four to eight min. The criterion for the original learning was to achieve 19 correct trials out of a possible 20 for each discrimination task over two successive days combined.

Half of the rats received the same training for a further 12 days after reaching the original learning criterion (Group OT). The other half received no further training on the original tasks once they had reached this criterion (Group NOT).

Phase 2 Extinction

After completing the original training, the rats in each group were divided into subgroups (W and P) matched with respect to the number of days to reach the criterion. For rats in Group W, both doors were locked on all trials on both the white-black discrimination and the vertical-horizontal stripe discrimination, although positive stimuli were still changed from side to side. Extinction continued for Group W rats until both positive and negative stimuli were chosen equally often over ten successive trials on each task. For Group P rats, both doors were locked on all trials on the vertical-horizontal stripe discrimination, but they continued to receive the original discrimination training on all trials in the white-black discrimination. Extinction continued for Group P rats until both stimuli were chosen equally often over ten successive trials on the vertical-horizontal stripe discrimination.

Phase 3 Reversal Learning

After reaching the extinction criterion, all rats of each groups were trained under the given reversal condition with a self-correction method until they achieved criterion. The criterion for reversal learning was the same as that in original learning. Group W was run under the whole reversal learning condition where both the white-black and vertical-horizontal stripe discriminations were reversed. On the other hand, Group P was run under partial reversal learning condition, where only the vertical-horizontal stripe discrimination was reversed but the white-black discrimination was not, and rats were given the same discrimination training on that task as for the original training. Other aspects of the conditions were the same as for the original training.

Results

Phase 1 Training

The mean number of days to reach criterion in Phase 1 of the experiment was as follows: 17.38 (SD = 6.63) on the black-white task (i.e., B-W) and 17.75 (SD = 6.42) on the horizontal-vertical stripe task (i.e., H-V) for Group W-OT; 17.88 (SD = 11.70) on B-W task and 18.38 (SD = 12.61) on H-V task for Group W-NOT; 16.75 (SD = 9.54) on B-W and 17.75 (SD = 9.27) on H-V task for Group P-OT; 19.75 (SD = 10.46) on B-W task and 20.63 (SD = 10.36) on H-V task for Group P-NOT. The results of an ANOVA using overtraining (OT vs. NOT), group (W vs. P), and task (B-W vs. H-V) performed on the number of days to reach criterion in the original learning were as follows: None of the main effects nor the interactions was significant, all Fs < 1.00. These results showed that there was no significant difference in learning ability among the four groups in this experiment.

Phase 2 Extinction

The mean number of days to reach criterion in Phase 2 of the experiment was as follows: 2.13 (SD = 0.78) on B-W task and 1.88 (SD = 0.60) on H-V task for Group W-OT; 2.25 (SD = 0.66) on B-W task and 2.25 (SD = 0.83) on H-V task for Group W-NOT; 5.13 (SD = 2.89) on H-V task for Group P-OT; 5.25 (SD = 2.49) on H-V task for Group P-NOT. An 2 x 2 ANOVA using overtraining (OT vs. NOT) and group (W vs. P) was performed on the number of days to reach criterion in extinction on the vertical-horizontal stripe discrimination task were as follows: The analysis yielded a significant effect of groups, $F_{(1,28)} = 18.81$, $p < .01$. That is, Group W took significantly fewer days to reach criterion in extinction on the vertical-horizontal stripe discrimination task than Group P both after overtraining, $t(14) = 2.47$, $p < .05$, and without overtraining, $t(14) = 2.81$, $p < .02$. Overtraining neither facilitated nor delayed extinction in either Group W, $F_{(1,28)} < 1.00$ or Group P, $F_{(1, 28)} < 1.00$. Some rats occasionally refused to respond, by not jumping across the gap within 60 sec from the start of the trial. The mean number of such nonchoice responses of each group on the first day in extinction was as follows: 4.00 (SD = 4.33) for Group W-NOT, 5.25 (SD= 5.97) for Group W-OT, 0.38 (SD = 0.70) for Group P-NOT, and 0.38 (SD = 0.70) for Group P-NOT. The analysis indicated that Group W made significantly more nonchoice responses than Group P, both after overtraining, $t(14) = 2.15$, $p < .05$, or without overtraining, $t(14) = 2.18$, $p < 0.05$.

Phase 3 Reversal Learning

The results for each group in Phase 3 reversal are illustrated in Figure 2. A 2 x 2 ANOVA using overtraining (OT vs. NOT) and group (W vs. P) was performed on the number of days to reach criterion in reversal learning of the vertical-horizontal stripe discrimination. The analysis yielded a significant overtraining x group interaction, $F (1,28) = 14.04$, $p < 0.01$. That is, overtraining significantly facilitated the reversal learning of Group W, $F (1,28) = 6.82$, $p < .05$, while it significantly delayed the reversal learning of Group P, $F (1,28) = 7.23$, $p < .05$. After overtraining, Group W took significantly fewer days to reach criterion than Group P, $F (1,28) = 5.88$, $p < .05$, while Group P took significantly fewer days to reach criterion than Group W did without the overtraining, $F (1,28) = 8.27$, $p < .01$. Overtraining significantly facilitated reversal learning of the white-black discrimination by Group W, $t (14) = 2.57$, $p < .05$.

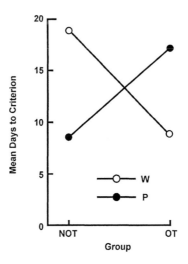

Figure 2. Mean days to criterion for each group in the Phase 3 as a function of overtraining trials.

Position Responses

In order to examine the tendency to adopt a position preference during reversal learning, a special criterion was devised: If rats chose a particular side (right or left) more than 16 times out of the 20 daily trials, the day was regarded as a positional-response day. The number of these days was counted for each rat. The mean number of days on which a position preferences was recorded for each group was as follows: 6.75 (SD = 5.50) for Group W-OT; 8.88 (SD = 7.71) for Group W-NOT; 7.38 (SD = 3.81) for Group P-OT; 3.13 (SD = 3.37) for Group P-NOT. Overtraining produced a significantly stronger position preference in Group P-OT than Group P-NOT, $t (14) = 2.50$, $p < .05$. On the other hand, there was no significant difference in this measure for Group W-OT and Group W-NOT, $t (14) < 1.00$.

Loss of Retention

In order to examine the degree of retention loss on the non-reversal discrimination task (the white-black task) of Group P, a special criterion was devised: If rats made more than three errors out of ten daily trials, the day was determined as a retention loss day. The number of those days was counted for each rat. The mean number of retention loss days on the non-reversal discrimination task for each group was as follows: 8.13 (SD = 5.30) for Group P-OT; 3.00 (SD = 3.13) for Group P-NOT. Overtraining significantly increased the retention loss days on the non-reversal discrimination task, t (14) = 2.39, p < .05.

Discussion

With regard to the number of days to reach criterion in extinction, overtraining neither facilitated nor delayed extinction in either Group W or Group P. This finding is not in line with the hypothesis of Sasaki and Shinoda (1969). Group W took significantly fewer days to reach criterion in extinction than Group P under both the overtraining and the non-overtraining conditions.

Overtraining did facilitate reversal learning in Group W and retarded reversal learning in Group P. Furthermore, Group W took significantly fewer days to reach criterion than Group P did under the overtraining condition, whereas in the absence of overtraining, Group P took significantly fewer days to reach criterion than Group W. These findings were not caused by the influence of overtraining on extinction, because there were no significant effects of this factor in the second stage of this experiment. Indeed, if differences in the rate of extinction are responsible for the speed of reversal learning, then the more rapid extinction by Group W than Group P implies that this learning should be faster in the former pair. However, this result was not observed. The findings are in line with previous findings of Sasaki and Shinoda (1969), Experiment 1 of the present study, and Nakagawa (1980a, 1980b, 1981) with young children. In addition, rats in Group P-OT showed a stronger position preference on both tasks and greater retention loss of the original white-black discrimination than their counterparts that were not overtrained, Group P-NOT. These additional findings are of interest since they indicate that following overtraining, performance on the two discriminations is no longer independent. Such an outcome can be understood if overtraining results in the development of associations between the discriminative stimuli that signal either reward, or non-reward, in the two tasks. As a consequence following overtraining, the extinction and subsequent reversal of one task should interfere with performance of the other. See also Experiment 1 of Nakagawa (1986).

EXPERIMENT 3

These findings of Experiments 1 and 2 make it clear that rats learn the whole reversal faster than the partial reversal after overtraining (i.e., the whole reversal versus partial reversal advantage effect), whereas they learn the partial reversal faster than the whole reversal after criterion training in concurrent discriminations (i.e., the partial reversal versus partial reversal advantage effect).

In spite of the reliability of the whole reversal versus partial reversal advantage effect following overtraining in either two go/no-go successive or two choice simultaneous concurrent discriminations, it remains unclear whether this advantage effect is due to a facilitation of reversal in the whole condition, a retardation of reversal in partial condition, or a combination of these two effects. The purpose of the present experiment was to determine the source of this advantage effect after overtraining by comparing reversal in the whole and partial reversal conditions with that in a control condition in which only a single discrimination was presented during reversal. If the whole condition facilitates reversal after overtraining, rats in this condition should reverse faster than those in the control condition. By contrast, slower reversal in the partial condition than in the control condition after overtraining would demonstrate that the partial reversal interferes with learning the reversed discrimination. This issue was examined in both simultaneous concurrent discriminations (Experiment 3) and go/no-go successive concurrent discriminations procedures (Experiment 4).

These findings of Experiments 1 and 2 indicate that rats have an ability to form stimulus classes between the discriminative stimuli of the same sensory modality (i.e., visual modality) during overtraining, which are heterogeneous associations (i.e., black-vertical stripes). A specific question, however, remains. Do rats form stimulus classes between the discriminative stimuli of two different sensory modalities, for example stimulus-stimulus associations between a visual stimulus (i.e., vertical lines or horizontal lines) and a tactual stimulus (i.e., rough or smooth)? Hence, the second purpose of the present experiment was to investigate the question of whether or not rats formed stimulus classes between the discriminative stimuli of two different sensory modalities during overtraining in concurrent discriminations (i.e., cross-modal stimulus classes). The two-thirds rats were concurrently trained to discriminate four simple stimuli [A (visual modality stimulus), B (visual modality stimulus), C (tactual modality stimulus), D (tactual modality stimulus) for example] where responses to the two stimuli were rewarded (A+C+ for example) and responses to the other stimuli were not rewarded (B-D- for example) to reach a criterion or were overtrained in a Y maze. After completing the original training, they were run under either a whole reversal condition (W) or a partial reversal condition (P) to reach a criterion in the shift learning. The remaining one-thirds rats were trained to discriminate two simple stimuli (C and D for example) where responses to the one stimulus were rewarded (C+ for example) and responses to the other stimulus were not rewarded (D- for example) to reach a criterion or were overtrained. After completing the original training, they were run a reversal condition to reach a criterion in the reversal learning (Control condition; C). The expectation according to the findings of Experiments 1 and 2 is that reversal is faster in the whole condition than in the control condition, which in turn is faster than in the partial condition after overtraining. Furthermore, the expectation according to the findings of Experiments 1 and 2 is that rats of the whole condition take fewer days to criterion in reversal after overtraining than after criterion training, whereas those of the partial condition take more days to criterion in reversal after overtraining than after criterion training, and that rats learn the whole reversal more rapidly than the partial reversal after overtraining, whereas they learn the partial reversal faster than the whole reversal after criterion training.

Method

Subjects

Forty-two experimentally naive Sprague-Dawley rats (20 females and 22 males) were used. They were about 150 days old with an initial average body weight of 266 g. Rats were handled for five min a day for 10 days. All details of the feeding schedule were the same as in Experiment 1. Rats were maintained on a 8:16-hr light: dark cycle, with lights off 9:00 p.m.

Apparatus

The apparatus (a modified Y maze) was basically the same as in Experiment 2. See Figure 1 of Nakagawa (2001a). The starting box measured 15 cm in height, 12,5 cm in width, and 16 cm in length. The distance from the starting box to the bifurcation was 46 cm. The arms of the Y maze were 87 cm in length. At the end of each arm was a goal box. Each goal box was 15 cm in height, 15 cm in width, and 22 cm in length. A guillotine door was located at the front of the starting box. At the entrance of the goal box a piece of cardboard was placed which served as a discriminandum. A gap over which rats had to jump (15 cm in depth, 12.5 cm in width, and 15 cm in length) was located 20 cm in front of the goal box. The apparatus was painted medium-gray inside and lit throughout the experiment by two 10-W fluorescent lamps suspended 45 cm above the top of both the arms. Brown Plexiglas except the starting box, each terrace and each goal box covered the apparatus.

Stimuli

Stimulus cards of a vertical-horizontal stripe discrimination task were 12-cm squares of cardboards. Each square was presented at the entrance of each goal box and served as an entrance door. They were arranged so that the card serving as the correct door could be pushed down easily, thus permitting rats to gain entrance into the goal box, while the card denoting the incorrect door was locked. For the vertical-horizontal stripe discrimination task vertically striped and horizontally striped squares were used, which had alternating black and white lines, 1 cm in width. A medium gray rubber mat having four projections of 3 mm in height per 1 cm^2 (12 cm in width and 20 cm in length) (rough stimulus) and a medium gray frosted glass plate (12 cm in width and 20 cm in length) (smooth stimulus) were used for a rough-smooth discrimination task. They were presented at 3 cm in front of the gap in the runway (see Figure 1 of Nakagawa, 2001a). The brown Plexiglas covering the apparatus and the frosted glass plate as the smooth stimulus allowed the colors of the different surfaces of the two tactual stimuli to be matched for luminance and they eliminated potentially different shadows cast by the two tactual stimuli as much as possible. Thus, both rough and smooth stimuli were detected solely on the basis of tactual receptors and not on the basis of visual cues. On the rough-smooth discrimination trials, a medium-gray stimulus was presented at the entrance of each goal box in place of the vertical and horizontal stripes. They were arranged so that the card serving as the correct door could be pushed down easily, while the card denoting the incorrect door was locked.

Procedure

Pretraining

Rats were given pretraining for eight days prior to the beginning of discrimination training. Rats were allowed to explore the apparatus for two periods of ten min on Day 1. All details of pretraining on through Day 2 to Day 8 were the same as in Experiment 2.

Phase 1 Discrimination Training (Original Learning)

Of 42 rats, 28 were concurrently trained for 12 trials a day with two discrimination tasks: smooth versus rough and vertical versus horizontal stripes. That is, they were concurrently trained for six trials a day with the smooth-rough discrimination task and for six trials a day with the vertical-horizontal stripes discrimination task at random. Training continued until a criterion had been reached of 11 correct trials out of a possible 12 for each discrimination over two successive days combined. A self-correction method was use in which, if rats made an error, they were allowed to return to the choice point and select a correct stimulus. The positive and negative stimuli were counterbalanced. The order of trials with the two tasks followed four predetermined random sequences. The position of a positive stimulus also followed four predetermined random sequences. The remaining 14 rats were run for six trials a day on only the rough-smooth discrimination with the self-correction method (Group C). At the end of a trial, rats were removed from the goal box by experimenter and placed to an individual cage. Rats were given two 45-mg milk pellets when they made a correct response. Intertrial intervals ranged from four to eight min.

Half of the rats received the same training for further 20 days after reaching the original learning criterion (Group OT), whereas the remaining rats received no further training in the original task once they had reached this criterion (Group NOT).

Phase 2 Reversal Learning

After completing the original learning, rats trained concurrently in Phase 1 were then divided into two subgroups (W and P), matched with respect to the number of days to criterion. The two discriminations were reversed in Group W. Only the rough-smooth discrimination task was reversed in Group P, and these rats continued to receive the same vertical-horizontal stripe discrimination training as in Phase 1. In Group C the rough-smooth task was reversed. Other aspects of the procedure were the same as during the original training.

Results

Phase 1 Training

The mean number of days to reach criterion in Phase 1 of the experiment was as follows: 21.43 (SD = 9.51) on the smooth-rough task (i.e., S-R) and 11.14 (SD = 4.29) on the horizontal-vertical stripe task (i.e., H-V) for Group W-NOT; 22.57 (SD = 9.08) on S-R task and 15.71 (SD = 7.85) on H-V task for Group W-OT; 21.14 (SD = 10.97) on S-R task and 11.86 (SD = 2.90) on H-V task for Group P-NOT; 23.57 (SD = 12.98) on S-R task and 14.00 (SD = 8.83) on H-V task for Group P-OT; 23.00 (SD = 13.11) on S-R task for Group C-NOT; and 20.00 (SD = 9.91) on S-R task for Group C-OT. An ANOVA using group (W vs. P vs. C) and overtraining (OT vs. NOT) was performed on the number of days to criterion on the smooth-rough discrimination task, which revealed that neither main effects nor the interaction were significant, all Fs < 1.

Rats in both Groups W and P learned the vertical-horizontal stripe task more rapidly than the rough-smooth task, F (1,24) = 17.92, p < .001. The percentage of errors during overtraining was 9.8 % for both Groups W and P, and 12 % for Group C.

Phase 2 Reversal Learning

Acquisition of Phase 2 reversal by Group OT was compared with acquisition of the corresponding reversal learning in Group NOT. These data are illustrated in Figure 3. An ANOVA using (W vs. P vs. C) and overtraining (OT vs. NOT) was performed on the number of days to criterion on the common reversal task (rough-smooth task), which is shown in Figure 3. The analysis yielded a significant group x overtraining interaction, F (2, 36) = 48.79, p < .001, and a significant main effect of overtraining, F(1, 36) = 21.31, p < .001, and a significant main effect of group F (1, 36) = 9.73, p < .001. Overtraining significantly facilitated reversals of both Groups W, F (1, 36) = 42.20, p < .001, and C, F (1, 36) = 47.55, p < .001, whereas it significantly retarded reversal of Group P, F (1, 36) = 29.67, p < .001. After overtraining there was a significant difference in the number of days to criterion among these three groups of W, P, and C, F (2,36) = 37.21, p < .001. A Scheffe test was run to analyze differences in the number of days to criterion among the three groups: Group W reversed more rapidly than Group P, F (1,18) = 90.56, p < .001, and Group C, F (1,18) = 9.35, p < .01. Group C also significantly reversed more rapidly than Group P did, F (1,18) = 41.72, p < .001.

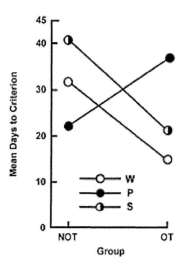

Figure 3. Means of days to criterion of each group in reversal learning as a function of overtraining trials. From "Cross-modal Stimulus Class Formation in Rats." Esho Nakagawa, 2001a, The Psychological Record, 51, pp.53-66. Copyright 2001 by The Psychological Record. Adapted with permission.

After criterion training there was a significant difference in the number of days to criterion among these three groups, $F (2,36) = 21.78$, $p < .001$. A Scheffe test was run to analyze differences in the number of days to criterion among the three groups: Group P significantly reversed more rapidly than either Group C, $F (1,18) = 35.39$, $p < .001$, or Group W, $F(1,18) = 9.95$, $p < .01$. Group W learned their reversal faster than Group C, $F (1,18) = 7.81$, $p < .05$.

Overtraining significantly facilitated reversal of the vertical-horizontal stripe task in Group W [mean days to criterion was 13.00 (SD = 2.27) for the OT rats and 25.43 (SD= 6.02) for the NOT rats], $t (12) = 4.73$, $p < .01$.

Loss of Retention

In order to examine the degree of retention loss on the non-reversal discrimination task (the vertical-horizontal stripe task) of Group P, a special criterion was devised: If rats made more than two errors out of six daily trials, the day was determined as a retention loss day. For Group P, only the smooth-rough task of the two discrimination tasks was reversed, whereas the other (i.e., the vertical-horizontal stripes task) was maintained as in original training. Thus, if performance on the two discriminations is independent, rats in Group P should make no error on the vertical-horizontal stripes task (i.e., non-reversal task) trials. If they made spontaneous errors for the reversal stage, they should make no more than one error out of six daily trials. Consequently, the retention loss measure implies that performance on the two discrimination tasks is no longer independent, that is, degree of the development of associations between the discriminative stimuli that signal either reward, or non-reward, in the two tasks. The means and SDs of retention loss day of Group P in the vertical-horizontal stripe task were follows: 9.00 (SD = 7.07) for Group P-OT and 2.14 (SD = 2.47) for Group P-NOT. Overtraining significantly increased the number of retention loss days in the vertical-horizontal stripe task, $t (12) = 2.24$, $p < .05$.

Discussion

The basic whole reversal versus partial reversal advantage effect was replicated in this experiment in that Group W reversed faster than Group P after overtraining, but not after criterion training. Comparisons with the performance of the control group, Group C, after overtraining indicate that both a facilitation of reversal in Group W and a retardation of reversal in Group P make a significant contribution to this effect. In addition, rats in Group P-OT showed greater retention loss of the original vertical-horizontal stripes discrimination than Group P-NOT. These findings make it clear that rats form stimulus classes (i.e., cross-modal stimulus classes) between the discriminative stimuli of the two different sensory modalities during overtraining.

The findings in the present experiment are not accordant with those in Experiment 1 of Nakagawa (1992). In Experiment 1 of Nakagawa (1992), there was not significant difference in the rate of reversal between Groups W and C (i.e., single discrimination group) after overtraining, whereas Group W reversed more rapidly than Group C after overtraining in the present experiment (Experiment 3). Overtraining did not significantly facilitate reversal in Group C in Experiment 1 of Nakagawa (1992), whereas it significantly facilitated reversal in Group C in the present experiment (Experiment 3). These differences may be due to difference in discrimination tasks (i.e., white-black and vertical-horizontal stripe tasks in Experiment 1 of Nakagawa, 1992; vertical-horizontal stripe and smooth-rough tasks in the present experiment, Experiment 3) employed in each experiment and to darkening the apparatus except the starting box, each terrace and each goal box by brown Plexiglas, so that a rough stimulus and smooth stimulus were detected solely on the basis of tactual receptors and not on the basis of visual cues in the present experiment (Experiment 3).

The findings of the present experiment are not readily explained by the categorization processes view on simple similarity between stimuli (Bhatt & Wasserman, 1989; Fersen & Lea, 1990; Vaughan & Hernstein, 1987). The categorization processes view (Bhatt & Wasserman, 1989; Fersen & Lea, 1990; Vaughan & Herrstein, 1987) has proposed that a concept comprises stimuli that are bound together by relations that are based solely on perceptual similarity. According to the categorization view, stimulus-stimulus associations or stimulus classes are due to categorization of stimuli based on simple similarity between stimuli. The two pairs of stimuli used in the present experiment have no simple similarity between them. Thus, it is very difficult for rats to categorize stimuli into a class on the basis of simple similarity between stimuli. The expectation according to the categorization processes view is that the basic whole reversal versus partial reversal advantage effect should not be confirmed in the present experiment. However, the basic whole reversal versus partial reversal advantage effect was replicated in the present experiment.

The present experiment has examined the effect of overtraining on reversal shifts in both two concurrent discrimination tasks and a single discrimination task. Mackintosh (1962, 1964, 1965a, 1965b) and Lawrence (1949, 1950) also have examined the effect of overtraining on reversal and non-reversal shift in a single discrimination task. Both Mackintosh and Lawrence have conceptualized the overtraining reversal effect (ORE) as being the result of overtraining enhancing animals' attention to the relevant dimension of the stimuli. That is, either Mackintosh' view or Lawrence' view has to do with changes in selective attention to the physical dimension of the stimuli. The expectations according to either Mackintosh' view or Lawrence' view are that overtraining should facilitate reversal learning of each condition: Group W, Group P, and Group C so that there should be no significant difference in the rate of reversal learning after overtraining. Or if there were significant differences in the rate of reversal learning among these three groups after criterion training, the same differences in the rate of reversal learning as after criterion training should then be observed among these three groups after overtraining. The findings of the present experiment, however, did not agree with these expectations.

The findings of the present experiment reported here make it clear that rats form stimulus classes between the discriminative stimuli of two different sensory modalities (e.g., visual and tactual modality) with the same response assignment during overtraining in two concurrent discriminations as well as between the discriminative stimuli of the same sensory modality. (See also Nakagawa, 2001a, 2002c).

These findings in the absence of overtraining of the present experiment are not consistent with the findings of Experiment 1 of Nakagawa (1992) that rats of Group P reversed faster than Group C, which in turn reversed faster than Group W (i.e., the partial reversal versus whole reversal advantage effect). These findings of the present experiment suggest that the partial reversal versus whole reversal advantage effect after criterion training is due to a facilitation of reversal in the partial condition. These findings also indicate that rats do not form stimulus classes between the discriminative stimuli after criterion training in concurrent discriminations.

Experiment 4

The findings of Experiment 3 indicate that both a facilitation of reversal in the whole condition and a retardation of reversal in the partial condition contribute to the whole reversal versus partial reversal advantage effect after overtraining. Furthermore, the findings of Experiment 3 demonstrate that overtraining has different effects on reversal learning in concurrent and single discriminations. Overtraining in concurrent discriminations produced an interaction between discrimination performances on the two tasks. The present experiment attempted to replicate the effects of overtraining on the reversal using a go/no-go successive discrimination procedure to test the generality of the whole reversal versus partial reversal advantage effect following overtraining observed in Experiment 3. To examine the question of which the presence of two discriminations is critical for the emergence of the whole reversal versus partial reversal advantage effect, either during acquisition or reversal, in addition to Groups W, P, and C, rats in a further control group (separated reversal group), Group S, received the same concurrent training as Group W before the one task was omitted and the other task reversed. Unlike Group C, the conditions during original learning in Group S matched exactly those in Groups P and W.

Method

Subjects

Forty-eight experimentally naive Sprague-Dawley rats (24 females, 24 males) were used. They were about 180 days old, with an average initial body weight of 425 g. All details of the feeding schedule and handling were the same as in Experiment 1. They were maintained on a 6:18-hr light: dark cycle, with lights off at 3:00 a.m.

Apparatus

The apparatus (a straight runway) was basically the same as that in Experiment 1. Only one difference in the apparatus between Experiment 1 and this experiment was the length of runway. That is, the length of runway of the apparatus used in this experiment was 50 cm, whereas it was 40 cm in the apparatus in Experiment 1. See Figure 3 of Nakagawa (1992). Separate starting time and running time were obtained on each trial by means of two electrical digital timers. When the experimenter raised the guillotine door, a micro switch activated the first timer. When rats interrupted a photo beam cell 7 cm down the runway, this timer stopped, and at the same time the second timer started. When rats interrupted the second photo beam cell 67 cm further down the runway, the second timer stopped. A running time is the time between the interrupting of the first and second photo beams.

Stimuli

The same stimuli as in Experiment 1 were used for the white-black and the vertical-horizontal-stripe discriminations.

Procedure

Pretraining

All details of pretraining were the same as in Experiment 1.

Phase 1 Discrimination Training (Original Learning)

Thirty-six rats were trained concurrently to criterion in original learning for 12 trials a day, six on each of the two discriminations: white versus black and vertical versus horizontal stripes. Two rats in each group were trained with B+H+, two rats with B+V+, one rat with W+H+, and one rat with W+V+. The order of the trials with the two tasks followed 4 predetermined random sequences. The remaining 12 rats were trained only on the vertical-horizontal stripe discrimination to criterion for six trials a day. Three rats were trained with V+, and three rats with H+. The order of rewarded trials and non-rewarded ones followed four predetermined, random sequences. Rats were given three rewarded trials and three non-rewarded ones per day on each task. On rewarded trials rats were given two 45-mg milk pellets as a reward in the goal box. On non-rewarded trials they were retained for 60 sec. in the runway after the guillotine door was opened. Intertrial intervals ranged from four to eight min. The criterion in original learning was that the median of the running time on the rewarded trials was shorter than the shortest running time on the non-rewarded trials for each task for two successive days.

Half of the rats received the same training for a further 20 days after reaching the criterion (Group OT). The remaining rats received no further training on the original learning task once they had reached the criterion (Group NOT).

Phase 2 Reversal Learning

After completing the original learning, rats trained concurrently during original learning were divided into the three groups: Groups W, P, and S. They were then trained under a given reversal condition until they achieved a criterion in reversal learning, which was the same as that in original learning. Group W was run under the whole reversal condition, Group P was run under the partial reversal condition, and Group C was run under the single reversal condition, as in Experiment 3. Group S was run under the separated reversal condition in which only the vertical-horizontal stripe discrimination task was reversed and the black-white task was omitted. Other aspects of the procedure were the same as during the original training.

Results

Phase 1 Training

The mean number of days to reach criterion in Phase 1 of the experiment was as follows: 10.17 (SD = 3.67) on the black-white task (i.e., B-W) and 10.83 (SD = 3.44) on the horizontal-vertical stripe task (i.e., H-V) for Group W-NOT; 10.10 (SD = 3.74) on B-W task and 10.50 (SD = 3.95) on H-V task for Group W-OT; 10.00 (SD = 3.42) on B-W task and 10.33 (SD = 3.15) on H-V task for Group P-NOT; 9.00 (SD = 2.28) on B-W task and 10.33 (SD = 2.98) on H-V task for Group P-OT; 10.33 (SD = 1.97) on B-W task and 10.17 (SD = 2.14) on H-V task for Group S-NOT; 9.83 (SD = 1.83) on B-W task and 10.67 (SD = 2.66) on

H-V task for Group S-OT; 11.83 (SD = 3.67) on H-V task for Group C-NOT; and 11.00 (SD = 3.37) on H-V task for Group C-OT. The results of an ANOVA using group (W vs. P vs. S vs. C) and degree of overtraining (OT vs. NOT) performed on the number of days to criterion on the vertical-horizontal stripe task were as follows: Neither the main effects nor the interaction was significant, all Fs < 1. Thus, there were no significant differences in the rate of learning among eight groups.

Phase 2 Reversal Learning

An ANOVA using group (W vs. P vs. S vs. C) and degree of overtraining (OT vs. NOT) was performed on the number of days to criterion on the vertical-horizontal stripe task, which is illustrated in Figure 4. The analysis yielded significant main effects of overtraining, $F(1,40) = 18.81$, $p < .01$, and of groups, $F(3,40) = 3.08$, $p < .04$. The overtraining x group interaction also was significant, $F(3,40) = 22.13$, $p < .01$. Overtraining significantly facilitated reversals in Group W, $F(1,40) = 41.46$, $p < .01$, Group S, $F(1,40) = 9.33$, $p < .05$, and Group C, $F(1,40) = 13.80$, $p < .01$. By contrast, it significantly delayed reversal in Group P, $F(1,40) = 20.62$, $p < .01$. After overtraining there was a significant difference in the number of days to criterion among the four groups, $F(3,40) = 9.21$, $p < .01$. A Scheffe test was run to analyze differences in the number of days to criterion among the four groups. Group W reversed significantly more rapidly than both Group P, $F(1,20) = 21.10$, $p < .01$, and Group C, $F(1,20) = 7.12$, $p < .05$, and marginally more rapidly than Group S, $F(1,20) = 4.08$, $.05 < p < .10$. Group S reversed significantly more rapidly, $F(1,20) = 6.36$, $p < .05$, and Group C marginally faster, $F(1,20) = 3.51$, $.05 < p < .10$, than Group P. The reversal performance of Groups S and C did not differ, $F < 1$.

In the absence of overtraining, there were significant differences in the number of days to criterion among the four groups, $F(3,40) = 16.01$, $p < .01$. Group P reversed significantly more rapidly than Group W, $F(1, 20) = 13.28$, $p < .01$, Group S, $F(1,20) = 8.82$, $p < .01$, and Group C, $F(1,20) = 14.85$, $p < .01$. However, there were no significant differences between Groups W, S, and C.

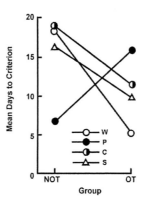

Figure 4. Means of days to criterion of each group in reversal learning as a function of overtraining trials. From "Effects of Overtraining on Reversal Learning by Rats in Concurrent and Single Discriminations." Esho Nakagawa, 1992, The Quarterly Journal of Experimental Psychology, 44B, pp.37-56. Copyright 1992 by The Experimental Psychology Society. Adapted with permission.

Overtraining significantly facilitated reversal of the white-black task in Group W [mean days to criterion was 4.50 (SD = 1.68) for the OT rats and 17.17 (SD = 2.85) for the NOT rats], t (10) = 8.56, p < .01.

Discussion

This experiment essentially replicated the pattern of results seen in Experiments 1, 2 and 3: the whole reversal versus partial reversal advantage effect was observed in that Group W reversed faster than Group P after overtraining, positive and negative OREs occurred in Group W and Group P, respectively. In addition, the facts that Group W reversed faster than group C, which in turn reversed faster than reversed marginally faster than Group P after overtraining confirm the conclusion from Experiment 3 that both a facilitation of reversal in Group W and a retardation of reversal learning in Group P contribute to the whole reversal versus partial reversal advantage effect.

In addition to generalizing these conclusions from a simultaneous to successive discrimination procedure, Experiment 4 also yielded further an important finding. That is, the comparable performance observed in the two control groups, Groups C and S, shows that it is the presence of two discriminations during reversal rather than acquisition that is critical for the emergence of the whole reversal versus partial reversal advantage effect.

In the absence of overtraining, Group P reversed more rapidly than Groups W, C, and S, whereas there were not significant differences in the rate of reversal among these three groups; W, C, and S. These findings suggest that a facilitation of reversal learning in Group P contributes to the partial reversal versus whole reversal advantage effect after criterion training. These findings are not in line with findings of Experiment 3. In Experiment 3, rats of Group W learned their reversal faster than group C after criterion training, whereas there were no significant differences between Groups W, S, and C in this experiment. This difference may be due to the difference in discrimination task used in each experiment (i.e., white versus black and vertical versus horizontal stripe tasks in Experiment 3; vertical versus horizontal stripe and smooth versus rough tasks in Experiment 4).

EXPERIMENT 5

These findings of Experiments 1, 2, 3, and 4 provide evidence for occurrence of the partial reversal versus whole reversal advantage effect after criterion training in concurrent discriminations in rats. That is, these findings of Experiments 3 and 4 suggest that the effect is caused by a facilitation of reversal in the partial condition. However, the findings of Experiment 1 of Nakagawa (1992) suggested both facilitation of reversal in the partial condition and a retardation of reversal of the whole condition contributed to the effect in the absence of overtraining.

In spite of the reliability of the partial reversal versus whole reversal advantage effect after criterion training that rats learn the partial reversal more rapidly than the whole (Nakagawa, 1978, 1986, 1992, 1998, 1999a, 2000, 2001a), it remains unclear whether this advantage effect is caused by a facilitation of reversal in the partial condition, a retardation of reversal in the whole condition, or a combination of the two effects. The purpose of the present experiment was to determine the source of the partial reversal versus whole reversal advantage effect by comparing reversal in the partial and whole conditions with that in a control condition. Either rats of Group C in Experiment 3 or ones of Groups C and S in Experiment 4 were trained on only one discrimination to criterion for six trials a day during the reversal stage, whereas rats of Groups W and P in either Experiments 3 or 4 were concurrently trained on two discriminations to criterion for 12 trials a day. The results after criterion training in Experiments 3 and 4 may be due to the difference in the number of training trials during the reversal stage. Thus, the present experiment was conducted to examine the source of the partial reversal versus whole reversal advantage effect under the condition that rats of either a whole condition, a partial condition, or a control condition were given the same number of training trials in a day in both the acquisition and reversal stages. At the same time, the present experiment examined the question of whether or not rats formed stimulus-stimulus associations between the discriminative stimuli with the same response assignment in two choice simultaneous concurrent discriminations after criterion training. Rats were concurrently trained with two discrimination tasks (A+ vs. B-; C+ vs. D-) to criterion. After completing Phase 1 training, they were transferred to either a whole reversal in which both tasks were reversed, a partial reversal in which only one of the two tasks was reversed but the other was not reversed, or a control reversal in which only one of the two tasks was reversed but the other was replaced for a new discrimination task. If the four connections (i.e., A with food, C with food, B with no food, and D with no food) in Phase 1 were independent of one another as Nakagawa (1978, 1986, 1992, 1998, 1999a, 1999b, 1999c, 1999d) postulated, rats for a partial reversal would have reversed faster than rats for a control reversal, which in turn would have reversed more rapidly than rats for a whole reversal, because rats for partial reversal and a control reversal had only two connections to relearn, whereas rats for a whole reversal had four connections to relearn. Furthermore, rats for a partial reversal have a non-reversal task that should inhibit their irrelevant responses such as positional responses, whereas rats for a control reversal have no such non-reversal task.

Method

Subjects

Twenty-four experimentally naive Sprague-Dawley rats (13 females and 11 males) were used. They were about 190 days old with an initial average body weight of 352 g. Rats were handled for five min a day for 12 days. All details of the feeding schedule were the same as in Experiment 1. Rats were maintained on a 8:16-hr light: dark cycle, with lights off 6:00 p.m.

Apparatus

An apparatus (a modified Y maze) was the same as in Experiment 2.

Stimuli

Stimulus cards were 12-cm squares of cardboard. Each card was presented at the entrance of each goal box and served as an entrance door. They were arranged so that the card serving as the correct door could be pushed down easily, thus permitting rats to gain entrance into the goal box; the card denoting an incorrect door was locked. For a white-black discrimination a white card and a black one were used. Vertically striped and horizontally striped cards were used for a vertical-horizontal stripe discrimination. Striped cards had alternating black and white lines one cm in width. For an additional discrimination used in the final phase of the experiment, an equilateral triangle with ten cm sides and a circle with a diameter of 7.5 cm were used.

Procedure

Pretraining
All details of pretraining were the same as in Experiment 2.

Phase 1 Discrimination Ttraining (Original Learning)
Rats were initially trained for 12 trials a day with two concurrent discrimination tasks: white versus black and vertical versus horizontal stripes. Training continued until a criterion had been reached of 11 correct trials out of a possible 12 for each discrimination task over two successive days combined. A self-correction method was used in which, if rats made an error, they were allowed to return to the choice point and select and stimulus. The positive and negative stimuli were counterbalanced. The order of trials with the two discriminations followed four predetermined random sequences. The position of a positive stimulus also followed four predetermined random sequences. Rats were given two 45-mg milk pellets when they made a correct response. Intertrial intervals ranged from four to eight min.

Phase 2 Reversal Learning
After completing the original training, rats were then divided into three groups (W, P, and C), matched with respect to the number of days to criterion. They were then trained under a given reversal condition until they achieved a criterion in reversal learning, which was the same as that in original learning. Group W was run under the whole reversal condition in which both discriminations were reversed. Group P was run under the partial reversal condition in which only one of the two discriminations (the vertical-horizontal stripe task) was reversed but the other (the white-black task) was not reversed. In order to equalize the number of exposures to the apparatus and the numbers of reinforcers obtained in the apparatus to those in both Groups W and P and further to examine the effect of a second problem on reversal of the first. Group C was run under the control reversal condition in which only one of the two discriminations (the vertical-horizontal stripe task) was reversed and a new discrimination task (triangle-circle task) was added instead of the other (the white-black task). Other aspects of the training procedure were the same as in the original training.

Results

Phase 1 Training
The mean number of days to reach criterion in Phase 1 of the experiment was as follows: 21.38 (SD = 9.94) on the white-black task (i.e., W-B) and 22.25 (SD = 9.19) on the horizontal-vertical stripe task (i.e., H-V) for Group W; 22.25 (SD = 7.50) on W-B task and 23.38 (SD = 8.79) on H-V task for Group P; 20.00 (SD = 6.04) on W-B task and 20.38 (SD =

6.32) on H-V task for Group C. An ANOVA using group (W vs. P vs. C) and task (W-B vs. H-V) was performed on the number of days to criterion, which revealed no significant min effects and no significant interaction, all Fs < 1.

Phase 2 Reversal

An ANOVA using group (W vs. P vs. C) was performed on the number of days to criterion on the vertical-horizontal stripe task, which is illustrated in Figure 5. The analysis yielded a significant main effect of group, $F (2, 21) = 41.39$, $p < .001$. A Scheffe test was run to analyze difference in the number of days to criterion among the three groups. Group P reversed significantly more rapidly than both Group C, $F (1,21) = 8.00$, $p < .05$. Group W reversed significantly more slowly than both Group C, $F (1,21) = 36.90$, $p < .001$, and Group P, $F (1,21) = 79.26$, $p < .001$. The means and SDs of days to criterion on both the white-black task in Group W and the triangle-circle task in Group C were as follows: 28.25 (SD = 6.92) for Group W and 14.13 (SD = 2.52) for Group C, respectively.

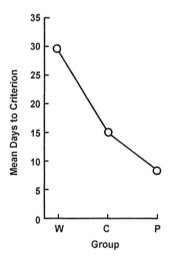

Figure 5. Mean days to criterion for each group in Phase 2 as a function of groups. From "Reversal Learning in Concurrent Discriminations in Rats." Esho Nakagawa, 2001b, The Psychological Record, 51, pp.251-269. Adapted with permission.

Stimulus Perseveration

In order to examine the extinction of the original discrimination after the beginning of Phase 2 reversal, a special criterion was devised: The number of days that a rat took to make more correct responses than three times out of six daily trials after beginning of Phase 2 was determined as a stimulus perseveration. The mean number of days to this criterion for the vertical-horizontal stripe task is plotted in Figure 6 for each group. An ANOVA using group (W vs. P vs. C) was performed, which revealed a significant main effect of group, $F (2,21) = 11.14$ $p < .001$. A Scheffe test was run to analyze differences in stimulus perseveration among these three groups. Group W made significantly stronger stimulus perseveration than Group C, $F (1,21) = 7.23$ $p < .05$, and Group P, $F (1,21) = 5.53$ $p < .05$. Group C also made stronger perseveration than Group P, but this difference just failed to reach significance, $F (1,21) = 4.07$, $.05 < p < .10$.

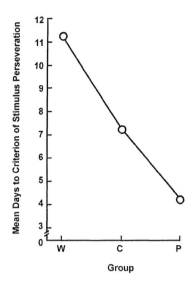

Figure 6. Mean days to criterion of stimulus perseveration for each group in Phase 2 as a function of groups. From "Reversal Learning in Concurrent Discriminations in Rats." Esho Nakagawa, 2001b, The Psychological Record, 51, pp.251-269. Adapted with permission.

In order to examine the tendency to adopt a position preference during reversal learning, a special criterion was devised: If rats chose a particular side (right or left) more than eight times out of 12 daily trials, the day was regarded as a positional-response day. The number of these days was counted for each rat, their means and SDs during reversal learning are illustrated in Figure 7 for each group. An ANOVA using group (W vs. P vs. C) was performed on the number of positional-response days, which revealed a significant main effect of group, $F_{(1,21)} = 20.15$, $p < .001$. A Scheffe test was run to analyze differences in the number of positional-response days among these three groups. Group P made significantly fewer positional-responses than Group C, $F_{(1,21)} = 13.67$ $p < .001$, which in turn made significantly fewer than positional –responses than Group W, $F_{(1,21)} = 6.86$, $p < .05$.

In order to examine the degree of interaction of performance between the non-reversal and reversal tasks in Group P, a special criterion was devised: If rats made more than two errors out of six daily trials on the non-reversal task, the day was determined as a retention loss day. The number of these days was counted for each rat. The mean and SD of the retention loss days in Group P were 1.50 (SD = 2.45).

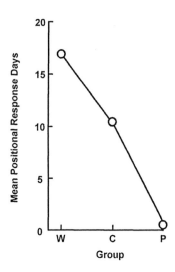

Figure 7. Mean positional-response days for each group in Phase 2 as a function of groups. From "Reversal Learning in Concurrent Discriminations in Rats." Esho Nakagawa, 2001b, The Psychological Record, 51, pp.251-269. Adapted with permission.

Discussion

These findings of Experiment 5 are consistent with the expectations according to the theory of Nakagawa (1992, 1998, 1999a, 1999b, 1999c, 1999d, 2000, 2001a, 2001b, 2002a, 2002b): Group P mastered reversal faster than Group C, which in turn mastered reversal faster than Group W. Comparisons with performance of the control condition indicate that both a facilitation of reversal in Group P and a retardation of reversal in Group W make significant contribution to the partial reversal versus whole reversal advantage effect. These findings are consistent with the findings of Experiment 1 of Nakagawa (1992).

The stimulus perseveration mirrored the partial reversal versus whole reversal advantage effect as measured by days to criterion. Group P showed more rapid reversal than the remaining groups, an effect that appeared to be caused by differences in stimulus perseveration. These findings are not in line with the findings of Experiment 1 of Nakagawa (1992). This discrepancy is because of difference in the measure of stimulus perseveration between the two experiments. That is, the number of trials that a rat took to make a first correct response after beginning the reversal was used as a stimulus perseveration measure in Experiment 1 of Nakagawa (1992), whereas the number of days that a rat took to make more correct responses than three times out of six daily trials after beginning of reversal was used a stimulus perseveration measure.

In addition, only two rats of Group P exhibited just two positional-response days, whereas the remaining rats did not exhibit any positional-response days. They made just a little retention loss on the non-reversed discrimination. These additional findings make it clear that rats do not form stimulus-stimulus associations between the discriminative stimuli with the same response assignment in the original training, that is, performance on two concurrent discriminations is independent of one another.

The analysis of positional-response days yielded a pattern that was very similar to the days to criterion measure for the partial reversal versus whole reversal advantage effect. Thus, it would appear that this effect is caused by variation in the degree of positional-response days.

EXPERIMENT 6

These findings of Experiment 5 provide evidence that both a facilitation of reversal in Group P and a retardation of reversal in Group W make significant contribution to occurrence of the partial reversal versus whole reversal advantage effect after criterion training, and that this effect is attributed to stimulus perseveration. These findings indicate that rats do not form stimulus-stimulus associations between the discriminative stimuli with the same consequence after criterion training in two simultaneous concurrent discriminations. The present experiment was conducted to replicate the partial reversal versus whole reversal advantage effect using a go/no-go successive discrimination procedure to test the generality of the conclusions from a simultaneous to successive discrimination procedure. Rats were trained with two go/no-go successive discrimination tasks to criterion. After completing Phase 1 training, they transferred to either a whole reversal or a partial reversal or a control reversal. The expectation according to the theory of Nakagawa (1992, 1998, 1999a, 1999b, 1999c, 1999d, 2000, 2001a, 2001b, 2002a, 2002b) is that rats of the partial reversal condition master reversal faster than rats of the control reversal condition, which in turn master reversal faster than rats of the whole reversal condition.

Method

Subjects
Twenty-four experimentally naïve male Sprague-Dawley rats were used. They were about 240 days old with initial average body weight of 542 g. All details of feeding schedule and handling were the same as in Experiment 1.

Apparatus
An apparatus (a straight runway) was the same as in Experiment 4.

Stimuli
The same stimuli as in Experiment 5 were used for the white-black discrimination task, for the vertical-horizontal stripe discrimination task, and for the triangle-circle discrimination task.

Procedure

Pretraining
Rats were given pretraining for eight days prior to the beginning of the training phase. All details of pretraining were the same as in Experiment 4.

Phase 1 Discrimination Training (Original Learning)

Rats were initially trained for 12 trials a day, six trials with each of the two discriminations: white versus black and vertical versus horizontal stripes. Rats were given three rewarded trials and three non-rewarded ones on each discrimination per day. On rewarded trials rats were given two 45-mg milk pellets as reward in the goal box. On non-rewarded trials they were retained for 60 sec. In the runway after the guillotine door was opened. Training continued until a criterion had been reached. The criterion was that the median of the running times on the rewarded trials was shorter than the shortest running time on the non-rewarded trials for each task for two successive days. The order of the trials with the two tasks followed four predetermined random sequences. The order of rewarded trials and non-rewarded ones also followed four predetermined sequences. Intertrial intervals ranged from four to eight min.

Phase 2 Reversal Learning

After completing the original training, rats were then divided into three groups (W vs. P vs. C), matched with respect to the number of days to criterion. They were trained under a given reversal condition until they achieved a criterion in the reversal learning, which was the same as in Phase 1 training. Group W was run under a whole reversal condition in which both tasks were reversed. Group P was run under a partial reversal condition in which only one of the two tasks was reversed but the other was not reversed and continued to receive the same discrimination training as in Phase 1. Group C was run under a control reversal condition in which only one of the two tasks was reversed and a new discrimination task (i.e., triangle-circle task) was given instead of the other (i.e., white-black task). Other aspects of the procedure were the same as during the original training.

Results

Phase 1 Training

The mean number of days to reach criterion in Phase 1 of the experiment was as follows: 6.50 (SD = 1.41) on the white-black task (i.e., W-B) and 6.38 (SD = 1.77) on the horizontal-vertical stripe task (i.e., H-V) for Group W; 6.38 (SD = 1.60) on W-B task and 6.25 (SD = 1.04) on H-V task for Group P; 7.25 (SD = 2.05) on W-B task and 6.25 (SD = 1.83) on H-V task for Group C. An ANOVA using group (W vs. P vs. C) and task (W-B vs. H-V) was performed on the number of days to criterion, which revealed no significant min effects and no significant interaction, all Fs < 1.

Phase 2 Reversal

An ANOVA using group (W vs. P vs. C) was performed on the number of days to criterion on the vertical-horizontal stripe task, which is illustrated in Figure 8. The analysis yielded a significant main effect of group, $F_{(2,21)} = 33.78$, $p < .001$. A Scheffe test was run to analyze difference in the number of days to criterion among the three groups. Group P reversed significantly more rapidly than both Group C, $F_{(1, 21)} = 5.52$, $p < .05$, and Group W, $F_{(1,21)} = 72.28$, $p < .001$. Group W reversed significantly more slowly than Group C, $F_{(1,21)} = 37.84$, $p < .001$.

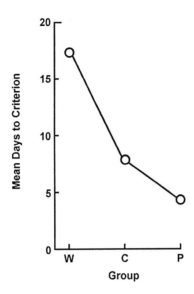

Figure 8. Mean days to criterion for each group in Phase 2 as a function of groups. From "Reversal Learning in Concurrent Discriminations in Rats". Esho Nakagawa, 2001b, The Psychological Record, 51, pp.251-269. Adapted with permission.

The means and SDs of days to criterion on both the white-black task in Group W and the triangle-circle task in Group C were as follows: 16.63 (SD = 4.66) for Group W and 7.63 (SD = 2.97) for Group C, respectively.

Stimulus Perseveration

In order to examine the extinction of the original discrimination after the beginning of Phase 2 reversal, a special criterion was devised: The criterion was that the median of the running times on the rewarded trials was shorter than the median of the running times on the non-rewarded trials for each task in the reversal learning. Number of days to reach this criterion was taken as a measure of a stimulus perseveration. The mean number of days to this criterion is plotted in Figure 9 for each group. An ANOVA using group (W vs. P vs. C) was performed, which revealed a significant main effect of group, $F_{(2,21)} = 3.50$, $p < .05$. An Scheffe test was run to analyze differences in stimulus perseveration among these three groups. Group W made significantly stronger stimulus perseveration than Group P, $F_{(1,21)} = 6.80$, $p < .05$. Group W also made stronger perseveration than Group C, but this difference just failed to reach significance, $F_{(1,21)} = 2.90$, $.05 < p < .10$. The mean and SD of the stimulus perseveration on the white-black task in Group W was 2.63 and 2.73, respectively.

In order to examine the degree of interaction of performance between the non-reversal and reversal tasks in Group P, a special criterion was devised: If any one of running times on non-rewarded trials became shorter than the mean of the running times on rewarded trials for the white-black task (i.e., non-reversed task), the day was determined as a retention loss day. The number of these days was counted for each rat. The mean and SD of the retention loss days in Group P were 1.13 and 0.46, respectively.

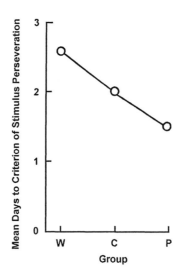

Figure 9. Mean days to criterion of stimulus perseveration for each group in Phase 2 as a function of groups. From "Reversal Learning in Concurrent Discriminations in Rats". Esho Nakagawa, 2001b, The Psychological Record, 51, pp.251-269. Adapted with permission.

Discussion

This Experiment 6 replicated the pattern of results seen in Experiment 5: The partial reversal versus whole reversal advantage effect was observed in that Group P reversed faster than Group C, which in turn reversed faster than Group W. These findings of the present experiment confirm the conclusion from Experiment 5 that both a facilitation of reversal learning in Group P and retardation of reversal learning in Group W, relative to the control condition, contribute to the partial reversal versus whole reversal advantage effect. These findings are in line with these findings of Experiments 3 and 4. These findings indicate that rats do not form stimulus-stimulus associations between the discriminative stimuli after criterion training in two successive go/no-go discriminations as well as in two choice concurrent discriminations. This is supported by the retention loss day data.

There were significant between-groups differences in stimulus perseveration among these three groups. According to Figure 9, as a whole, Group W made stronger stimulus perseveration than Group C, which in turn made stronger stimulus perseveration than Group P. These findings are in line with the findings of Experiment 5 and of Experiment 1 of Nakagawa (1992). However, these findings are not in line with the findings of Experiment 4. This discrepancy may be caused by differences in training procedures in Phase 2 reversal in the control condition between these two experiments. That is, in the present experiment, rats in Group C were concurrently given a reversed task and a newly added discrimination task, whereas, in Experiment 4 rats of Groups C and S were given only a reversed task.

GENERAL DISCUSSION

The six experiments reported here, using the whole reversal versus partial reversal procedure, have studied reversal learning in concurrent discriminations in rats. In Experiment 1 with go/no-go successive concurrent discriminations, rats of Group W reversed faster than Group P after overtraining (i.e., the whole reversal versus partial reversal advantage effect), whereas Group P reversed faster than Group W after criterion training (i.e., the partial reversal versus whole reversal advantage effect). Furthermore, overtraining facilitated reversal in Group W (a positive ORE), whereas it retarded reversal in Group P (a negative ORE). In Experiment 2 with two choice simultaneous concurrent discriminations, Group W reversed more rapidly than Group P after overtraining in Phase 3 after extinction training, whereas Group P reversed more rapidly than Group W after criterion training. These findings of Experiment 2 indicate that either the whole reversal versus partial reversal advantage effect after overtraining or the partial reversal versus whole reversal advantage effect after criterion training remain intact after extinction. In Experiment 3, rats of Group W took fewer days to criterion in reversal learning than Group C, which in turn took fewer days than Group P following overtraining, whereas Group P took fewer days to criterion than Group W, which in turn took fewer days than Group C after criterion training in two simultaneous concurrent discriminations of two different sensory modalities. In Experiment 4, rats of Group W learned their reversal faster than Groups C and S, which in turn learned their reversal faster than Group P after overtraining, whereas Group P learned their reversal faster than the other three groups of W, C, and S after criterion training. In Experiment 5 with two choice simultaneous concurrent discriminations, rats of Group P reversed more rapidly than Group C, which in turn reversed more rapidly than Group W in the absence of overtraining. Experiment 6 replicated the pattern of results seen in Experiment 5 in go/no-go successive concurrent discriminations. These findings of the six experiments in the present study provide evidence for occurrence of both the whole reversal versus partial reversal advantage effect following overtraining and the partial reversal versus whole reversal advantage effect in the absence of overtraining in concurrent discriminations in rats. Furthermore, these findings indicate that both a facilitation of reversal in the whole condition and a retardation of reversal in the partial condition make significant contribution to the whole reversal versus partial reversal advantage effect after overtraining in concurrent discriminations in rats, and that both a facilitation of reversal in the partial condition and a retardation of reversal in the whole condition contribute to the partial reversal versus whole reversal advantage effect after criterion training in the absence of overtraining. These findings also make it clear that overtraining has different effects on reversal learning in concurrent and single discriminations in rats.

As mentioned in the Discussion section in Experiment 1, the whole reversal versus partial effect following overtraining in concurrent discriminations are not explained by extant theories of discrimination learning. However, this effect are consistent with the expectation from the discrimination theory (i.e., reinforcement density theory) by Zentall (1998) and Zentall et al. (1991) that faster whole reversal than partial reversal is based on the difference in detectability of change in reinforcement across phases, between whole and partial reversal. According to the reinforcement density theory, for the rats of the whole reversal, there is a larger, and thus probably a more detected, change in the conditions of reinforcement from Phase 1 training to Phase 2 reversal than the rats for the partial reversal. For the whole reversal, responding on the basis of the rule acquired in the original training results in non-reinforcement. By contrast, for the partial reversal, responding on the basis of the rule acquired in the original training still results in reinforcement on half of trials. Indeed, reinforcement density changed from 100% to 0% in the whole reversal, whereas it changed from 100% to 50% in the partial reversal in the six experiments in the present study. Thus, Group W should reverse faster than Group P after overtraining. This result was observed in all the four experiments of 1, 2, 3, and 4. However, the reinforcement density theory could not explain the findings that both a facilitation of reversal in the whole condition and a retardation of reversal in the partial condition contribute to the whole reversal versus partial reversal advantage effect after overtraining. It is because reinforcement density changed from 100% to 0% in either the whole reversal or the control reversal (C or S), whereas it changed from 100% to 50% in the partial reversal. According to the reinforcement density theory, either Group W or Group C (or S) should learned their reversal than Group P after overtraining, whereas there should be not significant difference in the rate of reversal between Group W and Group C (or S). That is, the whole reversal versus partial reversal advantage effect should be caused by a retardation of reversal in Group P, but not by a facilitation of reversal in Group W. However, this result was not observed in Experiments 3 and 4.

Alternatively, the theory of Nakagawa (1992, 1998, 1999a, 1999b, 1999c, 1999d, 2000, 2001a, 2001b, 2002a, 2002b) can readily explain both the whole reversal versus partial reversal advantage effect and the findings that both a facilitation of reversal in the whole condition and a retardation of reversal in the partial condition contribute to the whole reversal versus partial reversal advantage effect after overtraining. According to the theory of Nakagawa, in concurrent discriminations, during the original training rats learn a connection between a positive stimulus and an approach response as well as a connection between a negative stimulus and an avoidance response for each discrimination task. During overtraining they also form associations between the discriminative stimuli with the same response assignment. Thus, rats learn to associate the two positive stimuli as well as to associate the two negative stimuli of the two independent discriminations. The associations between the two positive stimuli and between the two negative stimuli are called "stimulus-stimulus associations (i.e., cue-associations)". These stimulus-stimulus associations produce "an acquired equivalence" effect, whereby stimuli associated with the same consequence show enhanced generalization; that is, stimulus-stimulus associations mediate the transfer of appropriate responding from one positive (or negative) stimulus to the other positive (or negative) stimulus in reversal learning.

As a result of these stimulus-stimulus associations, the reversal of the one discrimination after overtraining in the whole condition should exert a synergistic influence upon the reversal of the other discrimination. Each reinforcement of the new positive stimulus in one discrimination should not only enhance the strength of the approach response to this stimulus but also augment the same response to the new positive stimulus in the other discrimination via the stimulus-stimulus associations between the positive stimuli formed during overtraining. Correspondingly, the consequences of non-reinforcement of the new negative stimulus should also transfer between discriminations. Consequently, reversal should be faster in the whole condition than in the control conditions in which this synergistic effect cannot operate. Overtraining on a single discrimination, as in Group C, precludes the development of stimulus-stimulus associations (i.e., cue-associations), whereas the omission of the second discrimination during reversal, as in Group S, removes the source of positive transfer via the stimulus-stimulus association (i.e., cue-associations). Furthermore, in agreement with the present data in Experiments 3 and 4, the theory of Nakagawa predicts a large positive ORE in the whole condition because in the absence of overtraining thee are no stimulus-stimulus associations (i.e., cue-associations) present to mediate the synergistic interaction between discriminations.

A parallel explanation can be given for the retarded reversal observed in the partial condition after overtraining. In the presence of stimulus-stimulus associations (i.e., cue-associations), continued training with the non-reversed discrimination during the reversal stages will lead to interference with the development of an approach response to the new positive stimulus and of an avoidance response to the new negative stimulus of the reversed discrimination. Consequently, Group P should exhibit both retarded reversal learning relative to the control conditions after overtraining and a negative ORE.

The two findings that rats learned their reversal in the partial condition faster than in the whole condition (i.e., the partial reversal versus whole reversal advantage effect) and that both a facilitation of reversal in the partial condition and a retardation of reversal in the whole condition significantly contributed to this advantage effect in the absence of overtraining are not readily explained by the reinforcement density theory. In Experiments 3, 4, 5, and 6, reinforcement density changed from 100% to 0% in either the whole reversal or the control reversal (C or S), whereas it changed from 100% to 50% in the partial reversal. According to the reinforcement density theory, either Group W or Group C (or S) should learned their reversal than Group P, whereas there should be no significant difference in the rate of reversal between Group W and Group C (or S). That is, the partial reversal versus whole reversal advantage effect should not occur, rather the whole reversal versus partial reversal advantage effect should occur, in the absence of overtraining. However, this result was not observed in the six experiments in the present study.

Alternatively, according to the theory of Nakagawa, rats do not form stimulus-stimulus associations between the discriminative stimuli after criterion training in concurrent discriminations. The reversal of the one discrimination in the whole reversal should not exert a synergistic influence upon the reversal of the other discrimination. Thus, performance on two discriminations is independent. For rats of Group P, continued training with the non-reversed discrimination during the reversal stage will lead to interference with the development of irrelevant responses such as positional responses, whereas rats of both Group W and Group C (or S) have non-reversed discrimination during the reversal stage so that they remove the source of interference with the development of irrelevant responses. Furthermore, either Group P or Group C (or S) has only two, rather than four, associations to relearn, whereas Group W has four associations to relearn. Consequently, Group P learns their reversal faster than Group C (or S), which in turn learns faster than Group W after criterion training.

The whole reversal versus partial reversal advantage effect following overtraining and the partial reversal versus whole reversal advantage effect in the absence of overtraining in concurrent discriminations seen the six experiments are peculiar to reversal learning in concurrent discriminations but not in a single discrimination. This is supported by the findings of Experiments 3 and 4.

These findings of the six experiments in the present study demonstrate that both a facilitation of reversal in Group W and a retardation of reversal in Group P significantly contribute to the whole reversal versus partial reversal advantage effect after overtraining, whereas both a facilitation of reversal in Group P and a retardation of reversal in Group W make significantly contribution to the partial reversal versus whole reversal advantage effect after criterion training in concurrent discriminations in rats. Furthermore, these findings indicate that rats do form stimulus-stimulus associations between the discriminative stimuli after overtraining, but not after criterion training. Finally, these findings make it clear that overtraining has different effects on reversal learning in concurrent and single discriminations in rats.

REFERENCES

Bhatt, R. S., & Wasserman, E. A. (1989). Secondary generalization and categorization in pigeons. *The Journal of the Experimental Analysis of Behavior*, 52, 213-224.

Coate, W.B. & Gardner, R.A. (1965). Source of transfer from original training to discrimination reversal. *Journal of Experimental Psychology*, 70. 94-97.

Delius, J.D., Ameling, M., Lea, S.E., & Staddon, J.E.R. (1995). Reinforcement concordance induces and maintains stimulus associations in pigeons. *The Psychological Record*, 45, 283-297.

Edwards, C.A., Jagielo, J.A., Zentall, T.R., & Hogan, D.E. (1982). Acquired equivalence and distinctiveness in matching-to-sample by pigeons: Mediation by reinforcer-specific expectancies. *Journal of Experimental Psychology: Animal Behavior Processes*, 8, 244-259.

Fersen, L., von, & Lea, S.E.G. (1990). Category discrimination with polymorhous feature. *The Journal of the Experimental Analysis of Behavior*, 54, 69-84.

Hall, G. (1973a). Response strategies after overtraining in the jumping stand. *Animal Learning and Behavior*, 1, 157-160.

Hall, G. (1973b). Overtraining and reversal learning in the rat: Effects of stimulus salience and response strategies. *Journal of Comparative and Physiological Psychology*, 84, 169-175.

Hall, G. (1974). Transfer effect produced by overtraining in the rat. *Journal of Comparative and Physiological Psychology*, 87, 938-944.

Hall, G., Ray, E., & Bonardi, C. (1993). Acquired equivalence between cues trained with a common antecedent. *Journal of Experimental Psychology: Animal Behavior Processes*, 19, 391-399.

Lawrence, D.H. (1949). Acquired distinctiveness of cues: I. Transfer between discrimination on the basis of familiarity with the stimulus. *Journal of Experimental Psychology*, 39, 770-784.

Lawrence, D. H. (1950). Acquired distinctiveness of cues: II. Selective association in a constant stimulus situation. *Journal of Experimental Psychology*, 40, 175-188.

Liu, S.W. & Zeiler, M.D. (1968). Independence of concurrent discrimination. *Journal of Comparative and Physiological Psychology*, 65, 61-65.

Mackintosh, N.J. (1962). The effect of overtraining on a reversal and a nonreversal shift. *Journal of Comparative and Physiological Psychology*, 55, 555-559.

Mackintosh, N.J. (1964). Overtraining and transfer within and between dimension in the rat. *Quarterly Journal of Experimental Psychology*, 16, 250-256.

Mackintosh, N.J. (1965a). Selective attention in animal discrimination learning. *Psychological Bulletin*, 64, 124-150.

Mackintosh, N. J. (1965b). Overtraining, reversal, and extinction in rats and chicks. *Journal of Comparative and Physiological Psychology*, 59, 31-36.

Mandler, J.M. (1966). Behavior changes during overtraining and their effects on reversal and transfer. *Psychological Monograph Supplement*, 1, 187-202.

Mandler, J.M. (1968). Overtraining and the use of positive and negative stimuli in reversal and transfer. *Journal of Comparative and Physiological Psychology*, 66, 110-115.

Mandler, J.M., & Hooper, M.R. (1967). Overtraining and goal approach strategies in discrimination reversal. *Quarterly Journal of Experimental Psychology*, 19, 142-149.

Nakagawa, E. (1978). The effect of overtraining on discrimination learning in the white rats (in Japanese). *Japanese Journal of Psychology*, 49, 70-77.

Nakagawa, E. (1980a). The effect of overtraining on concurrent discrimination learning in Kindergarten children (in Japanese). *Japanese Journal of Educational Psychology*, 28, 38-47.

Nakagawa, E. (1980b). Effects of the overtraining on concurrent discrimination shift in Kindergarten children (in Japanese). *Japanese Journal of Educational Psychology*, 28, 114-123.

Nakagawa, E. (1981). Effects of amount of initial discrimination learning on subsequent discrimination shifts in young children (in Japanese). *Japanese Journal of Educational Psychology*, 29, 95-l04.

Nakagawa, E. (1985). Effects of overtraining on discrimination learning in young children: Examination of Schaeffer & Ellis's cue-cluster hypothesis (in Japanese). *Japanese Journal of Educational Psychology*, 33, 261-266.

Nakagawa, E. (1986). Overtraining, extinction and shift learning in a concurrent discrimination in rats. *Quarterly Journal of Experimental Psychology*, 38B, 313-326.

Nakagawa, E. (1992). Effects of overtraining reversal learning by rats in concurrent and single discriminations. *Quarterly Journal of Experimental Psychology*, 44B, 37-56.

Nakagawa, E. (1998). Stimulus classes formation in concurrent discriminations in rats as a function of overtraining. *The Psychological Record*, 48, 537-552.

Nakagawa, E. (1999a). A factor affecting stimulus classes formation in concurrent discriminations in rats. *The Psychological Record*, 49, 117-136.

Nakagawa, E. (1999b). Transfer of learning between concurrent and matching (or non-matching)-to-sample discriminations in rats. *Quarterly Journal of Experimental Psychology*, 52B, 125-143.

Nakagawa, E. (1999c). Acquired equivalence of discriminative stimuli following two concurrent discrimination learning tasks as a function of overtraining in rats. *The Psychological Record*, 49, 327-348.

Nakagawa, E. (1999d). Mechanism of stimulus classes formation in concurrent discriminations in rats. *The Psychological Record*, 49, 349-368.

Nakagawa, E. (2000). Reversal learning in conditional discriminations is not controlled by reinforcer density. *The Psychological Record*, 50, 117-140.

Nakagawa, E. (2001a). Cross-modal stimulus class formation in rats. *The Psychological Record*, 51, 53-66.

Nakagawa, E. (2001b). Reversal learning in concurrent discriminations in rats. *The Psychological Record*, 51, 251-269.

Nakagawa, E. (2002a). *Whole-reversal and partial-reversal learning in conditional discriminations are not controlled by reinforcer density*. In Serge P. Shohov (Ed.). Advances in Psychology Research, 11, Chapter 5, 115-148. Nova Sciences.

Nakagawa, E. (2002b). *Cross-modal stimulus class formation in rats as function of overtraining*. In Serge P. Shohov (Ed.). Advances in Psychology Research, 13, Chapter 9, 169-187. Nova Sciences.

Pubols, B.H. Jr. (1956). The facilitation of visual and spatial discrimination reversal by overtraining. *Journal of Comparative and Physiological Psychology*, 49, pp. 243-248.

Reid, L.S. (1953). The development of noncontinuity behavior through continuity learning. *Journal of Experimental Psychology*, 46, 107-112.

Sanders, B. (1971). Factors affecting reversal and nonreversal shifts in rats and children. *Journal of Comparative and Physiological Psychology*, 74, 192-202

Sasaki, M. & Shinoda, A. (1969). *The whole reversal learning and the part reversal learning in hooded rats* (in Japanese). The Proceedings of the Department of Humanities, College of General Education, University of Tokyo, XLIX series of Psychology, pp.135-159.

Sutherland, N.S. & Mackintosh, N.J. (1971). *Mechanisms of animal discrimination learning*. New York: Academic Press.

Urcuioli, P. J., Zentall, T. R., Jackson-Smith, P., & Steirn, J. N. (1989). Evidence for common coding in many-to-one matching: Retention, intertrial interference, and transfer. *Journal of Experimental Psychology: Animal Behavior Processes*, 15, 264-373.

Vaughan, W., Jr., & Herrnstein, R. J. (1987). Choosing among natural stimuli. *The Journal of the Experimental Analysis of Behavior*, 47, 5-176

Zentall, T.R. (1998). Symbolic representation in animals: Emergent stimulus relations in conditional discrimination learning. *Animal Learning & Behavior*, 26, 363-377.

Zentall, T.R., Sherburne, L.M, Steirn, J.N, Randall, C.K., Roper, K.L., & Urcuioli, P.J. (1992). Common coding in pigeons: Partial versus total reversals of one-to-many conditional discriminations. *Animal Learning and Behavior*, 20, 373-386.

Zentall, .R., Steirn, J.N, Sherburne, L.M., & Urcuioli, P.J. (1991). Common coding in pigeons assessed through partial versus total reversals of many-to-one conditional and simple discriminations. *Journal of Experimental Psychology: Animal Behavior Processes*, 17, 194-201.

AUTHOR'S NOTE

Requests for reprints should be sent to E. Nakagawa, Department of Psychology, Kagawa University, 1-1 Saiwai-Cho, Takamatsu, Kagawa, 760-8522, Japan. E-mail: esho@ed.kagawa-u.ac.jp.

In: *Topics in Cognitive Psychology*
Serge P. Shohov (Editor) pp. 207-222

ISBN 1-59033-836-7.
© 2003 Nova Science Publishers, Inc.

Chapter 11

MATHEMATICAL-PROGRAMMING APPROACHES TO TEST ITEM POOL DESIGN

Bernard P. Veldkamp, Wim J. van der Linden[1] and Adelaide Ariel
University of Twente

ABSTRACT

This paper presents an approach to item pool design that has the potential to improve on the quality of current item pools in educational and psychological testing and hence to increase both measurement precision and validity. The approach consists of the application of mathematical programming techniques to calculate optimal blueprints for item pools. These blueprints can be used to guide the item-writing process. Three different types of design problems are discussed, namely for item pools for linear tests, item pools computerized adaptive testing (CAT), and systems of rotating item pools for CAT. The paper concludes with an empirical example of the problem of designing a system of rotating item pools for CAT.

Keywords: Item Pool, Item-Pool Design, Item Response Theory, Mathematical Programming, Optimal Test Assembly.

1. INTRODUCTION

In the early days of testing, tests typically had a linear format and once the test became obsolete, its items were just thrown away. In hindsight, this type of testing involved a waste of efforts and time. A more efficient type of testing is using item banking. In item banking, test items are written on a continuous based and tests are assembled to be optimal from pools of items in the item banking system. Items in the system are reused and after each

---

[1] This paper was written while the second author was a Fellow of the Center for Advanced Study in the Behavioral Sciences, Stanford, CA.

administration the response data can be used to update the estimates of their statistical properties.

The introduction of item banking in testing has led to the introduction of techniques of automated test assembly. These techniques allow test assemblers to declare a set of specifications for the test they want from an item pool and to delegate the actual assembly process to a computer algorithm. An important class of algorithms is known by the name of Optimal Test Assembly (OTA). The majority of these techniques are based on the application of mathematical programming. Typically, these techniques require the formulation of a test assembly model with an objective function that maximizes the measurement precision of the tests and a set of constraints to guarantee that the test meets its specifications, for example, with respect to test length, content, or test format. A review of these techniques is given in van der Linden (1998).

The fact that tests are assembled to be optimal does not necessarily imply that their quality is perfect. Generally, a test can never have a better quality than permitted by the item pool from which it is assembled. Because the technique of designing good item pools is still in its infancy, item pools currently in use in educational and psychological testing are often unbalanced. For example, they may consist of a small set of high-quality items that are often selected for administration, while the majority of the items are seldom used.

The disadvantages of using such item pools became most obvious when computerized adaptive testing (CAT) was introduced. The first real-life CAT programs appeared to be vulnerable to item security problems because of organized efforts to memorize the subset of popular items in the pool. These efforts were successful because only a small set of items needed to be memorized to compromise the pool. Though item-exposure control methods can be applied to guarantee a maximum exposure rate for the items in the pool, such methods do not fix another problem with unbalanced items pools, namely the waste of time and resources involved in writing and pretesting items that are seldom used.

The best way to overcome these problems is more systematic design and development of item pools. One of the avenues to improve item pool design is to begin with the calculation of an optimal *blueprint* for the item pool to guide the item-writing process. A blueprint is a document specifying what attributes the collection of items in the pool should have to serve its testing program in the best possible way. The current paper focuses on the problem of how to calculate an optimal blueprint for an item pool. Two different methods for calculating such blueprints will be presented, one method for item pools in a testing program with tests with a linear format and one for pools in a CAT program. In addition, we will present a method to design a system of rotating item pools for use in CAT.

The actual task of writing test items to a blueprint is difficult. The difficulty does not reside so much in the need to write items with predetermined content attributes of the items as well as to realize items with statistical attributes, such as p-values, item-test correlations, and IRT parameters, with predetermined values. It is common experience that the values of statistical attributes of *individual* items are only loosely predictable. At the same time, however, at the level of a pool of items, statistical attributes often show persistent patterns of correlation with content attributes. In this paper, these patterns are used to calculate the blueprint for a new item pool.

2. OVERVIEW OF THE LITERATURE

Boekkooi-Timminga (1991) presented a method of item pool design for the assembly of linear test forms. The method is based on the technique of integer programming. It can be used to optimize the design of item pools that have to support the assembly of a future series of linear test forms. The method assumes an item pool calibrated under the one-parameter logistic (1PL) or Rasch model. The methods in the current paper are also based on mathematical-programming techniques. One of the differences with the method in Boekkooi-Timminga is that Boekkooi-Timminga's method follows a sequential approach calculating the numbers of items required in the pool for each individual test form at a time, where the methods in the current paper use a simultaneous approach.

A description of the process of developing item pools for CAT is given in Flaugher (1990) and Segall, Moreno, and Hetter (1997). Both authors outline several steps in the development of item pools. Flaugher discusses current practices at these steps. Segall, Moreno, and Hetter explain the procedure that is followed to construct item pools for the CAT version of the Armed Services Vocational Aptitude Battery (ASVAB). A common feature of the process described in Flaugher and the method in the present paper is the use of computer simulation in the design process. However, in Flaugher's outline, computer simulation is used to evaluate the performance of an item pool once the items have been written and field-tested whereas in the current paper computer simulation is used to design an optimal blueprint.

A rather different approach is described by both Stocking and Swanson (1998) and Way, Steffen and Anderson (1998; see also Way, 1998). They address the problem of designing a system of rotating item pools for CAT. This system assumes the presence of a master pool from which operational item pools are generated. A basic quantity in this method is the number of operational pools each item should be included in. By manipulating this number, desired exposure rates for the test items can be set. The same goal is realized by one of the methods in the current paper; however, this method is based on the application of an entirely different type of mathematical programming.

3. ANALYSIS OF DESIGN PROBLEM

Before focusing on the problem of designing an item pool, we have a closer look at the notion of test specifications. Test specifications can be categorized in several ways. In optimal test assembly, test specifications are formulated as constraints in a mathematical programming model. Based on the mathematical shape of these constraints, test specifications can be characterized as constraints on categorical item attributes, on quantitative item attributes, and on inter-item dependencies (van der Linden, 1998).

3.1 Categorical Constraints

Categorical item attributes partition the item pool into a series of subsets. Examples of such attributes are item content, cognitive level, format, author, and answer key. A test specification that is formulated as a categorical constraint generally constrains the distribution of the items in the test over the subsets. If the items are coded by multiple attributes, their Cartesian product partitions the item pool. Test specifications can then also be formulated as a joint or conditional distribution over this partition.

A natural way to represent categorical item attributes is by a table. A fictitious example for a mathematics test is given in Table 1. One item attribute is content, C, with levels Geometry, Algebra, and Statistics); the other is item type, T (with levels Basic Skills and Application). In Table 1, the distribution of the items in the pool is represented by the numbers n_{ij}, $n_{i.}$, $n_{.j}$, and $n_{..}$, which are the numbers of items in cell (i,j), row i, column j, and the total table, respectively. If a test is to be assembled from this pool, a number of items have to be selected. Let the number of items to be selected from each subset be denoted as r_{ij}, $r_{i.}$, $r_{.j}$, and $r_{..}$. We may impose the following set of constraints on the selection of items in the test:

1. Number of Geometry items testing Application equal to eight ($r_{12} = 8$);
2. Number of Basic Skills items equal to nine ($r_{.1} = 9$);
3. Number of Geometry items equal to four ($r_{1.} = 4$);
4. Total number of items equal to 25 ($r_{..} = 25$).

Table 1. Sample Table with categorical Item Attributes

	Basic Skills	Application	
Geometry	n_{11}		$n_{1.}$
Algebra		n_{22}	
Statistics			
	$n_{.1}$		$n_{..}$

Note that this set of constraints not only fixes certain numbers of items from some of the cells in Table 1 directly, but also constrains the numbers from the other cells in the table. For example, the first and last constraints together imply that the number of Application items on Algebra or Statistics is equal to four. Mathematically, this constraint can be denoted as $r_{12}+r_{13}=4$. This example shows that the same set of test specifications can be represented by different sets of mathematical constraints. From the theory of mathematical programming it is known that some of these sets are more efficient than others. It is not the focus of this paper to discuss the efficiency of constraint formulation; for a paper on this topic, see Veldkamp (submitted).

3.2 Quantitative Constraints

Unlike categorical constraints, quantitative constraints do not impose bounds on numbers of items. Instead, they impose bounds on a function of the values of the items on a quantitative attribute, mostly on their sum or average. Examples of quantitative item attributes are: word counts, exposure rates, values for item response theory (IRT) information functions, expected response times, and such classical item parameters as p-values and item-test correlations.

As an example of a quantitative constraint, consider a constraint on response time that imposes a bound on the sum of the expected response times of the items in the test for the examinees. This type of constraints is useful if examinees have a fixed amount of time available to take the test. It is important to note that though each possible combination of items in the test defines a unique sum of expected response times, the reverse does not hold. Unlike categorical attributes, constraints with quantitative attributes have no one-one correspondences with item distributions. Instead, they imply sets of different distributions each of which feasible with respect to the constraint. Later in this paper, this property is exploited to choose a distribution to represent a quantitative constraint that is *optimal* with respect to an objective function.

Observe that it is possible to discretize quantitative item attributes and represent them by a table, just as categorical attributes. For example, if we discretize the expected response times of the items, t_i, their scales of possible values is replaced by a finite grid of values, t_{id}, with $d=1,...,D$. The number of points on the grid as well as their spacing is free.

Below, we will use Q to represent the table defined by the product of joint grid for all quantitative attributes in the test assembly model, which will have an arbitrary cell denoted by q. Likewise, the symbol C is used to represent the table defined by all categorical attributes in the model, with an arbitrary cell denoted by $c \in C$. A cell in the joint table defined by C and Q will be denoted as $(c,q) \in C \times Q$. An optimal blueprint for an item pool is a table $C \times Q$ with optimal values of n_{ij} for its cells.

3.3 Constraints on Inter-Item Dependencies

The defining characteristic for this type of constraints is that it deals with relations of exclusion and/or inclusion among items in the pool. Two items exclude each other, for example, if one item contains a clue to the answer to the other item. We will call such items "enemies". In test assembly, it is possible to constrain the test to have no more than one item from each known set of enemies. Usually, the occurrence of enemy sets in an item pool is not planned; they just happen to be there. In practice, we deal with such sets by distributing the items in them over different test forms. Also, in practice the number of enemy sets in an item pool is generally low. The position taken in this paper is that the presence of enemies is a problem of *test assembly*--not of item pool design. It will therefore be ignored in the remainder of this paper.

However, some other types of constraints on interdependent items have to be included in the design process. Items can be organized around common stimuli, for example, a reading passage in a reading comprehension test or a description of an experiment in a biology test. We will use "item sets" as a generic term for this item format. Typically, the items in the sets in the test are selected from larger sets available in the pool. If so, constraints have to be added to the test assembly process to define how many items in the item set can be selected in the test. Besides, selecting item sets often involves constraints on categorical (e.g., content) and quantitative (e.g., word counts) attributes of the stimuli. Methods for designing item pools should be able to handle such complicated relationships.

4. Methods of Item Pool Design

Design methods have been developed for item pools for different types of tests. In this section, we will describe methods for designing pools for linear tests with item sets and for use in computerized adaptive testing (CAT). In addition, a method for designing a set of rotating item pools in CAT will be discussed.

4.1 Linear Tests

A design method for pools for linear tests with item sets can be based on the following three-stage procedure introduced in van der Linden, Veldkamp and Reese (1998):

1. A blueprint for a pool of *items* is designed using an integer-programming model ignoring the item set structure. The blueprint is calculated using a mathematical programming model that constrains the distributions of the items over their categorical and quantitative attributes. The model has an objective function that minimizes the costs of item writing.

2. A blueprint for a pool of *stimuli* for the item sets is designed using the same methodology as for the pool of items. The model now constrains the distribution of the stimuli over their categorical and quantitative attributes and the objective function minimizes a cost function for writing the stimuli.

3. Items and stimuli in the two blueprints are assigned to the each other to form a new blueprint for a pool of *item sets*. The assignment is done using a separate mathematical programming model that constrains the assignment to deal with the numbers of items available in the various cells of the CxQ table and the numbers required in the item sets. The objective function is of the same type as above.

We will now discuss the mathematical programming models in somewhat more detail

4.1.1 Calculating Item Pool Blueprint

The objective function of the integer-programming model minimizes a cost function for writing the items. In general, costs of item writing are hard to assess. For some combinations of attributes it is easier to write items that for others. When no knowledge about the item writing process is available, a simple approach is to base the cost function on the distribution of the items in a typical previous pool.

Let x_{cq} denote the frequency of the items in cell (c,q) in a table for a previous pool. These frequencies contain information on the efforts involved in writing items for the various cells in the table. Cells with relatively large frequencies represent combinations of categorical and quantitative attribute values that tend to go together often; apparently, such items are easy to produce. On the other hand, empty cells seem to point at combinations of attribute values that are difficult to produce. A monotonically decreasing function of x_{cq}, denoted as $\varphi(x_{cq})$, will be used as an empirical measure of the efforts involved in writing items with the various possible combinations of attribute values. A simple cost function is $\varphi(x_{cq}) = x_{cq}^{-1}$, which requires $x_{cq} > 0$. Other choices are possible tough.

We assume that the item pool has to serve the assembly of $f=1,\ldots,F$ test forms, each with possible different specifications. The integer-programming model for designing a blue print for a pool of items for these forms can be formulated as follows:

$$\text{Minimize} \quad \sum_f \sum_c \sum_q \varphi_{cq}\, n_{fcq} \qquad \text{(minimizing costs)} \tag{1}$$

subject to

$$\sum_c \sum_q I_q(\theta_k)\, n_{fcq} \geq T_f(\theta_k) \quad ,f=1,\ldots,F,\ k=1,\ldots,K, \qquad \text{(test information)} \tag{2}$$

$$\sum_q n_{fcq} \geq n_{fc} \quad ,f=1,\ldots,F,\ c=1,\ldots,C, \qquad \text{(categorical constraints)} \tag{3}$$

$$\sum_c n_{fcq} \geq n_{f_q} \quad ,f=1,\ldots,F,\ q=1,\ldots,Q, \qquad \text{(quantitative constraints)} \tag{4}$$

$$n_{fcq}=0,1,\ldots,f=1,\ldots,F,\ c \in C,\ q \in Q. \qquad \text{(integer decision variables)} \tag{5}$$

The objective function in Equation 1 minimizes the sum of the item writing costs across all items in the F forms. For each form the constraints in Equation 2 require the test information function at θ_k, $k=1,\ldots,K$, to be larger than a predetermined set of target values. The objective function in Equation 1 guarantees that these bounds are approached from above. The categorical constraints imposed on the forms are in Equation 3. Lower bounds n_{fc} are set only; the objective function in Equation 1 guarantees that the constraints are always satisfied as equality at optimality. The same holds for the quantitative constraints in Equation 4.

Solving the model in Equation 1-5 gives us the set of optimal numbers of items in the table, n_{fcq}, that together constitute the blueprint for the item pool.

4.1.2 Calculating Stimuli Pool Blueprint

The method for calculating a blueprint for a pool of stimuli is formally similar to the one for designing the items. Tables C' and Q' are now defined for the sets of categorical and quantitative attributes that describe the stimuli in the test forms the item pool has to support. It should be observed that table Q' is expected to be much smaller than Q, because psychometric attributes for stimuli are rare. Sometimes item sets have to meet constraints with respect to *aggregated* statistical attributes, such as sums of p-values or average b_i values. However, such aggregates belong to the set of items associated with a stimulus--not to the stimulus itself. Constraints on aggregated attributes are therefore dealt with in the item-assignment model below.

The integer-programming model for the blueprint of stimuli follows directly from Equations 1-5. The cost function $\varphi_{c'q'}$ can be derived from the distribution of stimuli in the previous item pool. If the number of stimuli is small and the number of stimulus attributes large, taking the inverse of the table frequencies may not work well. If so, other cost functions must be considered. Just as in the previous model, the bounds in the categorical and quantitative constraints represent the specifications for the item sets in the various test forms.

4.1.3 Assigning Items to Stimuli

The final step is to assign the items in the CxQ table to the stimuli in the $C'xQ'$ table. A regular assignment model from mathematical programming can be applied to optimize this step. Such a model has decision variables for each combination of cell in CxQ and $C'xQ'$ that take the value 1 if an item from the cell in CxQ is assigned to a stimulus in the cell in $C'xQ'$ and the value 0 otherwise. The model also has an objective function that is to be maximized or minimized. Like the previous two models, a function representing the costs of assigning an item to a stimulus is used. The cost function, $\varphi_{cqc'q'}$, is defined on the Cartesian product of the tables CxQ and $C'xQ'$. This function represents the costs of writing an item with attributes (c,q) for a stimulus with attributes (c',q'). The constraints in the assignment model are needed: (1) to represent the maximum and minimum number of items and stimuli available in each cell; (2) to constrain the size of the item sets that have to be formed; and (3) to deal with possible aggregated quantitative items attributes that item sets are required to have. For a detailed example of an assignment model, see van der Linden, Veldkamp & Reese (2000).

4.2 Computerized Adaptive Testing

The process of designing on optimal blueprint for an item pool for use in CAT is somewhat more complicated. One of the reasons for this is that in CAT the goal is to have a test for each examinee with optimal information at his/her ability level. It is thus impossible to set a target for the test information function as in Equation 3. Another complication is that the number of different test forms is potentially as large as the number of examinees.

In Veldkamp and van der Linden (2000), an alternative method is described for designing a blueprint for CAT item pools. The method shares some of its logic with the method for developing blueprints for paper-and-pencil testing. Like the previous method, the set of specifications for the CAT is analyzed and all item attributes figuring in the specifications are identified. The result of this step is again a classification table that is the product of all categorical and quantitative item attributes. Each cell of the table represents a possible type of item in the pool.

However, unlike the design problem for linear tests, to obtain the optimal numbers n_{cq} for the table, we do not solve a mathematical programming model but run a computer simulation of the CAT for the ability distribution of the intended population of examinees. In this simulation, the "items" available are the cells in the table, the examinees are sampled from an ability distribution estimated from historic data, and the test specifications are imposed on the CAT through a shadow test approach. (The notion of CAT with shadow tests will be explained below.). During the simulation, the number of times an item is selected from a cell in the table is counted. The blueprint for the item pool is calculated from these counts.

4.2.1 CAT with Shadow Tests

The shadow test approach has been developed to guarantee that all test specifications in a CAT are met, even when the items are selected adaptively (van der Linden & Reese, 1998, van der Linden, 2000). The items in the CAT are selected using a two-stage procedure. First, a linear test (=shadow test) of the required length of the CAT that meets all constraints is assembled from the pool. The test is also required to contain all items already administered and is assembled to be optimal at the examinee's current ability estimate. Second, the item to be administered is selected from the free items in the shadow that is optimal contribution at the ability estimate. As a result of this two-stage selection procedure, each adaptive test meets all constraints and has items that are always optimal.

The algorithm for constrained CAT with shadow tests can be summarized as follows:

1. Choose an initial value of the examinee's ability parameter θ_k.
2. Assemble the first shadow test such that all constraints are met and the objective function is optimized.
3. Administer an item from the shadow test with optimal properties at the current ability estimate.
4. Update the estimate of θ_k as well as all other parameters in the test assembly model.
5. Return all unused items to the pool.
6. Assemble a new shadow test fixing the items already administered.
7. Repeat Steps 3-5 until all n items have been administered.

4.2.2 Integer Programming Model in CAT Simulations

In the CAT simulations, an integer-programming model is used to assemble the shadow test. The choice for an integer-programming model is motivated by the fact that in principle a shadow test may need more than one item from the same cell in the CxQ to be optimal at the current ability estimate.

To introduce the model, the following notation has to be introduced:

n_{cq}: integer variable for cell (c,q) in table CxQ, that is, $n_{cq}=0, 1, \ldots$;

θ_{k-1}: estimate of θ after k-1 items have been administered;

S_{k-1}: set of cells with nonzero decision variable after k-1 items have been administered;

$I_i(\theta)$: Fisher information in the response on item i for an examinee with ability θ;

n_c: number of items in category c to be selected in each CAT;

n_q: number of items in interval q to be selected in each CAT;

φ_{cq}: costs of writing an item for cell (c,q).

The model for the assembly of the shadow test for the selection of the kth item in the CAT simulation can be presented as:

$$\text{Minimize} \quad \sum_c \sum_q \varphi_{cq} n_{cq} \qquad \text{(minimizing costs)} \qquad \textbf{(6)}$$

subject to

$$\sum_c \sum_q I_q(\theta_k) n_{cq} \geq T(\theta_k) \quad , k=1,...,K, \qquad \text{(test information)} \qquad \textbf{(7)}$$

$$\sum_c \sum_q n_{cq} = k-1 \quad , (c,q) \in S_{k-1}, \qquad \text{(previous administered items in the test)} \qquad \textbf{(8)}$$

$$\sum_q n_{cq} \geq n_c \quad , c=1,...,C, \qquad \text{(categorical constraints)} \qquad \textbf{(9)}$$

$$\sum_c n_{cq} \geq n_q \quad , q=1,...,Q, \qquad \text{(quantitative constraints)} \qquad \textbf{(10)}$$

$$n_{cq} = 0,1,... \quad , c \in C, q \in Q. \qquad \text{(integer decision variables)} \qquad \textbf{(11)}$$

The model has an objective function (Equation 6) for the shadow tests that minimizes a cost function for writing the items in the pool. The information on the ability parameter at the ability estimate in the CAT is bounded from below by a target value, T, in Equation 7. The constraint in Equation 8 requires the k-1 previously administered items to be in the test. Because of this constraint, the attribute values of these items are automatically taken into account when selecting the kth item. Equation 9 and 10 guarantee that the CAT meets all categorical and quantitative constraints.

4.2.3 Calculating the Blueprint for the Item Pool

In the simulation study, it is counted how often an item in cell (c,q) is administered. The blueprint for the item pool is calculated from these counts. The idea is to calculate the blueprint such that all items will tend to have an equal exposure rate if the item pool is realized and used in operational testing. A uniform item exposure rate is generally considered to be ideal because it prevents both item security problems due to overexposure of a small number of items and loss of resources involved in the writing and pretesting of items that are hardly used at all.

Let the counts be equal to N_{cq} and let M be the maximum number of times an item can be exposed. The blueprint has the following number of items in cell (c,q):

$$I_{cq} = \left\lceil \frac{N_{cq}}{M} \right\rceil. \qquad \textbf{(12)}$$

This formula is justified by the following argument: If the ability distribution in the CAT simulations is a reasonable approximation to the true ability distribution in the population, N_{cq} predicts the number of items needed from cell (c,q). However, to meet the required exposure rates, these numbers should be divided by M. If I_{cq} is not an integer it should be rounded upward.

An empirical example of this method for designing item pools for CAT can be found in Veldkamp and van der Linden (2000).

4.3 COMPUTERIZED ADAPTIVE TESTING WITH ROTATING ITEM POOLS

A different way to deal with item security in CAT is to use a system of rotating item pools. The pools are taken from a master pool and assembled to be parallel. They rotate both over time and locations to prevent examinees from predicting what item pool they will get. The idea of rotating item pools was first described in Stocking and Swanson (1998). The main design question in this section approach is how to design a system of parallel rotating item pools.

In the method of Stocking and Swanson (1998), all the items are assigned to item pools using their weighted deviations model (Swanson & Stocking, 1993). The objective function in this method is to minimize the differences between the individual item pools and the average item pools with respect to (1) the number of items with the required categorical and quantitative attributes and (2) item information at a selected grid of θ values. The method requires the specification of a set of weights to reflect the importance of the differences. In Stocking and Swanson (1998) this method is applied to get both systems of overlapping and nonoverlapping item pools. The possibility of overlap between item pools is used to permit the selection of underused items in more than one pool. If the exposure rates of the items are known, the number of times they are assigned to an item pool can be used to approximate the ideal of uniform item exposure for all items in the master pool for the population of examinees.

Ariel, Veldkamp, and van der Linden (2002) present a different approach to assembling a system of rotating item pools. Their method is a two-step method based on the values of the item attributes instead of the observed exposure rates of the items. In the first step, items with similar attribute values are assigned to interim sets. In the second step, the items in the interim sets are assigned to item pools. The method was motivated by Gulliksen's (1950) matched random subsets method which was developed to split a test into two parallel halves to estimate a largest lower bound to the test reliability. A formalization of Gulliksen's method based on mathematical programming is given in van der Linden and Boekkooi-Timminga (1988).

We will discuss the method only for the case of the item difficulty and discrimination parameters and a system of two rotating item pools. The generalization to more attributes and larger numbers of item pools follows immediately. Let i and j be any two items in the master pool $(i, j=1,\ldots, I)$. The similarity between i and j is measured by a distance function

$$\delta_{ij} =| a_i - a_j |+w| b_i - b_j | \qquad \text{(distance function)} \quad (13)$$

where a denotes the item discrimination parameters, b the difficulty parameter, and w is a weight factor that can be used to correct for differences in scale between a and b.

4.3.1 Linear Programming Models

To find interim pairs of similar items the following linear programming problem has to be solved:

$$\text{Minimize} \quad \sum_{i=1}^{n-1}\sum_{j=i+1}^{n}\delta_{ij}*x_{ij} \qquad \text{(objective function)} \quad (14)$$

subject to

$$\sum_{i<j}x_{ij}+\sum_{i>j}x_{ji}=1, \quad j=1,...,I \qquad \text{(item pairs)} \quad (15)$$

$$x_{ij}=0,1, \; i,j=1,...,I. \qquad \text{(binary decision variables)} \quad (16)$$

The objective function in Equation 14 is minimized to get interim pairs that are as similar as possible. Equation 15 guarantees that every item belongs to only one interim pair.

In the second step of the method, items in the interim pairs, which we denote as Q_r, $r=1,...,R$, are assigned to the two item pools $p=1,2$. To make the pools parallel we want to minimize the difference in information in the pools at a selected grid of ability values, θ_k, $k=1,...,K$.

The decision variables in the model are variables y_{ip} which take the value 1 if item i is assigned to pool p and 0 otherwise. The following model for the assignment of the items is proposed:

$$\text{minimize } z \qquad \text{(objective function)} \quad (17)$$

subject to

$$\left|\sum_{i\neq j}I_i(\theta_k)y_{i1}-\sum_{j\neq i}I_j(\theta_k)y_{j2}\right|\leq z, \quad k=1,...,K \qquad , \qquad \text{(pool information)} \quad (18)$$

$$\sum_{i\in Q_r}y_{ip}=1, \quad p=1,2, \; r=1,...,R \qquad , \qquad \text{(each pool one item from each pair)} \quad (19)$$

$$\sum_{p}y_{ip}=1, \; i=1,...,I \qquad . \qquad \text{(each item assigned to one pool)} \quad (20)$$

$$y_{ip}=0,1. \qquad \text{(binary decision variables)} \quad (21)$$

The objective function in Equation 18 minimizes the difference in information between the two pools. To guarantee that each pool receives an item from each pair Equation 19 has been included in the model. Equation 20 requires that each item be assigned only once to an item pool.

If overlapping item pools are required, Equation 20 should be replaced by

$$\sum_p y_{ip} = n_i, \quad i = 1, \ldots, I$$

(item i assigned to n_i pools)   (22)

where $n_i \leq P$ denotes the number of pools item i is assigned to and P is the total number of pools.

Like the previous design models in this paper, the model in Equation 17-21 can be extended with constraints to deal with all possible kinds of categorical and/or quantitative constraints the items pool have to meet.

4.3.2. Empirical Example

An empirical example of the design problem of a rotating item pool system is given. (For the full example, see Ariel, Veldkamp and van der Linden, 2002). The master pool was a previous pool of 2,131 items from the Law School Admission Test (LSAT) all calibrated using the 3-parameter logistic model (Hambleton, Swaminathan & Rogers, 1991). The total number of categorical item attributes led to a content table with nine cells, which we label as $C_1, \ldots, C_9$. The number of items per cell ranged from 97 to 371. In addition to the item parameters in the 3-parameter response model, we had word counts per item as a quantitative attribute. Stocking's (1994) recommendation that an item pool have a size approximately 12 times the length of the test was followed in that we assembled a system of four nonoverlapping item pools.

In the first stage, the model in Equation 14-16 was solved using the heuristic approach of simulated annealing. A heuristic was used because the model was too large to find an optimal solution. For a description and application of the technique of simulated annealing, see Veldkamp (1999); for a theoretical introduction, see van Laarhoven and Aarts (1987).

In the second stage, items from the interim sets were assigned to the four nonoverlapping item pools. The software package AIMMS 3.2 (Paragon BV, 2000) was used to solve the model in Equation 17-21. The information in the pools in Equation 19 was constrained at $\theta_k = -1, 0, 1$. Also, the total word count for each item pool was set constraint to a reasonable value close to 20 percent of the total number of words in the master pool.

In order to evaluate the parallelness of the four item pools, CAT simulations from these pools were conducted. In addition, CAT simulations were conducted directly from the master pool. A shadow test approach was used to impose constraints on the CAT with respect to the content attributes, word counts, and length of the CAT. Both the shadow tests and the items picked for administration were selected to maximize the information at the current ability estimate. For each pool, 1,000 examinees were randomly sampled from a standard normal distribution for θ.

The average variances of the estimated ability parameters and the total number of items used in the CAT were used to compare the results (for these criteria, see Hambleton, Swaminathan & Rogers, 1991, p.94). The results are given in Table 2. They show the CAT simulations from the four pools yielded results that were closely enough to consider the pools to be parallel. In addition, the average variance of the ability estimates for each of the four pools was slightly higher than for the master pool, but that the total number of items used from the four pools (612) was dramatically larger than the number used from the master pool. These results are as expected: conducting a CAT directly from the master pool gives us more space to adapt the item selection to the examinees' abilities, but if we move to a system of four pools, the CAT is forced to spread its usage of the pools in much better way.

Table 2. Results form CAT Simulations

	Average Variance	Number of Items Used
Master Pool	.156	189
Four Item Pools		
Pool 1	.175	149
Pool 2	.181	157
Pool 3	.181	155
Pool 4	.182	151

5. DISCUSSION

Typically, item pools are no static entities. In most testing programs, tests are assembled from the pool and new items are pretested and added to the pool on a continuous basis. Hence, two important tasks of item pool management are: (1) monitoring the developments in the item pool; and (2) instructing item writers to write new items to complete the pool. The models in this paper can easily be adapted for use in item pool management. The only thing needed is to correct the decision variables in the models for the numbers of items and stimuli currently available in the pool.

The principle is illustrated for the model in Equations 1-6. Let v_{cq} be a constant representing the current number of items in cell (c,q) in the pool and η_{cq} a new decision variable denoting the number of items to be written for this cell. The only adaptation necessary is *substituting* $v_{cq} + \eta_{cq}$ for the old decision variables in the model.

If the current items in the pool reveal new patterns of correlation between categorical and quantitative attributes, the cost functions φ_{cq} can be updated by defining them on v_{cq} rather than the frequencies x_{cq} for the previous item pool, or perhaps on a weighted combination of both. This practice is recommended, for example, if the item writers form a categorical attribute in the definition of table CxQ and new item writers have been hired.

REFERENCES

Ariel, A., Veldkamp, B.P., van der Linden, W.J. (2002a). *Methods for constructing subpools*. Paper presented at the annual meeting of the Psychometric Society, Chapel Hill, NC.

Ariel, A., Veldkamp, B.P., van der Linden, W.J. (2002b*). Constructing rotating item pools for constrained adaptive testing*. Manuscript submitted for publication.

Boekkooi-Timminga, E. (1991). *A method for designing Rasch model-based item banks.* Paper presented at the annual meeting of the Psychometric Society, Princeton, NJ.

Flaugher, R. (1990). Item Pools. In H. Wainer, *Computerized Adaptive Testing: A primer* (pp. 41-64). Hillsdale, NJ: Lawrence Erlbaum Associates

Gulliksen, H. (1950). *Theory of mental tests*. New York: Wiley.

Hambleton, R.K., Swaminathan H., and Rogers, H.J. (1991). *Fundamentals of item response theory*. California, USA: Sage Publications.

Paragon BV (2000). *AIMMS (Version 3.2)* [Computer software and manual]. Haarlem, The Netherlands: Paragon BV.

Segall, D.O., Moreno, K.E., and Hetter, R.D. (1997). Item pool development and evaluation. In W.A. Sands, B.K. Waters, and J.R. McBride (Eds.). *Computerized adaptive testing: From inquiry to operation.* (pp. 117-130). Washington: Applied Psychological Association.

Stocking, M.L. (1994) *Three practical issues for modern adaptive testing item pools* (ETS Research Report No. 94-5) Princeton, NJ: Educational Testing Service.

Stocking, M.L., & Swanson, L. (1998). Optimal design of item pools for computerized adaptive tests. *Applied Psychological Measurement, 22,* 271-279.

Swanson, L., & Stocking, M.L. (1993). A model and heuristic for solving very large item selection problems. *Applied Psychological Measurement, 17,* 151-166.

van der Linden, W.J. (1998). Optimal assembly of psychological and educational tests. *Applied Psychological Measurement, 22,* 195-211.

van der Linden, W.J. (2000). Constrained adaptive testing with shadow tests. In W.J. van der Linden & C.A.W. Glas (Eds.). *Computerized adaptive testing: Theory and practice* (pp. 27-52). Boston: Kluwer.

van der Linden, W.J., & Boekkooi-Timminga, E. (1988). A zero-one programming approach to Gulliksen's matched random subtests method. *Applied Psychological Measurement, 12,* 201-209.

van der Linden, W.J., & Reese, L.M. (1998). A model for optimal constrained adaptive testing. *Applied Psychological Measurement, 22,* 259-270.

van der Linden, W.J., & Veldkamp, B.P. (2002). *Constraining item exposure in computerized adaptive testing with shadow tests*. Manuscript submitted for publication.

van der Linden, W.J., Veldkamp, B.P., & Reese, L.M. (2000). An integer programming approach to item bank design. *Applied Psychological Measurement, 24,* 139-150.

van Laarhoven, P.J.M., & Aarts, E.H.L. (1987). *Simulated annealing: theory and applications*. Dordrecht: Reidel.

Veldkamp, B.P. (1999). Multiple objective test assembly problems. *Journal of Educational Measurement, 36,* 253-266.

Veldkamp, B.P., & van der Linden, W.J., (2000). Designing item pools for computerized adaptive testing. In W.J. van der Linden & C.A.W. Glas (Eds.). *Computerized adaptive testing: Theory and practice* (pp. 149-162). Boston: Kluwer.

Way, W.D. (1998). Protecting the integrity of computerized testing item pools. *Educational Measurement: Issues and Practice, 17,* 17-26.

Way, W.D., Steffen, M., & Anderson, G.S. (1998, September). *Developing, maintaining, and renewing the item inventory to support computer-based testing.* Paper presented at the ETS Computer-Based Testing Colloquium, Philadelphia, PA.

INDEX